The

ECONOMISTS'
HOUR

The

ECONOMISTS' HOUR

BINYAMIN APPELBAUM

*How the False Prophets of Free
Markets Fractured Our Society*

PICADOR

First published 2019 by Little, Brown and Company,
a division of Hachette Book Group, Inc.

First published in the UK in paperback 2019 by Picador

This edition first published 2020 by Picador
an imprint of Pan Macmillan
The Smithson, 6 Briset Street, London EC1M 5NR
Associated companies throughout the world
www.panmacmillan.com

ISBN 978-1-5098-7913-7

Pan Macmillan does not have any control over, or any responsibility for,
any author or third-party websites referred to in or on this book.

1 3 5 7 9 8 6 4 2

A CIP catalogue record for this book is available from the British Library.

Printed and bound by CPI Group (UK) Ltd, Croydon, CR0 4YY

MIX
Paper from
responsible sources
FSC® C116313

Visit **www.picador.com** to read more about all our books
and to buy them. You will also find features, author interviews and
news of any author events, and you can sign up for e-newsletters
so that you're always first to hear about our new releases.

For my parents,
my partner,
and my children.

Contents

The

ECONOMISTS'
HOUR

Introduction

When modern science appeared, medieval Christianity was a complete, comprehensive system which explained both man and the universe; it was the basis for government, the inspiration for knowledge and art, the arbiter of war as of peace and the power behind the production and distribution of wealth — none of which was sufficient to prevent its downfall.

        — *Michel Houellebecq,* The Elementary Particles *(1998)*[1]

I can calculate the motions of the heavenly bodies, but not the madness of people.

        — *Isaac Newton (1720)*

In the early 1950s, a young economist named Paul Volcker worked as a human calculator in an office deep inside the Federal Reserve Bank of New York. He crunched numbers for the people who made decisions, and he told his wife that he saw little chance of ever moving up.[2] The central bank's leadership included bankers, lawyers, and an Iowa hog farmer, but not a single economist.[3] The Fed's chairman, William McChesney Martin, was a stockbroker with a low opinion of the species. "We have fifty econometricians working for us at the Fed," he told a visitor. "They are all located in the basement of this building, and there is a reason why they are there." They were in the building, he said, because they asked good questions. They were in the basement, he continued, because "they don't know their own limitations, and they have a far greater sense of confidence in their analyses than I have found to be warranted."[4]

Martin's distaste for economists was widely shared among the midcentury American elite. President Franklin Delano Roosevelt privately dismissed John Maynard Keynes, the most important economist of his generation, as an impractical "mathematician."[5] President Dwight D. Eisenhower, in his farewell address, urged Americans to keep technocrats from power, warning that "public policy could itself become the captive of a scientific-technological elite." Congress took testimony from economists but, as a rule, it did not take that testimony very seriously. "Economics was viewed generally among top policymakers, especially on Capitol Hill, as an esoteric field which could not bridge the gap to meet specific problems of concern," an aide to Wisconsin senator William Proxmire, a leading Democrat on domestic policy, wrote in the early 1960s.[6]

When C. Douglas Dillon, the U.S. Treasury secretary, commissioned two studies in 1963 of potential improvements to the international monetary system, he pointedly declined to consult academic economists. Another official explained their advice "was practically useless to those in charge of decision-making."[7]

That same year, the Supreme Court upheld the government's decision to prevent the merger of two Philadelphia banks despite evidence the merger would produce economic benefits. The court described the economic evidence as irrelevant.[8]

But a revolution was coming. Economists who believed in the power and the glory of markets were on the cusp of a rise to influence that transformed the business of government, the conduct of business, and, as a result, the patterns of everyday life.

As the quarter century of growth that followed World War II sputtered to a close in the 1970s, these economists persuaded political leaders to reduce government's role in the economy — to trust that markets would deliver better results than bureaucrats.

Economics is often called the "dismal science" for its insistence that choices must be made because resources are limited. But the real message of economics, and the reason for its popularity, is the tantalizing promise that it can help humankind to loosen those surly bonds of scarcity. Alchemists promised to make gold from lead; economists said they could do it ex nihilo, through better policy making.

In the four decades between 1969 and 2008, a period I call the "Economists' Hour," borrowing a phrase from the historian Thomas McCraw, economists played a leading role in curbing taxation and public spending, deregulating large sectors of the economy, and clearing the way for globalization.[9] Economists persuaded President Richard Nixon to end military conscription. Economists persuaded the federal judiciary largely to abandon the enforcement of antitrust laws. Economists even persuaded the government to assign a dollar value to human life — around $10 million in 2019 — to determine whether regulations were worthwhile.

Economists also became policy makers. The economist Arthur F. Burns replaced Martin as the Fed's chairman in 1970, inaugurating an era in which economists — including Volcker — led the central bank.[10] Two years later, in 1972, George Shultz became the first economist to serve as Treasury secretary, the job once held by Dillon.[11] The number of economists employed by the U.S. government rose from about two thousand in the mid-1950s to more than six thousand by the late 1970s.[12]

The United States was the epicenter of the intellectual ferment and the main laboratory for the translation of ideas into policies, but the embrace of markets as the cure for economic stagnation was a global phenomenon, seizing the imagination of politicians in countries including the United Kingdom, Chile, and Indonesia. America began to eliminate government price regulation in the mid-1970s. By the end of the decade, France was allowing bakers to set the price of baguettes for the first time in that nation's history.[13]

Even the world's largest Communist country joined the revolution. In September 1985, the Chinese leader Zhao Ziyang invited eight prominent Western economists for a weeklong cruise on the Yangtze River with a large chunk of China's economic policy-making elite. Mao Zedong had preached that economic considerations were always subordinate to political considerations. The discussions that week helped to persuade a new generation of Chinese leaders to place greater faith in markets, catalyzing China's construction of its own version of a market-based economy.[14]

This book is a biography of the revolution. Some leading figures are relatively well-known, like Milton Friedman, who had a greater influence on American life than any other economist of his era, and Arthur Laffer, who sketched a curve on a cocktail napkin in 1974 that helped to make tax cuts a staple of Republican economic policy. Others may be less familiar, like Walter Oi, a blind economist who dictated to his wife and assistants some of the calculations that persuaded Nixon to end military conscription; Alfred Kahn, who deregulated air travel and rejoiced in the cramped and crowded cabins on commercial flights as the proof of his success; and Thomas Schelling, a game theorist who persuaded the Kennedy administration to install a hotline to the Kremlin — and who figured out a way to put a dollar value on human life.

This book is also a reckoning of the consequences.

The embrace of markets lifted billions of people around the world from abject poverty. Nations have been tied together by the flows of goods and money and ideas, and most of the world's 7.7 billion people live wealthier, healthier, and happier lives as a consequence. Chinese businessmen eat salmon from Chile; children in India are treated with medicines made in Israel; Cameroonians watch their countrymen play basketball in the NBA. Infant mortality is lower today than it was in 1950 in every country on the face of the Earth.

Markets make it easier for people to get what they want when they want different things, a virtue that is particularly important in pluralistic societies which value diversity and freedom of choice. And economists have used markets to provide elegant solutions to salient problems, like closing a hole in the ozone layer and increasing the supply of kidneys available for transplant.

But the market revolution went too far. In the United States and in other developed nations, it has come at the expense of economic equality, of the health of liberal democracy, and of future generations.

Economists instructed policy makers to focus on maximizing growth without regard to the distribution of the gains—to focus on the size of the pie rather than the size of the pieces. Charles L. Schultze, the chairman of President Jimmy Carter's Council of Economic Advisers, said economists should fight for efficient policies "even when the result is significant income losses for particular groups — which it almost always is."[15] Keith Joseph, a key adviser to British prime minister Margaret Thatcher, declared that the United Kingdom needed more millionaires and more bankruptcies. "If we are to reduce poverty in this country and to raise our standard of living," he said, "we need more inequality than we have now."[16]

The medicine did not work. In the United States, growth slowed in each successive decade during the half century described in this book, from an annual average of 3.13 percent in the 1960s to 0.94 percent in the 2000s, adjusting for inflation and population.[17]

A few people became rich beyond the wildest dreams of Croesus, but the middle class now has reason to expect that their children will lead less prosperous lives.* My father was born in 1951. Seventy-five percent of American men born in that year made more money at the age of thirty than their fathers had made at that age. I was born in 1978. Only 45 percent of American men born in that year made more than our fathers at the age of thirty. For my children and their generation, the outlook is even bleaker.[18]

In the pursuit of efficiency, policy makers also subsumed the interests of Americans as producers to the interests of Americans as consumers, trading well-paid jobs for low-cost electronics. This, in turn, weakened the fabric of society and the viability of local governance. Communities mitigate the consequences of individual job losses; one reason mass layoffs are so painful is that the community, too, often is destroyed. The loss exceeds the sum of its parts.

And the emphasis on growth, now, has come at the expense of the future: tax cuts delivered small bursts of sugar-high prosperity at the expense

---

* Inequality has increased throughout the developed world, reflecting a variety of factors, including the march of technological progress and globalization. This book argues that economic policy — and the policies of the United States in particular — have played a starring role, both by encouraging those trends and by failing to ameliorate the consequences. I share the view of the economic historian Karl Polanyi that a crucial role of government is to limit the pace of change.

of spending on education and infrastructure; limits on environmental regulation preserved corporate profits — but not the environment.

Perhaps the starkest measure of the failure of our economic policies, however, is that the average American's life expectancy is in decline as inequalities of wealth increasingly have become inequalities of health. Life expectancy rose for the wealthiest 20 percent of Americans between 1980 and 2010. Over the same period, life expectancy declined for the poorest 20 percent of Americans. Shockingly, the difference in life expectancy between poor and wealthy American women widened over that period from 3.9 years to 13.6 years.[19]

The origins of economics as a discipline are closely intertwined with the rise of liberal democracy. Governments of the people, by the people, and for the people began to replace coercion with persuasion. Simon Schama, in his cultural history of the Dutch Republic in the seventeenth century, described a striking change in state ceremonies, which became "public rather than secluded, bombastic rather than magical, didactic rather than illusionist." The English economist William Petty, whom Karl Marx called the "founder of political economy," made himself useful, first to the Commonwealth and then to King Charles II, by taking the measure of private wealth to inform and justify the state's growing reliance on taxation.[20]

Partisans began to rely on the language of economics to muster public support for their views, and to shift government policy. The first great work of economics, published in 1776, was called *The Wealth of Nations* because Adam Smith had a recipe for increasing that wealth: free markets and free trade. A few decades later, in 1817, the economist David Ricardo sharpened the point, arguing that nations could prosper by abandoning production of some goods and focusing on areas of "comparative advantage." The other stuff could then be imported. This insight electrified opponents of Britain's Corn Laws, which limited imports of grain.* They spread Ricardo's gospel using a new technology, the postage stamp, which facilitated distribution of a new magazine, *The Economist*.[21] The 1846

---

* In British English, "corn" is a generic term for grain. The British ate wheat, not maize.

decision by Prime Minister Robert Peel to end the Corn Laws is probably the first significant example of economists reshaping public policy.

The influence of economists grew with the availability of data, like bean vines wrapped around cornstalks. Governments knew little about their own nations at the dawn of the modern age. They had only a rough idea of how many people lived in their countries, how much they earned, how much they owned.[22] Alexis de Tocqueville, in a memorable chapter-length harrumph in *Democracy in America* (1835), scoffed at the very idea that one could quantify the wealth of the United States. After all, he wrote, that kind of information wasn't even available about European countries. But nations gradually began to gather statistics — a word that originally meant information about the state. In 1853, the U.S. government hired one of the nation's first economics professors, James D. B. De Bow, to analyze the results of its decennial census, which had gathered more data than earlier iterations, including the first careful count of the number of acres under cultivation.[23]

De Bow's statistical work helped to transform the political debate about slavery. In a bestselling and hugely influential 1857 polemic, *The Impending Crisis of the South*, a young southerner named Hinton Helper used the census data to argue that slavery was bad for the South. In Helper's view, the critical problem with chattel slavery was not immorality but inefficiency.[24]

Over the next seventy-five years, the policy makers placed their faith in markets. The government slowly expanded its role in the economy, creating a national currency and then a central bank; establishing federal regulators, first for the railroads and then for a growing range of other industries; and legislating limits on monopolies. But the government remained a small and peripheral actor. As the country sank into the Great Depression, Congress still lacked basic information about the economy. In 1932, it commissioned an estimate of the decline in economic activity; the economist Simon Kuznets reported back in January 1934 that national income had fallen by half between 1929 and 1932. The data was two years old; it still seemed precious. The government printed forty-five hundred copies of the report, and quickly sold them all.[25]

*   *   *

From the first half of the twentieth century emerged a political consensus that governments should play a much larger role in managing the economy during the second half of the twentieth century. The excesses and inequalities of the early decades, and then the cataclysms of the 1930s and the 1940s, left people with little faith in markets. The economy had been treated as a rocking chair that might move forward or backward but reliably returned to the same place. Keynes made his mark by arguing the economy was more akin to a chair on wheels: after inevitable disruptions, the hand of government was needed to return the chair to its place. The economy required careful management both in good times, to prevent the unequal distribution of prosperity, and in bad times, to limit the pain. Conservatives in those years were people who argued for smaller increases in government regulation and in spending on social welfare.

The U.S. government extended regulation over large swaths of economic activity. Truckers licensed to carry exposed film by the Interstate Commerce Commission required a separate license to carry unexposed film. Antitrust regulators prevented midsized firms from merging and sought to break apart dominant firms like the Aluminum Company of America. Technology firms like AT&T were required to share discoveries with rivals. The banking industry, blamed for causing the Depression, was placed on probation.

Policy makers consciously sought to limit economic inequality. In 1946, Congress passed a law requiring the government to minimize unemployment. In addition, Congress imposed a steeply progressive income tax, and other levies, which collected more than half of the income of those who earned the most. The rise of the labor movement, legitimated by the government during the Great Depression, helped to ensure that workers prospered alongside shareholders. More than a quarter of American wage earners belonged to a union in the 1950s, including a fading movie star named Ronald Reagan, who served as the head of the Screen Actors Guild.

The government also sought to mitigate the effects of inequality by ensuring people had the opportunity to rise, and by catching those who fell.

Federal spending as a share of the nation's total economic output roughly doubled between 1948 and 1968, to 20 percent from about 10 percent. The United States built an interstate highway system, subsidized the expansion of commercial aviation, and laid the groundwork for the rise of the internet. The government also invested heavily in public education, public health care, and public pensions: America wanted to show it could produce better lives for ordinary people than its Communist rivals.

For roughly a quarter century, Americans enjoyed an era of plump prosperity. There were plenty of problems — including the legal, social, and economic subordination of women and of African Americans — but economic gains were broadly shared. Foreigners remarked on the egalitarian veneer of American society: bosses and workers drove similar cars, wore similar clothing, and sat in the same pews. America was a factory town, and Wall Street was the part of town where modestly compensated men managed other people's money. About a fifth of the American population moved to a new home in any given year, and most Americans succeeded in moving up the economic ladder during the course of their lives. In Detroit, car making carried a generation of workers into the middle class, and the cars carried them to the suburbs.

Economists began to enter government service in large numbers during the New Deal and World War II. They helped to calculate where roads and bridges should be built, and then they helped to calculate which roads and bridges should be destroyed. The economist Arnold Harberger recalled that a friend arrived in Washington during the war and found the National Mall filled with Quonset huts. "What is that?" he inquired. "Oh," came the response, "that's where the economists are."[26]

As policy makers and bureaucrats struggled to manage the rapid expansion of the federal government, they began to rely on economists to rationalize the administration of public policy. Gradually economists also began to exert an influence over the goals of public policy. The disciples of Keynes began to convince policy makers that the government could increase prosperity by playing a larger role in the economy. The apogee of this "activist economics" in the United States came in the mid-1960s under

Presidents John F. Kennedy and Lyndon B. Johnson, who deployed tax cuts and spending increases in an aggressive effort to stimulate economic growth and to reduce poverty.

For a few years, the effect seemed almost magical. Then unemployment and inflation began to rise together. By the early 1970s, the American economy was faltering—and Japan and West Germany were resurgent. "We can't compete in making cars, or making steel, or making airplanes," President Nixon fretted. "So are we going to end up just making toilet paper and toothpaste?"[27] Nixon and his successors, Gerald Ford and Jimmy Carter, kept trying the interventionist prescriptions of the Keynesians until even some of the Keynesians threw up their hands. Juanita Kreps, an economist who served as Carter's commerce secretary, told the *Washington Post* when she stepped down in 1979 that her confidence in Keynesian economics was so badly shaken that she did not plan to return to her position as a tenured professor at Duke University. "I don't know what I would teach," she said. "You do lose faith in the catechism."[28]

The economists who led the counterrevolution against Keynesian economics marched under a banner emblazoned "In Markets We Trust." In the late 1960s, they began to convince policy makers that the free movement of prices in a market economy would deliver better results than bureaucrats. They said the champions of activist economics had overstated the government's influence and their own competence. They said that managing capitalism to improve life on Earth ended up making things worse.

It required a certain arrogance to announce a better way of doing everything, but there was also a striking element of modesty. The new economists were not claiming to have the answers. Indeed, they were claiming *not* to have the answers. Their assertion was that policy makers should get out of the way instead of trying to make good choices. Governments should minimize spending and taxation, limit regulation, and allow goods and money to move freely across borders. Where policy was necessary—for example, in allocating the cost of pollution—governments should approximate the workings of a market with all possible fidelity. "If it is feasible to establish a market to implement a policy, no policy-maker can afford to do without one," J. H. Dales, an early advocate for using markets to reduce pollution, wrote in 1968.[29]

This call for faith in markets drew crucial support from other strains of conservatism in twentieth-century American life.[30] It appealed deeply to the "muscular right," which defined itself in opposition to communism and advocated for less government spending on everything except national defense. Midcentury liberals wrote about the resurgence of conservatism as a pathology gnawing at the fringes of society. But the historian Lisa McGirr has observed that the hotbeds of economic conservatism were in Sun Belt suburbs fattened on federal defense spending, including Orange County, California; Colorado Springs, Colorado; and Cobb County, Georgia. Its adherents were well-educated, prosperous people who thought of themselves as "thoroughly modern."[31] They took the view that things were going pretty well, and would continue to do so if government stopped messing around. (The dentists of Orange County did not acknowledge their dependence on the government that paid the contractors who came for cleanings twice a year.)

Economics was an affirming religion. Earlier faiths took a dim view of wealth, because it was generally assumed that one person's pleasure came at the expense of others' pain. And this was true in a world where productivity barely increased over time: the medieval system of guilds limited entry to skilled crafts because there was only so much demand for bread in Rouen.[32] But Adam Smith recognized that the industrial revolution had altered this reality. As productivity increased, wealth could be accumulated by increasing the size of the economy. Being selfish could be good for everyone. It's worth emphasizing that Smith did not think selfishness was *always* good for society. But economics has roughly the same relationship with its founding texts as the world's other great religions. Smith's nuanced accounting became "Greed is good," which has proved to be a world-conquering credo, among both the wealthy and the many who aspire to join them.

Proponents of faith in markets also developed a close relationship with the corporate elite, which was not as inevitable as it may seem in retrospect. Conservative economists like Friedman and his close friend George Stigler initially expressed fear of corporate power and argued that restraining corporate concentration was one of the few legitimate functions of government. Some conservative economists still do. But many decided to make common cause with corporations against government power. The economists provided ideas and the corporations provided money: underwriting research, endowing university chairs, and funding think tanks like the National Bureau of Economic Research, the American Enterprise Institute, and the Hoover Institution at Stanford University.

In a celebrated 1972 paper, the UCLA economists Armen Alchian and Harold Demsetz described corporations as the apotheosis of capitalism — the best possible mechanism for ensuring people were efficiently employed and fairly compensated. A footnote told readers the professors had reached these conclusions with funding from the pharmaceutical giant Eli Lilly.[33] Corporate executives and other wealthy Americans were only too delighted to see their beliefs and interests couched as scientific verities.

Economic conservatives had a more complicated relationship with the social conservatism of the "religious right" and with opponents of civil rights for minorities. Some of the most important early advocates for faith in markets, notably Friedman, a victim of anti-Semitic discrimination in his own academic career, argued that minority groups should embrace the turn toward markets as the best available defense against majoritarian persecution.[34] Markets made it easier to accommodate diverse needs and preferences, inhibiting discrimination on any basis other than the ability to pay. Friedman, and other leading economists, also expressed views that pained social conservatives, including support for immigration, the legalization of drugs, and gay rights. Many social conservatives had hesitations about the 1964 presidential campaign of the libertarian Barry Goldwater; many economic conservatives were pained by the racist agenda of George Wallace's 1968 presidential campaign. Yet by the 1970s the two camps had found a sufficient patch of common ground: social conservatives who feared for their moral values and economic conservatives who feared for their property values both felt profoundly threatened by the expansion of government. Religious leaders including Robert Schuller, pastor of the Garden Grove Community Church in Orange County, synthesized the two strains of conservatism by characterizing the pursuit of wealth as a moral enterprise. Schuller called his church a "shopping center for God" and told his congregants, "You have a God-ordained right to be wealthy." One congregant told McGirr that her previous minister "was talking about Cesar Chavez and the grape boycott, and you just don't want to go to church and hear that instead of the gospel."[35]

Conservatism was a coalition of the powerful, defending the status quo against threats real and imagined. And that coalition was crucial in generating sufficient political support for market-oriented policies. For social conservatives, however, the results were mixed. The turn toward markets made the United States a more diverse and permissive society, but it also helped to limit the speed and magnitude of those encroachments. The prioritization of efficiency and economic growth provided a value-neutral justification for resisting redistributive policies and welfare programs. And economic discrimination — not just tolerated but celebrated — was itself a powerful and durable proxy for other forms of discrimination. The historian Daniel T. Rodgers has observed that economists initiated a shift in public discourse from contests among groups to transactions among individuals.[36] Economists portrayed society as an egalitarian flatland where companies and workers, for example, interacted on even terms. People were reimagined as fully informed and empowered, masters of their own destinies. The most iconic chart in economics, which illustrates the relationship between supply and demand, shows a pair of curved lines that cross in an X on a field devoid of history or context. The prominence of the stock market — perhaps the nearest thing to a real-world example of a textbook marketplace — helped to cement the popular view of markets as cruel but fair, a stereotype that has worked against efforts to make the real world a little less unfair. If a black family took a subprime mortgage loan, the market view did not consider the parents and grandparents who had been unable to build wealth, or the mainstream lenders who refused to make loans in the neighborhood, or how hard it was to find and keep jobs that paid decent wages. The market view was that a borrower and a lender made a deal because both expected to benefit.

Economists are a diverse group. Any reasonable roster includes both Milton Friedman and Karl Marx, which is to say that membership cannot be defined in terms of support for any particular set of policies. In describing the influence of economists on public policy, I am cognizant that some economists vigorously opposed each of the changes described in this book. Indeed, it's quite likely that few economists, if any, supported all of the changes described in this book.

Yet I think it is possible to speak of economists, particularly in the United States in the second half of the twentieth century, as a homogeneous community. Most American economists — and in particular, those who were influential participants in public policy debates — occupied a narrow portion of the ideological spectrum.

American economists are sometimes divided into two camps, one of which is said to be headquartered in Chicago and to favor markets in everything, while the other is said to be headquartered in Cambridge, Massachusetts, and to favor the heavy hand of government. These camps are sometimes referred to as "freshwater" and "saltwater." Far too much is made of such distinctions; the leading members of both groups favored the key shifts described in this book. Although nature tends toward entropy, they shared a confidence that economies tend toward equilibrium. They agreed the primary goal of economic policy was to increase the dollar value of the nation's economic output. They had little patience for efforts to address inequality. A 1979 survey of the members of the American Economic Association found 98 percent opposed rent controls, 97 percent opposed tariffs, 95 percent favored floating exchange rates, and 90 percent opposed minimum wage laws.[37] Their differences were matters of degree, and while those differences are consequential — and are described in these pages — the degree of consensus was consequential, too. Critiques of capitalism that remained a staple of mainstream debate in Europe were seldom heard in the United States. The difference is nicely summarized by the political scientist Jonathan Schlefer: "Cambridge, England, saw capitalism as inherently troubled; Cambridge, Massachusetts, came to see capitalism as merely in need of 'fine-tuning.'"[38]

In time, the American consensus shifted the boundaries of debate in other countries, too.

The real differences between liberals and conservatives on matters of economic policy have tended to obscure the extent to which the Democratic Party, and the major left-of-center parties in other developed nations, supported the prioritization of economic efficiency. Conservatives often have been the most effective reformers, a dynamic Benjamin Disraeli famously encapsulated in his phrase "Tory men and Whig measures." But in recent decades, as reform pushed in a conservative direction, liberals often led the march toward goals conservatives could not reach on their own. In the United States, the reduction of taxation began under Kennedy and the reduction of regulation began under Carter. In Britain, Labour prime minister James Callaghan declared Keynesian ideas dead in 1976. In France, President François Mitterrand, a socialist, imposed fiscal austerity to prepare the country for monetary union with Germany.

The collapse of the Soviet Union solidified this political consensus. The division of the world between Communist and capitalist societies was one of history's great natural experiments, and the results seemed clear. "The Cold War is over, and the University of Chicago won it," the conservative columnist George Will exulted in 1991.[39] The leaders of left-of-center parties who came to power in the 1990s, like Bill Clinton in the United States and Tony Blair in the United Kingdom, largely continued the economic policies of their conservative predecessors. Capitalism became a self-satisfied monopolist in the marketplace of ideas, with predictable consequences: in the absence of alternatives, it was difficult to muster the will to deal with its evident shortcomings.

In the final years of the twentieth century and the first decade of the current century, the trust-in-markets revolution reached its apogee.

Political and social constraints on the role of markets were set aside. Governments pulled back from efforts to regulate the marketplace, to invest in future prosperity, or to limit inequality. The importance of economic growth became the nearest thing to an American ethos: as President George W. Bush told the nation after the September 11 attacks, "We must stand against terror by going back to work."

The triumph of free-market economics is sometimes illustrated by a satellite image of the Korean peninsula at night, the southern half illuminated by electricity, the northern half black as the surrounding ocean. It is a powerful image, but its significance has often been misrepresented. South Korea, like other wealthy nations, rose to prosperity by carefully steering its economy. This is the story of what happened when nations decided to take both hands off the wheel.

PART I

Chapter One

Markets in Everything

To keep the fish that they carried on long journeys lively and
fresh, sea captains used to introduce an eel into the barrel. In the
economics profession, Milton Friedman is that eel.

— *Paul Samuelson (1969)*[1]

In late 1966, Martin Anderson, a young Columbia University economics professor with libertarian leanings, found himself seated at a dinner party next to a lawyer from Richard Nixon's law firm. Nixon had joined the New York firm after announcing his first retirement from politics, telling reporters, "You don't have Nixon to kick around anymore." The lawyer did not like Nixon and, by the end of the night, he also didn't like Anderson. "With views like that," he told Anderson, "you should be working for my boss — not me." A few days later, Anderson received a call from Leonard Garment, a partner at Nixon's firm and a close adviser. Garment told Anderson he'd heard there was a Columbia professor saying crazy things, and he invited Anderson to pay a visit. Soon, Anderson was meeting regularly with the small group plotting Nixon's political resurrection in the 1968 presidential election.[2]

At a meeting in March 1967, the Nixon group turned its attention to military conscription. The United States had drafted men to fight in most of its major wars but, after the end of World War II, Congress for the first time had authorized an ongoing draft. The nation was shouldering global responsibilities; no one was quite sure how many soldiers were needed to fight a Cold War. Over the next quarter century, the government annually conscripted tens of thousands of men.

Popular support for the draft had started to wane by the 1960s. While military service was described as a universal obligation, significantly less than half of American men served in the military. As fighting in Vietnam intensified, so did objections to the basic unfairness of picking some men to serve and perhaps to die. Reformers floated ideas like replacing local draft boards with a national lottery, or requiring all men to attend military training, but those plans did not address the basic inequity.

"I have an idea," Anderson told the Nixon men. He had just read an article by the University of Chicago economist Milton Friedman, who argued that the government should end conscription and instead recruit an all-volunteer military by offering competitive wages. "What if I could show you how we could end the draft and increase our military strength at the same time?" Anderson asked the group. "Let me put together a paper on this."[3]

The world changes and it's hard to say why. The United States ended conscription in 1973 because Americans had a lot of babies in the 1950s and because an insecure man named Lyndon Baines Johnson doubled down on a losing hand and because it kept getting harder to teach recruits how to operate new military technology and because the voting age dropped to eighteen and because young men in an increasingly prosperous nation did not want to fight. All of that was important. But it is also true that the United States ended conscription because Milton Friedman persuaded Anderson, who persuaded Nixon, who won the 1968 presidential election.

Friedman was a formidable academic, crowned with a Nobel Prize in economics in 1976, yet he deserves to be remembered chiefly as one of the most influential ideologues of the twentieth century, the forceful prophet of a conservative counterrevolution that reshaped life in the United States and around the world.

He wrote in his 1998 memoirs that economists exert influence "by keeping options available when something has to be done in a time of crisis" — by ensuring the refrigerator is well stocked when policy makers open the door.[4] His role in ending military conscription marked the first time he shifted policy in the direction of his beliefs. More celebrated triumphs followed, but Friedman, toward the end of his life, said he remained most proud of the first. "No public policy activity that I have ever engaged in," he said, "has given me as much satisfaction."[5]

Milton Friedman skittered disruptively through the twentieth century like a loose electron, leaving behind a world reconfigured by his ideas. He was a small man with large glasses and the boyish enthusiasm of a natural salesman. Great scientists often are portrayed as singularly bad at communicating with other humans; indeed, this is held to be a mark of their brilliance. Great economists, by contrast, tend to be the popularizers of their own ideas and, in this art, Friedman had few peers. His animating idea was simple and universal: the open marketplace was the best possible system of human governance — certainly much better than traditional forms of government, which ought to be kept to an absolute minimum. He joked that if government bureaucrats should ever gain control of the Sahara, there soon would be a shortage of sand.

In *Free to Choose*, a ten-part exposition of Friedman's views broadcast on PBS in 1980, the economist held up a simple yellow pencil and rhapsodized over its construction. "Literally thousands of people cooperated to make this pencil," Friedman told viewers. He listed the workers who provided the wood and graphite, the yellow and black paint, the rubber eraser, and its metal band. "People who don't speak the same language," he said, "who practice different religions, who might hate one another if they ever met." And what, he asked, tapping the pointed tip, brought them together? "It was the magic of the price system."

He was also a ferocious debater, prompting one colleague to observe it was best to argue with Friedman when he was not in the room.[6] He listened to opponents with a Cheshire cat's smile, waiting for them to stop talking so he could help them understand why they were wrong.

During the first half of his career, Friedman produced the majority of his significant academic research. During the second half, he emerged as "the most creative social political thinker of our age," in the words of Daniel Patrick Moynihan, the New York senator and public intellectual who was well equipped to judge Friedman, since they worked in the same line.[7] Even those who disagreed with Friedman found themselves unable to ignore his broadsides. "Only a small minority of the profession is persuaded by his opinions," the liberal economist Robert Solow said in the 1960s, but "around any academic lunch table on any given day, the talk is more likely to be about Milton Friedman than about any other economist."[8]

A half century later, economists still were talking about Friedman — but many more of them had come to agree. Lawrence H. Summers, a Harvard economist who served as a senior official in the Clinton and Obama administrations, wrote in 2006 that Friedman had been a "devil figure" in his youth, but he had come to view Friedman with great admiration. "He has had more influence on economic policy as it is practiced around the world today than any other modern figure," Summers wrote.[9] A Harvard colleague, Andrei Shleifer, wrote in 2009 that the period between 1980 and 2005 had been "the Age of Milton Friedman."[10]

Milton Friedman's parents came from the same small Austro-Hungarian city, Beregszász, but they met in Brooklyn, where Milton was born on July 31, 1912. He grew up in Rahway, New Jersey, where the family owned small businesses including, at various times, a clothing factory, a dry-goods store, and an ice cream parlor. At the age of sixteen, Milton left home and enrolled at Rutgers University, where he had his only brush with military service. The school then required students to enroll in the Reserve Officers' Training Corps; Milton completed the required two years and dropped out of the training program.* Years later he wrote, "I regarded ROTC as a burden to be borne with no significant benefits for me or for the country."[11]

He started out studying mathematics, intending to become an actuary.

---

* The Morrill Act of 1862, which endowed colleges in each state with grants of federal land, required recipient institutions to teach military tactics. In 1916, the ROTC program was created to standardize these efforts. At many land-grant schools, training was mandatory until the 1960s — consistent with the older view of military service as a responsibility. Rutgers, in 1960, was one of the first schools to make participation voluntary.

But in the midst of the Great Depression, he decided economics was more interesting, and one of his professors helped him to secure a place in the Ph.D. program at the University of Chicago.[12] Friedman headed west in 1932 with a little money in his pocket: during his undergraduate years, he and a classmate had obtained permission from the dean at Rutgers to sell white socks and green ties to the college's freshmen, who then were required to wear both.[13] They soon expanded into selling used textbooks, prompting a protest from the campus bookstore. Fortunately for Friedman, the dean's letter of permission was not overly specific about what they could sell.

The money, however, was not enough to get Friedman through graduate school. In 1935, Friedman and the woman he later married, a fellow Chicago economics graduate student named Rose Director, moved to Washington, D.C., where they joined the rapidly expanding army of economists employed in the administration of the federal government's New Deal programs. "Ironically, the New Deal was a lifesaver for us personally," Friedman wrote. "The new government programs created a boom market for economists, especially in Washington. Absent the New Deal, it is far from clear that we could have gotten jobs as economists."[14]

Rose, born in Russia in 1910 or 1911, moved to the United States with her family just before World War I. She grew up in Portland, Oregon, and enrolled at Reed College before transferring to the University of Chicago to join her brother, Aaron Director, who was then a graduate student in economics and who went on to become one of the most important and uncompromising libertarians of his generation. Rose met Milton in Professor Jacob Viner's seminar on economic theory; they were seated next to each other because Viner organized students by last name. They were married in 1938. When Rose wrote her brother to share the news, Aaron responded, "Tell him I shall not hold his very strong New Deal leanings — authoritarian to use an abusive term — against him."[15] It was a marriage of economists. Said Milton, "I can recall many a pleasant summer evening discussing consumption data and theory in front of a blazing fire." The Friedmans also assigned numbers to frequent arguments, because that was more efficient. To the end of their lives, they said "Number 2" instead of "I was wrong and you were right."[16] Rose never finished her thesis; she became Milton's collaborator, particularly on public policy issues; his editor, particularly of his popular works; and his intellectual commissar. Even after a half century of marriage, Rose said she had never forgiven Milton for his role as a young Treasury Department official in the early 1940s in facilitating the growth of government by devising the requirement that employers must withhold taxes from paychecks.[17]

During the war years, Friedman also worked at a government-funded think tank that applied math to military questions. For example: Was it better for a fighter plane to have eight smaller machine guns or four larger guns?[18] One of Friedman's projects involved testing alloys for the blades of jet engine turbines. Friedman saw a shortcut: he crunched the data and came up with a new alloy, which he asked a laboratory at the Massachusetts Institute of Technology to mix and test. Friedman's calculations showed the blade should last for two hundred hours. It lasted two hours.[19] Friedman later said the experience shaped his lifelong skepticism of complicated formulas and forecasting. Indeed, a basic theme in his public policy prescriptions was that governments operated in darkness, and that the appropriate response to most problems was to do very little, and to do it slowly and steadily. Ambitious interventions, he said, tended to make matters worse.[20]

By contrast with his skepticism about the future, he had a deeply romantic view of the past, forever comparing the fallen condition of modern society to an earlier era in which he imagined people had cared for themselves and prospered to the best of their abilities. Meritocracy is an idea that appeals deeply to talented outsiders, and Friedman chose to see the role of individual initiative rather than the context of public support. He celebrated drivers and took roads for granted.

Throughout his career he enjoyed the support of wealthy patrons eager to find intellectuals who would champion the cause of limited government. The National Bureau of Economic Research, which published his doctoral dissertation and later supported his most influential work on monetary policy, was the first and most important. It was created in 1920 to gather and publish economic data, in the days before the government had embraced that role, with financial backing from the Rockefellers and other oil barons. Friedman's dissertation criticized licensing requirements for physicians, arguing that the government was helping doctors to limit competition at the expense of their patients. This was a bit much for the bureau. Licensing was widely regarded as a necessary form of quality control, and the bureau refused to publish the study until Friedman softened the language. It finally appeared in 1945, allowing Friedman to obtain his doctorate.[21]

That year, Friedman briefly joined the faculty at the University of Minnesota, where he shared an office with another young professor, George Stigler. The two men, who had first met as graduate students at Chicago, co-authored an attack on rent control playfully entitled *Roofs or Ceilings?* for the libertarian Foundation for Economic Education. Friedman and Stigler began by describing the rapid reconstruction of San Francisco after the 1906 earthquake that destroyed much of the city. Then they jumped ahead forty years, writing that San Francisco once again needed a wave of new construction to house a booming population. But this time, they said, the government was standing in the way. They argued that rent controls discouraged construction of new apartments and maintenance of existing apartments. By restraining the profits of landlords, they said, the government was harming tenants, too.[22]

The Foundation for Economic Education objected to a passage in which Friedman and Stigler wrote that reducing economic inequality was a legitimate goal of public policy, even though they added that rent control was the wrong way to pursue that goal. The foundation inserted a note, without the authors' permission, describing the pamphlet as all the more compelling for showing that even a pair of bleeding hearts like Friedman and Stigler opposed rent control. A trade group for real estate agents distributed half a million copies.[23]

By the time the pamphlet appeared in the fall of 1946, Friedman already had left Minnesota to join the economics faculty at the University of Chicago. Shortly after his arrival, in the spring of 1947, he traveled with Aaron Director and Stigler to Switzerland for the first meeting of the Mont Pelerin Society, a group created by the libertarian economist Friedrich Hayek to bring together the lonely apostles of the free market, who labored in an environment of unremitting hostility to their ideas, which were widely viewed as dangerous and old-fashioned. "Nobody in Europe believes in the American way of life, that is, private enterprise, or rather, those who believe in it are a defeated party which seems to have no more future than the Jacobites in England after 1688," the British political commentator A. J. P. Taylor said on a BBC radio broadcast in 1945.[24] In the early years after World War II, it was also hard to find Americans who believed in that version of the American way of life.

Hayek, who was born in Austria in 1899, and whose career took root before the Great Depression, was raised in the free-market faith and never abandoned it. In his most famous book, *The Road to Serfdom*, published in 1944, Hayek attacked the interventionist brand of economics associated with John Maynard Keynes. Hayek argued that socialism was bad and that the expansion of government's role in managing the economy was a slippery slope that would end in socialism.

Hayek's attack on the logic of socialism was powerful and enduring. He argued that prices in an open marketplace conveyed far more information than any bureaucracy could possibly compile, and transactions based on those prices allocated resources far more efficiently than any bureaucracy could possibly achieve. His slippery-slope thesis, by contrast, was a flawed piece of alarmism: as Keynes noted in an acerbic rebuttal, Hayek acknowledged the necessity of some government functions but offered little explanation of the line between his preferred forms of intervention and the kinds that led to socialism. Keynes thought it was not only possible but necessary for societies to strike a balance between markets and management.*

Friedman found friends and respite at the Mont Pelerin meeting, which became an annual event. He recalled, "It provided a week when people like that could get together and open their minds and not have to worry about whether someone was going to stick a knife in their back."[25]

---

* Western democracies settled the theoretical argument by massively expanding social welfare spending after the war. Not even Sweden has slipped back into serfdom. Hayek, however, is still quoted by those concerned that the next government intervention will prove to be one step too far.

In a 1951 essay, Friedman predicted the public, too, would soon begin to run out of patience with what he described as the Western world's turn toward collectivism. He perceived a latent appetite for liberalism, in the old sense of a commitment to free markets and minimal government. "The stage is set for the growth of a new current of opinion to replace the old, to provide the philosophy that will guide the legislators of the next generation even though it can hardly affect those of this one," he wrote. "Ideas have little chance of making much headway against a strong tide; their opportunity comes when the tide has ceased running strong but has not yet turned.

"This is, if I am right, such a time."[26]

Walter Oi's War

Friedman first condemned military conscription in a June 1956 speech at Wabash College in western Indiana. He was the star attraction at a summer camp for young economics professors staged by the William Volker Fund, a foundation endowed by a Kansas City window-shade maker that was one of the most important sources of funding for the dissemination of free-market ideas in the midcentury United States. The speech was a wide-ranging attack on government. The critique of conscription was the eleventh item on a list of fourteen misguided public policies that also included national parks, the postal service, and public housing. Friedman said the government was "interfer[ing] with the freedom of young men to shape their lives."[27]

Rose Friedman took that speech and several others and turned them into Milton's first book, *Capitalism and Freedom*. Its publication in 1962 marked Milton's emergence as a public intellectual. It became one of the most important books of the twentieth century, not least because Ronald Reagan numbered among its fans. The royalties covered the cost of the Friedmans' Vermont summer home, which they named "Capitaf." But first, *Capitalism and Freedom* helped to connect Friedman with Senator Barry Goldwater.

Goldwater, the Republican presidential nominee in 1964, was the beta version of Reagan. He ran against government, proposing to end federal oversight of the energy, telephone, and airline industries; to cut taxes; and to privatize the Tennessee Valley Authority, which provided cheap electricity to a big chunk of the Southeast.

Goldwater endorsed Friedman's book, boosting sales; Friedman wrote parts of the speech Goldwater gave to formally launch his general election campaign on September 3, 1964. "Republicans will end the draft altogether, and as soon as possible," Goldwater said. "That I promise you."[28] He said military service should be a career like anything else.

A few weeks later, Friedman elaborated on the theme in an article for the *New York Times Magazine* entitled "The Goldwater View of Economics."[29] He described conscription as a tax: the government was taking people's time, and it was manifestly compensating them inadequately, as evidenced by the fact they had not volunteered. In Friedman's view, it was the same system of forced labor Egyptian pharaohs had used to build the pyramids and Britannia had used to rule the waves — and it was unconscionable. Friedman's son, David, had turned nineteen in 1964, lending an edge to his father's outrage. "How can we justify paying him less than the amount for which he is willing to serve?" Friedman wrote a few years later, in the essay that reached Anderson and then Nixon. "How can we justify, that is, involuntary servitude except in times of the greatest national emergency? One of the great gains in the progress of civilization was the elimination of the power of the nobleman or the sovereign to exact compulsory servitude."[30]

Friedman's argument would have puzzled America's founding fathers. Thomas Jefferson wrote of "the necessity of obligating every citizen to be a soldier; this was the case with the Greeks and Romans, and must be that of every free state."[31] George Washington regarded an army of professional soldiers as posing a much greater danger to democracy than an army of conscripts. But opposition to conscription is an old tradition, too. During the English Civil War in the seventeenth century, the radical Levellers — a political movement rooted in the urban middle class and committed to republican government — proposed an end to military conscription as one of their signature reforms. They argued no man should be required to fight unless he was "satisfied in the justness of that cause wherein he hazards his life, or may destroy an others."[32]

Even in the immediate aftermath of World War II, support for the draft was by no means uniform. Senator Robert A. Taft, an Ohio Republican, went to Gettysburg National Cemetery in 1946 to deliver a Memorial Day speech condemning the continuation of the draft as "essentially totalitarian."[33] The liberal economist John Kenneth Galbraith helped to persuade Adlai Stevenson, the Democratic nominee in 1956, to raise the possibility of ending the draft in a speech delivered just a few months after Friedman's Wabash speech.[34] Wags said it was the only thing Friedman and Galbraith ever agreed about.*

Still, in 1964, opponents of conscription remained solidly in the minority. There were many people campaigning to change the draft, but few seeking to end it. Communism loomed; the military was the bulwark of democracy, and experts generally agreed there was no other way to find enough soldiers. After Goldwater's speech, President Johnson created a study group to blunt what his advisers saw as yet another instance of the Republican candidate promising free lunches to voters. Its conclusion was unequivocal: "Increases in military compensation sufficient to attract a volunteer force cannot be justified."[35]

But as Bob Dylan sang that same year, the times were a-changin'. President Kennedy's famous plea in his 1961 inaugural address — "Ask not what your country can do for you. Ask what you can do for your country" — resonated precisely because the opposite tendency was taking hold. People increasingly were inclined to prioritize the rights of individuals over the needs of the community. Some of the earliest manifestations of the new mood were small acts of local defiance. The Dallas suburb of Richardson voted in the early 1960s to charge seven cents for milk in school cafeterias, rather than accepting federal aid and charging two

---

* Friedman and Galbraith actually agreed about a wide range of policy questions. Their differences tended to be narrow, but very much in the public eye. Galbraith once described Friedman as "a man who is not reliably wrong except on monetary policy."

cents. The mayor of Lakeland, Florida, declined federal money to rebuild the city's water system, explaining, "It breeds apathy, destroys initiative and opens the door to the invasion of individual rights."[36] The pollster Samuel Lubell, among the first to take notice, wrote that the priorities of Americans were shifting "from those of getting to those of keeping."[37] Nixon, among the first politicians to grasp the implications, reworked Kennedy's challenge in his 1973 inaugural. "Let each of us ask — not just what government will do for me, but what can I do for myself?"

Other changes also were at work. After World War II, Americans started making a lot of babies; in 1964, the nineteenth anniversary of that baby boom, the pool of draft-eligible young men expanded dramatically. Among the 1.2 million American men born in 1938, 42 percent served in the military. Among the 1.9 million men born in 1947, only 27 percent served in the military — notwithstanding the escalation of the Vietnam War.[38] One of the many groups convened to study the draft posed the obvious question in the title of its report, "Who Serves When Not All Serve?"

The answer in 1964 rested with local draft boards. In Wisconsin, draft boards often declined to conscript mechanics who specialized in farm equipment; in Alaska, draft boards passed over ophthalmologists "because they happen to have a lot of eye trouble up there."[39] The Selective Service Administration celebrated this idiosyncratic process, boasting for example that it was filling the nation's classrooms by offering deferments to men who took teaching jobs.[40] But some of those were men who did not want to be teachers. Draft boards also displayed a taste for sending minorities to war, which was perhaps connected to the fact that no local draft board in the state of Mississippi had an African American on its panel.

Technology also was reducing the need for manual labor, in war as in factories, and the work that remained increasingly involved the operation of sophisticated machines. The military needed well-trained and experienced hands, not conscripts who fled after two years.

And there was Vietnam. On the morning of March 8, 1965, roughly thirty-five hundred U.S. marines landed on a beach north of the city of

Da Nang, where they were greeted by Vietnamese women holding garlands of flowers and a large sign that read "Welcome, Gallant Marines!" President Johnson had decided to commit ground troops to the burgeoning war and more than 2.7 million Americans would end up going over there. Public anger about the draft and the war would intertwine and grow until Nixon moved to end both.

On the evening of May 11, 1966, several hundred University of Chicago students occupied the campus administration building, barring entry to everyone except reporters, janitors, and the women who worked the university's telephone switchboard, which happened to be in the basement. Disinclined to take them seriously, the *New York Times* reported that the students brought food, bedrolls, and "at least one banjo," and illustrated its account with a photograph of a woman holding a squirming child on her lap, captioned, "Protester's son protests."[41] The students, if not the son, were protesting a change in the rules of the draft. Lewis Hershey, the seventy-two-year-old general who had headed the Selective Service Administration almost from its inception in 1940, had decided to end a blanket exemption for pretty much anyone enrolled in college classes. The best and the brightest still could stay in class; the rest might better serve their country by serving their country.

In response to the protests, the Chicago faculty senate announced it would hold a conference on the draft. The three-day event, held in early December 1966, attracted an all-star cast: General Hershey and the executive secretary of the Central Committee for Conscientious Objectors; the cartoonist Bill Mauldin, famous for drawing beleaguered grunts; a nun who delighted in relating that she represented one of the oldest volunteer armies; and two of the youngest members of Congress, Senator Edward Kennedy of Massachusetts, a Democrat, and Representative Donald Rumsfeld of Illinois, a Republican.

There were papers and presenters, but mostly a freewheeling discussion around a series of questions: What was good about the draft? What might be improved? What might take its place? At the outset, the vast majority of the 120 participants indicated they did not see an alternative to conscription. By the end, Friedman and his allies persuaded half the participants to sign a petition calling for an all-volunteer force.[42]

The person most responsible for winning over the crowd was Walter Oi, an economist who had started going blind in the fourth grade and, by the time he rose to speak in Chicago, could barely tell the difference between night and day. Oi was born in Los Angeles in 1929, the son of Japanese immigrants.[43] The family was imprisoned during World War II at the Granada internment camp in southeast Colorado, an experience that informed Oi's lifelong concern about government overreach. Despite his deteriorating vision, he completed a bachelor's and a master's degree at UCLA and then, in 1962, completed a doctorate in labor economics at Chicago. In 1964, he landed a fellowship at the Pentagon, working on the recruitment study Johnson had ordered in response to Goldwater.

Oi was undeterred by the loss of vision. Assistants recorded papers and Oi listened, first on reels and later on cassettes and later still on digital devices. He dictated calculations to research assistants or his wife, whom he taught to perform regressions and other statistical techniques. He gave speeches from memory, reeling off facts and figures as if he were reading from a script, and perhaps there was one in his head. For pleasure, he would sit in the stands at stock car races, rocking in the waves of heat and noise as the cars roared past. He even hitched a ride in a pace car at the Atlanta Motor Speedway so he could feel what it was like to hurtle around the track.

In later years, Oi told his daughter that he had decided not to pursue a career in bench science because he was afraid he might blow something up, but Oi did like to cause a little chaos. One of his favorite jokes involved two dignitaries watching a military parade. At the very end, after all the tanks and missiles and marching men, came a wagon with a few shabby civilians inside. "Who are they?" the first man asked the second. "Oh," the second man replied. "Those are the economists. You wouldn't believe the damage they can cause." Oi would unsettle visitors by making nonsensical pronouncements, then press his assistants to describe the looks on the visitors' faces. That kind of belligerence played well with economists, a discipline with an outsized share of macho intellectuals. For many years,

Chicago's economics department gave an annual award in Oi's name to the graduate student who asked the most ridiculous question.

Oi's presentation at the Chicago conference was a detailed attack on the Pentagon study he had helped to produce. The Pentagon had pegged the additional cost of a volunteer military at a minimum of $5.5 billion — roughly a 10 percent increase in annual defense spending. Oi argued that this was both overstated and misleading. The actual cost, he said, would be no more than $4 billion; the Pentagon had failed to consider the likelihood that volunteers would serve for longer, reducing the need for new recruits. The Pentagon study also ignored the economic benefits of allowing men to pursue other lines of work, which Oi estimated at more than $5 billion. An all-volunteer army, in other words, would be good for the economy.[44]

Sol Tax, an anthropology professor who organized the Chicago conference, wrote that Oi persuaded the gathering "that abandonment of conscription entirely might not be an outlandish alternative."[45] Others offered similar praise. "Thanks to the sessions and the papers and the arguments in the past few days, I'm a convert to the idea of a volunteer Army, to the idea of taking as a real goal the ending of the draft," said Harris Wofford, associate director of the Peace Corps. After returning to Washington, Congressman Rumsfeld introduced legislation to end the draft and read Oi's presentation into the Congressional Record.

But the Johnson administration had no interest. In March 1967, Johnson requested a four-year extension of the draft, insisting there was no realistic alternative. The bill quickly passed both chambers of Congress by large margins. Only nine members of the House and two members of the Senate voted no. "A substantial percentage of the members of Congress at that time were veterans of military service," recalled John J. Ford, then the staff director of the House Armed Services Committee.* "They had lived with the Selective Service law in effect

---

* In 1967 and 1969, 75.1 percent of the members of Congress were veterans, the highest level in modern times. Then began a long decline. By 2015, just 17 percent of the members of Congress were veterans.

virtually all their adult life. They had a sense of the moral rightness, if you will, of service to your country, or at least being liable for such service."[46]

The Mercenary Professor

Among the economists who played a leading role in ending the draft, Martin Anderson was the only who had served in the military: he enrolled in the ROTC program at Dartmouth College and then spent 1958–1959 as a second lieutenant in army intelligence.[47] After returning to academia, he earned a doctorate in economics at MIT and joined the faculty at Columbia's business school, where he taught finance. Anderson, quick-witted and gregarious, had a contrarian bent. In 1964, he published *The Federal Bulldozer*, which called for the end of urban renewal projects, then widely regarded as the epitome of progressive urban policy. Anderson argued the government was destroying far more housing than it was creating, and he mocked the premise that poor families were finding better housing. If such housing existed, he wrote, "wouldn't it be far simpler and much cheaper to advise people of these attractive bargains without going to all the trouble of tearing their homes down?"[48] Anderson liked jabbing the establishment in person, too. That fall, Anderson and his future wife, Annelise, campaigned door-to-door for Goldwater on the Upper West Side of Manhattan.

Milton Friedman arrived at Columbia that same autumn to spend a year as a visiting professor, and Anderson cultivated a relationship. One night at Friedman's apartment, they started arguing around 11:00 p.m.; three hours later, Anderson said he was too tired to continue. "All right," Friedman responded with a big smile. "I win."[49] Anderson also joined the loose circle of libertarians that revolved around the novelist Ayn Rand. The group included a flashy economist named Alan Greenspan who had gone into business rather than academia and therefore had a posh apartment and a blue Cadillac Eldorado convertible.

In the spring of 1967, Anderson read a printed version of the arguments Friedman and Oi had made against conscription at the Chicago conference and raised the idea with Nixon's advisers. He then recruited Greenspan to help him draft a memo for Nixon. The two men delivered a seven-page version in April and a thirty-page version by the Fourth of July. They began by asserting that no one liked conscription. "It has been tolerated reluctantly," they wrote, "only because it has been thought to be absolutely necessary to preserve and protect the national security of the United States." The memo then described Oi's work: the effective tax imposed on conscripts, and the relatively modest cost of recruiting volunteers instead. Anderson and Greenspan concluded: "Because it is moral and fair, because it increases our national security, and because it is economically feasible, we should give high priority to the goal of establishing an all-volunteer armed force with fair, decent wages that will offer the young men of our country the opportunity to participate in its defense with dignity, with honor and as free men."[50]

Nixon described the memo as "very interesting," and circulated copies among his advisers. Some liked the idea; others responded with alarm, warning that Nixon would anger conservative voters. That concern was heightened in late September 1967, when 320 prominent liberals — including the Nobel laureate Linus Pauling, the poet Robert Lowell, and Dr. Benjamin Spock, the author of the era's bible of baby care — signed "A Call to Resist Illegitimate Authority" in support of men who refused to serve in the military. Then, in mid-October, came a week of nationwide antidraft protests culminating in a march on Washington. Patrick Buchanan, a top Nixon adviser, warned his boss that endorsing an end to the draft was tantamount to siding with the protesters. He wrote, "Will it be said that RN is giving these guys the means to avoid service?" Across the bottom of the memo, Nixon scrawled, "Ike thinks so."[51] Notwithstanding Dwight Eisenhower's reservations, Nixon decided to take the plunge. At the University of Wisconsin on November 17, 1967, a student asked about the draft. Nixon responded by calling for "an entirely new approach" to recruitment. The nation, he said, must "move toward a volunteer army by compensating those who go into the military on a basis comparable to those in civilian careers."[52] There was an important caveat: he said he would end the draft only after he ended the war in Vietnam.

Still, it was a risky stand for Nixon to take. Congress had just voted to reauthorize the draft, and conscription remained popular with the general public. Opinion polls wouldn't swing in favor of Nixon's position for another three years.[53]

In his 1978 memoirs, Nixon portrayed the decision as rooted in economic ideology. "When I came into office, one of the severest and most unfair restraints on the free market was the military draft, which is a way of compelling service from everyone rather than hiring service from those who supply it voluntarily," he wrote. "Thus the elimination of the draft and the introduction of a volunteer Army in January 1973 were also major steps to meaningful economic freedom."[54]

In August 1968, when the Republican Party nominated Nixon as its presidential candidate, ending the draft became a plank in the party's campaign platform.[55]

Hubert Humphrey, the Democratic nominee, denounced the idea as "highly irresponsible," echoing the language Eisenhower had used in 1956 and Johnson had used in 1964. Humphrey said the cost was prohibitive; Nixon was teasing young Americans with "vain hopes."[56] Nixon responded by giving a national radio address declaring even more forcefully that he intended to end the draft. "This is my belief," Nixon said on October 17, 1968, "once our involvement in the Vietnam War is behind us, we move toward an all-volunteer armed force."[57]

Three weeks later, Nixon was elected the thirty-seventh president of the United States.

Nixon brought into his White House a group of advisers who were older than his campaign staff, more embedded in the political establishment, and less inclined to end military conscription. Henry Kissinger, the national security adviser, and his military assistant, Colonel Alexander Haig, strongly opposed the idea. "The only reason I am not more concerned about this campaign promise is I know that a Republican budget could not sustain the economics of such a force even if the Vietnam conflict were settled tomorrow," Haig wrote Kissinger in a memo that described ending the draft as "totally incompatible with the traditions of the military and our society."[58]

Anderson, who became an aide to Arthur F. Burns, Nixon's top economic adviser, immediately set to work reminding anyone who would listen that the President had made a promise, and he rallied others to the cause. In mid-December 1968, even before Nixon had taken office, Burns got a call from W. Allen Wallis, the president of the University of Rochester. Wallis was an economic prodigy, so talented that he didn't even have a doctorate. He had been on the verge of completing his work at the University of Chicago in 1946 when the university offered him a professorship on the condition that he drop out of school, because Chicago did not grant degrees to its own faculty. During World War II, he was Friedman's boss at Columbia and the two men had remained friends and allies. At Rochester, Wallis had begun to build a new center of market-oriented economics; among his recruits was Walter Oi, who joined the faculty in 1967. Wallis regarded the draft as "immutably immoral" and inefficient, and he offered to send Burns a summary of the latest research on conscription. Burns agreed to share it with Nixon, but he told Wallis that it had to fit on a single page, it had to show the cost would be less than $1 billion per year, and it had to be delivered by the end of the year.

Oi already had left Rochester for California, to introduce his fiancée to his father; the couple returned to Rochester on the next available airplane. Oi and some colleagues finished the report on Christmas Eve and paid a graduate student to carry it to Burns in New York City. Unable to restrict themselves to a single page, the economists filled twenty-five pages. They settled for stapling a one-page summary to the front and labeling the rest an appendix.[59]

Nixon acted on the idea shortly after taking office. "I have concluded that it would be desirable to end the draft as soon as it can be done responsibly," the new president wrote his defense secretary, Melvin Laird, on February 2, 1969, instructing him to assemble a panel of experts.[60] Presidential commissions were all the rage in the late 1960s, just like music festivals and marijuana. President Johnson established roughly two dozen. On March 27, 1969, Nixon created his first: the President's Commission on an All-Volunteer Armed Force, known as the Gates Commission after its chairman, Thomas S. Gates Jr., who had been Eisenhower's last defense secretary. The White House was careful to include a diversity of views, but the outcome was predetermined. "I want to move in that direction," Nixon told Gates during a private meeting in the Oval Office.[61] To help the commission along, the bulk of the staff—including Oi—was imported from Rochester, the hotbed of antidraft academia.

Still, there was a genuine debate. Lauris Norstad, a retired air force general and the former supreme allied commander for Europe, simply didn't see a problem that needed to be fixed: he had served, and it had done him no obvious harm. He also worried that using money as an inducement would draw a lower quality of people into the military. Crawford Greenewalt, the former chief executive of the chemical conglomerate DuPont, asked for assurances at the first meeting that he would not be required to support an end to the draft, and he continued to express hesitation right through the last meeting. Greenewalt was, like Friedman, a member of Hayek's Mont Pelerin Society. But Greenewalt's minimalist conception of social obligation included military service. He suggested the government should raise military pay while leaving conscription in place, thus eliminating the tax on those who served.

Friedman and the research staff, who had a rejoinder to every concern, pointed out that paying an average wage still would not adequately compensate men who could earn more in civilian life—a group that included the likes of Private Willie Mays and Sergeant Elvis Presley. Friedman also sought to humanize the debate. At one meeting, he asked the staff to distribute a letter from a young conscript. "The atmosphere of my new unit is truly depressing," the young man wrote. "There is no one here who has a kind word or thought for the Army—everyone hates his work, his officers and his obligation to wake up every morning."[62]

A defining moment came on a Sunday morning in December 1969. Gates invited the heads of the various branches of the military to meet with the commission. General William Westmoreland, the army's chief of staff, regarded the commission's work as an assault on the army, the only branch of the service that relied on conscription.

"I do not relish the prospect of commanding an army of mercenaries," Westmoreland told the commissioners.

Friedman, smelling blood in the water, responded, "General, would you rather command an army of slaves?"

Westmoreland: "I do not like to hear patriotic draftees referred to as slaves."

Friedman: "I do not like to hear patriotic volunteers referred to as mercenaries. After all, in that same sense I am a mercenary professor, who has his hair cut by a mercenary barber, his ills taken care of by a mercenary physician, and his legal affairs handled by a mercenary lawyer. And — if you will pardon me — you, sir, are a mercenary general."[63]

Two months later, the commission voted unanimously to end the draft. They presented their report to the President on February 21, 1970. The meeting was scheduled for thirty minutes but Nixon, engaged, kept them for ninety minutes.[64] Oi's guide dog, Genie, had a habit of growling at strangers, but she let the President pat her head.

The report, drafted by Friedman and polished by Richard J. Whalen, a conservative writer hired for the purpose, was a forceful polemic against conscription, and the administration arranged to publish 100,000 copies.[65] The enumeration of grievances, in particular, had the flavor of the Declaration of Independence: "It has been a costly, inequitable and divisive procedure for recruiting men for the armed forces. It has imposed heavy burdens on a small minority of young men while easing slightly the tax burden on the rest of us. It has introduced needless uncertainty into the lives of all our young men. It has burdened draft boards with painful decisions about who shall be compelled to serve and who shall be deferred. It has weakened the political fabric of our society and impaired the delicate web of shared values that alone enables a free society to exist. These costs of conscription would have to be borne if they were a necessary price for defending our peace and security. They are intolerable when there is an alternative consistent with our basic national values."[66]

The alternative, of course, was a volunteer force, ensuring soldiers wanted to be soldiers — and that other men could pursue other dreams.

From "Who Fights?" to "Who Cares?"

The march toward a volunteer army encountered the first real resistance when it reached Congress. Representative F. Edward Hébert of Louisiana, the chairman of the House Armed Services Committee, set the tone. "The only way to get an all-volunteer army is to draft it," he said as he opened hearings.[67] Vietnam burned on in the background and, in the minds of many protesters, the two issues, draft and war, were fused into one incandescent outrage. But that was not the standard view on Capitol Hill. The politicians most committed to ending the draft tended to be proponents of the war. Indeed, some saw ending the draft as a way to mute criticism of the war. By contrast, many of those who opposed the war still regarded conscription as an important civic institution. "Ending the draft will not end this war, and it will not prevent future wars. All it will do is make this and future wars the business of the poor," said Senator Thomas F. Eagleton, a Missouri Democrat. "If we allow this to happen, Vietnam will be an even greater tragedy."[68]

The administration had complicated its own sales job by persuading Congress in November 1969 to replace the judgment of local draft boards with a national lottery. The first drawing was broadcast to the nation on December 1. Representative Alexander Pirnie of New York, a retired colonel, drew a blue capsule from a glass bowl. It said "September 14," which meant young men born on that date were first in line for Vietnam.[69] But only those with high draft numbers were at risk, so the lottery also had the effect of instantly reassuring much of the nation's population of young adult males that they would not be going to war.

Anderson fretted that the lottery would ease political pressure to end the draft without resolving the economic or ideological shortcomings. But Nixon remained committed to ending the draft, and the administration struck a pair of bargains with Congress. The first deal extended the draft for two years while gradually raising salaries, allowing Congress to test the waters. It also limited the increase in total spending, since military pay would rise as the United States pulled out of Vietnam. The "peace dividend" would fund the volunteer army.[70]

The second deal was a "private agreement" with Hébert. The administration agreed to build a training facility for military doctors: the F. Edward Hébert School of Medicine.[71]

As Congress deliberated, public opinion moved against conscription. Lieutenant William Calley was convicted in the spring of 1971 of murdering twenty-two Vietnamese civilians at the village of My Lai. A few months later, the *New York Times* began to publish the Pentagon Papers — excerpts from an internal government history documenting the duplicity of the Kennedy and Johnson administrations in escalating the war. And on July 1, 1971, the Twenty-Sixth Amendment to the Constitution became law, allowing Americans between the ages of eighteen and twenty-one to vote in the next national election.[72]

The House voted on August 4 to end conscription, but the margin was so fine in the Senate that the death of Senator Winston Prouty of Vermont on September 10 left the administration one vote short. The governor of Vermont quickly appointed Representative Robert Stafford, a longtime supporter of the all-volunteer military who had already voted for the legislation in the House, to fill the vacancy. The White House sent a plane to bring Stafford back to Washington, where he voted for the bill again, this time in the Senate. Nixon signed it into law on September 28, 1971.

The last conscript to serve in the American military was Dwight Elliott Stone, a twenty-four-year-old plumber's apprentice from Sacramento, California, who did not report for basic training at Fort Polk, Louisiana, until June 30, 1973 — the last day, up to the present moment, that military conscription was legal in the United States. Stone did not want to be there. He had missed appointments and call-up dates until he was indicted by the government, which offered him a choice between two kinds of uniforms. Stone grudgingly chose green and spent sixteen months and fifteen days in the military, mostly working as a radio repair-man. "I wouldn't have joined," he told a reporter. "I wouldn't recommend it for anyone. I didn't like it."[73]

The U.S military did not share the view of Oi, Friedman, and other econo-mists that recruits made rational decisions. Instead it sold the army as a life-style brand. "Let advertising do for the Army what it has done successfully for business," William K. Brehm, the assistant secretary for manpower, told his superiors in the late 1960s, as the army began to brace for the end of con-scription.[74] The early efforts were not subtle. "Take the Army's 16-Month Tour of Europe," urged one ad that showed a man sitting in a café with a blonde raising a lipstick to her mouth.* The army's campaign inspired one of the most famous lines in advertising. The Marine Corps responded by roll-ing out ads under the tagline "If you just want to be one of the boys, stick with the boys. The Marines are looking for a few good men."[75]

Critics warned the military would fill its ranks with Americans who lacked choices. "One could almost accuse this group of conspiring to develop a system to exclude themselves," J. Timothy McGinley, a young Labor Department official, said at the Chicago conference in 1966.[76] Instead the military has remained a selective employer. Technology, and the end of the Cold War, reduced the need for recruits even as the population grew and women started signing up in larger numbers.[77] It also became harder to find blue-collar jobs. Military recruits today come disproportion-ately from middle-income census tracts, and the military excludes those who score in the bottom third of the population on aptitude tests. In 1989, Dwight Elliott Stone's oldest son enlisted in the marines.[78]

When the United States first eliminated the draft, Helmut Schmidt

---

* The University of Chicago economists Gary Becker and George Stigler demon-strated to their own satisfaction in a famous 1977 paper, "De Gustibus Non Est Disputandum," that the purpose of advertising is to convey information to rational consumers. The firm that created the army ad apparently had a different theory of human behavior.

of West Germany complained it was setting a bad example.[79] Since the end of the Cold War, most European countries have decided they, too, do not need a draft. Germany ended conscription in 2011.

The elimination of an obligation to serve has had consequences.

On Armed Forces Day in 1970, thousands of people flooded Rowan Park in Fayetteville, North Carolina, to protest the Vietnam War. The protesters included the actress and antiwar activist Jane Fonda, and several hundred soldiers stationed at Fort Bragg, the massive base that abuts the city. Indeed, some soldiers were involved in planning the protest. And so it went at bases around the country that Saturday in May: military personnel, in uniform, protesting the war they were charged with fighting. A 1971 study commissioned by the army found, rather astonishingly, that 37 percent of enlisted personnel had engaged in some act of dissent.[80]

More than three decades later, in March 2005, several thousand people gathered in the same Fayetteville park to protest the war in Iraq. They draped cardboard coffins with American flags to mark the deaths of soldiers based at Fort Bragg. They said many of the same words their predecessors had said about Vietnam. But this time, no soldiers in uniform numbered among the protesters.[81] Since service is voluntary, there is less internal dissent.

Increasingly, market-rate soldiers serve and fight alongside market-rate contractors. In the last three major deployments of the American military, in the Balkans, Iraq, and Afghanistan, the United States employed military personnel and contractors in roughly equal numbers.[82]

The Gates Commission argued that a market-rate military would inhibit conflict. "Recent history," the commission wrote, "suggests that increased taxes generate far more public discussion than increased draft calls."[83] Instead, by making war more efficient and more remote from the lives of most Americans, the end of the draft may also have made war more likely. We live in an era of permanent, low-grade conflict. The occupation of Afghanistan is the longest sustained war in American history, but it commands little public attention. War, once an abnormal act of national purpose, has become a regular line of work.

Chapter Two

Friedman v. Keynes

The common-sense attitude toward change was discarded in favor of a mystical readiness to accept the social consequences of economic improvement, whatever they might be. The elementary truths of political science and statecraft were first discredited then forgotten.

— *Karl Polanyi*, The Great Transformation (1944)[1]

On the last day of 1933, the British economist John Maynard Keynes published an open letter in the *New York Times* pleading with President Franklin Delano Roosevelt to embark on a spending spree. He advised the President to build more railroads — though, really, anything would do. The government, he said later, could even bury money in old mines and sell digging rights.[2]

Roosevelt's inauguration in March 1933 had boosted spirits after three long years of depression, as had the repeal of Prohibition in early December 1933. The crowd gathered on New Year's Eve in the square outside the Times Building in midtown Manhattan was the largest since the end of the Great War. Yet the economic situation remained grim. One in four workers had been jobless during 1933, the highest rate in the nation's modern history.

Most Americans — certainly most members of the political elite — did not hold the federal government responsible. They did not think the government could increase growth by borrowing money from private citizens and spending it on public works. This was widely seen as equivalent to moving money from the left pocket to the right pocket of the same pair of pants.

Keynes's letter was an attack on this faith in markets. In his view, no invisible hand ensured markets automatically would deliver the best possible outcomes. Businesses uncertain about the future would refrain from investing; people would remain unemployed. The government, he said, needed to borrow and spend until "animal spirits" were revived.[3]

Keynes wrote that if Roosevelt followed his instructions, the President could spark a global recovery. "If you succeed, new and bolder methods will be tried everywhere," he wrote, "and we may date the first chapter of a new economic era from your accession to office."

In 1936, Keynes elaborated on this new economics in *The General Theory of Employment, Interest and Money*, a book whose influence has significantly exceeded its readership. "The *General Theory* caught most economists under the age of thirty-five with the unexpected virulence of a disease first attacking and decimating an isolated tribe of South Sea islanders," wrote the American economist Paul Samuelson, one of the most consequential casualties.[4] The assertion that people could improve upon nature was well matched to its era. And if humankind had the ability to remedy recessions and promote prosperity, who could deny the moral imperative to do so?

Yet the new era dawned slowly. Roosevelt was wary of deficit spending. After Keynes's letter appeared in the *Times*, Roosevelt asked a mutual friend, Felix Frankfurter, to tell "the professor" that the President agreed the economy needed help, but "there is a practical limit to what the government can borrow."[5] Frankfurter arranged for the men to meet at the White House a few months later, in May 1934. This only served to reinforce Roosevelt's initial impression. "I saw your friend Keynes," he told Frances Perkins, the secretary of labor. "He left a whole rigmarole of figures. He must be a mathematician rather than a political economist."[6]

The U.S. unemployment rate was still 17 percent at the onset of World War II.[7]

Keynes, who died in 1946, had regarded his work as an effort to salvage capitalism as a viable alternative to communism — to show that the market economy needed help, but that it did not need to be replaced. After World War II, that project gained new urgency for the Western democracies as they confronted the rise of the Soviet Union.

In Britain, both major parties wrote full employment into their platforms after the war. The Conservative Party's 1950 manifesto declared, "We regard the maintenance of full employment as the first aim of a Conservative Government."[8] In the United States, Democrats pushed a landmark law through Congress in 1946 that instructed federal policy makers "to promote maximum employment, production, and purchasing power." The law also established a special role for economists, creating the White House Council of Economic Advisers: three economists at the president's elbow.[9] But conservatives — then a substantial congregation in both parties — never fully signed on. The most outspoken decried Keynesianism as a kissing cousin of communism. One of these critics was Rose Wilder Lane, a fiery libertarian who edited and shaped the memoirs of her mother, Laura Ingalls Wilder, into the Little House series of children's books.[10] Pioneer families had traveled on government-backed railroads, staked claims to public lands, and relied on the army's protection; the books celebrated self-sufficiency.[11] In 1947, Lane published a withering review of the first Keynesian economics textbook, which she described as Marxist propaganda. She was particularly outraged by its celebration of government spending. "This is not an economics text at all; it is a pagan-religious and political tract," Lane wrote. "It inspires an irrational faith and spurs it to political action. From cover to cover there is not a suggestion of any action that is not political — and Federal." A letter-writing campaign discouraged adoption of the textbook, leaving the field to Paul Samuelson, who published a more centrist economics textbook the following year.

At first there wasn't much need for Keynesian advice. A wave of pent-up innovation propelled rapid economic growth after the war, and the prosperity was broadly shared: machines let women escape household work more quickly than machines eliminated factory jobs. Economists seemed as useful as Maytag repairmen; in 1952, Republicans sought to shutter the Council of Economic Advisers. It was preserved, but not with any great enthusiasm.

Undaunted by the indifference of policy makers, economists during the 1950s continued to refine their ideas and to make increasingly audacious claims. By the end of the decade, Keynesian economics had entered the high summer of its self-regard. Leading economists insisted governments could adjust economic conditions like the settings on a thermostat. The economist A. W. Phillips plotted the relationship between unemployment and wages in the United Kingdom over the previous century, and found wages tended to rise when unemployment was low. Enthusiastically conflating correlation and causation, economists concluded governments could glide up and down a "Phillips curve," trading off unemployment and inflation. In an influential paper published in 1960, Samuelson and Robert Solow, two of the most important economists of the postwar era, said the American government could choose from a "menu" of unemployment and inflation rates. The available options included 5 to 6 percent unemployment with no inflation or, if one preferred, 3 percent unemployment with 4 to 5 percent inflation.[12] In Great Britain, one economist recalled a meeting in the early 1960s that devolved into an emotional confrontation between those wanting to limit unemployment to 1.25 percent and those favoring 1.75 percent: "There was a figure called Professor Frank Paish who proposed 2.5 percent, who was regarded as, more or less, a Nazi."[13]

Washington's embrace of economics began in the engine rooms of government. Policy makers and bureaucrats struggling to manage the rapid expansion of the government's role in American life turned to economists, particularly in complex areas like taxation. "The stuff was just over my head," said one member of the House Ways and Means Committee, which was charged with writing the nation's tax laws. Said another, "This was calculus and I hadn't had arithmetic yet."[14] The trend prompted

President Eisenhower's warning in his farewell address against allowing technocrats to make political decisions. But other politicians saw opportunity. Wilbur Mills, the chairman of Ways and Means from the late 1950s to the mid-1970s, thought economics could help transcend partisan differences by providing lawmakers with clear and indisputable facts.

Mills, who began life in 1909 as the son of the most powerful man in a small Arkansas town, was sometimes described as the most powerful man in Washington by people who were not entirely joking. He studied law at Harvard before entering Congress in 1939 at the tender age of twenty-nine. A few years later, in 1942, he landed a coveted seat on Ways and Means, arriving at the dawn of modern federal income taxation. The government began to tax the incomes of rich people in 1913, but until World War II, only about 6 percent of American households had ever paid anything.[15] Broad income taxation was initiated to fund the war, then was continued to fund America's arms race against the Soviet Union, as well as the expansion of social welfare spending in the postwar years. Mills immersed himself in the intricacies of the law. He also sought an education in economics, amusing more than one tutor by switching into a southern accent when he answered the phone on his desk. Mills was a rising star among southern Democrats, who dominated Congress, and in 1957, still just forty-eight years old, he was handed the gavel of Ways and Means after the previous chairman died of a heart attack.

The tax code he inherited was a mess. The federal government taxed personal income at rates that topped out above 90 percent: for every dollar of taxable income above $200,000 in 1957, the government took 91 cents and the taxpayer kept 9 cents.* But the key words were "taxable income." The rules were riddled with loopholes; only about 40 percent of personal income was subject to any federal taxation.[16] The situation was similar in other developed nations. The top tax rate in the United Kingdom offended the Beatles so much they wrote a song about a greedy "Taxman" who wanted to collect 95 percent of income. Quoth the Taxman, "Should five

---

* An income of $200,000 in 1957 is the equivalent of an income of about $1.8 million in 2019.

per cent appear too small / Be thankful I don't take it all." But the Beatles, like most rich people, legally avoided much of the burden.[17]

Mills hired an economist named Norman B. Ture, who had been one of Milton Friedman's first graduate students at Chicago, and began to work on a plan to make the tax system more fair and efficient. Mills compared the system to a triangle. The government had constructed a tall, thin triangle, with high rates and a narrow tax base. Mills said the government could raise the same amount of money by constructing a short, wide triangle — lowering tax rates while broadening the share of income subject to taxation. He said lower rates would encourage economic activity, an early articulation of what came to be called supply-side economics.

One Shining Moment

The 1957 launch of Sputnik, the Soviet satellite all too visible in the evening sky as it passed over the United States, heightened worries that the Soviet Union was pulling ahead in an economic race widely regarded as a referendum on the merits of rival political systems. Kennedy played on those fears in the 1960 presidential race, promising to increase economic growth to an annual rate of 5 percent — roughly twice the average pace during the second half of the 1950s.

He had few fixed ideas about how to deliver on that promise. As a senator, he had wrangled an appointment to the prestigious Joint Economic Committee and then skipped almost every meeting.[18] During the campaign, he told advisers he had earned a C in his only college economics class, so they should start at the beginning and explain everything.[19] Kennedy did, however, have fixed ideas about professors: he collected them, respected them, and sometimes even listened to them. He hired the best available minds and asked for directions. When the Yale economist James Tobin expressed reluctance to sign on because he was "an ivory-tower economist," Kennedy responded, "That's all right, professor. I am what you might call an ivory-tower president."[20] Samuelson, who served as an informal adviser, plaintively asked a presidential aide whether Kennedy could be prevailed upon to stop calling him "professor."[21]

The economist most responsible for shaping the Kennedy administration's policies was a tall, clean-cut midwesterner named Walter W. Heller. He was forty-five years old in 1960, a tenured professor at the University of Minnesota and a well-regarded expert on taxation, but he was not on anyone's list of the nation's top economists — he was described by one contemporary as "a colonel in the Keynesian army" — and he very nearly missed his train to prominence. When Kennedy swung through Minneapolis for a campaign rally in October 1960, Heller decided at the last minute to put on a suit and head downtown. In the lobby of the old Leamington Hotel, he ran into Hubert Humphrey, then the state's senior senator, who took him to meet the candidate.

Kennedy was changing his shirt when the two men walked in. Humphrey introduced Heller by joking that some smart people lived west of the Mississippi River; Kennedy started asking questions.[22] Was it realistic to promise 5 percent growth? How could small changes in fiscal policy affect the economy? Why was West Germany prospering despite high interest rates? "He just stood there scratching his chest while we talked and everybody else fell away," Heller recalled.[23]

A few months later, Kennedy asked Heller to lead his Council of Economic Advisers. Kennedy liked the economist's quick wit and conversational style, and Heller's midwestern roots counted as diversity in the Kennedy White House. But it was not obvious that Heller would play a particularly significant role. Economists never had. One acquaintance innocently asked Heller, "Will you handle this from Minnesota, or will you have to go to Washington?"[24]

Heller, the son of German immigrants, was born in Buffalo in 1915 and raised in Wisconsin, where his father, an engineer, moved the family in search of work. He completed his doctorate at the University of Wisconsin in 1941, writing his dissertation on the administration of state income taxation. Rejected by the army for bad eyesight, he took a job at Treasury working on the same project as Milton Friedman: the administration of federal income taxation. After the war, he settled in Minnesota, raising a family and developing a reputation as a lucid expositor. President Johnson once brandished a Heller memo, telling the rest of his advisers, "That's the way I want you all to write your memos."[25] Heller's tongue could cut, too, as in his later description of President Reagan as "charming, disarming, and sometimes alarming."[26]

In Washington, Heller argued relentlessly that the government should cut taxes to promote job growth. The economy was growing, but he said it could be growing more quickly if the government left people with more money to spend. Heller described the difference between actual economic growth and the frontier of what was possible as an "output gap," and he made an impression by telling Kennedy the gap was roughly the size of the Italian economy.

Heller's ideas marked a tactical break with the traditional Keynesian emphasis on increased government spending. In the traditional view, the government could invigorate the economy by borrowing money from the private sector and then spending it.[27] Heller was proposing to borrow money from the private sector and then give it back to the private sector to spend it. In both cases, the idea was to draw money from savings, by selling Treasury securities to investors, and then put the money back into circulation. Heller acknowledged his plan was less direct, and less effective, than the standard Keynesian approach. But Kennedy already had ruled out a big increase in spending as politically untenable, and Heller recognized conservatives might be more willing to cut taxes. They liked the idea of less government as the best government could do.[28] Heller also sweetened his sales pitch by predicting the stimulus would be so effective that it would pay for itself. As the economy grew, he said, tax revenues would increase even at lower tax rates. In effect, the government would be getting a smaller share of a larger economic pie. There was a precedent. During the 1920s, the plutocratic Treasury secretary Andrew W. Mellon had engineered a series of cuts in income tax rates; as growth had boomed, federal tax revenue had increased.[29]

Kennedy initially resisted. He had inaugurated his presidency by calling on Americans to sacrifice for the collective good and a tax cut seemed to strike a dissonant chord. But the unemployment rate remained around 5.5 percent, and, as the next presidential election hove into view, Kennedy warmed to the premise that the economy was not living up to its potential.[30] In December 1962, Kennedy floated the idea for a tax cut in a speech before business leaders in New York, pledging to "cut the fetters which hold back private spending."[31] The audience responded with enthusiasm. Afterward, Kennedy called Heller and rhapsodized, "I gave them straight Keynes and Heller, and they loved it."[32]

Wilbur Mills was ready to make a deal. He saw an opportunity to increase the efficiency of taxation, and he was willing to accept a larger deficit as the price of lower tax rates. The Kennedy administration, in turn, agreed to permanent cuts in tax rates as the price of a larger deficit. Historians and partisans have wrestled ever since over the nature of the Kennedy plan, some describing it as the apogee of Keynesianism, others as the birth of supply-side economics. It was both. Secretary of the Treasury Douglas Dillon privately called it a "happy coincidence."[33]

Much of the political establishment, however, still recoiled from the premise that a larger budget deficit could be good for the economy. Balancing the budget — matching revenue and spending — remained the standard measure of responsible governance. Eisenhower wrote a member of the House Republican leadership that the plan was "fiscal recklessness." Former president Harry Truman told reporters, "I am old-fashioned. I believe you should pay in more than you spend."[34] And Senator Harry Byrd, the Virginia Democrat who chaired the Senate Finance Committee — and who believed Roosevelt had been a decent president until "this fellow Keynes got ahold of him" — refused to move the bill. "He hated public debt with a holy passion," a colleague said.[35]

It took the death of Kennedy and the legislative prowess of Lyndon Baines Johnson to see the plan into law. Johnson appeased Byrd by agreeing to a package of spending cuts that reduced the size of the deficit. Mills told fellow conservatives that the tax cuts would force further spending cuts, an early articulation of the strategy later dubbed "Starving the Beast."[36]

Heller, who had stayed on under Johnson, was disheartened; he did not want to cut government spending and, in his view, increasing the deficit was the point to the plan. But Johnson privately assured Heller that it would be easy to increase spending after the votes were counted. "Once you have the tax cut," Johnson said, "you can do what you want."[37]

Johnson did. With the tax cut in hand, federal spending rose sharply as the administration pursued a war in Vietnam and what Johnson called an "unconditional war on poverty."

About a fifth of the American population, some 30 million people, then lived in destitution with little prospect of betterment. Both liberal and conservative administrations had taken the view that poverty was best treated by pursuing broad economic growth.[38] But by the early 1960s, scholars and journalists were focusing public attention on the inadequacy of this strategy — a project intertwined with the rise of the civil rights movement, since deprivation was concentrated in minority communities.

Heller was unusual among economists of his generation in his belief that redistributive policies were necessary to address inequality.[39] At his first meeting with Johnson, Heller found his new boss agreed. Johnson, raised in poverty, added $500 million to the budget as a down payment on antipoverty programs. He brought Heller to his Texas ranch for the winter holidays in 1964, put him in a cabin with another adviser, and demanded a plan. "I wanted original, inspiring ideas," Johnson wrote in his memoirs.[40] Three main efforts eventually emerged: the Medicare and Medicaid health insurance programs, food stamps, and subsidies for schools in poor communities.

Heller's tax cut delivered on its premise. Growth roared along as Americans spent the windfall, and the unemployment rate sharply declined, finding a new level at around 3.5 percent in the late 1960s — two percentage points lower than at the beginning of the decade. The difference meant that about 1.6 million more Americans were able to find paid work. The long economic expansion also fostered palpable optimism that "modern economics" could perpetuate growth, world without end, amen. "I do not believe recessions are inevitable," Johnson told Congress in

January 1965. At the end of that year, *Time* put Keynes on the cover and credited the adoption of his ideas for the "most sizable, prolonged and widely distributed prosperity in history."[41]

The new social welfare programs also succeeded, sharply reducing poverty.[42]

No one asked the economists who followed Heller as presidential advisers whether they planned to work in Washington.[43] As Johnson observed at the swearing-in ceremony of James Duesenberry, whom he named to the Council of Economic Advisers in 1966, "Dr. Duesenberry is, as we all know, one of this nation's leading economists. When I was growing up, that didn't seem to mean very much, but since I grew up we have learned the error of our ways."[44]

But the triumph of the Keynesians was short-lived. By late 1965, the economy was beginning to overheat and inflation was rising. The Johnson administration's aggressive efforts to stimulate economic growth, and its spending on the war in Vietnam, were reprising one of humankind's oldest discoveries: add wood to a fire, and it will burn more brightly; add too much wood, and it will burn out of control.

Inflation is a loss of purchasing power. If annual inflation is 2 percent, a person with enough money to buy 100 hamburgers on New Year's Day would be able to afford only 98 hamburgers by Christmas. Consumers do not like the idea that the money in their pocket is losing value. Lenders also dislike inflation: it means the money they get back will be less valuable than the money they loaned. And economists dislike inflation because it reduces the informational value of market prices.

The Keynesians argued the government should raise taxes to hold down inflation. But a theory rooted in what its proponents described as a more realistic assessment of human behavior was curiously blind to the realities of politics. Johnson did not want to raise taxes, and did not agree to seek a tax hike until 1967.

The long-serving chairman of the Federal Reserve, William McChesney Martin, was the Shakespeare of tough-talking central bankers, still remembered for his description of the central bank as the nation's designated adult. Its job, he said, was to take away the punch bowl "just when the party was really warming up."[45] In June 1965, Martin signaled the moment had come. In a speech at Columbia University, he compared the optimism of the 1960s to the years before the Great Depression. "Then, as now," he observed, "many government officials, scholars and businessmen were convinced that a new economic era had opened, an era in which business fluctuations had become a thing of the past."[46] The Fed began to raise interest rates, which infuriated Johnson. In December 1965, he summoned the Fed chairman to his Texas ranch and pushed Martin around the room, shouting, "Boys are dying in Vietnam, and Bill Martin doesn't care!" Martin got the message. The Fed raised rates a little higher and then stopped.[47]

The only method of inflation control that appealed to Johnson was the Alice in Wonderland idea that the government could dictate what prices would be, no more and no less. Instead of raising taxes or allowing the Fed to raise interest rates, the President set out to personally suppress inflation. "Shoe prices went up, so LBJ slapped export controls on hides to increase the supply of leather," recalled Joseph A. Califano Jr., a senior aide. "Domestic lamb prices rose. LBJ directed [Defense Secretary Robert] McNamara to buy cheaper lamb from New Zealand for the troops in Vietnam."[48] When lumber prices rose, Johnson ordered the government to buy metal furniture for federal offices. When egg prices rose in the spring of 1966, Johnson told the surgeon general to issue warnings about the dangers of cholesterol consumption.

But inflation, like Vietnam, proved to be a fight Johnson couldn't win. By the end of 1968, inflation was up to 4.7 percent, the hottest annual pace since the Korean War.

Don't Just Do Something. Stand There.

Milton Friedman never met John Maynard Keynes. Their only interaction came in 1935, when Friedman submitted his first academic paper to a British journal edited by Keynes, and Keynes refused to publish it.[49] But as governments embraced responsibility for active management of economic conditions, and specifically for minimizing unemployment,

Friedman built a case for a counterrevolution. He wanted to restore the pre-Keynesian consensus that governments could not stimulate economic growth and should not try. He pressed his argument in the surprising form of a campaign to increase the power of a government agency: the Federal Reserve.

The Fed is the central bank of the United States, a backstop for the financial system created by Congress in 1913 to prevent the banking crises that had repeatedly plunged the economy into recession. Its special power is the ability to create money, or to remove money from circulation. Printed across the top of every dollar are the words "Federal Reserve Note."

Keynes and his followers thought the Fed had failed its great test: it had tried to end the Great Depression by pumping money into the economy, and its efforts had been unavailing. Keynes drew the conclusion that relying on monetary policy to revive economic growth was like "trying to get fat by buying a larger belt." What really mattered, he said, was not the number of dollars the Fed put into circulation, but the number of transactions: a dollar could languish for years in a porcelain piggy bank, or it could be spent several times by successive owners in a single day. This meant that the Fed's influence over economic conditions was quite limited, while fiscal authorities could stimulate growth by borrowing and spending. Truman's chief economic adviser, Leon Keyserling, dismissed the Fed's control over the supply of money as "no more than one mild tool among many in the quest for economic stability."[50]

Friedman's most famous work of economic scholarship was a history of the Great Depression, which he wrote with the economist Anna Jacobson Schwartz, in which they argued that the Keynesians were wrong about the facts, and therefore had drawn the wrong conclusions. The Fed, they wrote, had allowed the supply of money to fall by more than a third between August 1929 and March 1933. The cause of the contraction was not the Fed's impotence, but its malpractice: it had held a pillow over the face of the economy. "The contraction," the authors wrote, "is in fact a tragic testimonial to the importance of monetary forces."[51]

In upholding the power of the Fed, Friedman was consciously seeking to show that it didn't really matter what happened to money after it was printed. The Keynesians claimed that Congress and the president, by spending money, could lift an economy from recession and lift people from unemployment. Friedman denied that this was possible. He said the only effective form of macroeconomic policy was to provide an appropriate supply of money.

The British economist A. A. Walters, who helped to translate Friedman's ideas into public policy as an adviser to Margaret Thatcher, later observed the idea had "obvious appeal" for Friedman, because it was the least intrusive form of macroeconomic policy.[52]

Friedman began to spar with the ghost of Keynes in the late 1940s. At first, the argument was not about the best way to increase growth, because the American economy was growing robustly. Instead, it was an argument about the other side of the coin: how to reduce inflation.

Keynesians regarded inflation as a complex phenomenon with many potential causes and many potential remedies. The problem might be too much government spending, or a sharp drop in the oil supply, or unions pressing for higher wages. And each cause had its own cure.

Friedman, by contrast, had a radically simple view: governments caused inflation by printing too much money — by expanding the quantity of money in circulation faster than the growth of the economy — and governments could reduce inflation only by printing less money.* In January 1948, Friedman and seven other members of the Chicago economics

---

* Friedman's Keynesian contemporaries were focused on building economic models that captured the complexity of the real world. Friedman's monetarism was rooted in a very different approach. He argued that the test of an economic theory was not the verisimilitude of its assumptions, but the accuracy of its predictions. This emphasis on results became a defining feature of modern economics, helping to justify the rise of increasingly abstract models that treated people as rational actors — not because anyone thought people were rational, but because the pretense was said to produce better results. See Milton Friedman, "The Methodology of Positive Economics," in *Essays in Positive Economics* (Chicago: University of Chicago Press, 1953).

faculty published a letter in the *New York Times* asserting that the "chief cause" of rising prices was that the amount of money in circulation in the United States had roughly tripled between 1939 and 1948. This view came to be known as monetarism.[53] Friedman would later summarize the idea in a famous turn of phrase: "Inflation is always and everywhere a monetary phenomenon."[54]

Later that year, Friedman received a golden invitation to prove his point. Arthur F. Burns, his former professor, had taken over the National Bureau of Economic Research, which funded work on the ups and downs of the economy. The Rockefeller Foundation, which provided much of the bureau's funding, wanted a study examining the role of bank lending in economic cycles — reflecting the Keynesian view that what mattered was the movement of money, not the quantity. Burns asked Friedman to tackle the project together with Anna Schwartz, then a Columbia graduate student with a growing reputation for wizardry in data collection.

Friedman took the job but rewrote the marching orders. In a letter to the head of the Rockefeller Foundation in January 1949, he explained his view that quantity was more important than velocity — and therefore that monetary policy was important, while Keynesian-style fiscal policy was not. Friedman sketched for the first time the idea that the Fed turned a garden-variety economic downturn into the Great Depression by failing to pump enough money into the economy. He also predicted the research would take eight months; it took fourteen years.[55]

Even as Friedman sought evidence, he continued to broadcast his conclusions. "The primary task of our monetary authorities is to promote economic stability by controlling the stock of money," he told Congress in March 1952.[56] The next year, Friedman published a revised version of an essay on inflation that he wrote in the early 1940s. The original had described inflation in Keynesian terms, as the result of too much government spending. The new version emphasized that the root cause of inflation was the overexpansion of the money supply. Friedman included an apologetic footnote: "As I trust the new material makes clear," he wrote, "the omission from that version of monetary effects is a serious error which is not excused but may perhaps be explained by the prevailing Keynesian temper of the times."[57]

Friedman's professional stature was sufficient to win him a ready audience for his views on monetary policy, but there were not a lot of early converts.* Keynesian economics was ascendant. Per Jacobsson, the head of the International Monetary Fund, who personified the prevailing confidence in Keynesian mechanics, invited Friedman to speak at his research institute in Basel, Switzerland. The visit devolved into the academic version of a bar brawl, both men "standing, shouting, gesticulating, and banging their chairs on the floor."[58]

The environment in Britain was, if anything, even more hostile. Roy Harrod, Keynes's official biographer and the chief economic adviser to the Conservative prime minister Harold Macmillan, wrote his boss regarding monetarism in 1957, "I do sincerely hope that no government speaker would use words implying that the government subscribes to such an antiquated doctrine." The following year, Macmillan accepted the resignations of three treasury officials who had proposed regulation of the money supply.[59] The year after that, 1959, a government commission issued a report concluding "monetary policy had little to do with inflation, and was largely ineffective as an instrument of demand management."[60]

Even as he struggled to convince his contemporaries, however, Friedman set out to educate the next generation of economists, launching a "workshop" on money and banking at the University of Chicago. Participating students pursued research on monetary issues under Friedman's

---

* In 1951, Friedman was named the third winner of the John Bates Clark Medal, created to honor the most important American economist under the age of forty. He had little public profile, but, among economists, he was clearly marked as a rising star. He was honored for his early work at the intersection of statistics and mathematics, contributions that had nothing to do with his work on monetary policy. Indeed, Friedman grew increasingly suspicious of the use of sophisticated mathematical and statistical techniques. Eleven of the first twenty recipients of the Clark Medal later won Nobel Prizes in economics. Friedman is unique among that group in winning the two prizes for unrelated bodies of work.

guidance. The idea, soon adopted by other members of the economics faculty, was an attempt to emulate the structure that the laboratory model provided for scientific research. Friedman ran his workshop for a quarter century, raising an army of monetarists.[61]

In 1963, Friedman and Schwartz finally heaved their research into the public square, publishing *A Monetary History of the United States, 1867–1960*. The book found a receptive audience, in part because by the early 1960s, the Fed's reputation was on the upswing. The impotence of the central bank had been a matter of federal policy during World War II. The Fed operated under the direction of the Treasury, with a mandate to create enough money so the government could borrow at low interest rates. But in 1951, the Fed had established operational independence with support from Congress.[62] In the intervening decade, the Fed had begun to demonstrate its ability to influence economic conditions. Keynesians did not accept Friedman's account of the mechanics. In their view, the Fed encouraged (or discouraged) economic activity by lowering (or raising) interest rates, not by controlling the money supply. But they were ready to acknowledge that monetary policy mattered. "Prevailing economic doctrine has only recently — prodded by Professor Friedman, among others — swung around from the view that monetary phenomena are not very important to the view that perhaps they are," the Keynesian economist Robert Solow wrote in an open-minded review of *A Monetary History*.[63]

But Friedman's triumph was incomplete. Two important differences remained. First, while Keynesians increasingly accepted the importance of monetary policy, they did not accept the impotence of fiscal policy. "The issue is not whether money matters — we all grant that — but whether only money matters," said Walter Heller.[64] Paul W. McCracken, the first chairman of Nixon's Council of Economic Advisers, described his views on macroeconomic policy as "Friedmanesque" — the quantity of money was important, but it wasn't the only thing.

The Fed, too, was reluctant to accept sole responsibility for macroeconomic policy. Friedman and Paul Samuelson started writing alternating columns for *Newsweek* in 1966, bringing Friedman's ideas before a broader audience.[65] Some members of Congress soon started asking questions about monetarism. In response, Fed officials downplayed the idea that monetary policy alone could deliver slower inflation. They insisted the rest of the government still needed to help. One Fed official later observed tartly that Congress had a natural affinity for monetarism because it shifted responsibility from Congress to the Fed.[66]

The second dispute was about the limits of monetary policy. Friedman and Schwartz's book was widely interpreted as a firefighting manual. Their conclusion that the Fed had caused the Depression by failing to print enough money implied that the Fed could stimulate economic growth by printing more money. Keynesians began to talk about monetary policy as another tool that could be used to manage the economy.

For Friedman, this was worse than being ignored. He had intended to argue against activist economic policy; instead he had convinced policy makers that printing money was another way to create jobs. When the *Wall Street Journal*'s reliably conservative editorial page endorsed this reading in 1963, Friedman lost his temper. "Is there no one on your paper perceptive enough to realize what our book is really about?" he wrote to Vermont Connecticut Royster, the editorial page editor.* Friedman insisted the lesson of the Depression was that central banks should avoid crises by increasing the money supply at a steady pace approximating the rate of economic growth.[67] The Fed's job, he said in a speech a few years later, was to "prevent money itself from being a major source of economic disturbance."[68] The market would deliver stable economic growth; the role of government, he said, was to get out of the way. Friedman suggested the Fed should be replaced by three functionaries in an office at the Treasury. In later years he updated that imagery, telling audiences the Fed

---

* Royster was named in keeping with a long-standing family tradition. His male relatives included Iowa Michigan Royster, Arkansas Delaware Royster, and Wisconsin Illinois Royster. His female relatives included Virginia Carolina Royster and Indiana Georgia Royster.

should be replaced by a computer. "Economic stability is too serious a matter to be left to central bankers," he said.[69]

This was a flawed argument, and Friedman knew it. Everyone could agree that crises should be avoided, but crises happened all the same. Friedman had not explained why the government should remain passive in a time of crisis — or indeed why it should refrain from printing more money as a remedy for any period of lackluster economic growth.

In December 1967, Friedman delivered the missing piece of his argument in a landmark address to the American Economic Association. One of his most important critics, James Tobin, later lamented that the printed version of Friedman's speech was "very likely the most influential article ever published in an economics journal."[70] The occasion was Friedman's presidential address to the association, delivered at its annual meeting in Washington, D.C. Standing just a few miles from Congress, the seat of fiscal policy, and from the Fed, the seat of monetary policy, Friedman agreed with his critics that both kinds of economic policy should be regarded in the same light. Both, he said, were useless for tinkering with the nation's economic circumstances.

His focus was on monetary policy. He acknowledged printing money could boost employment and growth, but only by tricking people into thinking that the economy was growing. Friedman said that people would soon realize what had happened, and the only way to maintain faster growth would be to fool them again by printing even more money. The gains in growth and employment would be ephemeral, he said. The price would be not just inflation, but accelerating inflation.[71]

Imagine that the government tomorrow sends every American ten hundred-dollar bills. Suddenly there is more money, and people go shopping. As books fly off the shelves at the neighborhood bookstore, the owner places an order for more — and hires a high school kid to stock the shelves — because she concludes, quite reasonably, that the winds have shifted in her favor. But her good fortune is an illusion. The supply of goods and services remains unchanged. As the bookstore begins to run out of books, the bookseller raises her prices. Good thing, too, because when she stops by the grocery store she finds the price of milk also is up. The money printed by the government has caused inflation but not economic growth. The bookstore sells the same number of books at higher prices, which allows the owner to buy the same amount of milk. She fires the high school kid. Everyone has more money, but they're just treading water.[72]

Friedman conceded the journey from confusion to clarity, and therefore the benefits of printing money, might last for years. But he cautioned against trying to take advantage. The historical record, he said, showed the effects of monetary policy spread at an unpredictable pace. Governments struggled to calibrate their efforts: they ended up doing too little or too much.[73]

Friedman and the Keynesians were arguing about the best way to travel through darkness. Friedman maintained that in the face of uncertainty, it was best to pick a line and sail as straight as possible. The Keynesians insisted it was better to navigate each part of the journey on its own terms. Debating Friedman in 1969, Heller acknowledged active management of the economy was imperfect, but he said the record of the 1960s spoke for itself. "The more active, informed, and self-conscious fiscal and monetary policies have become, by and large," he said, "the more fully employed and stable the affected economies have become."[74] Heller said Friedman's approach would sacrifice clear opportunities to improve well-being in the near term — and he was right. He also pointed to mechanical problems with monetarism — and he was right again. Central banks would find it difficult to measure the money supply, let alone to control its growth.

But as economic conditions soured, so did faith in Heller's "activist economics."

Friedman's 1967 presidential address electrified many of the economists who had gathered in Washington. "It was instantly clear that this was a big deal," recalled the economist Robert Hall. He said conversation swirled as people passed into the corridors of the conference hotel, debating the merits and parsing the implications.[75]

Friedman's showmanship stoked the debate. He publicly pitted his monetarist forecasts against the predictions of the Keynesians. In 1967, for example, Friedman said the Fed was stimulating the economy because the money supply was increasing, while Fed officials insisted they were hitting the brakes, because interest rates were rising. Friedman was right and the economy boomed.[76] In 1968, Friedman predicted a temporary tax increase would not check growth because the money supply continued to expand. He was vindicated again. One wit observed that the coincidences were becoming harder for the Keynesians to explain.[77]

Word crossed the ocean, too. A. A. Walters invited Friedman to speak in the United Kingdom in 1969, writing, "You must realize that you have become almost a household name in Britain."[78] The following year, Friedman made the trip. Keynes had carried ideas to America; Friedman was returning the favor. He told his audience that if Keynes had lived to read *A Monetary History*, "he would no doubt be at the forefront of the counter-revolution."[79]

In December 1969, Friedman made the cover of *Time* — four years after Keynes.

The clear focus of federal economic policy at the end of the 1960s still was to ensure that Americans had jobs, even at the expense of inflation. By the beginning of the 1980s, the clear focus of economic policy would be on getting rid of inflation, even at the expense of jobs.

That shift, which carried around the globe, was Friedman's most important legacy.

Chapter Three

One Nation, Under Employed

High unemployment represents a waste of resources so colossal
that no one truly interested in efficiency can be complacent
about it. It is both ironic and tragic that, in searching out ways to
improve economic efficiency, we seem to have ignored the biggest
inefficiency of them all.

— *Alan Blinder,* Hard Heads, Soft Hearts *(1987)*[1]

R ichard Nixon campaigned for Republican congressional candidates
in 1966 by railing against "the High Cost of Johnson," and Republicans distributed "Great Society Funny Money" to underscore the threat
of inflation. During the 1968 presidential campaign, Nixon blazed away
again, invoking stereotypes of profligate Democrats and prudent Republicans. But he didn't mean it. Nixon was not well versed in economics but,
like most Americans of his generation, his basic frame of reference was
Keynesian. He believed the government faced a choice between inflation
and unemployment, and he knew what he wanted to order from that
menu. He explained to aides that nobody lost elections because of inflation, telling them, "Unemployment is always a bigger issue."[2]

When the economy faltered in 1971, Nixon pulled the lever marked
Deficit Spending. In January 1972, the President ordered cabinet departments to spend money as quickly as possible to boost economic growth in
an election year. Agencies were required to document their profligacy at
weekly meetings.[3] "This is an activist administration," he told a reporter a

few months later. "Where I think that action can be taken to stimulate the economy, we are going to take it."[4]

Much of Europe also doubled down on Keynesianism. Helmut Schmidt, then the West German finance minister, said Germans could better endure 5 percent inflation than 5 percent unemployment. The Great Depression, after all, was a more recent trauma than the Weimar hyperinflation.

In the pursuit of growth, Nixon named his favorite economist, Arthur Burns, to replace William McChesney Martin as chairman of the Federal Reserve. Burns was an uncanny amalgam of the kinds of people Nixon professed to hate: urbane, professorial, Jewish. He lectured everyone, including the President. "Arthur was a magnificent talker — one cannot say conversationalist," observed a wry friend.[5] Yet to the enduring amazement of other aides, Nixon listened. Burns "talks slowly but thinks fast," Nixon told the president of France.[6] Burns, for his part, found politics intoxicating — "Arthur would have been a great economist if he hadn't been so interested in politics," Milton Friedman once opined — and Nixon was the politician who took Burns most seriously.[7] The relationship had been cemented during the 1960 presidential campaign. Burns warned the economy was weakening and urged a tax cut. Eisenhower refused, a recession ensued, and Nixon was narrowly defeated. Nixon, who never forgave Eisenhower, concluded Burns was "a good prophet."[8]

Friedman was delighted by Nixon's choice of Burns. He celebrated by printing mock dollar bills with Burns's face in place of Washington's.[9] Burns was the first economist to lead the Fed, and he understood monetarism: Friedman regularly sent his papers to Burns before publication, seeking comments from his old professor.[10]

But Burns did not believe in Keynesianism or monetarism. He came from an older tradition that viewed the economy as a complex organism irreducible to stable formulas. His was the economics of the age of biology, and he did not regard the age of physics as an improvement. "Subtle understanding of economic change comes from a knowledge of history and large affairs, not from statistics or their processing alone — to which our disturbed age has turned so eagerly in its quest for certainty," Burns wrote in 1969.[11] The world was nuanced and confusing, and the work of a central banker was necessarily judgmental. He loved to gather data, but in the entrails he saw answers to specific problems, not eternal verities. "The argument between the Friedmanites and the Keynesians is a false argument," he told a friend in the 1970s. "It's an argument about how well this or that group of economists can forecast the future. They cannot do so, and thank God they can't."[12]

Burns told Congress he doubted the Fed had the power to control inflation, which he blamed on the excessive wage demands of labor unions.[13] He also knew Nixon did not want him to try too hard. The President had embraced the Keynesian version of monetarism — the view that printing money was one more way to stimulate job growth — and he pressed Burns relentlessly to keep the printing presses running, particularly before the 1972 presidential election.[14] "Err toward inflation," Nixon told Burns during one Oval Office meeting.[15] Nixon's chief domestic adviser, John Ehrlichman, summoned two of Burns's lieutenants and told them, "When you gentlemen get up in the morning and look in the mirror while you are shaving, I want you to think carefully about one thing. Ask yourselves, 'What can I do today to get the money supply up?'"[16]

To control inflation without raising interest rates or reducing the growth of the money supply, Burns and Nixon agreed the government should try to restrain prices directly. In August 1971, Nixon announced the first peacetime wage-and-price restrictions in American history.[17] Knowing that this would infuriate Friedman, Nixon dispatched George Shultz, a former Chicago economics professor then serving as head of the Office of Management and Budget, to tell Friedman the administration was preempting congressional Democrats from doing something worse. Friedman didn't think there was anything worse. Nixon tried to laugh it off when Friedman visited the following month. "Don't blame George," he said, pointing at Shultz. Friedman responded, "I don't blame George. I blame you, Mr. President." That was Friedman's last visit to the Nixon White House.[18]

The price controls were popular and briefly effective, but distortions soon burst into view. In June 1973, the evening news showed footage of workers at an east Texas chicken farm drowning forty-three thousand chicks by dumping them into oil drums because the price of feeding chickens had climbed above the price of chicken. "It's cheaper to drown 'em," the owner explained.[19]

In the mid-1960s, as the United Kingdom suffered both slow growth and rising inflation, the British politician Iain Macleod coined a new word to describe the problem. "We now have the worst of both worlds — not just inflation on the one side or stagnation on the other, but both of them together," Macleod told the House of Commons. "We have a sort of 'stagflation' situation."[20]

In the mid-1970s, Americans were introduced to stagflation, too. The shock of the oil embargo that Arab nations imposed on Israel's allies in 1973 sent the U.S. economy sliding into the deepest downturn since the Great Depression. Much to the surprise of Keynesian economists, unemployment and inflation both increased. It was as if both sides of a scale were moving upward at the same time. Nixon's price controls had been scrapped, but the idea that inflation could be talked into submission remained irresistible to politicians. In October 1974, President Gerald Ford went before Congress to try again, telling the nation, "We must whip inflation right now." Ford's plan consisted of coining an acronym, WIN, printing it on millions of red buttons, and urging people to plant vegetable gardens, wear sweaters, and ride in carpools. None of it worked — not even the red buttons. The unemployment rate peaked at 9 percent in May 1975. By then, inflation had been above 10 percent for more than a year.

For Friedman, the explanation was obvious. Unemployment was rising because the economy was weak, and inflation was rising because the government kept printing money. The U.S. money supply rose 23 percent in the 1950s, 44 percent in the 1960s, and 78 percent in the 1970s.[21]

The apparent breakdown of Keynesian economics began to increase interest in Friedman's ideas.[22] In 1974, the West German central bank, the Bundesbank, which was more insulated from political influence than its American counterpart, became the first institution to try monetarist mechanics. The Bundesbank announced that it would aim to expand the supply of money by 8 percent in 1975.[23] In 1976, Friedman was awarded the Nobel Prize in economics for "the renaissance of the role of money in inflation and the consequent renewed understanding of the instrument of monetary policy."[24]

The combination of American ideas and West Germany's example exerted a powerful influence on Keith Joseph, a conservative British politician who was a kind of John the Baptist figure in Margaret Thatcher's rise to power. In 1974, he gave a landmark speech declaring inflation a larger problem than unemployment. Two years later, in April 1976, Joseph proposed for the first time that Britain should adopt the West German approach, which he said was already proving its worth in reducing inflation.[25] Surprisingly, this quickly became a bipartisan consensus. James Callaghan, the new Labour prime minister, delivered a eulogy for Keynesianism at a party conference in September 1976 in the fading resort town of Blackpool. "We used to think that you could spend your way out of a recession and increase employment by cutting taxes and boosting government spending," Callaghan told the party's leadership, who were probably confused by his use of the past tense to describe something they still believed. "I tell you in all candor that that option no longer exists, and that insofar as it ever did exist, it only worked on each occasion since the war by injecting a bigger dose of inflation into the economy, on every occasion, followed by higher levels of unemployment as the next step." Callaghan's government turned toward monetarism, instructing the Bank of England for the first time to regulate the growth of the money supply.[26]

But Friedman had yet to convince the leaders of his own country. President Ford invited Friedman to a White House conference on inflation in 1974, where the Chicago economist delivered a televised jeremiad: "If that disease is not checked," Friedman said of inflation, "it will take a heavy toll including, in my opinion, the very likely destruction of our personal, political and economic freedoms." Friedman said there was "one, and only one, way to cure the disease" — printing less money.[27] He was, however, the only economist at the conference who favored a focus on reducing inflation. In the midst of a recession, most thought that job creation was more important.[28]

Friedman was particularly frustrated by his inability to sway Burns. Increasingly estranged from his former professor, he sometimes adopted the device of writing to friends and sending copies to Burns. The letters were long, prescriptive, and seething with frustration. "I feel like an unimaginative dullard to say the same thing over and over again," Friedman wrote. He urged the Fed to focus on the money supply. "As you know, this was my view one year ago, two years ago, and longer ago still." He simply could not understand why it was not Burns's view, too. "There has never been any excuse," he wrote, "and there still is none."[29]

Jimmy Carter made perfectly clear during the 1976 presidential campaign that he had no interest in monetarism. "My own belief is that the best way to control inflation is not to make money scarce," he said in September 1976. Instead he advocated economic growth as the cure for inflation.[30] The following month, just a few weeks before the election, Carter placed an order from the Samuelson-Solow menu, pledging to reduce unemployment to 4 percent and inflation below 4 percent by the end of his first term.[31]

Once in office, Carter backed up his rhetoric about unemployment by replacing Burns as Fed chairman with a handsome, pleasant manufacturing executive named G. William Miller, who sometimes laughed so hard at his own jokes that he couldn't get to the punch line, and who passionately expressed a determination to stimulate job creation, particularly for minorities.[32]

Democrats also sought to write Keynesian economics more firmly into law by passing the Humphrey-Hawkins Full Employment Act in 1978, which enshrined "full employment" and "reasonable price stability" as the goals of fiscal and monetary policy. For proponents of activist economics, it seemed like a second sunrise, and they confidently predicted an economic revival.

Instead it was the final act of the Keynesian era. Inflation rose inexorably during Carter's first two years. Then the Iranian revolution sparked a second oil crisis and prices rose faster. By the summer of 1979, inflation once again topped 10 percent, while unemployment hovered persistently around 6 percent. Truckers angry about high oil prices staged paralyzing strikes; protesters in Levittown, Pennsylvania, built a bonfire of cars and tires in the middle of that iconic postwar suburb.[33]

Policy makers had tolerated inflation because the cure was held to be more painful than the disease. Wages had climbed roughly as fast as prices during the 1970s, preserving the purchasing power of the typical household.[34] Most Americans were borrowers more than lenders, and inflation reduced the burden of their debts: paying a thirty-year mortgage required a smaller share of income with each passing year. Home ownership rose during the 1970s — indeed, in 1978, the share of Americans who owned homes was higher than it would be in 2018.[35] Nobody liked inflation, but the idea of driving the economy into a recession seemed like unnecessarily strong medicine. It "amputates the hand to relieve the hangnail," said the Keynesian economist Joseph Minarik.[36]

But Americans were losing patience with inflation. People tended to see higher wages as just rewards, and higher prices as theft. They dreamt of what their increased wages could have purchased if prices had just stayed the same. Terry McLamb, a bread salesman from Raleigh, North Carolina, told a reporter in 1978 that he had abandoned his dream of buying a home. He didn't seem to realize that his income had outstripped inflation by 14 percent over the previous five years.[37]

Many Americans also disliked the sensation of rapid change. Conservatives described inflation as both a symptom and a cause of moral decay. In a 1977 essay, the conservative economists James M. Buchanan and Richard E. Wagner blamed inflation for a litany of ills, including "a generalized erosion in public and private manners, increasingly liberalized attitudes toward sexual activities, a declining vitality of the Puritan work ethic, deterioration in product quality, explosion of the welfare rolls, widespread corruption in both the private and the governmental sector."[38]

And there was a growing sense of exhaustion with promises of policy makers. Friedman's simple narrative that the Great Depression and the

Great Inflation were bookend failures of government — too little money the first time; too much money the second time — struck many as an illuminating diagnosis.

Carter, recognizing his political peril, abandoned his earlier promise to prioritize jobs, and declared that inflation was the nation's primary domestic problem. But he didn't know where to turn. Henry Thomassen, who had been Carter's chief economic adviser during his term as governor of Georgia, told him the administration's efforts to persuade companies and unions to restrain prices and wages were not working. Carter responded, "Hank, I understand from this what will not work. What will?"[39] In July 1979, the beleaguered president retreated to Camp David for several days, emerging on Sunday, July 15, to tell the nation it was suffering from a crisis of confidence. Americans, he said, should embrace austerity to escape inflation and other woes. "We've discovered that owning things and consuming things does not satisfy our longing for meaning," Carter told the congregation. This was a Keynesian prescription dressed up in religious clothes. The President was arguing inflation would slow down if people bought less stuff.

Carter also decided to replace the Fed's Miller with someone who might inspire greater confidence among investors.[40] He settled on Paul Volcker, who had been serving since 1975 as president of the Federal Reserve Bank of New York, the second-most-powerful position at the central bank. Carter made the choice with some reluctance: Volcker was known to favor a crackdown on inflation. He had spent the previous four years impersonating a teapot on a hot stove, getting more and more angry about the Fed's desultory efforts to control inflation until steam came whistling out of the top. At a meeting of the Fed's policy-making committee in July 1978, Volcker told colleagues that Fed policy had become "something of a farce."[41] Some of Carter's aides warned the President he was placing his prospects for reelection in Volcker's hands. Before accepting the job, Volcker also tried to be clear. Slumped on a couch in the Oval Office, cigar in hand, Volcker gestured at Miller, who was in the room, and said, "You have to understand, if you appoint me, I favor a tighter policy than that fellow."[42] Carter said he understood. "I in effect told him,"

Carter later wrote, "'I need to get somebody in here who will take care of the economy — let me take care of the politics.'"[43]

Volckerevolution

Paul Adolph Volcker Jr. stood six feet seven in socks and looked a bit like a lamppost — with a grumpy face hanging where the lamp would have been. He was also an imposing presence intellectually.

He was born on September 5, 1927, and raised in Teaneck, New Jersey, where his father was hired as the town manager after the town fell into a financial crisis. Upon graduating from high school in 1945, he was rejected by the army for being too tall, so he enrolled at Princeton. His father warned that the other students would be very smart, and urged him to choose a lesser school. The younger Volcker later observed, "They weren't as smart as my father thought."[44]

Princeton's economics department, where Volcker found an intellectual home, was dominated by Austrian émigrés shaped and scarred by the hyperinflation that followed World War I. They had never stopped believing in the importance of the money supply, and they had little use for John Maynard Keynes. In four years of economics classes, Volcker said he hardly heard the name. His senior thesis, submitted in 1949, was a 256-page analysis of Federal Reserve policy in the aftermath of World War II that argued the Fed should have taken stronger measures to control inflation. The young Volcker sounded a lot like the Volcker who became chairman of the Fed three decades later. "A swollen money supply presented a grave inflationary threat to the economy," he wrote in one portentous passage. "There was a need to bring this money supply under control if the disastrous effects of a sharp price rise were to be avoided."[45]

Volcker also got a personal lesson in the perils of inflation during his Princeton years. When his older sister, Ruth, attended Simmons College in the late 1930s, the Volckers had given her twenty-five dollars a month. When Paul went to Princeton a decade later, they offered him the same stipend. Paul protested — the dollar had lost 40 percent of its purchasing power in the interim — but the Volckers were unyielding. Ruth later joked of her brother, "He learned central banking on twenty-five dollars."[46]

Volcker went on to graduate school at Harvard, where he got a full dose of Keynesianism. It passed through his system. "I remember sitting in class at Harvard listening to [Professor] Arthur Smithies say, 'A little inflation is good for the economy.' And all I can remember after that was a word flashing in my brain like a yellow caution sign: 'Bullshit,'" Volcker told a biographer.[47] Over the years, he described Keynesian ideas as "bullshit" often enough to make it his official position.

He went to London to write his doctoral thesis but ended up touring the continent instead; upon returning to the United States in 1952, he landed a job in the New York Fed's research department, on the British desk. He spent the next five years in the bowels of the Fed before concluding that his prospects were limited and taking a job at Chase Manhattan.

John F. Kennedy's election pulled Volcker back into public service: his former boss at the New York Fed took a Treasury job and persuaded Volcker to join him. Volcker arrived in Washington in 1962, just as America's postwar hegemony was starting to crumble. He spent much of the next half century trying to limit the damage. "One of my old friends from abroad once told me — I think he meant it as an ironic compliment — that he thought of my career as a long saga of trying to make the decline of the United States in the world respectable and orderly," Volcker said.[48]

He struck many as aloof and intimidating; those who knew him said he was shy. His first wife waited vainly for a proposal until, finally, she asked Volcker to marry her. He was famously frugal, fond of cheap suits and drugstore cigars.[49] For years, he drove an old Nash Rambler with a chair jammed behind the driver's seat so it wouldn't collapse. He sometimes shared Chinese takeout with an old friend, Robert Kavesh, who recalled, "I would pay, and he would eat."[50]

He worked as a Treasury Department official under Presidents Kennedy, Johnson, and Nixon before leaving Washington in 1974.

He intended to return to the banking industry, but Arthur Burns asked him to become president of the New York Fed. Volcker thought about it while fishing for salmon in Canada, then he called Burns, collect, to accept.

In December 1970, *Time* magazine put a picture of a dollar bill on its cover, with a tear running down Washington's cheek and a red scrawl that read "Worth 73¢." By the time Volcker was sworn in as Fed chairman in August 1979, that dollar was worth just 39 cents. Inflation had taken the rest; Americans told pollsters it was the nation's top problem.

During his time as president of the New York Fed, seeking to strengthen the Fed's resolve to fight inflation, Volcker had begun to flirt with Friedman's monetarism. He did not want to be replaced by a computer, but he had long regarded the quantity of money as important. In a 1976 speech, he argued for "practical monetarism" — policy makers would set targets for the growth of the money supply while retaining discretion to address changes in economic conditions.[51] Volcker thought inflation was rising in part because Americans expected inflation to keep rising. A public commitment to monetarism might reset those expectations. Monetarism, he said, was "a new, and in many ways, more sensible and comprehensible symbol of responsible policy."[52] He also was ready for the pain. Senator William Proxmire, a populist in the old Wisconsin tradition, opened Volcker's confirmation hearing in July 1979 by asking for assurances Volcker would not raise interest rates to levels that would be "very difficult for small business, the farmer, and the working people." Volcker, chomping on a cheap cigar, offered little comfort. "I don't think we have any substitute for seeking an answer to our problems in the context of monetary discipline," he said.

In late September 1979, a few weeks after Volcker was sworn in, Arthur Burns delivered an apologia at an international conference in Belgrade for his failure to control inflation. Burns blamed everyone else, including the American public, which in his view had not wanted him to control inflation.[53] Volcker arrived late and found a seat on the floor, along the back wall. He later told a biographer, William Silber, that he had listened to Burns with sadness. Volcker's mind wandered back to a weekend at Camp David in the early 1970s when Burns had urged Nixon to include one more tax break in a stimulus package. The President had smiled and said, "You are too softhearted, Arthur, to be a banker."[54]

Two of Volcker's top aides had remained in the United States to hammer out a plan for cracking down on inflation. After Burns's speech, feeling "bored and itchy," Volcker left Belgrade and flew home to finalize the details.[55] On Friday morning, October 5, he told the presidents of the Fed's twelve regional banks they needed to be in Washington for a meeting the next day. Each president was booked into a different hotel, and Volcker encouraged them to lie about the purpose of the last-minute trip if they were asked questions, even by their own staffs.[56]

The following day, October 6, Volcker told Fed officials it was time to embrace monetarism.

In technical terms, it amounted to a relatively minor change. Before monetarism, the Fed sought to influence economic conditions by managing the level of short-term interest rates. During the first half of 1979, for example, the Fed targeted a range between 9.75 percent and 10.5 percent for its benchmark rate, the federal funds rate.* In manipulating interest rates, the Fed also was manipulating the money supply, but the Fed was not trying to stabilize the growth of the money supply. The Fed controlled the funds rate like a dad holding a kid by the hand. The money supply followed like a dog on a leash, free to wander from side to side.

---

* The Fed manipulated short-term interest rates through a narrow channel. Commercial banks were required to keep some money in reserve in proportion to the deposits they collected from customers. At the end of every banking day, banks that needed more reserves could borrow from banks that had extra. The prevailing interest rate on those loans, which was determined by the availability of reserves, was called the "federal funds rate." The Fed controlled the availability of reserves, and thus the federal funds rate, like the lord of a bathtub determining the level of the water. To increase the supply of reserves, the Fed bought Treasury securities from banks and paid by creating reserves. The availability of reserves reduced the funds rate, encouraging banks to expand their own lending. Banks sought customers by offering lower interest rates, and economic growth increased. Conversely, to reduce the supply of reserves, the Fed sold Treasury securities to banks. This increased the federal funds rate, which prompted banks to reduce lending, which slowed economic growth.

Under Volcker, the Fed tried to hold hands with the dog. It sought to stabilize the growth of the money supply while allowing the federal funds rate to wander. The Fed adopted Friedman's advice to focus on the quantity of money, and to let markets determine the price.

In Volcker's view, the mechanics were less important than the message. The Fed had initiated anti-inflation campaigns in 1965, 1969, 1973, and 1975, raising interest rates and wrapping its hands around the neck of the economy only to let go, each time, as soon as the economy began to choke. Volcker needed to convince the public this time would be different.

He was, in effect, hoping to borrow Friedman's credibility.[57]

After Volcker concluded his meeting with Fed officials, Joseph Coyne, the Fed's spokesman, raced to summon reporters to an evening news conference. But when Coyne reached a producer at the CBS Washington bureau, he ran into a problem. The producer politely told Coyne the bureau had one camera crew on duty, and Pope John Paul II was visiting the White House. "Send your crew here," Coyne insisted. "Long after the Pope is gone, you'll remember this one."[58]

By the appointed hour, a couple of dozen ruffled reporters had materialized in the boardroom on the second floor of the Fed's marble headquarters. Volcker entered and joked in a gravelly growl that he was neither dead nor resigning.[59] Then he declared war on inflation. "The basic message we tried to convey was simplicity itself," he said later. "We meant to slay the inflationary dragon."[60]

The execution was painful. As the Fed tightened the money supply, interest rates climbed sharply. The prime rate — the rate banks charged the best customers — topped out above 20 percent. Other rates went much higher. Consumers stopped buying cars and washing machines; millions of workers lost their jobs. Without jobs, many lost their homes and hopes of a comfortable retirement.[61]

Factory workers suffered most. Unemployment in the auto industry reached 23 percent. Among steelworkers, it hit 29 percent. And the damage was enduring: a study of Pennsylvania workers who lost jobs in the mass layoffs found that six years later they were still earning 25 percent less than before the recession.[62]

At the July 1980 meeting of the Fed's policy-making committee, Nancy Teeters, the most liberal of the Fed's governors, asked how much harder the Fed needed to squeeze the money supply.

"We don't know," responded Governor Emmett Rice. "We will keep bringing it down until we find out."

"We don't know," Teeters repeated, and history does not record if her tone was sarcastic or wondering.

"It must be lower than what we've had," offered Volcker.

"Or we have to do it longer," said another of the governors.[63]

Volcker insisted low inflation was worth the price. "You just have to tell yourself that somehow it's in the larger interest of the country — and even of these people — to get this straightened out," he told the journalist William Greider.[64] Reversing Keynesian writ, he said low inflation was the best way to deliver low unemployment. "I give you one conviction," Volcker said. "Over time, you can move unemployment lower if we purge inflation and inflationary expectations than if we don't."[65] But he wasn't sure that the pain would be sufficient. Years later, he said that he wore a path in his office rug pacing back and forth, wondering when inflation finally would stop rising.[66]

As Americans suffered, they noticed a new kind of pilot was guiding the economy. Auto dealers sent Volcker the keys to cars they could not sell. Home builders sent chunks of two-by-four wooden beams. "Dear Mr. Volcker," one wrote on a block with a knothole. "I am beginning to feel as useless as this knothole. Where will our children live?"[67] A home builders' association in Kentucky published a wanted poster for Volcker. His crime: Murder of the American Dream.

On December 20, 1981, Senate Democrats held a public forum on the effects of the high interest rates. The *CBS Evening News* aired several minutes from the hearing, almost entirely devoted to a lengthy outburst by a Detroit home builder named Manny Dembs, who told the senators that Volcker was driving him out of business. "We've got the executive, we've got the legislative, we've got the judicial, but we don't have the Federal Reserve Board as a fourth branch of government," Dembs shouted. "I don't even know these people — with the Milton Friedmans and the… the Volckers! I'm reading about all these people. These people scare me! I'm worried about my country and I'm worried that I'm going to go down the drain."[68]

Freedom from Inflation

More than 8 million Americans were out of work when Ronald Reagan delivered his first inaugural address on January 20, 1981, but the new president was focused on a different problem. "We suffer from the longest and one of the worst sustained inflations in our national history," Reagan said. "It distorts our economic decisions, penalizes thrift, and crushes the struggling young and the fixed-income elderly alike. It threatens to shatter the lives of millions of our people." He listed this even before the burden of high taxes and, for both, he famously offered the same prescription. "Government is not the solution to our problem; government is the problem."

Carter had blamed inflation on the profligacy of the American people; Reagan was blaming inflation on the profligacy of the government. Monetarism had reached the White House. The new Treasury secretary, Donald Regan, said he went looking for "the best monetarist I can get" to serve as under secretary of monetary affairs. His choice, Beryl Sprinkel, was a Chicago-trained economist and a monetarist of the purest faith. Sprinkel once joked, before an audience of French policy makers and economists, that his views were easily summarized: "Only money matters. Control the money supply and everything else falls into place. Thank you, and good night."[69] Explaining the new administration's view of monetary policy to a congressional committee, Sprinkel reworked Keynes's metaphor that printing money was like buying a larger belt. Actually, Sprinkel said, it was like feeding a child. "Stuffing a kid with too much food doesn't make him grow faster," he said. "It makes him sick."[70]

Some conservatives wanted Reagan to confront inflation by adopting a gold standard, meaning that the United States would promise to exchange gold for dollars at a fixed rate. Jude Wanniski, the *Wall Street Journal's* lead editorial writer on economic issues during much of the 1970s, told Reagan in a 1981 letter that a gold standard would end inflation without pain, by convincing the public that the government would maintain the value of the dollar. Reagan was prone to nostalgia about the gold standard, which Nixon had ended in 1973, but he wrote back to Wanniski that he couldn't embrace the idea "with one of my favorite people Milton F. opposed." Reagan had learned his monetarism directly from Friedman, whom he had known since the early 1970s, and he put Friedman's ideas into his own words in the radio commentaries he wrote and delivered in the mid-1970s, after his two terms as governor of California.[71] In the early days of the Reagan administration, Bryce Harlow, an old Nixon hand who served as an informal adviser, cautioned White House colleagues against leaving Friedman alone with the President "because he was just too persuasive."[72] But on monetary policy, it was too late: the President was persuaded. Reagan tossed a bone to the goldbugs by creating a commission, but he fixed the outcome by naming Anna Schwartz, Friedman's research partner, as the director. Wanniski was left to fume. "Milton Friedman is my adversary," he wrote a friend in 1982. "At moments I feel a loathing for him as great as my loathing for the Kremlin."[73]

Crucially, Reagan was willing to accept the pain required by the monetarist approach. He had warned after the 1976 presidential election that the country faced a big "bellyache" as punishment for inflationary excess. In mid-1978, Reagan told a reporter visiting his southern California home, "Frankly, I'm afraid this country is just going to have to suffer two, three years of hard times to pay for the binge we've been on."[74] Reagan's advisers battled successfully to temper his public remarks during the 1980 campaign — he was the sunshine candidate; let Carter talk about bellyaches — but they did not change his mind.[75] Volcker doubted whether Reagan understood the details of monetarism, but he did not doubt Reagan's determination. "He said this to me directly," Volcker recalled, "that he learned in this little college he went to, his economics professor taught that inflation was the end of the world."[76]

Volcker later said that one of Reagan's most important contributions to the war on inflation was his decision to fire hundreds of striking air traffic controllers, a stiff blow to the faltering labor movement. "The significance was that someone finally took on an aggressive, well-organized union and said no," Volcker said.[77] Friedman, the high priest of monetarism, had long preached that wage demands did not drive inflation, but Volcker thought this defied common sense. Volcker carried in his pocket a card on which he kept track of union wage deals. Like many economists of both political persuasions, he regarded unions as blackmail artists who interfered with market forces, thereby reducing economic efficiency and growth. He thought a free market would benefit everyone. "The prospects for sustained economic growth and increases in real wages for all Americans will improve as we achieve greater productivity and moderation in the demand for nominal wage increases," he said in September 1981.[78] In fact, American workers did not recover from the Volcker shock. The median income of a full-time male worker in 1978, adjusted for inflation, was $54,392. That number was not matched or exceeded at any point in the next four decades. As of 2017, the most recent available data, the median income of a full-time male worker was $52,146.[79]

The nation's annual economic output, adjusted for inflation, roughly tripled over those same four decades. Yet the median male worker made less money.

On the other end of the economic spectrum, the Volcker recession was hugely profitable for the financial industry. As Volcker drove interest rates into the sky, banks that had been delighted with 4 percent profit margins found themselves earning as much as 9 percent. The banking industry's profits rose by one quarter during the recession years, while other corporations saw profitability decline by one third.[80] That golden moment did not last but, in the era of low inflation, lenders continued to prosper — and the financial industry became the engine of a new economy.

Volcker began to ease his campaign against inflation in the summer of 1982, telling a Senate committee, "The evidence now seems to me strong that the inflationary tide has turned in a fundamental way."[81] As the Fed lowered interest rates, the economy rebounded, and Reagan began to cel- ebrate. "The long nightmare of runaway inflation is now behind us," the President said in January 1983. Soon he was talking about "morning in America."

But monetarism did not survive the celebration. The Fed quietly abandoned monetary targets and returned to a policy of targeting interest rates. Friedman's simple instructions had proved hard to follow. More- over, one of his most basic assertions was wrong. Friedman had said pol- icy makers could count on stability in the velocity of money — the frequency with which money was used. Indeed, velocity was stable between 1948 and 1981.[82] But as the Fed targeted the money supply, velocity began to jump around. Ironically, the stability Friedman had taken for granted was undermined by the unwinding of rules he regarded as unnecessary: financial deregulation was shifting patterns of money use. The instability meant Friedman had overstated the central bank's power to influence economic conditions. It also meant that Friedman had been wrong to dismiss the potential power of fiscal policy to influence conditions.

Other central banks ran aground on the same shoals. The Bank of Canada, which adopted monetary targets in 1975, discarded those tar- gets in November 1982. "We didn't abandon monetary aggregates, they abandoned us," said Gerald Bouey, the bank's governor.

In Britain, Margaret Thatcher had intensified the government's com- mitment to monetarism. "We had learned at Milton Friedman's knee," she said, "that inflation is a monetary phenomenon; that it can only be controlled and reduced by a gradual squeezing of the money supply."[83] As in the United States, the result was a recession that lowered inflation at the cost of high unemployment. By 1980, Thatcher was under growing political pressure to ease the squeeze.* That October, at a Conservative Party conference, she declared that monetarism was the only possible

---

* After Friedman met briefly with Thatcher in February 1980, the Labour Party's leader, James Callaghan, told Parliament he was "thankful that the prime minister was able to spend only a short time yesterday with Professor Milton Friedman."

solution. "You turn if you want to," she said. "The lady's not for turning."[84] Yet Britain soon began to back away from monetary growth targets. The Bundesbank alone persisted, publishing monetary targets until the creation of the euro in 1999.[85]

Some who had suffered Friedman's verbal lashings now returned the favor. "I feel sorry for him," said Fed governor J. Charles Partee. "He's an old man now. He spent his life on this theory. Now it's destroyed."[86] Friedman responded by blaming failures of execution. His tart formulation was that the conduct of monetary policy "would not have been different if they had deliberately set out to give monetarism a bad name."[87] He also predicted that abandoning monetary targets would lead to a resurgence of inflation, a mistake that further emboldened his critics.

But Friedman had won the war, even if he seemed incapable of celebrating. He had persuaded policy makers that central banks should play the central role in macroeconomic policy, and that they should focus on controlling inflation even at the expense of unemployment. As Reagan put the matter in 1982, "I have the greatest sympathy, I think anyone does, for those people who are unemployed.... But the people today have a lower interest rate than they had when we started. The inflation rate is sizably lower." In the United Kingdom, Chancellor of the Exchequer Norman Lamont celebrated the same trade-off a decade later, telling Parliament in 1991, "Rising unemployment and the recession have been the price that we have had to pay to get inflation down. That price is well worth paying."[88]

A telling record of Friedman's victory is preserved in the successive editions of Samuelson's bestselling economics textbook. The 1955 edition presented the high Keynesian view that monetary policy was a sideshow. By 1973, Samuelson conceded "both fiscal and monetary policies matter much." The 1995 edition completed the shift, informing its readers that "fiscal policy is no longer a major tool of stabilization policy in the United States. Over the foreseeable future, stabilization policy will be performed by Federal Reserve monetary policy."[89]

(Im)moderation

A replacement for monetarist mechanics emerged from an unexpected quarter: New Zealand. The island nation had grown and prospered by shipping mutton, wool, and butter to Britain, but access to that market was limited after the United Kingdom joined the European Community in 1973. As the economy faltered, the conservative New Zealand government administered doses of Keynesian-style stimulus and froze wages and prices to control inflation. To no avail. When the Labour Party swept into power in 1984, the new finance minister, Roger Douglas, embarked on a free-market program inevitably dubbed "Rogernomics." He floated the New Zealand dollar, he slashed farm subsidies, and — seeking to drive down inflation, which topped 15 percent in 1985 — he sent aides around the world to shop for a better approach to monetary policy. They brought back the next big thing, a policy so new no other nation had tried it. It was called inflation targeting.[90]

The idea was simple: instead of seeking to control inflation by targeting interest rates or the money supply, central banks should target inflation itself. Like modernist architecture, this was said to eliminate ornamentation, leaving a form of policy defined by its function. Economists were increasingly convinced that public expectations about inflation had the quality of a self-fulfilling prophecy. Lenders wanted an interest rate that was sufficient to cover inflation over the period of a loan. A country with 2 percent annual inflation would not realize the full benefits unless lenders were convinced inflation would remain at 2 percent. Germany and France had similar inflation in the late 1980s, but interest rates remained significantly higher on French government debt. The head of the Bundesbank, Karl Otto Pöhl, told one of New Zealand's scouting parties that the explanation was simple: "Savers don't yet know whether they can trust those French bastards."[91]

In December 1989, New Zealand passed a law making price stability the sole responsibility of its central bank, sweeping away a 1964 law that, characteristically for its time, had instructed the central bank to pursue a laundry list of goals including economic growth, employment, social welfare, and trade promotion. The man picked to lead New Zealand's experiment was an economist named Don Brash, who ran one of the nation's largest banks and then one of its largest trade groups, the Kiwifruit Authority.[92] His job description was simple: deliver inflation between 0 percent and 2 percent. If he failed, he could be fired.[93]

Brash was a believer in price stability. After reading Milton and Rose Friedman's 1980 book, *Free to Choose*, which he described as "enormously influential" in shaping his views, he had invited the Friedmans to visit New Zealand for a speaking tour and escorted them around the country.[94]

In his new role, Brash made his own speaking tour, appearing before any group willing to listen. During one barnstorming swing he gave twenty-one talks in two weeks. Often he told audiences about his uncle, an apple farmer who had sold his orchards in 1971 and plowed the proceeds into government bonds paying 5.4 percent interest. Unfortunately, over the next two decades, inflation rose about 12 percent a year, eroding his uncle's retirement savings.[95]

Brash started raising interest rates and, predictably, the economy convulsed. The unemployment rate spiked to 11 percent, the highest since the Great Depression. A farm group reported that fifty-two farmers in financial distress had committed suicide in the worst year of the downturn.[96] A property developer wrote to request Brash's weight, for the purpose of constructing a sufficient gallows. But Brash kept his job. Inflation fell into the target range by the end of 1991, and stayed there. New Zealand reaped the benefits in the form of lower interest rates, which fell by half between 1987 and 1997.

Central bankers are members of a small and intimate fraternity — they gather every other month at the opulent offices of the Bank for International Settlements in Switzerland[97] — and other countries soon moved to emulate New Zealand, granting their central banks the same combination of operational independence and an inflation target. By 1994, Australia, Canada, Chile, Israel, Spain, and Sweden were doing it. Brash took particular pleasure in advising Britain on the overhaul of its monetary policy regime in 1997. When the European Central Bank opened in 1998, it, too, adopted a 2 percent inflation target.

The drive to eliminate inflation had become a religious phenomenon. Friedman's elegant theory had been tested and found wanting, yet it didn't seem to matter. The central bankers of the world, moving en masse, had decided that inflation was worse than unemployment.

Alan Greenspan, the economist who succeeded Volcker as Fed chairman in 1987, resisted the adoption of an inflation target, but his objections were tactical. He was committed to keeping his foot on the neck of inflation, but he doubted the power of words. At a meeting of the Fed's policy-making committee in 1989, Greenspan dismissed a proposal to adopt an inflation target. Don Kohn, his trusted lieutenant, then serving as head of the Fed's monetary affairs department, drew a contrast with President George H. W. Bush's 1988 campaign promise not to raise taxes. "It's what we do more than what we say," he told Fed officials. "Read our actions rather than our lips."[98]

What Greenspan tried to do was to eliminate inflation. As inflation fell below 3 percent in the 1990s, he insisted further declines would increase prosperity. "The lower the inflation, the higher the productivity growth rate," Greenspan told Congress in 1994.[99] His theory was that low inflation made it harder to raise prices, forcing companies to chase revenue growth by becoming more efficient. The difficulty, which Greenspan freely conceded in private, was that he had no evidence. He told colleagues that the theory was "probably going to be determined to be correct eventually."[100] Meanwhile, in public, Greenspan admitted no such uncertainty. "Not only is it important to bring the inflation rate down from 10 percent to 5 percent, which everyone agrees to," he told Congress, "but it's increasingly becoming evident that the lower we get under 5 percent, the more stable and growing the economy." Greenspan was insisting that reducing inflation from 3 percent to 2 percent would increase economic growth, and that reducing inflation from 2 percent to 1 percent would further increase economic growth. The price of this crusade was paid by millions of Americans. By one estimate, in its pursuit of low inflation, the Fed left more than one million people unnecessarily unemployed in the average month between 1979 and 1996.[101]

Bill Clinton ran for president in 1992 on the unofficial slogan "It's the economy, stupid." On the day he took office in January 1993, the unemployment rate was 7.3 percent, and Clinton was eager to start spending money to stimulate job growth. But a cadre of centrist advisers persuaded the new president to abandon his Keynesian instincts and place his faith in monetary policy instead. The leading figure was Robert Rubin, a former Goldman Sachs executive whom Clinton installed as the head of a new policy shop called the National Economic Council.[102] Rubin argued that Clinton should focus on reducing annual federal deficits by raising taxes and restraining spending. By borrowing less money, the government would reduce competition for available funds, allowing people and businesses to borrow more money at lower interest rates. The government also would ease inflationary pressures, allowing the Fed to maintain lower interest rates. Clinton's initial reaction was disbelief. "You mean to tell me that the success of the program and my reelection hinges on the Federal Reserve and a bunch of fucking bond traders?"[103] But he was a quick study, and, soon enough, he was bowing at the altar of macroeconomic minimalism.

Clinton did try to get the Fed to show more concern for the plight of those without jobs, tapping a leading Keynesian, Alan Blinder, as the Fed's vice chairman in June 1994. Blinder, a Princeton professor, was the author of a scorching attack on the Fed's indifference to human suffering. In a 1987 book, Blinder had argued that Volcker's cure for inflation had been much worse than the disease. He described the effects of inflation as "quite modest — more like a bad cold than a cancer on society." By contrast, Blinder quoted Martin Luther King Jr.'s description of unemployment as "murder, psychologically." Blinder added, "The Fed killed the economy in order to save it from inflation." He also addressed economists on their own terms: if the government's goal was efficiency, surely its top priority should be jobs. Unemployment, he noted, was "the biggest inefficiency of them all."[104]

Greenspan asked his outgoing vice chairman, David W. Mullins Jr., to look into Blinder's work. Mullins came back with a full report, telling Greenspan, "It's not like he's a Communist or anything." The journalist Bob Woodward reported that Greenspan responded, "I would have preferred he were a Communist."[105]

But Blinder left his ammunition at Princeton. He did not accuse his new Fed colleagues of psychological murder, instead adopting the bloodless language of central banking.[106] And in truth, it didn't matter what Blinder thought. Greenspan ran the Fed, and Clinton, who could have replaced him, made his own priorities clear in February 1996 by nominating Greenspan to a third term.[107]

A more successful effort to check the drive toward zero inflation was mounted by another Clinton appointee to the Fed's board, a University of California, Berkeley, economics professor named Janet Yellen.

In July 1996, seeking to build consensus, Greenspan set aside the metronomic routine of the Fed's policy meetings for a debate about the optimal level of inflation. He asked Yellen to explain to her colleagues why she thought a little inflation was a good thing.

Yellen's explanation was rooted in her experience hiring a babysitter for her son in the early 1980s. Yellen and her husband, the economist George A. Akerlof, decided to pay more than the going rate, reasoning that a happier babysitter would provide better care. Generalizing from that experience, Yellen and Akerlof presented evidence in their academic work that companies often seek to boost morale, and productivity, by paying workers more than the cost of a replacement.* Similarly, during recessions, employers refrain from cutting wages because lower morale would diminish pro-

---

* In the early 1990s, the Yale economist Truman Bewley took the extraordinary step of talking with other human beings, traveling around New England during a sharp regional recession to interview corporate executives and workers. He found exactly what Akerlof and Yellen predicted. "Wage rigidity stems from a desire to encourage loyalty," Bewley wrote. See Truman Bewley, *Why Wages Don't Fall During a Recession* (Cambridge: Harvard University Press, 1999), 1.

ductivity. They prefer to fire workers rather than cut pay, because they would not save money if productivity fell, too. In economic models, people can always find jobs by offering to accept lower wages, as employers are always seeking to pay the lowest possible wages. But that logic breaks down if employers are not willing to reduce wages. And that is where a little inflation comes in: it allows employers to gradually reduce the cost of labor without reducing the number of dollars their employees take home. For example, the school board in Anchorage, Alaska, agreed to give teachers an annual 1 percent raise each year from 2013 through 2018. During those years, annual inflation averaged 1.25 percent. The number of dollars, or nominal pay, increased, while purchasing power, or real pay, declined.[108]

Yellen, in 1996, argued the available research suggested the Fed should not seek to reduce inflation below 2 percent. Indeed, she suggested Canada, which had reduced inflation to around 1 percent, already was suffering the ill effects. Other Fed officials found Yellen persuasive. "She was the one who really brought the story that inflation could be too low, and she was very effective. Once she said it, it seemed so obvious and sensible," said Fed governor Laurence H. Meyer.[109] Greenspan did not concede but, recognizing the argument could not be won, he proposed the Fed should cut inflation to 2 percent, then decide what came next.[110]

Bad luck played an underappreciated role in the failures of Keynesianism in the 1970s. The Vietnam War, a pair of oil shocks, and a slump in productivity growth all contributed to the unraveling of confidence in "activist economics." Conversely, in the 1990s, the winds seemed permanently at the back of trust-the-market economics. The "peace dividend" from the end of the Cold War made it easier to reduce federal spending; globalization weighed on wages and prices; new technologies drove a surge in productivity and prosperity. By the early years of the twenty-first century, the victory over inflation appeared complete. In the developed world, inflation had declined from an annual average of 9 percent between 1980 and 1984 to just 2 percent between 2000 and 2006. In the developing world, inflation had declined from an annual average of 31 percent to just 7 percent during the same windows.[111]

The journalist Greg Ip observed in 2005 that central bankers were no longer differentiated by their tolerance for inflation, but only by their forecasts about the likely trajectory of inflation.[112] There also was little remaining difference between the two political parties in the United States. Most Democrats no longer argued the government should prioritize unemployment. They, too, wanted to focus on inflation. "Any honest Democrat will admit that we are now all Friedmanites,"[113] Larry Summers, the Harvard economist who had served as Treasury secretary in the Clinton administration, wrote in 2006.

Ben S. Bernanke, who succeeded Greenspan as Fed chairman in 2006, spoke of a "Great Moderation," a new era in which stable inflation was the linchpin of broader economic stability. Economists once again celebrated the triumph of economics, ignoring the lessons of history. The Nobel laureate Robert Lucas, a founding father of the new minimalism, noted in his presidential address to the American Economic Association in 2003 that macroeconomics had begun in an effort to develop the knowledge and expertise to prevent a recurrence of the Great Depression. "Macroeconomics in this original sense has succeeded," Lucas declared. "Its central problem of depression prevention has been solved, for all practical purposes."[114] The following year, Lucas penned an essay celebrating the success of economics in delivering prosperity — and warning against any return to public policies focused on the distribution of wealth. "Of the tendencies that are harmful to sound economics, the most seductive, and in my opinion the most poisonous, is to focus on questions of distribution," he wrote. "Of the vast increase in the well-being of hundreds of millions of people that has occurred in the 200-year course of the industrial revolution to date, virtually none of it can be attributed to the direct redistribution of resources from rich to poor."[115]

Even at the time, these celebrations should have rung a little hollow. The average rate of unemployment in developed nations between 1992 and 2007 was 7 percent — more than twice the average rate of 3 percent between 1959 and 1975.[116] The benefits of low inflation, meanwhile, were concentrated in the hands of the elite. In the United States in 2007, the top 10 percent of households owned 71.6 percent of the nation's wealth.[117]

By punishing workers and rewarding lenders, monetary policy was contributing to the rise of economic inequality.

There was another problem, too: low inflation had not delivered economic stability. The Great Moderation was about to give way to the Great Recession.

As the economy tipped over the edge of the waterfall, some Fed officials still kept their eyes on prices. "Containing inflation is the purpose of the ship I crew for," Richard Fisher, the president of the Federal Reserve Bank of Dallas, declared in March 2008, three months after the start of the recession in the United States. "If a temporary economic slowdown is what we must endure while we achieve that purpose, then it is, in my opinion, a burden we must bear."[118]

Chapter Four

Representation Without Taxation

What is called sound economics is very often what mirrors the
needs of the respectably affluent.

—*John Kenneth Galbraith,*
Money: Whence It Came, Where It Went *(1975)*[1]

I n April 1971, some of the world's leading economists and bankers
gathered in Bologna, Italy, to talk about stagflation. The developed
world found itself on the horns of a dilemma. The known remedies for
inflation were regarded as likely to increase unemployment, while the
known remedies for unemployment were regarded as likely to increase
inflation.

As the attendees worked their worry beads, the University of Chicago economist Robert Mundell startled the gathering by insisting both
problems could be solved at once. He said he had a recipe to reduce inflation and unemployment simultaneously. Better yet, prosperity could be
restored without pain.

The main ingredient in this elixir, he said, was a big tax cut.

Mundell was a brilliant, abrasive, and eccentric academic whose
insights had transformed the study of international economics, but his
remarks in Bologna were met with incredulity. Keynesians agreed tax
cuts could spur job growth, but only at the price of inflation; monetarists
thought tax cuts didn't have anything to do with inflation. The two sides
agreed that Mundell wasn't making sense.

The response was so hostile that Mundell stiffly compared himself to

St. Sebastian, an early Christian martyr whom the Romans riddled with arrows. Willard Thorp, the venerable conference chairman, who had helped to write the Marshall Plan and saw no cause to regret that act of High Keynesianism, allowed a few final salvos before concluding, "Since it's time for us to adjourn, the chairman will save St. Sebastian from any further arrows."[2]

But Mundell was not destined for martyrdom. In the space of a single decade, his proposal moved from the fringes of academia to the mainstream of American politics. Half a century later, Mundell's supply-side case for tax cuts remains a pillar of Republican economic ideology.

Mundell, born in Ontario, Canada, on October 24, 1932, took an interest in economics while studying at the University of British Columbia. He enrolled in graduate school at the University of Washington and began a rapid professional ascent, finishing his doctorate at MIT and then joining the Stanford faculty. There, "on that Sunday afternoon in November 1958, in my Menlo Park apartment, just a month before the birth of my first son," Mundell had the epiphany that shaped his career. The young professor was hunched over a table, drawing graphs, when into his mind popped the kernel of a new model of the global economy. He later wrote, "I was so taken with the idea — elated might be a better word — that I put pencil and paper down, to prolong the enjoyment of the suspense about what would, with a little more work, unfold."[3]

Economists at the time studied national economies as self-contained systems, every nation an island. Mundell's model provided a framework for examining interactions among countries. One of his conclusions was that some nations might benefit by sharing a currency, an idea that later influenced the creation of the euro.

Another conclusion, which he presented in a 1962 paper, was that the Kennedy administration was mismanaging the U.S. economy. The White House was seeking to maintain fiscal discipline to keep a lid on inflation, while simultaneously reducing interest rates to encourage economic growth. Mundell wrote that the policy should be inverted. The government should cut taxes to stimulate the economy, and raise interest rates to control inflation.[4] Mundell wrote the paper during a stint at the International Monetary Fund and some of his colleagues there argued against publication of such heresies. They were right to worry; it circulated widely. Treasury Secretary Douglas Dillon shared an annotated copy with the President. In December, after Kennedy proposed a tax cut before business leaders in New York, Mundell's boss at the Fund stopped by his desk and said, "Well, I guess you must be happy."[5]

But the happiness was fleeting. Kennedy and the Keynesians had happened to agree with Mundell about the need for a tax cut, but they had not accepted his underlying critique of Keynesian mechanics. Mundell wanted to cut taxes instead of lowering interest rates and increasing spending; during the rest of the 1960s, Keynesian economists persuaded U.S. policy makers to do all three things at once, delivering a massive jolt of stimulus.

By the late 1960s, inflation was on the rise, but still, no one had much interest in Mundell's alternative mechanics. When the Johnson administration raised taxes in 1968, in a bid to control inflation, Mundell predicted the government would succeed only in slowing growth. Following Nixon's victory in the 1968 presidential election, Mundell urged the new administration to reverse the tax increase and instead to adopt his recipe of higher interest rates and lower taxes. But Friedman and other conservative economists firmly opposed any move to cut taxes, and Mundell did not have Nixon's ear.[6] Frustrated and convinced of the wisdom of his own advice, he paid ten thousand dollars for a run-down palazzo outside Siena, Italy, in 1969, reasoning that inflation was inevitable, and property would be a good hedge.[7]

The conference in Bologna two years later, and about one hundred miles from Mundell's palazzo, gave him the opportunity to try again. His main target was the Keynesian view that the Federal Reserve could stimulate economic growth by holding down interest rates — basically accepting more inflation as the price of more jobs. Mundell, like Friedman, argued that inflation "is neither necessary for, nor conducive to, full employment."[8] Indeed, he argued inflation could increase unemployment. But Mundell also opposed the monetarist view that the cure for inflation was to sharply restrict the growth of the money supply, driving the economy into a recession. He noted dryly that if the monetarists were right about the cure for inflation, the American people might reasonably prefer to live with the disease. Instead, Mundell described his third way: a tax cut to spur economic activity, combined with higher interest rates.

The key point of Mundell's argument was the case for cutting taxes. He said growth was a natural force and taxation was the cork. Everyone agreed that handing out money would increase the demand for goods and services; Mundell argued it would also increase the supply. Companies would increase investment, seeking profits subject to a lower rate of taxation.

Tax cuts also would increase the federal deficit. The standard fear is that deficits will force governments either to print money, driving up inflation, or to borrow from the private sector, driving up interest rates. Mundell said the United States could borrow the money from other countries, avoiding both problems. "Suppose it does mean a budget deficit in the United States," he said at the Bologna conference. "Who cares?"[9] Later he put a finer point on the matter, telling a friend who raised the issue, "The Saudis will finance that."[10]

After the Bologna conference, the wounded Mundell left Chicago for the University of Waterloo in Ontario. Former colleagues joked that Waterloo had found its Napoleon. Mundell found a more receptive audience. Canada, like most countries with income taxes, used a system of tax brackets that imposed progressively higher rates on higher levels of income. This system automatically increased government revenues as inflation rose, because the rise of nominal incomes pushed people into higher tax brackets. But inflation did not increase real incomes — the number of hamburgers people could buy — so, as people were taxed at higher rates, their hamburger purchasing power declined. Keynesians did not regard this "bracket creep" as a drag on growth, because the government could spend the money instead. But Mundell argued incentives were important, too: higher taxes made each hour of work less lucrative, so people worked less.

In 1973, the Canadian Parliament voted to adjust tax brackets automatically to keep pace with inflation. The legislation was presented as a straightforward application of Mundell's work: Canada was cutting taxes because taxes impeded growth. "This proposal is a major innovation in tax philosophy and practice," John Turner, the minister of finance, told Parliament in introducing the measure. "It will take some time for people and governments to adjust to it."[11]

By the time Mundell returned to the United States in 1974, to take a job at Columbia University in New York, the American economy had descended into stagflation. As the Keynesians fiddled and Milton Friedman fumed, Mundell renewed his campaign for tax cuts.

At a conference in Washington that spring, Mundell suggested the government should cut taxes by $15 billion. By September, he was arguing for a $30 billion cut. President Ford instead proposed a 5 percent tax increase, embracing the standard Keynesian cure for inflation.

Fortunately for the cause of supply-side economics, a pair of Technicolor Boswells emerged to help Mundell sell his ideas in the United States. The first was Arthur Laffer, an irrepressibly cheerful economist blissfully untroubled by the on-the-one-hand, on-the-other-hand tendencies of his tribe. When offering economic advice, Laffer had only one hand.

Laffer was born in 1940 to a wealthy Cleveland family, raised in an affluent suburb of that mighty industrial city, and educated at Yale and Stanford. He liked life as he found it and saw little purpose in government meddling. "My worldview is not to try to find all the flaws in the competitive model of the world," Laffer told me when I visited him in 2018 in Nashville, where he lived in a large home stuffed with antiquities and fossils. "People have this incredible desire to tinker with the system. Keep your stinking hands off the economy!"

Laffer followed Mundell's path, studying international economics at Stanford and becoming a tenured University of Chicago professor at the tender age of twenty-eight. When Congress raised taxes in 1968 to curb inflation, Laffer joined Mundell in decrying the decision.

Two years later, in 1970, Laffer went to Washington to work for George Shultz, the former dean of Chicago's business school, whom Nixon had named to lead a new agency overseeing the federal bureaucracy, the White House Office of Management and Budget.[12] Shultz was engaged in a futile effort to dissuade Nixon from trying to stimulate the economy. Laffer built a simple forecasting model and predicted the economy would grow at a healthy clip the following year without any additional federal help — a conclusion that made him the target of attacks by proponents of the fiscal stimulus plan. The *New York Times* published a mocking poem in its Sunday business section that began, "They laughed at Laffer's money machine / Such a quaint econometric model has seldom been seen." Paul Samuelson gave a lecture on Laffer's home court at Chicago entitled "Why They Are Laughing at Laffer." The young professor's torment was deepened when his critics discovered he had not completed his Stanford doctorate. Laffer quickly finished the process in 1971, and returned to the University of Chicago the following year.[13]

During the forecasting kerfuffle, Laffer was interviewed by Jude Wanniski, then a young journalist, who made Mundell seem conventional and Laffer seem shy. Wanniski, born in 1936, came from a line of Pennsylvania coal miners with socialist tendencies. He began his newspaper career in Las Vegas before arriving in Washington in 1962 in a lamé suit, driving a Buick convertible with a Vegas showgirl in the passenger seat.[14] Relentless, ingratiating, and a quick study, Wanniski thrived in the world of Washington journalism. He began to write about economic issues and, in 1972, he was offered a plum job on the *Wall Street Journal*'s editorial page. Wanniski uncharacteristically hesitated, telling his new boss he didn't know how to write editorials. "Jude," the editor responded, "all it takes is arrogance."[15] That he had in abundance. He shared his opinions in editorials — and in letters to policy makers. One, to President Ford's chief of staff, began, "First I want you to get comfortable with the idea that I may be the smartest man in the United States."[16]

Wanniski, smart enough to know he needed a better education in economics, cultivated a relationship with Laffer. "Art was the only economist I knew who would answer silly questions," Wanniski said. When Wanniski asked Laffer to name the greatest living economist, Laffer named Mundell.[17] In the spring of 1974, Laffer introduced the two men at a conference in Washington. Wanniski, who did nothing by half measures, later wrote he spent several hours that afternoon in Mundell's hotel room, peppering him with questions. He added that he had found his purpose: he would be the hype man of the supply-side movement.[18]

In December 1974, Wanniski introduced supply-side economics to a popular audience in a *Journal* column entitled "It's Time to Cut Taxes." The thoughts were the thoughts of Mundell, who carefully reviewed every word before publication. But the voice was unmistakably the voice of Wanniski: "The national economy is being choked by taxes — asphyxiated."[19]

Over the next five years, Wanniski used the *Journal*'s megaphone to make that point as often as possible. He also published a book, *The Way the World Works*, elaborating on the theme. It was a bestseller; Laffer said it was the best book ever written about economics.

Wanniski's most effective piece of propaganda, however, was his immortalization of a napkin. In November 1974, Laffer and Wanniski invited Dick Cheney, President Ford's deputy chief of staff, to meet for drinks at Two Continents, a restaurant across the street from the Treasury Department. The economy was mired in a deep recession and Republicans, tarred by the crimes of the Nixon administration, had just suffered a crushing defeat in the midterm elections. Laffer and Wanniski, picking up where Mundell had left off, told Cheney the economy needed a tax cut. Laffer told Cheney that cutting tax rates would generate so much economic activity that the government would actually collect more revenue. To illustrate the point, Laffer grabbed a cocktail napkin and sketched a curve that looked like the nose of an airplane. Wanniski dubbed it the "Laffer curve" and made it so famous that the Smithsonian museum now displays a replica inscribed by Laffer. The curve illustrated the claim that high tax rates are counterproductive. Higher tax rates produce higher revenues until a certain point — the nose of the airplane — but as rates are raised above that point, revenues fall. If a government raised tax rates to 100 percent, people would stop working and soon it might not collect anything at all. On Laffer's curve, the nose of the airplane was not labeled. He said he did not know the rate at which taxation became counterproductive — but he was confident tax rates in the United States were above that level, and therefore tax cuts would increase revenues. He wrote a little ditty on the Smithsonian's napkin: "If you tax a product less results / If you subsidize a product more results / We've been taxing work, output and income and subsidizing non-work, leisure and unemployment. / The consequences are obvious!"[20]

Laffer's emphasis on the idea that tax cuts would encourage people to earn more money was a simplification of Mundell's original theory. Laffer further sharpened the point by arguing that the government should focus on reducing the highest tax rates. This was a direct attack on the government's use of taxation as a powerful tool to redistribute income. Instead of helping those who needed the most help, Laffer and Mundell argued the government should focus on helping those who needed the least. They said the benefits would trickle down: the wealthy would work harder and invest more, the economy would grow, and everyone would prosper. "Supply-side economics made the argument that steeply progressive tax rates reduced the size of the pie to be distributed," Mundell said. "The poor might be better off with a smaller share of a larger pie than with a larger share of a small pie."[21]

Mad as Hell

Lewis F. Powell, one of America's most prominent corporate lawyers, drafted an alarmist memo for the U.S. Chamber of Commerce in August 1971, warning, "No thoughtful person can question that the American economic system is under broad attack." Powell's memo was a catalog of woes: Capitalism, he said, was threatened by radicals like Ralph Nader who wanted the federal government to protect consumers. It was threatened by environmentalists, by liberals who favored higher taxes, by college students whose minds were poisoned by radical professors. Students at the University of California, Santa Barbara, had pushed a flaming dumpster into the local Bank of America in February 1970, burning the bank to the ground. One of the students explained, "It was the biggest capitalist thing around."[22] Powell bemoaned this lack of respect for private property. Companies spent vast sums advertising their brands; he said they needed to advertise capitalism, too. They needed to reshape public opinion in order to reshape public policy.[23]

The beer magnate Joseph Coors said he was inspired by Powell's memo to create the Heritage Foundation.[24] The next year, 1972, the National Association of Manufacturers moved to Washington. "We have been in New York since before the turn of the century, because we regarded this city as the center of business and industry," it said. "But the thing that affects business most today is government."[25]

Powell and his patrons were particularly upset about taxation, which they said was weighing on economic growth. Economic output is determined by the productivity of the average worker, and productivity growth was slowing in the early 1970s; in 1974, the productivity of the average American worker fell for the first time in two decades. Standard economic theory treated productivity growth as a direct consequence of investment, and business leaders said taxation was discouraging investment. They said proposals for corporate tax cuts, widely portrayed as giveaways to the rich, would deliver prosperity to everyone. The Chamber of Commerce hired Norman Ture, the economist who had helped Wilbur Mills shape the Kennedy-Johnson tax cuts in the early 1960s, to collect examples of corporations oppressed by high rates of taxation.

Cutting taxes to encourage investment is shortsighted. A company with five workers may be able to increase productivity by purchasing five computers, but it cannot continue to increase productivity by purchasing more computers. At some point, continued gains can come only from better computers. Productivity growth ultimately is driven by innovation, and fostering innovation requires public investment in education and research and infrastructure. It requires tax dollars. But corporations were focused on the immediate problem; the costs of tax cuts were many years in the future.

The concerns of the business community found a champion in Jack Kemp, who led the Buffalo Bills to a pair of AFL championships as the team's quarterback, then claimed a seat in Congress before the cheering died down. He was a politician in search of a cause and in December 1974 — the month Wanniski introduced supply-side economics in the *Journal* — Kemp introduced a bill to cut corporate taxes. He told of an ad in a Buffalo paper that read "Lathe Operators Wanted — Bring Your Own Lathe."[26] The bill did not attract much support, but it did attract Paul Craig Roberts, an economist with a doctorate from the University of Virginia, who joined Kemp's staff the following year. Roberts, in turn, hired Ture, and together they produced a more sophisticated bill. Kemp dubbed it the Job Creation Act and insisted the increase in economic growth would "generate additional tax revenues that will wipe out the initial revenue loss."*

Wanniski, focused on personal income taxation, initially ignored the bill, but in January 1976 he showed up in Kemp's office without an appointment. Kemp appeared almost immediately. "Wanniski!" he said. "I've just been thinking about how I was going to meet you!" The two men started talking at ten in the morning and, when it was time to go home, Wanniski went home with Kemp, where they ate macaroni and cheese and talked until midnight.[27]

It was also in early 1976 that the economist Herbert Stein described

---

* In the public mind, the assertion that cutting taxes was a free lunch came to be regarded as the central claim of supply-side economics, but supply-siders did not regard 100 percent revenue recovery as a universal property of tax cuts. The Laffer curve went up and it went down — some cuts would pay for themselves, others not. And the claim was generally more complicated than "the government will collect more revenue." It actually had three parts: some revenue would be recouped from faster economic growth; that growth also would reduce government spending on safety-net programs; and the increase in savings would hold down interest rates, reducing the government's borrowing costs. See Paul Craig Roberts, *The Supply-Side Revolution* (Cambridge: Harvard University Press, 1984), 31.

the proponents of these tax cuts as "supply-side fiscalists," a term he did not mean in a nice way. Wanniski, delighted to be noticed, took the epithet and made it his own.[28] Wanniski and friends, now dubbed "supply siders," began to gather in Kemp's offices, laying plans for the revolution.

Congress created the Congressional Budget Office in 1974 to wrest control of economic analysis from the White House.[29] Senate Democrats wanted to appoint Alice Rivlin, a liberal economist at the Brookings Institution, as the first director, but the chairman of the House Budget Committee, Al Ullman, said he wouldn't accept a woman. The impasse was resolved by Wilbur Mills. On a Monday night in early October 1974, police in Washington, D.C., stopped a speeding car. The passengers included a drunken Mills and his mistress, an exotic dancer named Fanne Foxe, who jumped out of the car and into the Tidal Basin. When Mills was forced to resign the chairmanship of Ways and Means, Ullman took the job — and Ullman's successor on the Budget Committee agreed to hire Rivlin.[30]

Rivlin was a small woman full of a force and energy that was only partly obscured by her calm and succinct style. She was born Georgianna Alice Mitchell in Philadelphia in 1931, and raised in Bloomington, Indiana, where her father was a professor at the state university. She enrolled at Bryn Mawr intending to study history, but, during her first summer home from college, she took an introductory economics course and changed her mind. "The appeal of economics was that it was important for the future of the world rather than being more backward-looking, like history," she said.[31] She spent her final college summer working on the Marshall Plan, wrote her senior thesis on Europe's economic integration, and enrolled at Radcliffe College to pursue a doctorate in economics. While in Boston, she married Lewis A. Rivlin, a lawyer, and followed him to Washington in the summer of 1957 "with an unfinished dissertation and a five-month-old baby." Unable to find a job teaching economics — "In those days," she recalled, "colleges simply said they didn't hire women" — she landed at Brookings instead.[32]

At the time, barely one in three women in the United States held a paying job, and Rivlin was even more unusual in maintaining her career while raising three children.

Economists in the 1950s were just beginning to study the government's rapidly expanding role in the economy; Rivlin worked on that frontier, analyzing federal spending on social welfare programs. In 1965, President Johnson ordered federal agencies to start analyzing their own budgets — a story told in chapter 7 — and agencies responded by hiring hundreds of economists, stripping Washington's think tanks. Rivlin became deputy assistant secretary for policy planning at the Department of Health, Education, and Welfare. When Nixon ended the Johnson program, Rivlin returned to Brookings, where she joined the official who had overseen the budgeting program, the economist Charles Schultze, in creating a shadow budget office. They published an annual report analyzing federal spending, just as they had inside the government.

When Congress decided that it wanted its own economists, Rivlin jumped at the chance. She told the *Washington Star* that she cooked dinner every night for her husband and three children. With her new job, she said they would eat more takeout.[33]

A key part of Rivlin's new job was evaluating the economic impact of proposed legislation, taking advantage of the growing power of computers to run simulations.[34] Rivlin and the computer programs were reliably Keynesian; in calculating the effects of a tax cut, neither gave credence to Mundell's theory that people would respond to lower tax rates by working harder, increasing economic growth. Because the budget office did not accept the premise of supply-side economics, it reliably concluded tax cuts would reduce tax revenue.

Paul Craig Roberts, deeply frustrated, persuaded John Rousselot, a sympathetic Republican congressman from southern California, to send a letter to Rivlin inquiring about the omission of supply-side effects from the budget office's analyses; Rivlin responded that such effects were too small to significantly alter the results.[35] Next, Roberts persuaded Senator Orrin Hatch, a young Utah Republican who had arrived in the Senate in 1976, to request that the Budget Committee hold hearings on the budget office's models. Hatch pressed the issue with the chairman, Edmund Muskie, a Democrat from Maine, who said he'd be glad to hold hearings, but kept postponing the date. When Hatch declared that he smelled a rat, Muskie accused him of being "paranoid." Shortly thereafter, someone provided Hatch with a memo Rivlin had sent to Muskie's staff describing the supply-siders as an "extreme right-wing claque who should not be given an audience." At the committee's next meeting, Hatch read it into the record.[36]

The ferocity of the fight reflected an uncomfortable truth: the assumptions used in the economic models dictated the results. Supply-side tax cuts would not look palatable until the models were retooled. In the words of Senator Russell Long, a Louisiana Democrat who wanted to cut taxes, "Something has to be done to try to find somebody who knows more how to put the answer in the computer so that it comes out the right way."[37] Long, the chairman of the Senate Finance Committee, decided the committee would pay for the construction of its own supply-side model.[38]

Milton Friedman did not accept the supply-side rationale for tax cuts, but he was in favor of less government, and he had concluded that liberals were taking advantage of the conservative commitment to fiscal discipline. Liberals kept increasing spending, confronting conservatives with a choice between raising taxes or accepting deficits. It seemed to Friedman that conservatives should adopt the mirror strategy: cut taxes, and confront liberals with a choice between cutting spending or accepting deficits. "By concentrating on the wrong thing, the deficit, instead of the right thing, total government spending, fiscal conservatives have been the unwitting hand-maidens of the big spenders," Friedman wrote in a broadside for the Heritage Foundation.[39] He had reached a new conclusion: "I now say, 'Let's get taxes cut under any and all circumstances.'"[40] Like a general laying siege to a city, he had tried negotiation and now was ready to try starvation. He predicted liberals would surrender and tax cuts would lead to spending cuts.

In the mid-1970s, Friedman helped to form a National Tax Limitation Committee to press for constitutional restrictions on taxation at the state level. On October 14, 1976, he flew from Chicago to Detroit for a day of campaigning for a proposed state constitutional amendment to limit state spending. When he arrived at the first scheduled news conference, he was surprised to find an unusually large number of reporters waiting for him.

"Tell me," one of the reporters said, "what is your reaction to the award?"

That was how Friedman learned he had won the Nobel Prize in economics.[41]

The following year, Friedman turned sixty-five and retired from the University of Chicago, joining his brother-in-law, Aaron Director, at the Hoover Institution on Stanford's campus.

Laffer also had left Chicago for California, fleeing his critics to become a professor at the University of Southern California in 1976.[42] His academic peers continued to describe his ideas as half baked, which bothered Laffer, but he found solace in a burgeoning corporate consulting business. He bought a sprawling house outside Los Angeles, and stocked it with three hundred kinds of cacti and a menagerie of pets including a green macaw named Molly who often perched on his shoulder. He was becoming something of a celebrity. *People* magazine, not a publication that usually spotlights economists, ran a mostly flattering profile, although it did quote Laffer's wife as saying she liked to take long runs because "it's the only way I can stay married to a lunatic."[43]

In 1978, both Laffer and Friedman — fresh additions to the rolls of California taxpayers — agreed to back Proposition 13, an amendment to the state constitution to restrict property taxation. A rapid rise in home values, partly driven by inflation, was causing large increases in property taxation. The amendment reduced the average tax burden from 2.67 percent of a home's value to a maximum of 1 percent.

Howard Jarvis, the combative businessman who spearheaded the campaign, said his goal was to protect property owners, even at the expense of public services. "The most important thing in this country is not the school system, nor the police department nor the fire department," Jarvis said. "The right to have property in this country, the right to have a home in this country, that's important." He said he was inspired by the 1976 film *Network*, in which the lead character memorably yells, "I'm as mad as hell and I'm not going to take this anymore."[44]

The campaign borrowed a needed measure of gravitas from Laffer and Friedman. Laffer said the measure "would go a long way toward revitalizing California's economy." Friedman called it "the best chance we have to control government spending." Jarvis paraded around telling critics the two most important economists in California were on his side. The *Appeal-Democrat*, the local paper in Marysville, a small town north of Sacramento, noted in April 1978, "When an economist of Milton Friedman's status endorses the Jarvis-Gann property tax initiative, those who have scornfully dismissed the proposition as a screwball idea that would bankrupt California government are forced to give it more careful consideration."[45] The measure passed by a margin of 2 to 1. The liberal economist John Kenneth Galbraith, playing off Jarvis's indifference to public safety, wrote *Newsweek* to suggest that people should ring Friedman if the fire department didn't take their calls. "It would be inconvenient indeed," he said, "were there no one at all to respond."[46]

Jimmy Carter promised during the 1976 presidential campaign to revive economic growth the old-fashioned way, and congressional Democrats quickly moved a Keynesian stimulus package to the floor of the House in February 1977. The bill included a fillip of federal spending and a $50 rebate for taxpayers who made less than $30,000 a year. When Rousselot, the congressman from southern California who had questioned Rivlin, rose on the House floor during the final debate, Democrats expected an argument against profligacy. Instead, Rousselot proposed to replace the Democratic plan with a supply-side stimulus: a uniform 5 percent reduction in personal income tax rates.

Astonished Democrats dismissed the idea as "trickle-down economic theory," and the amendment was easily voted down, but the supply-siders were just getting started.

Kemp, seeking to upstage Rousselot, introduced legislation with Senator William Roth a few months later to reduce tax rates by 10 percent a year for three years: "10-10-10."[47] In September 1977, the Republican National Committee endorsed the bill despite the discomfort of fiscal conservatives. Greenspan recalled a lunch at which Kemp asked him,

"Why can't we be a little irresponsible ourselves? Why can't we cut taxes and give away goodies before they can?"[48] This was a line from Wanniski's pitch book and it didn't please the deficit-averse Greenspan. Others were a little wary, too, including Dick Cheney, who was running for the House in 1978. "I'm spreading the word on Kemp-Roth," Cheney wrote Wanniski from the campaign trail. "You guys better know what you're talking about."[49]

Political support for tax cuts increased as the second oil crisis in 1979 deepened the symptoms of stagflation. Monetarists and supply-siders viewed their ideas as alternative treatments for the nation's economic maladies; antsy politicians grabbed both bottles off the medicine shelf, embracing monetary discipline and tax cuts.

The first bill to break through was a measure reducing capital gains taxation on investment income, introduced by William Steiger, a Wisconsin Republican who worried the American economy was losing its entrepreneurial mojo. Steiger wanted to spur investment in the technology sector by reversing a 1969 increase in the capital gains tax. He cited research by Martin Feldstein, a Harvard economist who was a rising star in conservative policy circles, that found the 1969 increase had discouraged such investment.[50] Steiger was a young, ambitious moderate who wrote the law creating the Occupational Safety and Health Administration; his interest in tax cuts was a clear sign supply-side ideas were entering the mainstream. The White House attacked Feldstein's research as "fundamentally flawed," and Carter railed against "tax windfalls for millionaires," but Congress was resolved to try something new. In November 1978, the tax cut passed into law.[51]

In 1980, the Joint Economic Committee, chaired by the Texas Democratic senator Lloyd Bentsen, issued its annual report unanimously, breaking with its usual practice of issuing a pair of partisan reports. "The 1980 annual report signals the start of a new era of economic thinking," it began. "The past has been dominated by economists who focused almost exclusively on the demand side of the economy and who, as a result, were trapped into believing that there is an inevitable trade-off between unemployment and inflation." The new economics, it said, "can reduce inflation significantly during the 1980s without increasing unemployment."

Bentsen also convened the long awaited hearings on economic models, forcing Rivlin to surrender in classic Washington fashion — by pretending there had never been a dispute.

"We are intensely interested in the supply side," she said.[52]

Reaganomics

Ronald Reagan made little mention of taxation during his failed 1976 presidential campaign, nor in the early months of his 1980 campaign. But after losing the Iowa caucuses to George H. W. Bush, Reagan headed into the New Hampshire primary in February 1980 needing a victory to reestablish himself as the front-runner. He found traction with voters by promising to cut taxes, debuting a series of ads that proved hugely popular.

> Announcer: Ronald Reagan believes that when you tax something, you get less of it. We're taxing work, savings and investment like never before. As a result, we have less work, less savings and less invested.
>
> Reagan: I didn't always agree with President Kennedy. But when his 30 percent federal tax cut became law, the economy did so well that every group in the country came out ahead. Even the government gained $54 billion in unexpected revenue. If I become president, we're going to try that again.[53]

Reagan's opponents did not conceal their frustration that voters took him seriously. Bush, a proponent of old-fashioned fiscal discipline, mocked Reagan's "voodoo economics." John Anderson, a moderate Republican congressman from Illinois, described Reagan as a charlatan. He said the only way Reagan could deliver on his promises to cut taxes, increase defense spending, and balance the budget was with "blue smoke and mirrors."

But the political moment was ripe. The government was collecting the largest share of the nation's economic output since World War II.

This was partly the result of an increase in payroll taxation to provide more funding for Social Security and Medicare.[54] It was partly the result of inflation, which pushed people into higher income tax brackets. And the population of the top tax bracket was rising thanks to a trend that didn't get much attention until the 1980s: the best-paid Americans were earning a lot more money, especially in finance, creating a new class of influential and unhappy taxpayers.

Carter missed the change in the political weather. He told voters that cutting taxes would be irresponsible, writing in his diary in June 1980, "We'll continue to wrap the Kemp-Roth proposal around Reagan's neck as best we can."[55]

Voters liked the guy with the tax cuts wrapped around his neck. They liked Reagan's mix of sunshine and sternness. And on January 20, 1981, Americans listened as the nation's first supply-side president promised, "In the days ahead I will propose removing the roadblocks that have slowed our economy and reduced productivity." The unemployment rate was 7.5 percent, and inflation was 11.4 percent. The crowd, tired of stagflation, roared its approval.

Reagan continued, "It is time to reawaken this industrial giant, to get government back within its means, and to lighten our punitive tax burden. And these will be our first priorities, and on these principles there will be no compromise."

Reagan had broken with the hoary tradition that presidents were inaugurated on the east side of the Capitol. He stood on the west side on that cold January morning, facing in the direction of American progress as he promised a return to prosperity. "And after all," he asked, "why shouldn't we believe that? We are Americans."

The festivities that evening contrasted with the President's description of the nation's dire straits. A delegation of Indiana Republicans arrived on a private railroad car once owned by J. P. Morgan. Washington National Airport ran out of parking spaces for private jets.* Limousine companies sent rentals from as far away as Atlanta. "These people have

---

* In 1998, the airport was renamed Ronald Reagan Washington National Airport.

really fine taste," said one giddy caterer. "Rather than shrimp salad, they want the whole shrimp."[56] The Reagan administration said private donors paid for everything; two years later, it emerged that the final bill was roughly double the reported cost, and much of the difference was paid by the Defense Department.[57]

There was eight years in a nutshell: proclamations of prosperity, excesses of profligacy — a new Gilded Age. Reagan asked White House staff to hang a portrait of President Calvin Coolidge in the Cabinet Room.

Reagan's distaste for taxation predated the rise of supply-side economics in the 1970s, Mundell's epiphany in the 1960s, and even Ture's research in the 1950s. In Reagan's telling, it was rooted in his experience as a highly paid Hollywood actor during an era when the government taxed income at rates above 90 percent. Reagan said he turned down roles because he wouldn't work "for six cents on the dollar." The story doesn't check out — among other things, he was in the army the only year the top rate hit 94 percent — but the pain apparently was real enough.[58]

Reagan burst onto the national political scene in 1964 when he delivered an impassioned defense of conservatism on national television during the closing days of Barry Goldwater's presidential campaign. "No nation in history has ever survived a tax burden that reached a third of its national income," Reagan declared. (This was not true: France then collected about a third of national income in taxes; by 2017, the average across developed nations was 34 percent.[59]) Two years later, Reagan promised to cut taxes during his successful campaign for governor of California. He didn't follow through, in part because of opposition from the state legislature. In 1973, approaching the end of his second term, he called a special election on a state constitutional amendment capping the share of personal income California could collect in taxes. Friedman helped to craft the amendment, and he spent a long day with Reagan barnstorming California by airplane. It was the first time the two men talked at any length.

The amendment was soundly defeated in November 1973, but Reagan vowed to try again. "This idea will become a reality," he said. "It must prevail because if it does not, the free society we have known for two hundred years, the ideal of a government by consent of the governed, will simply cease to exist."[60]

After Arthur Laffer moved to southern California in 1976, Justin Dart, a drugstore magnate and a member of Reagan's "kitchen cabinet" of old friends, introduced the economist to the former governor.[61] Laffer became a regular visitor at Reagan's ranch. By the fall of 1977, Reagan was offering supply-side justifications for tax cuts in his syndicated radio commentaries. The following year, after Kemp's bill was defeated, Reagan told his radio audience, "Kemp-Roth is not dead. Ideas do not die. It is simply waiting for the wisdom of the people to be accepted by the majority in Congress."[62]

Laffer still had doubts about Reagan's commitment to the supply side. He urged Kemp to run in the 1980 Republican primaries; Kemp, after a visit to Reagan's ranch, decided to support Reagan instead, judging him "90 percent" in the supply-side camp.[63] His faith was rewarded. Once Reagan was in the White House, Treasury Secretary Donald Regan, a Wall Street executive who had shown little interest in supply-side economics, filled the top tax jobs at Treasury with economists who had worked for Kemp, including Norman Ture.* "I read what President Reagan said during the campaign, and he made clear he was in favor of what is called supply-side tax cuts," Regan said. "I tried to find the best men with those views."[64]

The administration worked quickly, avoiding messy internal disputes by proposing large cuts in both personal income taxes and corporate income taxes. It helped that Republicans riding on Reagan's coattails had

---

* In an article on Ture's appointment, the *New York Times* advised readers that the name was pronounced too-RAY. This was incorrect; the family pronounced it TOO-ray. But according to Ture's wife, the article changed his mind, and he began to pronounce his name the way it appeared in the *Times*. See Irvin Molotsky, "Norman B. Ture, Architect of the 1981 Tax Cut, Dies at 74," *New York Times*, August 13, 1997.

taken control of the Senate in 1981, for the first time in twenty-six years. Resistance among House Democrats weakened after Reagan was shot that March.

But some Democrats and Republicans still expressed lingering concern that cutting taxes would result in larger budget deficits. The President responded by making the argument he had often heard from Laffer and other supply-siders. He said tax cuts would catalyze such an increase in economic growth that federal tax revenues would increase, too. Some of Reagan's closest advisers, notably the economist Martin Anderson, his top domestic policy aide, later insisted Reagan had never claimed that the 1981 tax cuts would pay for themselves. This is risible revisionism. Reagan made the claim both on the campaign trail and in the White House. "It's true that I believe, as President Kennedy did, that our kind of tax cut will so stimulate our economy that we will actually increase government revenue," he said in a speech on July 7, 1981, as the legislative debate was in its final stages.[65]

Reagan signed the tax cut on August 13, 1981, in the yard of his California ranch, dressed in denim and cowboy boots, and using twenty-four pens to create a sufficient number of mementos. He wrote in his diary that it was "the greatest pol[itical] win in half a century."[66]

The Reagan tax cuts should have discredited supply-side economics.[67] The evidence of failure was not the Volcker recession, which was already under way when the tax cuts passed into law. Rather, it was the fact that even after growth resumed toward the end of 1982, the promised supply-side benefits did not materialize. Everyone agreed handing out money would boost economic growth. The supply-side claim was that lower tax rates also would encourage people to work harder and invest more. The administration specifically predicted Americans would save about 40 percent of the tax cut — an astonishing figure, given the 6 percent savings rate for other kinds of income. Instead, the average savings rate did not budge.[68]

The bill also sought to encourage investment by slashing corporate taxation, particularly for manufacturers. Between 1960 and 1980, the effective tax rate on machinery already had been reduced from 59 percent to 18 percent. Under the 1981 law, the effective rate fell to negative 5.5 percent. The federal government, in essence, was subsidizing investment in machinery.[69] A study of 250 large corporations found slightly more than half paid no taxes in at least one year between 1981 and 1983. General Electric — which the study dryly described as "Ronald Reagan's former employer" — earned $6.5 billion and did not pay a penny in taxes.[70] But investment declined across the economy. In a defining moment, U.S. Steel announced in November 1981 that it would buy Marathon Oil for $6.3 billion instead of upgrading its aging steel mills.

Taxes change behavior: up to 45 percent of cigarettes smoked in New York are illegally imported from other states because New York has the nation's highest taxes on cigarettes.[71] But supply-siders overestimated the influence of taxation. Milton and Rose Friedman built their summer home, Capitaf, on the Vermont side of the Connecticut River even though they acknowledged that, "as economists, we should have looked for land in New Hampshire," where taxes are lower.[72] After Reagan's election, William J. DeLancey, chief executive of Cleveland's Republic Steel, rejoiced that tax cuts would open "a whole new era of greater productivity and profitability for the steel industry."[73] Republic Steel did not survive Reagan's first term.

Even the impact of tax cuts on demand — the direct benefit of handing out money — proved modest. When the dust had settled at the end of the decade, the combination of recession and recovery produced average annual growth of 2.2 percent during the 1980s, adjusting for population and inflation — slightly slower than the annual average for the 1970s.[74] "I'm not convinced that the Reagan tax cuts worked," Dick Cheney told a friend in the late 1980s.[75]

The failure of Reagan's tax cuts to deliver faster economic growth forced the government to borrow money on the largest scale since World War II. Some conservatives, including Friedman, were not surprised by the government's predicament: they had scoffed at the predictions of the supply-siders. They also were not dismayed. They had supported the tax cut because they wanted to blow a hole in the federal budget, and then close it with spending cuts.[76]

David Stockman, Reagan's budget director, knew exactly what he wanted to cut. Stockman was a wiry thirty-four-year-old who looked and dressed like the earnest Hill staffer he once had been, although his hair had started to show traces of gray. He was not an economist; instead, he was an example of the evolution of trust-the-market economics from a set of esoteric critiques into a political movement, a parade in which anyone could march. Raised on a Michigan farm, Stockman landed at Harvard Divinity School in the late 1960s, where he babysat for Daniel Patrick Moynihan's kids, which he parlayed into a seat in a seminar taught by the journalist David Broder, who introduced him to Congressman John Anderson, a rising star in the Republican Party who needed an aide to focus on economic issues. Stockman knew nothing about the subject, but he started reading, and so he encountered the ideas of Hayek and Friedman in the mid-1970s. He recalled, "Everything the free market scholars said would happen — shortages, bottlenecks, investment distortions, waste, irrationality, and more inflation — did happen right before my eyes."[77]

Stockman won one of Michigan's House seats in 1977 and befriended Kemp, bonding during late-night discussions about subjects like West Germany's postwar economic reforms. But he never joined Kemp's inner circle.[78] The supply-siders did not care about deficits. Stockman described himself as a "compleat supply sider"; he wanted to cut taxes and spending.

Stockman got his heart broken. Reagan and most members of Congress liked tax cuts more than spending cuts. Reagan refused to back Stockman's plans for cuts in federal entitlement programs; meanwhile, the President backed large increases in military spending. "I heard the President say more than once, 'Between cutting back on defense and incurring a deficit, I'll incur a deficit,'" said James C. Miller III, who followed Stockman as budget director.[79]

As federal borrowing mushroomed, supply-siders pleaded for patience, arguing the annual deficits would not last and were not important. William Niskanen, a member of Reagan's Council of Economic Advisers, channeled Mundell, declaring in a December 1981 appearance at the American Enterprise Institute that there was little connection between larger deficits and inflation or higher interest rates. Several Senate Republicans, committed to the old-fashioned view that deficits were dangerous, called for his resignation.[80]

Niskanen had a point. The Japanese proved particularly eager to loan money to the United States.[81] The Reagan administration helped matters along by encouraging Congress in 1984 to create a new kind of Treasury security for foreign buyers.[82] These remarkable bonds were designed to facilitate tax fraud against foreign governments by allowing bondholders to collect interest payments anonymously. They simply needed to certify they were not American. This, in turn, allowed the United States to pay lower interest rates. The Treasury sent senior officials to Japan and Europe to market the bonds. Reagan hailed the United States as "the investment capital of the world." But Americans paid a price: the massive reliance on foreign money eroded the nation's industrial base, a story told in chapter 8.

In late 1981, Bob Dole, the Kansas Republican who chaired the Senate Finance Committee, found himself at a dinner party with Frederick Schultz, the Federal Reserve's vice chairman, who regarded the administration's profligacy with horror, and Walter Wriston, Citicorp's chief executive, who was an outspoken defender of Reaganomics. A few days later, encountering Schultz in an elevator, Dole confided, "You won the debate. I think we are going to have to do something on the fiscal side."[83] Dole also added a new joke to his repertoire: "Good news is, a bus full of supply-siders went over a cliff last night. Bad news is, there were three empty seats."[84]

It took most of the next two decades to repair the damage to the government's finances.

Still Reagan and the supply-siders won an enduring political victory. The most visible change was the permanent reduction of tax rates for those with high incomes. The 1981 law reduced the top rate to

50 percent. In 1986, Congress further reduced the top rate, to 33 percent.[85] Since the 1980s, the top rate has tended to rise under Democratic presidents, and to fall under Republican presidents, but it has remained below 40 percent.

During the mid-twentieth century, the government had used income taxation as a corrective for economic inequality. Taxation was a bulldozer that made the tallest mountains noticeably shorter and the shortest hills a little taller. In 1979, under Carter, the inequality of income distribution after taxation was 10.2 percent smaller than the inequality of income distribution before taxation. The Reagan tax cuts substituted a much smaller bulldozer. By 1986, the inequality of income distribution after taxation was just 5.1 percent smaller than the inequality before taxation.[86]

After-tax income inequality in the United States rose faster during the mid-1980s than during any other period in the postwar era.[87] The gulf between the wealthy and everyone else was yawning wider — and the federal government was no longer fighting back.

Other developed nations emulated America, though few went as far. The British conservative ideologue Keith Joseph had wholeheartedly endorsed the need for reductions in top tax rates in a 1976 speech tellingly titled "Monetarism Is Not Enough":

> By taxation, by inflation, by the remorseless flood of regulations
> and legislation, by controls and by the constant and arbitrary
> interventions of authority, successive governments since the war
> have cumulatively taken away both the pleasure and the rewards
> that once made risk-taking worthwhile.[88]

Under Prime Minister Margaret Thatcher, the United Kingdom reduced the top rate of personal income taxation from 80 percent to 40 percent. Japan's top rate dropped from 75 percent to 50 percent. The average top tax rate in a group of twenty-five developed nations fell from 66 percent in 1979 to 50 percent a decade later.[89] "The bottom line," Mundell said in a 2011 valedictory, "is that no one is advocating putting back tax rates to what they were in the late 1970s. And I think this is the victory."[90]

The Lean Years

Reagan's tax cuts marked the end of an era in which the federal government's role in the economy steadily increased. Federal spending as a share of the nation's economic output rose from less than 10 percent before the Great Depression to 22.8 percent in 1983. That was the peak. Over the next two decades, the deals Democrats and Republicans hashed out to repair the government's finances significantly reduced the economic footprint of the federal government.[91]

Dole and other Republicans joined with Democrats in 1982 to force the Reagan administration to roll back some of the tax cuts passed less than a year before. The congressional pressure exposed differences among the administration's supply-siders. Some, like Ture, wanted to preserve the corporate tax cuts. He saw stronger evidence that cutting corporate taxes could stimulate long-term economic growth, and he mocked Laffer's emphasis on personal income tax cuts. "The cocktail napkin has nothing to do with supply-side economics," Ture said dismissively.[92]

But Laffer's version of supply-side economics was more attractive politically. Reagan agreed to reverse roughly half the cuts in corporate and investment taxes enacted just eleven months earlier. To seal the deal, he promised to send House Democrats who voted for the plan a letter of thanks they could publicize during the 1982 midterm elections, as a shield against voter anger.[93]

The corporate case for tax relief, which the administration and Congress had embraced with such enthusiasm, suddenly seemed unaffordable. "The fundamental merit of our proposal was not even debated," said one outraged corporate lobbyist.[94]

In 1984, a majority of congressional Republicans once again voted with Democrats for a bill, once again endorsed by Reagan, that cut deficits mostly by increasing taxation.[95]

But in 1987, a majority of congressional Republicans voted against a third round of tax hikes.* Vice President George H. W. Bush, running to succeed Reagan, heeded the change in his party's mood, telling the roaring crowd at the 1988 Republican National Convention, "Read my lips — No. New. Taxes."

Bush, however, was still an old-school Republican, more worried about deficits than taxes, and in 1990 he struck a deal with Democrats on a new package of tax increases and spending cuts. Just one third of the money came from tax increases, but most Republicans still opposed the measure; Bush barely mustered the necessary support to push it through Congress. The last vote, on a Saturday afternoon in October 1990, turned out to be one for the history books. Senator Pete Domenici turned from a conversation on the Senate floor, caught the eye of a clerk by raising his right hand, and then signaled his vote in favor. It was the last time for more than a quarter century that any congressional Republican voted to raise income taxes.

In 1993, President Clinton pushed a tax hike through Congress without a single Republican vote. Supply-siders insisted raising tax rates would not increase federal revenues. Jack Kemp told conservative activists that the Clinton tax hike would backfire. "Will raising taxes reduce the deficit? No, it will weaken our economy and increase the deficit."[96] This was intellectually consistent; it was also wrong. Under Clinton, the economy boomed and deficits vanished.

Republicans won some spending cuts. Representative Richard Armey of Texas, a former economics professor, played a leading role. Armey was born in 1940 in a North Dakota town called Cando. (The town's name is pronounced just the way a libertarian would want it to be.) His father was the mayor; his

---

* The 1986 tax bill, which reduced the top tax rate to 33 percent, was designed to be revenue neutral: neither increasing nor decreasing the deficit. It was the embodiment of the goal first articulated by Wilbur Mills in the 1950s: cutting tax rates while broadening the tax base. The legislation is still regarded as a triumph of bipartisanship — and of economic policy making. It did nothing, however, to resolve the basic mismatch between federal spending and revenues.

mother kept the books at the family grain elevator and insisted she had no use for government. Armey took after his mother. "The market is rational and the government is dumb," he liked to say. He got a doctorate in economics from the University of Oklahoma and began a teaching career that reached its climax when he became department chair at North Texas State University. He was, he said, a "bush league professor at a bush league school." But along the way, he spent the summer of 1969 at the University of Chicago, which he described as "my first real exposure to the discipline of economics."[97] In the early 1980s, a big Republican donor named Eddie Chiles, who sat on the North Texas board, asked a college official whether the faculty included "anything like a free market economist."[98] Chiles helped Armey to enter politics.

When Armey landed in Washington in 1985, he tried to sleep on a cot in the House gym, to make the point that he didn't want to get comfortable. He made his name in 1990 by rallying opposition to President Bush's tax plan, in defiance of the party's leadership. Three years later, installed as a member of the party's leadership, he helped to ensure not a single House Republican voted for President Clinton's tax plan.

Armey was serious about spending cuts, supporting reductions in farm subsidies and the closure of military bases in the wake of the Cold War. But Armey, who numbered a letter from Milton Friedman among his treasured possessions, shared Friedman's view that Congress lacked the fortitude to cut spending. He and his allies tried to solve this problem with a pair of contracts. The first was dreamed up by Grover Norquist, an antitax activist who said he wanted to reduce the size of government until it was small enough to drown in a bathtub. Beginning in the mid-1980s, he pressed Republican candidates to sign a "Taxpayer Protection Pledge" in the presence of two witnesses, promising not to vote for tax increases of any kind at any time. During the 1994 midterm election campaign, Norquist collected signed pledges from the vast majority of Republican congressional candidates. He said he kept them in a fireproof vault.[99]

The second contract, crafted by Armey and Newt Gingrich as a campaign platform for the 1994 midterms, was billed as the "Contract with America." It included a constitutional amendment mandating a balanced budget, which they hoped would force significant spending cuts. After voters gave Republicans a House majority for the first time in forty years, Armey pushed the balanced-budget amendment to the verge of congressional approval. It failed by just a single vote in the Senate on March 2, 1995 — but President Clinton avoided the shackles in part by pledging to cut spending. "The era of big government is over," he said in his 1996 State of the Union. Federal spending declined from 21.2 percent of the nation's economic activity in 1990 to 17.6 percent in 2000.[100]

The government's austerity during the Clinton years is often listed among the reasons the economy boomed, because it helped to hold down interest rates. But the government's greater contribution to economic growth in the 1990s was its spending in earlier decades on education, research, and infrastructure. Americans who entered their prime working years in the 1990s were far more likely to have college degrees than adults in the rest of the developed world. The rise of Silicon Valley was a triumph of government-sponsored research, government investment in infrastructure, and the government's development of human capital.

The austerity of the Clinton years, by contrast, meant the government was reducing its investment in future growth.

Federal spending on research declined. Samuel Broder, the head of the National Cancer Institute, left for the private sector in 1995. "When I first came here twenty-two years ago, government service was still something that people generally admired," Broder told the *Washington Post*. "And I think it might be good to take a few steps back and remember that although we do have to make government more efficient and face fiscal realities… there are certain core functions of the government that are extremely important, including scientific research for the alleviation of suffering."[101]

Federal spending on infrastructure declined. The federal gas tax, a major source of funding for transportation improvements, has not increased since 1993. On an inflation-adjusted basis, the bite of the tax has declined by 40 percent over that period. But despite broad support for spending on roads and bridges — and support for a tax increase among business groups — ideological opposition to taxation prevents any change to this day.

Federal spending on human welfare declined. Indeed, the overall diminution of the government's role in the economy obscured an even larger decline in spending to help the poor, as policy makers shifted welfare spending toward the elderly and the middle class. A milestone in that shift was Clinton's promise to "end welfare as we know it." Instead of providing direct aid to poor families, the federal government began to divide $16.5 billion among the states each year. More than two decades later, the sum remains the same, but inflation has eroded the value by more than a third.

And America lost its edge in education. The cost of a university education in the United States is now among the highest in the developed world, and it is not a coincidence that Americans who entered their working primes in the 2010s were less likely to have college degrees than the citizens of eleven other developed nations. Four decades after Wanniski warned that taxation was asphyxiating the American economy, it is the absence of taxation that has proven more damaging.

If at First You Don't Succeed

Sometimes ideas slip their moorings. Supply-side economics was developed as a corrective for the economic doldrums of the late 1950s and was revived as a corrective for the stagflation of the late 1970s. The third generation of supply-side proponents shucked that context in the late 1990s. In their view, tax cuts were like logs that could be thrown onto the fire at any time.

When George W. Bush first proposed a major tax cut in December 1999, as a candidate in the Republican presidential primaries, the economy had been growing for almost a decade. Both inflation and unemployment were low and, while those at the top continued to reap an outsized share of the gains, workers' wages were rising, too.

Bush argued that a tax cut was necessary to keep the good times rolling. "Putting more wealth in the hands of the earners and creators of wealth — now, before our trouble comes — would give our current expansion a timely second wind," the Texas governor told an Iowa audience.[102] He had a compelling political reason for that argument. He needed to convince Republican voters he was another Reagan and not another Bush. "This is not only 'No new taxes,' this is, 'Tax cuts, so help me God,'" he said during a January 2000 debate.

Bush's controversial victory in the 2000 election strengthened his resolve. The new president and his advisers decided the best way to put questions about legitimacy in the rearview mirror was to plow ahead with his agenda. On Inauguration Day in 2001, unemployment was just 4.2 percent, inflation was 2.6 percent, investment was increasing, and productivity was rising — and still Bush declared that he would push for tax cuts "to recover the momentum of our economy and reward the effort and enterprise of working Americans."

The following month, Bush added another justification. The federal government collected 20 percent of the nation's economic output in 2001 — the largest share since World War II — while spending just 17.6 percent. "The people of America have been overcharged," Bush said, "and, on their behalf, I'm here asking for a refund."

None of this made sense. The economy did not need help. Reagan had shown tax cuts could not provide significant help, at least not on the supply side. And Americans had not been overcharged. Setting aside the question of whether the government should have been spending more in 2001, the government clearly needed more money to fully fund the retirement benefits that had been promised to the baby boomers.

Bush's Treasury secretary, Paul O'Neill, a fiscal conservative, argued tax cuts should be contingent on continued budget surpluses, and he sought support from Fed chairman Alan Greenspan. Greenspan's opposition had helped to kill a Republican tax cut plan in 1999 that was only half as large as the 2001 plan, and O'Neill, whose friendship with Greenspan dated back to the Ford administration, sought to convince him a larger cut was even more irresponsible.[103] But Vice President Cheney, also a Ford alum and friend of Greenspan, rejoined that surpluses were dangerous because Congress would spend the money.[104]

Greenspan told both men he agreed with them. Before Congress on January 25, 2001, he endorsed large tax cuts conditional on the government's fiscal health. All anyone heard was that Greenspan had changed his mind about tax cuts. "I'm a Baptist. We have a hymnal. We have a song in our hymnal, 'The Anchor Holds,'" drawled Senator Robert Byrd, an octogenarian Democrat from West Virginia. "I have listened to you over the past several years, that we need to pay down the debt, that is the basic need. I believe that you were right then and I am somewhat stunned by the fact that the anchor seems to be wavering."[105]

When the economy entered a mild recession in the spring of 2001, Bush added a Keynesian rationale to his collection, tacking on a $600 rebate check to broaden political support. That was enough to push the cuts through Congress.

The government's fiscal health deteriorated quickly in 2001, replicating the outcome of the 1981 tax cuts. But the political environment was very different. Bush refused to emulate Reagan's retreat. "Not over my dead body will they raise your taxes," Bush told a cheering crowd in January 2002. Leading Democrats responded with indignation. Tom Daschle, the Senate majority leader, insisted that he did not want to raise taxes either.

This time around, there also was no effort to cut spending. Instead, Bush went on a spending spree. In a surprisingly faithful imitation of Lyndon Johnson, he plunged into an unwinnable war in Asia, this time in Iraq, and backed the addition of a prescription drug benefit to Johnson's Medicare program, which provides health insurance to senior citizens.

Then the President announced the economy needed more tax cuts.

Cheney took the lead in constructing a supply-side plan focused on encouraging investment. "He got this idea from Art Laffer on capital-gains reductions and he was just hot on that," said his top economic aide, Cesar Conda.[106] Cheney had shed his wariness of supply-side ideas; that was no longer a viable position for a Republican. "It was our belief that taxes ought to be as low as possible," Cheney later wrote, "especially when it came to those elements of the tax code that affected savings and investment, economic growth, and job creation."[107] In fact, Cheney wanted to go further than Bush, who omitted the capital gains cut from the package the administration sent to Congress. So Cheney persuaded House Republicans to pass the capital gains cut. Then, after the Senate passed the Bush version of the plan, Cheney and the President sat together, alone, in the Oval Office and decided to support Cheney's version.[108]

O'Neill, for his part, was determined to fight harder against the second round of cuts. He told Bush in September 2002 that the plan was "not responsible," which briefly paused its progress. But Republican victories in the midterm elections emboldened the White House to move ahead. The final internal showdown came on November 15, 2002, at a meeting convened by Cheney. O'Neill argued strenuously that the country was "moving toward a fiscal crisis." The government had just posted its first annual deficit in five years. "Reagan proved deficits don't matter," Cheney responded.[109]

Proponents and opponents of the tax cut plan both insisted that economics validated their position. Four hundred and fifty economists signed a statement, printed as a full-page ad in the *New York Times*, that opposed the plan, concluding it would expand the federal debt but not the American economy. Two hundred and fifty economists responded with a statement in support of the plan, taking the opposite view that it would expand the economy but not the debt.

The general public had more information than ever to judge these internecine fights, including the record of the Reagan tax cuts, but, as the historian Michael Bernstein has observed acutely, the explosion of data in recent decades has tended to confuse rather than clarify. The availability of overwhelming quantities of information not only has made people mistrust their own judgments, it has contributed to a suspicion that no one is up to the challenge.[110]

Greenspan was among the economists who came out publicly against the second round of tax cuts, albeit in his typically equivocating style.[111] He fought harder in private, bringing Cheney an analysis concluding larger deficits would raise interest rates and reduce growth.[112]

Cheney told Conda to prepare a critique arguing Greenspan was crying wolf.[113] The memo, circulated around the White House, reprised Niskanen's argument in 1981. It said many factors determined the level of rates, and there was little evidence the deficit was particularly important. In May 2003, the cuts passed by the narrowest possible margin. Cheney cast the deciding vote, joking afterward that he didn't vote often, but when he did, he always prevailed. "The Republican Party is now a supply-side party. It's a tax-cut party," crowed Stephen Moore, a longtime antitax crusader. "It has evolved over the past forty years from being a party of Eisenhower balanced-budget Republicans into a party of Reaganite pro-growth advocates."[114]

Tax cuts once again were a political triumph and an economic failure. Bush won reelection in 2004, but growth was tepid, investment declined, and Americans, particularly prime-aged men, continued to drop out of the workforce. Andrew Samwick, the chief economist on Bush's Council of Economic Advisers in 2003 and 2004, later concluded in a postmortem, "There is, in short, no first-order evidence in the aggregate data that these tax cuts generated growth."[115]

As federal borrowing soared, the United States once again found ready lenders. This time China played the leading role instead of Japan, but the effects were the same. The codependent relationship with China undermined American manufacturing, eliminating millions of jobs.

The Bush tax cuts also continued to flatten the distribution of taxation. In 1961, the roughly 112,000 Americans with the highest incomes paid an average of 51.5 percent of that money in local, state, and federal taxes. In other words, from each dollar of income, the government took roughly half. Meanwhile, the great mass of Americans — the bottom 90 percent, ranked by income — paid an average of 22.3 percent of income. From each dollar of income, the government took less than a quarter. Half a century later, the gap was much smaller — almost entirely because of a massive reduction in the taxation of rich people.* In 2011, top earners paid 33.2 percent of their income in taxes, while the bottom 90 percent paid 26 percent of their income in taxes.[116]

It is an important fact — a marker of the supply-side movement's political success — that many less affluent Americans supported this

---

* Because of the rapid growth of income at the top of the economic ladder, the share of taxes paid by the most affluent Americans has increased even as the share of their income paid in taxes has declined. By "massive reduction," I mean the wealthy would have paid much more in taxes if they were still subject to the law of 1960 or of 1980.

shift in the tax burden. The share of Americans who said high-income households paid too little in taxes fell from 77 percent in 1992 to 62 percent in 2012, even as inequality rose to the highest levels since the Great Depression.[117]

Laffer surprised friends by moving in 2006 from his longtime home in California to Nashville, Tennessee. He said he wanted to find a state that shared his view of taxation, and there is almost no state that asks less from its residents than the Volunteer State. Only Alaska, South Dakota, and Wyoming collect a smaller share of income in state and local taxes.[118] Laffer likes to say the money he saved on taxes in the first year alone paid for his $1.55 million mansion in ritzy Belle Meade, where his neighbors include Al Gore. "It's a great line and it's very close to being true," Laffer told me. Shortly after moving, however, Laffer made an alarming discovery: Tennessee still had an estate tax. "It was a good place to live," Laffer said. "But it was not a good place to die." So Laffer launched a campaign that persuaded the Tennessee legislature to eliminate estate taxation. "And now," Laffer told me, "it's okay to die here, too."

PART II

Chapter Five

In Corporations We Trust

There is a saying that economists make bullets that lawyers fire
at one another.

— Merton J. Peck (1978)[1]

In April 1952, dozens of engineers from some of the world's largest companies, and from companies so new they had no products, boarded buses in New York City and headed under the Hudson River. They were guests of AT&T, which had patented a new electronic device called a transistor just a few months earlier, and had invited its potential rivals to spend nine days learning exactly how they could make transistors, too. The company even provided a two-day tour of its state-of-the-art manufacturing facility in Allentown, Pennsylvania. Then, for good measure, AT&T published the complete instructions in two volumes, a reference work known to a generation of electrical engineers as "Mother Bell's Cookbook."[2]

One group of engineers at the AT&T classes came from Texas Instruments, a small company just turning to electronics from oil work. Two years later, in 1954, the company produced the first silicon transistor, which led to the development of microprocessors, which allowed the creation of personal computers. The Japanese company Tokyo Tsushin Kogyo did not send engineers to the AT&T seminar, which was restricted to companies from NATO countries, but it licensed the technology in 1953 and soon began to produce one of the first blockbuster products of the consumer electronics era: the Sony transistor radio.

Indeed, the transistor is the building block of virtually all modern electronic devices. But AT&T reaped only modest rewards: companies paid $25,000 to license the technology.

There was a simple explanation for AT&T's generosity: the federal government forced the company to share its inventions as part of an aggressive, carefully considered, and wide-ranging campaign to prevent large and powerful companies from hoarding innovations.[3]

To "open up the electronics field," regulators required more than one hundred companies to license patents between 1941 and 1959.[4] General Electric shared the secrets of its lightbulbs; IBM published the recipe for its mainframe computer.[5] A generation later, the federal government intervened again, forcing IBM to let others write software for its computers. New companies sprouted, including Micro-Soft, founded by Bill Gates and Paul Allen in April 1975.

The mythology of the computer revolution, of libertarians developing ideas in Silicon Valley garages, is usually narrated without any mention of the role played by government. It was antitrust regulation that opened the market and allowed those ideas to bloom.

Limiting the market power of large corporations was a distinctly American tradition.

Americans in the nineteenth century saw themselves as a nation of yeoman farmers, craftsmen, and storekeepers, where every man was his own master, or had reason to believe he could be someday. Nor was this pure fantasy: while the ideal of economic autonomy excluded blacks and women and quite a few white men, ownership of land and capital in the United States, particularly in the Northeast and Midwest, was distributed much more broadly and evenly than in Europe.

The rise of railroads and other large corporations in the second half of the nineteenth century struck many Americans as a direct threat to this way of life. Size itself was the problem: the new behemoths absorbed smaller rivals, squeezed suppliers, overcharged customers. A handful of men reaped outsized profits and exercised outsized political influence; for everyone else, the dream of economic independence seemed to be fading away. America was becoming a society of unequals. By the end of the nineteenth century, two thirds of manufactured goods were produced by corporations, and two thirds of wage earners worked for corporations.[6]

The political backlash birthed the Sherman Antitrust Act in 1890, the nation's first antitrust law, which criminalized the abuse of market power. "If we will not endure a king as a political power, we should not endure a king over the production, transportation and sale of any of the necessaries of life," said Senator John Sherman, the Ohio Republican who sponsored the legislation.[7]

In time, the law would come to be portrayed as an early, misguided attempt to maximize the efficiency of the American economy. This was a rewriting of history. The law was a conscious effort to subordinate economic efficiency to politics. It was intended to preserve the autonomy of small business owners. More than this, it was meant to safeguard the viability of democratic government.[8]

Two decades later, in 1911, the federal government used its power to break John D. Rockefeller's Standard Oil Company into thirty-four pieces.[9] Rockefeller had embodied and celebrated a new vision of American life, writing in 1882, "The day of combination is here to stay. Individualism has gone, never to return." The Supreme Court, in upholding the atomization of his company, made clear that the government wasn't ready to concede the point. Three years later, in 1914, Congress prohibited a broader range of anticompetitive practices, including mergers of rival firms that substantially reduced competition.

Concerns about corporate concentration were reheated by the Great Depression. The board game Monopoly — invented in 1904 as antitrust propaganda — was repackaged for a mass audience in the 1930s, and became a bestseller.[10] President Franklin Roosevelt, thundering that Americans "must have equal opportunity in the marketplace," expanded the Justice Department's antitrust staff from eighteen people to nearly five hundred.

After World War II, antitrust enforcement also was championed as an antidote to both fascism and communism. In a much quoted 1947 speech, Representative Estes Kefauver, a Tennessee Democrat, warned corporate concentration would fuel populist demands for more and more government — until capitalism and freedom were lost. Kefauver delivered his warning in language that would seem strikingly contemporary in almost every decade since the 1940s.

> The control of American business is steadily being transferred from local communities to a few large cities in which central managers decide the policies and the fate of the far-flung enterprises they control. Millions of people depend helplessly on their judgment. Through monopolistic mergers the people are losing the power to direct their own economic welfare. When they lost [sic] the power to direct their economic welfare they also lose the means to direct their political future.[11]

The Truman administration, concluding German monopolies had played a key role in bringing Hitler to power, broke up some of the largest German conglomerates. The most important, I.G. Farben, was divided into nine pieces, including BASF and Bayer. But West Germany developed a different approach to constraining corporate power than the United States. The government, influenced by the "Ordoliberal" school of economic thought — which held that government needs to regulate markets to ensure optimal results — embraced the practice of preserving smaller companies through the creation of state-sanctioned cartels. It also sought to counterbalance corporate power through state support for strong labor unions.

The United States required Japan to create an antitrust law, too, but it had even less effect.

Throughout this period, American policy makers showed little interest in the views of economists. When in 1920 the government had the novel idea of calling an economist to testify in an antitrust case against U.S. Steel, the Supreme Court mocked the man's "philosophical deductions" as an inferior grade of evidence.[12] In a 1963 decision blocking the merger of two Philadelphia banks, the court offered a more polite explanation for its aversion, explaining judges lacked the competence to assess economic evidence. This was the jurisprudential version of "It's not you, it's me."

Meanwhile, the government continued to treat size itself as un-American. A dominant company might provide the best service at the lowest price, but economic efficiency was not the goal of public policy. In 1962, the Supreme Court ruled unanimously that the Brown Shoe Company could not buy the G. R. Kinney Company because the deal would let the combined company sell shoes at lower prices, and that would place its smaller competitors at a disadvantage. "We cannot fail to recognize Congress' desire to promote competition through the protection of viable, small, locally-owned business," wrote Chief Justice Earl Warren. "Congress appreciated that occasional higher costs and prices might result from the maintenance of fragmented industries and markets. It resolved these competing considerations in favor of decentralization."[13]

The rise of economics transformed the role of antitrust law in American life. During the second half of the twentieth century, economists gradually persuaded the federal judiciary — and, to a lesser extent, the Justice Department — to set aside the original goals of antitrust law and to substitute the single objective of providing goods and services to consumers at the lowest possible prices.

As in other areas of public policy, economists began to gain influence in the early 1960s by arguing that economic principles could be used to rationalize the administration of antitrust law. This argument found a receptive audience because there was a growing concern among policy makers that the government was not applying a clear standard in its enforcement decisions. Supreme Court Justice Potter Stewart, dissenting from a 1966 decision to prevent the merger of two midsized Los Angeles grocery chains, carped that the "sole consistency" in the federal government's lawsuits against proposed mergers was that "the Government always wins."[14]

Seeking to address such complaints, the Johnson administration installed Donald Turner to run the antitrust division at the Justice Department. Turner, like all his predecessors, was a lawyer. Unlike any of his predecessors, he also was a trained economist. Before enrolling at Yale Law, he had completed a doctorate at Harvard. In a 1959 book that caught the attention of Johnson's aides, Turner argued the government should establish a uniform antitrust standard to discipline its interventions in the marketplace. Turner spent three years at the Justice Department battling his own staff of lawyers to create the department's first antitrust guidelines, which enshrined economic analysis as the proper method for judging the legality of corporate conduct. The immediate consequences were limited. In Turner's view, economic theory justified wide-ranging restrictions on corporate conduct. The department started hiring economists, and it began to explain its decisions in the language of economics, but the conclusions, for the most part, were unchanged: the government continued to block a wide range of mergers.

The role of economists was captured in a 1972 report:

> There is another kind of professional at the Division: economists. They are second-class citizens. They have little or no say in the type of cases brought, the legal theories used, or the relief sought. In general, they neither conduct long-range studies nor work closely with the policy-planning staff. Mostly they aid attorneys in the preparation of statistical data for trial, and they occasionally testify. They are technicians — "statisticians," as nearly all the lawyers call them — and act like it. One broke off an interview with us because, he explained as he hurried off to confer with an attorney, "my master called."[15]

But Turner's guidelines created a clear path for changes in the academic understanding of corporate concentration to become changes in the enforcement of antitrust law. And during the course of the 1970s, trust-the-market economists would seize the opportunity.

Anti-antitrust

George Stigler, the economist most responsible for overturning the postwar view of corporate concentration, was conservative by nature, once described by his longtime assistant as the last man on the University of

Chicago campus who persisted in wearing a fedora when he walked outside.[16]

Some of the great minds of his generation were drawn to economics as a tool kit for improving the human condition. For Stigler, the austere beauty of economics was its confirmation that such efforts were futile: the work of economists was to "pronounce the harsh verdict of economic logic" on schemes for social improvement.[17] He believed markets delivered the best outcomes, and that politicians, philanthropists, and other kinds of meddlers only made things worse.

This faith found its most pristine expression in Stigler's "survival principle" — his assertion that profitable business practices were also, generally speaking, optimal. Companies survived by adapting to market conditions.[18] The analogy with evolution was explicit: The megacorporation, like the duck-billed platypus, might offend aesthetic sensibilities, but its existence was its justification. The government should stop trying to fix what wasn't broken.

Stigler was born in a small city outside Seattle in 1911, the year the government diced up Standard Oil. His father, a German immigrant, was a brewer put out of business by Prohibition, then a modestly successful real estate investor who moved the family through sixteen homes by the time George turned sixteen. Stigler graduated from the University of Washington in 1931, which was not a good year for finding a job, so he headed east, enrolling in business school at Northwestern. There he discovered economics, then completed a doctorate at the University of Chicago in 1938.[19]

Stigler met Friedman at Chicago, but the two men became friends during World War II, working together at Columbia. In 1945, both landed at the University of Minnesota, where they wrote their pamphlet on rent control. The following year, they interviewed for the same job at the University of Chicago. Friedman was hired, and Stigler went into exile at Brown and then at Columbia. While they never published another joint piece, the men remained close. They corresponded constantly, each serving as an editor and sounding board, although Stigler sometimes chided his pen pal for stinting on gossip. In later years, they also shared a car and a gym locker.

George Shultz, who knew both men well, said Friedman hammered at the logic of an argument while Stigler would "get everybody laughing at you."[20] The liberal economist Robert Solow, who happened to take a sabbatical at Stanford alongside the two men, found Friedman to be an unredeemed ideologue — "Not a saving spark of humor in him," Solow wrote to a friend — but he found he couldn't help but like Stigler. "He's got a genuine humorous streak," Solow allowed, "and he doesn't take his laissez faire dead seriously every minute of the day."[21] When a reporter observed to Stigler that he had written one hundred papers while another economist, Harry Johnson, had written some five hundred, Stigler replied, "Mine are all different."[22] Stigler, who was tall, observed of the liberal economist John Kenneth Galbraith, also tall, and of Friedman, who was not, "All great economists are tall. There are two exceptions: John Kenneth Galbraith and Milton Friedman."

Stigler liked to argue that the work of academic economists had little impact on public policy and that Friedman was wasting his time by trying to teach economics to the general public. "Milton wants to change the world; I only want to understand it," Stigler said.[23] But those who knew Stigler marked the scope of his ambition. "He thought he was going to change the world," said his longtime colleague Ronald Coase.[24] The real difference was that Stigler focused on winning over his fellow economists. He continued to produce significant work, and to battle academic opponents with gusto, long after Friedman had turned to a life as a public intellectual. "A scholar is an evangelist seeking to convert his learned brethren to the new enlightenment he is preaching," Stigler wrote in his memoirs. "A new idea proposed in a halfhearted and casual way is almost certainly consigned to oblivion."[25]

Fittingly, Stigler launched his defense of markets in 1948 with a scathing attack on a fellow economist delivered in a series of lectures at the London School of Economics. The target, Edward Chamberlin, a Harvard professor, had made a name for himself in the 1930s by arguing that monopoly power was a pervasive feature of the economic landscape. Relatively few industries were dominated by large companies, but Chamberlin argued that even in apparently competitive industries, companies often had some degree of monopoly power — some ability to squeeze their suppliers, their competitors, or their customers. Consider the example of a beach boardwalk with an ice cream parlor, a frozen yogurt stand, and a pushcart selling shaved ice. None of those businesses monopolizes the trade in frozen treats; if the ice cream store doubled its prices, people could eat more yogurt and ices. But Chamberlin said the ice cream store could charge somewhat higher prices, because some customers preferred ice cream, and it could cultivate those preferences, for example through advertising or a loyalty card offering the tenth cone free of charge. This had the effect of segmenting the market, creating what Chamberlin called "monopolistic competition." And he warned that the economy was moving toward more monopoly and less competition.

Chamberlin's view of markets as highly fragmented and imperfectly competitive offended Stigler's aesthetic sensibilities and his political inclinations. His primary objection, however, was that Chamberlin's view of markets was useless. Chamberlin's model might superficially resemble the real world, in which adjacent gas stations often charged different prices, but Stigler said that was literature. Stigler, like Friedman, wanted to judge economic models by the accuracy of their predictions. Economics, in his view, required the distillation of general theories, not carefully rendered portraits of idiosyncratic realities. Markets were not perfectly competitive, but Stigler said economists — and policy makers — would achieve better results by pretending most markets were.[26]

At this early stage in his career, Stigler still regarded the relatively rare instances of actual monopolies as dangers to the economy. In a 1952 essay in *Fortune* magazine, he called for the government to break such companies into pieces.[27] But Stigler's motive was distinct from the traditional rationale for antitrust enforcement. Instead of the corruption of government and society, Stigler feared the corruption of the marketplace. He warned that the rise of big business was being used to justify the rise of labor unions and of regulation. "More and more," he wrote, "big businesses are being asked to act in the 'social interest' and more and more, government is interfering in their routine operations."

Stigler and Friedman reunited in 1957 by arranging simultaneous sabbaticals at Stanford, where they split the $300 cost of a 1950 Buick so they could drive to a tennis court to hit volleys on most weekdays.[28]

The next year, Stigler joined the University of Chicago faculty on a princely salary of about $25,000,* plus a large research endowment.[29] The money was provided by Charles Walgreen, a local drugstore magnate who had made a fortune selling prescription whiskey during Prohibition. Walgreen had withdrawn his niece from the University of Chicago in 1935, accusing the institution of teaching communism and free love. The Illinois legislature duly investigated but found little evidence of either at the university. Two years later, Walgreen mended fences by donating $550,000 to "foster greater appreciation of American life and values among University of Chicago students."[30]

Potted in the Chicago hothouse, Stigler's critique of antitrust enforcement blossomed. In his rebuttal of Chamberlin, he had not provided an explanation for price disparities. How could drugstores in the same city sell the same toothpaste at difference prices? Would not rational consumers seek out the best price? In 1961, he offered his answer in a paper he described as his "most important contribution to economic theory."[31] It opened, "One should hardly have to tell academicians that information is a valuable resource: knowledge is power. And yet it occupies a slum dwelling in the town of economics. Mostly it is ignored."[32] Stigler said people made imperfect decisions because information had a price, just like anything else. People were unlikely to invest the necessary time and energy to thoroughly research the cost of toothpaste.

One implication, Stigler argued in a 1964 paper, was that the govern-

---

* The median salary for a male college professor in 1957 was $7971, according to the 1960 census. Professors of economics were not yet regarded as particularly valuable. The Columbia economist John M. Clark complained in the mid-1950s that he made about the same as a skilled carpenter.

ment should worry less about corporate concentration. The paper was a direct rebuttal of a sacred text, Adam Smith's *The Wealth of Nations*, in which Smith famously observed, "People of the same trade seldom meet together, even for merriment and diversion, but the conversation ends in a conspiracy against the public, or in some contrivance to raise prices." By the 1960s, this observation had been formalized by academics who shared the prevailing distrust of markets, and adopted as policy by the federal government, which assumed that the odds of collusion increased as competition declined. In its 1963 decision blocking the merger of two Philadelphia banks, the Supreme Court established a presumption that any increase in market share above 30 percent was anticompetitive. Enter Stigler. It was true, he wrote, that companies in relatively concentrated industries could increase profits by simulating a monopoly — by reaching an agreement to restrict output and raise prices. But it was even more profitable for any given company to participate in the creation of such a cartel and then cheat its partners by quietly offering discounts. Building on his earlier work, Stigler argued that preventing such cheating was costly — because it required the acquisition of information about others' sales — so companies instead would avoid cheating by refusing to participate in cartels. The fear that cartels would destroy markets was backward; the market destroyed cartels. "Competition," Stigler wrote, "is a tough weed, not a delicate flower."[33]

One of the earliest and most important translators of trust-the-market theory into legal theory was Aaron Director, Friedman's brother-in-law, who became one of the first economists to teach at an American law school when he joined the University of Chicago faculty in 1946.

Director, born in 1901 in Eastern Europe, arrived in Portland, Oregon, with his family in 1913, speaking barely a word of English. Eight years later, he won a scholarship to Yale.[34] He went east with a friend named Mark Rothkowitz, who later dropped out, dropped the last four letters of his last name, and became a famous artist. Director graduated and, after dabbling in socialism for a few years, enrolled as a graduate student in economics at the University of Chicago in 1927. He never completed a doctorate, but he left Chicago in 1934 with a convert's fervent faith in the cause of free-market economics. During World War II, Director persuaded the University of Chicago Press to publish an American edition of Hayek's book *The Road to Serfdom*. In 1946, Hayek returned the favor by persuading his friends at the Volker Fund — the Kansas City nonprofit devoted to libertarian causes — to cover the cost of a position for Director at Chicago's law school.[35]

Thus began an unusual academic career. During his two decades on the Chicago faculty, Director published almost nothing, yet the mark he left on a generation of Chicago-trained lawyers made him one of the most important legal thinkers of his time. For years, Director taught the law school's antitrust course with Edward H. Levi, later U.S. attorney general under President Ford. Levi would give four lectures, and then Director would give one. "Aaron Director would tell us that everything that Levi had told us the preceding four days was nonsense," recalled one student. For some it was a religious experience. "We became Janissaries," said Robert Bork, an early student who was one of the most influential popularizers of Director's ideas.* Ronald Coase, a colleague who later won the Nobel Prize in economics for his work integrating economics into legal theory, also counted himself a disciple of Director, saying, "I regarded my role as that of Saint Paul to Aaron Director's Christ. He got the doctrine going and what I had to do was bring it to the gentiles."[36]

Director's trademark was his skepticism that corporate behavior was anticompetitive. He began by assuming markets were efficient, then tried to deduce explanations for corporate behavior. In the standard view, big companies roamed the marketplace preying on weaker rivals, suppliers, and consumers; in Director's view, companies were just trying to survive. Even behemoths like AT&T or Alcoa, which faced no obvious competition, were restrained by the fear that inefficiency would attract new rivals.

Consider the classic case of Standard Oil. The government accused the company of trying to create a monopoly by selling kerosene at a loss in

---

* The Janissaries were Christians captured by the Ottomans, converted to Islam, and sent into battle.

cities where it faced competition, to drive smaller rivals out of business. Director argued this was illogical. A company seeking a monopoly could simply reach an agreement to acquire its rivals, by offering to split the extra profits that could be earned by operating as a monopoly. He argued that it only made sense for Standard Oil to sell kerosene at lower prices if the company actually enjoyed an advantage in the form of lower costs. In 1953, Director urged John McGee, a graduate student in economics at Chicago, to examine the government's evidence against Standard Oil. McGee was skeptical — "Like everyone else, I knew full well what Standard had really done," he wrote — but after digging into the archives, he concluded Director was right. In 1958, McGee published a celebrated article asserting Standard Oil was innocent. The company sold kerosene at lower prices, McGee said, because it produced kerosene at lower cost. The article appeared in the first issue of the *Journal of Law and Economics*, created by Director to disseminate his ideas.[37] The University of Chicago, endowed with Rockefeller money, had found a way to return the favor.

Director and his acolytes spent the 1960s taking potshots at lawyers who largely ignored them. They were particularly outraged when the Supreme Court in 1967 rode to the rescue of the Utah Pie Company. As Americans began to purchase refrigerators with freezer compartments in the 1950s, one consequence was a rapid rise in the sale of bake-at-home frozen pies. Utah Pie, facing an equally rapid decline in sales of its fresh pies, built a factory in 1958 to make frozen pies in flavors including apple, cherry, boysenberry, peach, pumpkin, and mince.

The company sold its pies to local supermarkets for $4.15 per dozen, below the prices charged by national brands like Carnation and Pet Milk. The national brands responded by cutting prices, and capitalism ensued: over the next four years, the number of pies sold in the Salt Lake City area more than quadrupled, while the average price fell by one third. Utah Pie's sales and profits rose each year, but its profit margins shrank. In 1961, the company sued its rivals for predatory pricing, alleging the larger firms had slashed pie prices in an effort to drive Utah Pie out of business.

The case presented a clear choice: competition was reducing the price of pie, but it was also threatening to reduce the number of competitors. The Supreme Court, in siding with Utah Pie, once again emphasized that the law was written to protect companies.[38] Indeed, in 1936, Congress had reinforced the Sherman Act by passing the Robinson-Patman Act, which specifically prohibited large companies from charging lower prices to undermine local rivals.

Robert Bork described the verdict as a violation of the laws of economics. The defendants, he wrote, "were convicted not of injuring competition but, quite simply, of competing."[39] Stigler, testifying on Capitol Hill, urged Congress to rewrite the laws of the United States. "I hope the subcommittee will reflect upon the fact," he said, "that if all the prominent economists in favor of the Robinson-Patman Act were put in a Volkswagen, there would still be room for a portly chauffeur."[40]

Director retired from the University of Chicago in 1965, moving to California, where he kept an office at Stanford. In the fall of 1968, Richard Posner, a new professor at Stanford Law School, saw the familiar name on an office door and seized the chance to introduce himself. Posner, as a clerk for Supreme Court Justice William Brennan, had drafted the majority opinion in the 1963 *Philadelphia National Bank* case, in which the court memorably declared it lacked the ability to assess economic analysis. But he had developed an interest in the subject while working as a lawyer at the Federal Trade Commission and then in the solicitor general's office, which represents the government before the Supreme Court. Arriving at Stanford as a twenty-nine-year-old wunderkind, he eagerly sought an education from Director. The old economist and the young lawyer spent long hours in Posner's office, Director perched on a filing cabinet, lecturing, while Posner sat behind a typewriter, taking notes.[41]

That winter, Stigler arrived at Stanford as a visiting scholar, and two became three. Stigler and Director made almost weekly appearances at Posner's seminar on antitrust law. Posner later developed a reputation as a fearsome instructor who delighted in grilling students, but that first year the students escaped unscathed. The professors mostly talked to one another.[42]

By spring, Director and Stigler had arranged a marriage between Posner and the University of Chicago. One year after moving across the country from Washington to California, Posner moved most of the way back.

Just a few years later, in 1973, Posner published *Economic Analysis of Law*, a book that one reviewer memorably compared to *Huckleberry Finn*, describing Posner's book as a serial adventure in which the hero, economics, encountered a new problem in each chapter and prevailed in clever fashion.[43] Posner insisted the common law had economics in its bones. Centuries of Anglo-American jurisprudence, much of it predating economics as a mode of thought, almost all of it formulated without any input from economists, had accumulated in a body of precedents that, in Posner's view, was roughly what you would have gotten if you had dressed economists in black robes. Posner expressed this view somewhat cautiously in the book's first edition, but in the second edition, in 1977, he wrote that economic efficiency is "perhaps the most common" meaning of justice.

> We shall see, among many other examples, that when people describe as "unjust" convicting a person without a trial, taking property without just compensation, or failing to require a negligent automobile driver to answer in damages to the victim of his negligence, they can be interpreted as meaning nothing more pretentious than that the conduct in question wastes resources.[44]

Furthermore, Posner argued that where the law was inefficient, it should be changed.

In a second book, *Antitrust Law*, published in 1976, Posner applied that lesson, arguing that economic efficiency should be the sole standard of antitrust policy, which in his view, echoing Director, meant the government mostly should let corporations do as they pleased.

Law professors who wrote and thought about grand theories of the law mostly reacted with outrage to Posner's attempt to chisel "Justice" off the face of the nation's courthouses and carve "Efficiency" in its place. Many subscribed to some version of the theory that justice meant fairness, which the philosopher John Rawls had elegantly updated in his 1971 book, *A Theory of Justice*. Rawls introduced a twist on the Golden Rule, suggesting the test of fairness was to ask what a person would think of a policy if she did not know her own circumstances, a perspective Rawls described as a "veil of ignorance." He also rejected the idea that one person's gains could justify another person's losses. Justice, he wrote, "does not allow that the sacrifices imposed on a few are outweighed by the larger sum of advantages enjoyed by many."

The outrage served Posner's purpose. Looking back on what followed, Douglas Baird, a longtime professor at Chicago's law school, said Posner and his allies would write papers asserting that the standard view of some legal issue was 100 percent wrong — for example, that courts adjudicating bankruptcy cases needed to account for the concept that a dollar today is worth more than a dollar tomorrow — and the rebuttals would insist the conventional approach was only 80 percent wrong. "Posner never got things exactly right," Baird said, "but he always turned everything upside down, and people talked about law differently."[45]

"Posner, Baxter, Bork"

Support for antitrust enforcement began to wane in the 1970s. In part, the law was a victim of its own failure. It was increasingly hard to ignore that blocking mergers had not prevented the rise of large corporations. Take the case of beer. In the midcentury, there were several hundred small and midsized companies that brewed beer in the United States, and the government sought to prevent those companies from merging. In 1959, it blocked Anheuser-Busch from buying a Florida brewery. That same year, the Supreme Court forced two midsized Milwaukee breweries, Pabst and Blatz, to reverse a merger. "If not stopped," the court wrote, "this decline in the number of separate competitors and this rise in the share of the market controlled by the larger beer manufacturers are bound to lead to greater and greater concentration of the beer industry into fewer and fewer hands."[46] But the government's efforts were unavailing. The industry consolidated without mergers. Over the next two decades, Anheuser-Busch built a national network of breweries without making a single acquisition. Meanwhile, Blatz and many other smaller brewers went out of business. In 1960, the top four firms had brewed 27 percent of the beer; by 1980, the top four firms brewed 67 percent.[47] And economists pointed out the price of beer had steadily declined.

Consumer advocates like Ralph Nader increasingly took the existence of large corporations for granted; rather than trying to break companies apart, they sought to strengthen federal regulation.

The rise of the Japanese economy also began to shift public debate. Japan treated industrial conglomerates as a source of strength, not a threat to society and the state. American corporations argued consolidation was necessary to compete, and some politicians began to sound sympathetic notes. "The world is changing, and we must change with it," John Connally, an economic adviser to President Nixon, said in a 1973 speech advocating relaxation of antitrust rules. The speech was remarkable for its pessimism about America's economic prospects. Connally asked the audience, "Can we continue to exist in the face of competition from other nations that are not faced with the same constraints that we are?"

"Why not?" someone shouted.

"Why not?" repeated Connally. "I'll tell you why not. Because you just can't do it."[48]

But antitrust law was not rewritten by Congress; it was vitiated by the judiciary.

Four pro-business conservatives joined the Supreme Court in Nixon's first term. One of them, Lewis Powell, was the prominent corporate lawyer who wrote the alarmist 1971 memo for the Chamber of Commerce warning that capitalism was under attack.

In 1976, Powell persuaded his colleagues to hear a case brought by a San Francisco retailer, Continental T.V. The court initially voted against taking the case, but Powell persisted, seeing an opportunity to undermine antitrust law. A television manufacturer, GTE Sylvania, had decided to limit competition among its dealers by dividing the nation into sales territories. When Continental sought permission to sell televisions in Sacramento, GTE Sylvania refused, and Continental filed an antitrust suit. A lower court ruled against GTE Sylvania, noting the Supreme Court had ruled against the bicycle maker Schwinn in a similar case just a decade earlier. The court then held that manufacturers could not impose restrictions on retailers. If Continental T.V. wanted to sell TVs at a lower price than other retailers in Sacramento, that was surely the definition of competition.

In the late 1950s, Director had encouraged one of his students, Lester G. Telser, to consider why manufacturers sought to impose such restrictions on retailers. Telser's theory, published in Director's journal in 1960, was that manufacturers wanted retailers to spend money on advertising and repair facilities, so they sought to prevent discounters from free riding "at the expense of those who have convinced consumers to buy the product."[49] Posner described Telser's reasoning in his 1976 book, adding that the *Schwinn* ruling was "an intellectual failure of imposing dimensions."[50]

Powell agreed with Posner. He told his law clerk it was "important to demonstrate the economic illiteracy of *Schwinn*."[51] In his majority opinion, Powell went beyond the legitimation of sales territories. He wrote that it had been wrong to make Continental prove that it was acting legally. The burden was on the government, he said.[52] The significance was not just in the particulars, but in the willingness to consider particulars. Powell was adopting Stigler's view that markets should get the benefit of the doubt. The case opened a new era in which the court set aside sweeping bans on anticompetitive practices in favor of case-by-case evaluations. The judges were ready to hear from the economists.

To reinforce this trend, Henry Manne, another of Director's disciples, created a "boot camp" for law professors in 1971 at the University of Rochester. Manne paid professors from prominent law schools $1000 to attend classes on economics. The money came from companies including Exxon, General Electric, and IBM. Manne explained, "General counsels of many of these companies were aware by then of how helpful 'Chicago Economics' was in antitrust cases."[53] He insisted on annual donations rather than long-term gifts because he said he wanted to be held accountable to the marketplace. Manne soon moved the program to the University of Miami, a more attractive destination, and, in 1976, he added a two-week course for federal judges.

Manne recruited some of the nation's most prominent economists as lecturers. Armen Alchian, who co-authored the 1972 paper describing corporations as the apotheosis of capitalism, usually taught the first three days. A visiting journalist narrated one of the professor's performances: "Racing up and down in front of the fascinated judges, Alchian cried, 'I'm trying to change your view of the world, to show you that what you thought was bad really may not be.'"[54] Milton Friedman addressed the judges after receiving the Nobel Prize in 1976. Paul Samuelson also was a frequent speaker. After one of Samuelson's speeches, some of the judges asked Manne to explain the difference between the liberal and conservative economists "since Paul Samuelson seemed to be teaching the same economics as Armen Alchian."[55]

By 1980, almost 20 percent of federal judges had attended Manne's program; by 1990, the figure was 40 percent. An examination of judges' rulings before and after attendance found a significant shift toward trust-the-market rulings.[56] A. Andrew Hauk, a U.S. District Court judge in California, told the *Washington Post* the lessons he learned in Miami induced him to issue a ruling that ended a federal system of quotas for contracts with minority vendors. "More and more," Hauk said, "life is best explained not by religion, not by law, but by economics."[57]

To justify the insertion of economics into antitrust law, Robert Bork rewrote history. After graduating from Chicago, Bork had become a professor at Yale Law School — where his students dubbed his class on antitrust law "protrust" — and then served as Nixon's solicitor general.[58] After returning to Yale, he wrote *The Antitrust Paradox*, a popular 1978 book that asserted the original purpose of the Sherman Antitrust Act was to maximize consumer welfare. Bork insisted that nothing in the

Congressional Record suggested legislators had wanted to impose higher prices on consumers to preserve small business or to prevent the concentration of political power.[59]

This was shoddy scholarship. To take just one example, consider the remarks of Representative William Mason of Illinois, a leading proponent of the Sherman Act, just before the final vote in 1890: "Some say that the trusts have made products cheaper, have reduced prices; but if the price of oil, for instance, were reduced to 1 cent a barrel it would not right the wrong done to the people of this country by the trusts which have destroyed legitimate competition and driven honest men from legitimate business enterprises."[60]

But policy makers across the political spectrum wanted to believe Bork was right. Americans, who had first defined themselves as a nation of farmers, and then as a nation of factory workers, increasingly defined themselves as a nation of consumers. And as consumption replaced work as the quintessence of American identity, one consequence was a growing intolerance for public policies that aimed to preserve the welfare of producers.

Judges wanted to believe Bork, too. They were struggling to deal with increasingly complex antitrust cases, and the "Chicago School" approach of Director and his disciples offered a clear and consistent standard, even for more liberal jurists. Stephen Breyer, the future Supreme Court justice, wrote in 1983, while serving on the First Circuit Court of Appeals, that economics "offers objectivity — terra firma — upon which we can base decisions."[61]

The year after Bork's book was published, the Carter administration intervened in an antitrust lawsuit against a hearing aid maker, Sonotone, to assert that the legality of corporate conduct should be based on consumer welfare. The court agreed unanimously. "Congress designed the Sherman Act as a 'consumer welfare prescription,'" wrote Chief Justice Warren Burger. The footnote read, "R. Bork, *The Antitrust Paradox*."[62]

Some legislators tried to prevent the shift, but they did not have the votes. Senator Philip A. Hart of Michigan introduced a bill in 1976 instructing the courts to ignore economics; it went no further.[63] When regulators did bring cases, the courts increasingly ruled in favor of the accused corporations. The Federal Trade Commission, which shared with the Justice Department the power to bring antitrust cases, won 88 percent of its lawsuits during the first half of the 1970s. Between 1976 and 1981, the agency won 43 percent of the time.[64]

In the early twentieth century, the great Chicago stockyard, 320 acres of cows in the middle of a crowded city, was home to five of the nation's largest meatpacking firms, and they were blissfully unaware of Stigler's dictum that collusion was all but impossible. They underpaid suppliers and over-charged customers until, in 1920, the government brought them to heel under the Sherman Act. For the next six decades, through the 1970s, the five largest cattle-killing companies provided no more than 25 percent of the nation's beef.

That chapter ended on June 24, 1981, when William French Smith, Ronald Reagan's longtime personal attorney and the nation's new attorney general, walked up to a Washington podium and declared the federal government planned to get out of the way of corporate concentration. "We must recognize that bigness in business does not necessarily mean badness, and that success should not automatically be suspect," said Smith, whose expensive suits and carefully combed white hair spoke of his former life as a corporate lawyer.

In 1982, the Justice Department issued new antitrust guidelines that embraced the tolerant Chicago view of corporate concentration.[65] The meatpackers accepted the invitation. The agribusiness giant Cargill agreed to buy three midwestern meatpacking plants from an agricultural cooperative. When a rival meatpacker, Kenneth Monfort, sued to block the deal, the Justice Department rushed to Cargill's defense, describing the merger as good for the economy. The Supreme Court agreed and, for good measure, limited challenges of future mergers. Monfort promptly sold out to another agribusiness giant, ConAgra.[66] By 1992, the market share of the top meatpacking firms was up to 71 percent from 25 percent.

There is little evidence that consolidation in the meatpacking indus-try has come at the expense of either the ranchers who raise the cattle or the people who eat the beef. There was only one clear group of losers: the people who worked in the packing plants. Hourly wages declined by 35 percent, adjusted for inflation, as companies shuttered unionized plants and used the threat of closure to squeeze concessions from workers.[67]

Other industries consolidated, too. Robert Tollison, the chief economist at the Federal Trade Commission, told a trade publication early in the Reagan years that he intended to conduct "a natural experiment in the economy." In theory, he said, mergers were good, so "you would allow a lot of mergers to go through. You would allow a lot of people to put their money on the line, and we'll see what happens."[68] If things did not go well, Tollison continued, the government could "try to unscramble the eggs." Between 1981 and 1984, the FTC signed off on the nine largest mergers in American history to that time.

Reagan also overhauled the federal judiciary. In the fall of 1981, Reagan nominated both Posner and Bork to serve as federal judges, part of a generational changing of the guard. By the time Reagan left office in January 1989, he had appointed almost half of the federal judiciary.[69]

The Reagan administration did complete a long-running effort to break up AT&T. William F. Baxter, a Stanford law professor named by Reagan to lead the Justice Department's antitrust division, was committed to the Chicago view of antitrust law, but he saw breaking up AT&T as primarily an act of deregulation. He wanted to separate the regulated local telephone monopolies from AT&T's long-distance business, opening the way for competition in the long-distance market.[70]

The staff of the antitrust division was halved under Reagan. Dozens of attorneys were dispatched to serve in the "war on drugs"; the remainder were enrolled in mandatory economics classes. The membership of the American Bar Association's antitrust division peaked at 13,500 lawyers in 1982–1983. As enforcement lapsed, so did corporate demand for their services.[71]

James C. Miller III, the first economist to head the FTC (before he succeeded David Stockman as White House budget director), dropped investigations of collusion among the big three automakers, the big oil companies, and the big breakfast cereal companies. Instead he sued Minneapolis and New Orleans to end regulation of taxicabs.[72]

Miller said the shift in priorities was a response to the rise of a service economy. But he didn't go after doctors, whom Friedman regarded as the outstanding example of a harmful cartel, nor real estate agents, who all charged the same commission rates. Instead the FTC sued a group of Washington, D.C., lawyers who represented indigent defendants, and who had staged a two-week strike in 1983 seeking $35 an hour from the city, which since 1970 had paid $30 for each hour the lawyers spent in court. The FTC took the case to the Supreme Court, which barred the lawyers from organizing in pursuit of a raise.[73]

Some corporate cases were still too egregious to ignore, but these were handled gently. Howard Putnam, the chief executive of Braniff Airways, gave the government a recording of a phone conversation with Robert Crandall, the president of American Airlines. Crandall called Putnam to complain about price competition between the two airlines on flights from Dallas. "I think it's dumb as hell, for Christ's sake, all right, to sit here and pound the shit out of each other and neither one of us making a fucking dime," Crandall began.

> Putnam: Do you have a suggestion for me?
> Crandall: Yes, I have a suggestion for you. Raise your goddamn fares 20 percent. I'll raise mine the next morning.
> Putnam: Robert, we —
> Crandall: You'll make more money and I will too.
> Putnam: — we can't talk about pricing.
> Crandall: Oh, bullshit, Howard, we can talk about any goddamn thing we want to talk about.[74]

The government, unable to avoid the conclusion that such talk was illegal, had to do something, so it threw a book at Crandall, requiring him to keep records for two years of his conversations with other airline executives.

Two weeks after Reagan left office, the government approved the largest merger of the 1980s, allowing the private equity firm Kohlberg Kravis Roberts to merge RJR Nabisco and Beatrice in a $25 billion deal that created one of the world's largest food companies. In a show of concern about the integrity of the marketplace, regulators required the combined company to divest three product lines: Chinese food, ketchup, and peanuts.

"Antitrust Is Dead, Isn't It?"

On a chilly evening in November 1992, an executive of the agribusiness giant Archer Daniels Midland (ADM) sat in a car outside his home, the fanciest house in Moweaqua, Illinois, alongside an agent from the Federal Bureau of Investigation. The executive, Mark Whitacre, had requested the meeting. He had a confession to make. He told the astonished agent that ADM and its ostensible competitors were fixing the price of lysine, an amino acid added to animal feed to increase muscle growth. Whitacre met regularly with his counterparts at the other four major lysine producers to divvy up the international market. ADM had a saying, Whitacre told the agent: "The competitors are our friends, and the customers are our enemies."[75]

Whitacre agreed to tape price-fixing conversations with the other companies, based in Japan and South Korea, creating an astonishingly detailed record of the brazen conspiracy. The government broke up the cartel in 1995. Three ADM executives were convicted of violating the Sherman Antitrust Act and sent to federal prison.

During its investigation, the FBI discovered ADM also was part of a cartel fixing the price of citric acid, a staple ingredient in laundry detergents and soft drinks. That led investigators to another cartel, created by some of the world's largest drugmakers, to fix the prices of a wide range of food additives. The members called it "Vitamins, Inc."

Stigler's 1964 paper had popularized the view that collusion was rare and unstable. The Reagan administration had embraced that premise in its permissive 1982 merger guidelines. Now the real world was intruding.

"I was shocked," said Robert Litan, an economist and lawyer who oversaw civil nonmerger antitrust litigation in the early years of the Clinton administration. "I was shocked that there was as much cartel activity as what was going on. I thought it was almost impossible. I thought that people don't do this anymore. Most economists — and I brought this prejudice with me — we didn't think it existed. And it was massive. It was all over the place."[76]

In 1994, while the ADM investigation was under way, partners from a Philadelphia law firm traveled to Washington to meet with Litan and his boss, Anne K. Bingaman. They brought research by a pair of financial economists identifying a suspicious pattern in the fees charged by stock brokers on the NASDAQ exchange. The exchange allowed pricing in increments of an eighth of a dollar, but on larger transactions, the brokers were rounding their fees up to the nearest quarter, systematically over-charging their customers. The consistency of this pattern — and the absence of price competition — suggested collusion on a grand scale. Litan asked how many brokers dealt, for example, in Microsoft stock. The answer was as many as thirty-six. "I said, 'You can't maintain a price-fixing conspiracy among thirty-six people!'" Litan recalled. The subsequent investigation, including recordings of internal conversations, made clear that the brokers could.[77]

The evidence that collusion was common led the Justice Department to announce a clever new program that offered leniency to the first company in a cartel that tattled. Jim Loftis, a leading antitrust lawyer, recalled that he prevailed upon a client to rush to Dallas for a meeting with prosecutors. As he left the building with the company's executives, they ran into a lawyer he knew escorting executives from another company in the same cartel. "Rats, Jim," said the other lawyer. "You beat us to it."[78]

What the government did not do, however, was reconsider its tolerance for corporate consolidation. One reason was that the deregulation of finance, transportation, and telecommunications was sharply increasing competition in a number of highly visible industries.[79]

Economists also argued that globalization was diminishing the importance of national antitrust enforcement: if an American company sought to raise prices, foreign companies could enter the American marketplace. And even as the United States was pulling apart politically in the late 1990s, it was united in accepting the priority of economic efficiency. When Posner published a new edition of *Antitrust Law* in 2001, he dropped the previous edition's subtitle, *An Economic Perspective*, because, he wrote, "other perspectives have largely fallen away."[80]

The decline of antitrust enforcement freed corporate America to follow the advice of Jack Welch, General Electric's chief executive, who preached that you should be first or second in your market, or you should get out. The merger wave of the Clinton years was surpassed by the merger wave of the Bush years, which was surpassed by the merger wave of the Obama years. The country was left with four major airlines, three big car rental companies, two big beer makers — the list of industries emulating the meatpacking business kept growing.

The courts, meanwhile, continued to roll back antitrust law. Each precedent had to be popped separately, as on a sheet of bubble wrap, but the pattern was the same. Judges replaced the presumption of guilt with a presumption of innocence, and then defined the offense narrowly, rendering illegal conduct unlikely. In 1993, for example, the Supreme Court decided a predatory pricing case for the first time since *Utah Pie*. Liggett, the smallest of the major tobacco companies, struggling to survive, had introduced a line of discount cigarettes in 1980 called "black and whites," which it sold in unadorned packages for 30 percent less than its name brands. It was a success, prompting a rival firm, Brown and Williamson, to introduce its own generic cigarettes, which it sold to distributors at a lower price than Liggett's. Sales of both products boomed, but profit margins narrowed and Liggett sued, just like Utah Pie had a quarter century before.

Brown and Williamson, represented by Robert Bork, argued Liggett was attempting to suppress competition, and that ruling in its favor would teach companies that "it is dangerous to compete."[81]

In ruling against Liggett, the court agreed, ruling that Brown and Williamson's tactics might have hurt Liggett, but there was no evidence consumers had been harmed, or that consumers would be harmed by less competition.[82]

In 1998, the Clinton administration sued Microsoft for using the dominant market position of its Windows operating system to encourage adoption of its web browser, Internet Explorer. That kind of coercion, known as tying, was on the shrinking list of practices still officially regarded as anticompetitive, so a federal judge ruled against Microsoft and ordered the company broken in two. Democrats and Republicans took turns bemoaning the ruling. "Only the United States would consider breaking up a company that has done this much economically to advance our national interest," said Senator Robert Torricelli, Democrat of New Jersey. "I'd rather break up the Justice Department," said Representative Dick Armey, Republican of Texas.[83] But the politicians needn't have worried: an appeals court set aside the order.*

George Stigler had died in 1991. But in the wake of the Microsoft case, Milton Friedman picked up the torch. He said he had concluded the government should eliminate antitrust enforcement. "I was a great supporter of antitrust laws," he wrote. "I thought enforcing them was one of the few desirable things that the government could do to promote competition." That had changed. "Over time, I have gradually come to the conclusion that antitrust laws do far more harm than good and that we would be better off if we didn't have them at all."[84]

Public policy has moved in that direction over the last two decades. Regulators brought a dwindling number of enforcement actions; courts kept chipping away at the law.

In March 2017, the University of Chicago's Stigler Center held a conference on antitrust. The featured lunchtime speaker was Richard Posner, the last of the revolutionary vanguard. Posner, a few months from retirement, puckishly professed to be puzzled by the gathering.

"Antitrust is dead," he said. "Isn't it?"[85]

---

* The prosecution of Microsoft still had consequences. The company was prevented from using similar tactics to ward off the rise of new rivals like Google. It's easy to imagine an alternative universe in which Microsoft's Bing became the world's top search engine.

*   *   *

We live in a new era of giant corporations, and there is little evidence consumers are suffering.

But the narrow focus of public policy on consumer welfare is causing other kinds of economic damage. The concentration of the corporate sector is tilting the balance of power between employers and workers, allowing companies to demand more and to pay less.[86] Workers have less leverage because they have fewer alternatives. In 2007, Steve Jobs, Apple's chief executive, learned Google was recruiting one of his engineers, so he sent an email to his Google counterpart, Eric Schmidt. "I would be extremely pleased if Google would stop doing this," Jobs wrote. Schmidt forwarded the email to his recruiting department. "I believe we have a policy of no recruiting from Apple and this is a direct inbound request," Schmidt wrote. "Can you get this stopped and let me know why this is happening? I will need to send a response back to Apple quickly so please let me know as soon as you can." The response was that the Google recruiter had been fired. Jobs replied with a smiley face.[87]

Corporate concentration also is taking a toll on democracy. At the Stigler Center's 2017 conference, the University of Chicago economist Luigi Zingales told the audience that he'd been studying a rewrite of the nation's bankruptcy laws in 2004. Previous overhauls had required carefully negotiated compromises between advocates of lenders and borrowers. This time, he said, the financial industry simply won. The sheer size of the largest banks, he said, was translating into political power. Senator Sherman's fears were coming true.

The focus on consumer welfare may even be taking a toll on economic efficiency, by reducing innovation. Large companies, particularly in the tech sector, increasingly respond to the emergence of young rivals by imitating the Greek god Kronos, who swallowed his newborn children. Amazon swallowed Zappos. Facebook swallowed WhatsApp. Between 2010 and 2018, Google announced an average of eighteen acquisitions per year. YouTube, which might have disrupted the Google-Facebook online advertising duopoly, now lives inside Google.

The United States also has steadily increased protections for patent holders, reversing its mid-twentieth-century effort to make dominant firms share innovations. The government forced AT&T to make room for IBM; it forced IBM to make room for Microsoft; it forced Microsoft to make room for Google. But the federal government has not forced Google to make room.

State ownership of dominant industrial firms was widespread in Western Europe through most of the twentieth century—big was government policy. "By comparison with Europe, we have the most perfect of perfect competition," Friedman wrote Stigler during a visit in the 1950s.[88] But in the twenty-first century, Europe increasingly has dissented from America's tolerance for corporate concentration.

The divergence is particularly stark in the technology sector. In 2017, European regulators slapped Google with a record fine of 2.4 billion euros for manipulating search results to display its own price-comparison website more prominently than rival services. The next year, 2018, Europe fined Google 4.3 billion euros for requiring phone manufacturers to install Google software, including its search engine, on phones using its Android operating system.

In a 2017 article on the *Yale Law Journal*'s website, a Yale Law student named Lina Khan argued for the revitalization of antitrust enforcement in the United States, spotlighting Amazon as a prime example of a company that was amassing market power it could abuse to the detriment of its suppliers, its workers, and its customers.[89] The piece struck a chord among a younger generation of scholars increasingly concerned about the erosion of antitrust enforcement. "We've been living through this natural experiment for the last forty years and we should be able to agree that something is wrong," Khan told me. "I'm under no illusions that the previous eras of antitrust enforcement were ideal, but I think we should be having a conversation about what we should do differently."[90]

The tech companies, and their advocates, say they are under attack for the sin of creating superior products, just like Standard Oil. They say that Google dominates online searches because it has the best search engine, and it is free, so there is little point in using the second-best search engine. And the tech companies like to emphasize their fragility. Tech companies rise and fall. The truth, they say, is that their dominance will last until someone comes up with a better idea. In the words of Google cofounder Larry Page, "Competition is one click away."

But the popular image of a perpetual internet revolution is a remembrance of things past. The revolution is over; the major technology companies are middle-aged and fat. And the best argument for stricter antitrust enforcement is not that history has reached some kind of end point, but that no one can know what tomorrow might bring.

Chapter Six

Freedom from Regulation

The market has some good points. It keeps people on their toes,
it rewards the best. But at the same time it creates injustices,
establishes monopolies, favors cheaters. So don't be blind to the
market. You mustn't imagine that it alone will solve all problems.
The market isn't above the nation and above the state. It's up to
the state, the nation, to keep an eye on the market.
— *Charles de Gaulle, letter to Alain Peyrefitte (1962)*[1]

I n the mid-1930s, the fledging airline industry hired Colonel Edgar
Gorrell, a decorated army aviator, to convince Congress that competition was threatening the industry's survival. Gorrell painted a bleak picture for Congress: new airlines kept entering the business, as all it took was a pilot and a plane; existing airlines kept adding routes; companies competed vigorously to offer the best prices and service. It was "economic anarchy," said Gorrell — chaotic, cutthroat, and unprofitable. He pleaded for the government to tuck the airlines under its wing.[2]

Congress obliged Gorrell in 1938, creating the Civil Aeronautics Authority, which issued licenses to sixteen airlines and then refused to let anyone else enter the business for the next four decades.[3] "For the first time," the authority declared in its initial report in 1940, "American air carriers and the public are safeguarded against uneconomic, destructive competition."[4]

Even as the United States sought to increase competition across much of the economy in the mid-twentieth century through invigorated

161

enforcement of antitrust laws, it was widely accepted that some industries were "natural monopolies" — sectors in which healthy competition was impossible. Electric companies, for example, could compete only by running multiple lines into the same homes, and all but one of those lines would be wasted. The result would be either too much competition, which was bad for the companies, or too little competition, which was bad for consumers. So governments intervened.*

In some cases, particularly in other developed nations, the government became the major provider of utilities and transportation. By the 1950s, even tiny Luxembourg had a national airline. In the United States, popular aversion to state ownership meant most utilities and transportation companies remained in private hands. Instead, the government established vast supervisory bureaucracies to limit competition and protect customers. Economic regulation started with the republic — the eleventh law passed by Congress, in 1789, just before the act creating the Treasury Department, restricted the coasting trade to ships built and owned by Americans — but it was the creation of a railroad regulator a century later, in 1887, that opened a new era of intensive regulation.[5] By the mid-twentieth century, truckers needed to obtain federal licenses that specified both the routes they could travel and the products they could carry. One company complained that its trucks, licensed to carry tomatoes from California to a pizza factory in Tennessee, could not get permission to carry pizzas back to California.[6] Federal law prevented banks

---

* Economists in the midcentury defined natural monopolies as industries in which multifirm production was more expensive than single-firm production. The government didn't observe the finer points of this theory in selecting which industries to place under regulation. President Theodore Roosevelt offered to place Standard Oil under federal regulation before seeking its dismemberment. Trucking was placed under regulation at the urging of railroads, which feared the rise of a rival. Airlines were included at their own behest, but Congress was receptive in part because airlines were seen as railroads by other means. Prices were set at the same level as first-class passenger fares on the same railroad routes, and early airline maps looked like railroad maps: thick, straight lines along the ground, rather than the arcs used on modern maps.

from operating in more than one state, and fifteen states did not allow banks to have more than one location. In the case of *62 Cases, More or Less, Each Containing Six Jars of Jam v. U.S.,* the Supreme Court defined the meaning of "jam."[7]

Few industries were watched as closely as aviation. A board of five bureaucrats met daily in a Washington office building to decide the routes airlines could fly and the prices they could charge. One board member told of receiving a frantic call from a Virginia farmer demanding action on an application to fly sheep to England. The issue was urgent: the sheep were in heat.[8]

The era of regulation often is remembered as a golden age for passengers: fine dining on china; plenty of room for knees; an abundance of nonstop, half-empty flights.[9] Less remembered is that passengers paid for the empty seats as well as their own. Flying remained exotic and expensive; the average American today flies roughly eight times more often than in 1960.[10]

In December 1964, George Stigler stood before the American Economic Association as its president and complained that his peers were not paying enough attention to the government's role in the economy. How was it possible, he asked, that economists still knew so little about the costs and benefits of regulation?

Stigler had sparked controversy in 1962 by publishing an article in Aaron Director's journal concluding that the regulation of electric companies did not reduce prices. The study, written with Claire Friedland, was based on a comparison of prices in regulated and unregulated markets in the early twentieth century, before regulation became universal. Stigler speculated that market forces had restrained unregulated utilities from raising prices, perhaps because utilities feared industrial customers would build their own power plants or move to an area served by a different utility.[11]

In the spring of 1964, Stigler had published a second article on regulation, attacking a holier cow. "It is doubtful whether any other type of public regulation of economic activity has been so widely admired as the regulation of the securities market by the Securities and Exchange Commission," he wrote, before concluding that the SEC also was impotent.[12]

The first paper, in particular, was deeply flawed. Prices were quite different in regulated and unregulated states, and the paper's conclusion — that this could be explained by factors other than regulation — rested on some odd assumptions. Price changes during the first three years after regulation began, for example, were not attributed to regulation. Two decades later, a Chicago graduate student asked Friedland for the data and found a basic math error.[13] Stigler's most important disciple, Sam Peltzman — whom Stigler feted as "the best purchase the Walgreen foundation has yet made" — later described Stigler's work on regulation as propaganda.[14] "He was very much the kind of a person who would say, 'I'll state this result as strongly as I possibly can, even if it's not completely justified by the evidence,'" Peltzman said of Stigler. "He was using a bully pulpit that he had acquired from his stature in the profession."[15]

The propaganda worked. Researchers began to examine regulation across a wide range of industries. In 1967, the Brookings Institution launched a major initiative on the economic impact of regulation, backed by $1.8 million from the Ford Foundation and directed by a panel that included Stigler. Between 1967 and 1975, Brookings published twenty-two books, sixty-five journal articles, and thirty-eight dissertations attacking regulation.[16]

The economist Roger Noll, who wrote one of those studies, testified before Congress in the early 1970s that he knew of no reputable economic study published in the previous decade that had landed on the side of regulation. He joked that the work was easy: "You never have to run the risk of being dead wrong saying regulation has been foolish."[17]

But this wave of research contradicted an important aspect of Stigler's original theory. He had asserted that regulation was ineffective, but the accumulating evidence showed regulation could be very powerful. Peltzman, for example, estimated in his 1965 dissertation that regulation had reduced the creation of new banks by almost half since the Great Depression. Another economist pointed to the example of New York

City taxi medallions: it was quite obvious the government determined the value by deciding how many medallions to issue.[18]

The new critique was that regulation was doing more harm than good.

In 1971, Stigler pushed his way back to the front of the parade that he had started, publishing a second landmark paper in which he made the conventional wisdom his own. "As a rule," Stigler wrote, "regulation is acquired by the industry and is designed and operated primarily for its benefit." The innovation in Stigler's paper was his conclusion that government should stop trying. He wrote that regulators inevitably became the servants of the industries. Criticizing regulators for protecting businesses, he wrote, "seems to me exactly as appropriate as a criticism of the Great Atlantic and Pacific Tea Company for selling groceries."[19]

The historian William J. Novak has described Stigler's call for government to surrender as a remarkable departure from the American political tradition. James Madison, in *Federalist No. 10*, described special interests as the great threat to American democracy, and curbing those interests as the great work of government. Generations of legislators had accepted that duty: they wrote rules, and when those rules came up short, they tried to write better rules.[20]

Stigler was proposing to trust the markets instead.

U.S. Air

The first time Michael Levine flew to California, in the early 1960s, he was surprised by the diversity of the passengers he saw at the San Francisco airport. Back east, where Levine was a student at Yale Law School, people dressed up to fly. It was an event. But in San Francisco, a lot of people in casual clothing were waiting for flights on Pacific Southwest Airlines (PSA).

Levine's confusion was understandable: he was looking at America's first discount airline. PSA offered regular flights between northern and southern California at prices well below the major airlines like United and Western. By the end of the decade, PSA had made the Los Angeles–San Francisco corridor the most heavily traveled airline route in the world.

Levine was an aviation geek: as a kid, he would slip under the fences at New York's Idlewild Airport to get a better view; as a law student, he spent leisure hours reading *Aviation Week*. And one of his favorite law school professors, Robert Bork, had sparked his interest in the application of economics to legal questions. As a result, Levine had spent a fair amount of time thinking about airline regulation, and he was inclined to accept that it was valuable. "This was the era of Bob McNamara," he recalled. "I believed that really smart people could figure out the way that the world was supposed to work."[21] But Levine also was familiar with the argument made by some economists that airline regulation had created a state-sponsored cartel, driving up prices and restricting service. These economists said the government was protecting companies when it should be protecting competition.[22] As Levine learned more about PSA, he decided the discount airline was living proof that those economists were right.

PSA, founded in 1949, was not subject to federal regulation because none of its flights left California. It launched service with a weekly round-trip between San Diego and Oakland — up on Friday, back on Sunday. Tickets in the early days were sold from a renovated latrine at the San Diego airport; luggage was weighed on a bathroom scale; and fares were less than half the going rates on United and Western, the federally licensed carriers between San Diego and the Bay Area. By the mid-1960s, the airline had added other north-south routes, and business was booming in what had just become the nation's most populous state.[23]

Levine had gone to California to visit his girlfriend; mixing business and pleasure, he persuaded the dean of Yale's law school to pay for another trip to California. In 1965, Levine published his conclusions in the *Yale Law Journal*: "Regulation of United States air transportation is predicated upon erroneous economic assumptions and results in unnecessarily high fares."[24] The solution was straightforward: open the skies to competition.

The chairman of the Civil Aeronautics Board (CAB) offered Levine a job, explaining that he wanted to hear different perspectives. But Levine quit after less than a year. The only person at the board who seemed interested in his perspective was his office-mate, who began to keep a picture of Milton Friedman on his desk.[25]

Unable to compete by cutting prices, airlines instead increased spending. In the spring of 1971, American Airlines removed forty seats from coach class on some of its 747s and installed a wall-to-wall lounge with a bar, armchairs, and cocktail tables for passengers on transcontinental flights. United responded by installing two lounges on its 747s. So American put a piano on each plane. Ads showed smiling people having a midair cocktail party, with the tagline "Our passengers get the best of everything." That prompted United to announce its 747s would feature live performances by musicians. A *Wall Street Journal* reporter sent to interview United management found guitarists waiting to audition.[26]

This kind of competition also shrank profit margins, and the airlines complained that they were not making enough money. So Robert D. Timm, appointed by President Nixon to head the CAB, decided to raise fares. He explained that he was focused on maintaining a "healthy industry."[27] Economists warned, correctly, that raising prices would not improve profits because airlines would spend the additional money. By the mid-1970s, the CAB was talking about the need for another round of increases in airfares. At a 1974 conference on the economics of regulation, one despairing economist suggested that everyone should bring the same papers to another conference a decade later, and present them again, because there was little prospect anything would change.[28]

That was not a good prediction. Some on the political left had come to agree with Stigler that Americans might benefit from less regulation. The most influential figure was Ralph Nader, the slender zealot who had emerged as the icon of the nascent consumer movement. Nader had made his reputation campaigning for more health and safety regulation; by the early 1970s, he was also campaigning for less economic regulation, which in his view protected companies at the expense of consumers. He described economic regulators as servants of the capitalist elite, echoing Marx, except that Nader's proletariat was comprised of consumers rather than workers.

The capitalist elite, meanwhile, was starting to have its own doubts about economic regulation. The perpetual struggles of the airline industry were not unique, although the exact pressures varied by industry. Railroads, for example, had been struggling for years to adapt to the rise of trucking, a process made more difficult by federal constraints on raising prices or cutting costs. When the Southern Railway in 1961 introduced a giant hopper car that could carry one third more grain than existing freight cars, it asked for permission to offer discounts on grain shipments. Regulators refused. A few years later, in 1968, the government approved the merger of two failing northeastern railroads, perhaps on the theory that the drowning should seek comfort in each other's arms. The resulting company, Penn Central, lasted two years, then filed the largest bankruptcy in U.S. history.

Ted Kennedy could read the political winds. In the second decade of his Senate career, the Massachusetts Democrat had commandeered a subcommittee of the Judiciary Committee to conduct wide-ranging investigations. One staffer described it as a "fire brigade for liberal causes," forever arriving with lights and sirens at the scene of the latest outrage against the common man.[29] In 1974, Kennedy lured Stephen Breyer, then a rising star at Harvard Law School, to spend a sabbatical year in Washington. Breyer proposed a pair of possible investigations. The first, on post-Watergate reforms, Breyer described as "more likely to receive publicity." The second, airline deregulation, he described as "a non-glamorous, detailed, intricate, 'good government' job."[30] Kennedy chose deregulation. When the committee held a hearing in Boston a few months later, a local woman asked the senator, "Why are you having hearings on airlines? I've never been able to fly." Kennedy replied, "That's why I'm having the hearings."[31]

Soon after starting his new job, Breyer read in the *Washington Post* that President Ford's transportation secretary, Claude Brinegar, was meeting with airline executives to discuss the plight of Pan American Airways, which was struggling with rising fuel prices. Breyer crashed the meeting, arriving in time to hear Brinegar urging uniform increases in airfares to restore Pan Am to profitability. Breyer recalled the moment with wonder: "It was a cartel, a simple cartel being organized by the government."[32] He persuaded Kennedy to hold a hearing in November 1974 that featured Freddie Laker, a bubbly British entrepreneur who had been fruitlessly seeking permission for a low-cost transatlantic airline.[33] Laker blasted Brinegar's plan as "PanAmania," which he gleefully defined as the madness of propping up a dying airline at public expense.

The main hearings, held in February 1975, were more subdued. Breyer eschewed testimony about what he called "frozen dog" stories — anecdotes about horrific customer service — in favor of detailed explorations of the economics of airline regulation. The second day of hearings highlighted the contrast between intrastate airfares in California and Texas and the cost of interstate travel over similar distances.* Kennedy, prompted by Breyer, pressed executives and regulators to explain why a ticket from San Francisco to Los Angeles on PSA cost $18.75 in 1974, while a ticket between Boston and Washington on American Airlines cost $41.67.[34] The flights covered roughly the same distance; the carriers used the same airplane. Explanation after explanation was examined and discarded until one remained: regulation.

Breyer summarized the hearings in a 328-page report, which he said thirty years later was "probably the best thing I ever wrote."[35] The hearings and the report resonated with politicians and voters who were increasingly skeptical about the value of the government's efforts to police the marketplace. President Ford spoke of 100,000 regulators employed by the government in a "bureaucrat's dream of heaven," and said they were preventing small businesses from becoming big businesses. "Rules and regulations

---

* Texas got its own discount carrier in 1971, when Southwest Airlines began flying between Dallas, Houston, and San Antonio. The new airline borrowed Pacific Southwest's business plan and half its name. It also borrowed equipment, including pilot manuals.

churned out by federal agencies were having a damaging effect on almost every aspect of American life," Ford wrote in his memoirs. "Red tape surrounded and almost smothered us; we as a nation were about to suffocate."[36]

The government had placed the airlines under federal regulation in the 1930s because there was a consensus that competition was destructive. Now there was an emerging consensus that competition was the very thing the economy needed. The pendulum was swinging.

Jimmy Carter's political career was built on persuading voters he was a different kind of Democrat. One of the most striking shifts was his emphasis on Americans as consumers, rather than Americans as workers. During the 1976 presidential campaign, he accepted an invitation from Ralph Nader to address a gathering of consumer advocates, telling them, "Consumers will now have a voice in the Oval Office." He skipped the Labor Day rally on Detroit's Cadillac Square, where Democratic candidates traditionally opened their general election campaigns.[37]

Carter and Nader both wanted the government to stop sheltering industries from competition. The two men, a matched pair of intense introverts, also formed a personal bond. Carter invited Nader to spend a night at his house in Plains, Georgia, where they dined on black-eyed peas. Later, when Carter and his staff played a softball game against the press corps, Nader served as umpire, calling balls and strikes in a suit and tie. After Carter won the election, he appointed a number of Nader's lieutenants to top positions at regulatory agencies.

Carter particularly disliked trucking regulation, which had cost him money as a farmer. Australia had deregulated trucking in 1954, reducing prices in a nation with important similarities to the sprawling American market. "Newcomers entered the industry as fast as new trucks could be purchased or released from other commitments," one observer reported.[38] In 1969, Britain had started to deregulate trucking with similar success. But Carter's aides feared the politics of deregulating an industry with thousands of companies scattered across the country. They advised Carter to start with airlines instead.[39] The glamorous industry commanded public attention, but it was not particularly large, and Kennedy's hearings had primed the public. Simon Lazarus, who had known Breyer since law school and received a personal copy of his report, and Mary Schuman, a former staffer on the Senate Commerce Committee, told Carter that airline deregulation could serve as a springboard for battles over trucks and telecommunications.

In February 1977 — on the same day the first supply-side tax cut bill was introduced in the House — the White House launched a push to deregulate commercial aviation. Seizing on a new government report that estimated airline regulation was inflating ticket costs by $1.8 billion a year, Carter sent a message to Congress urging legislation to set the industry free.[40] "Regulation, once designed to serve the interests of the public, now stifles competition," the President wrote. To hasten the process, he picked a new head for the aeronautics board. Carter might have picked Breyer or a like-minded lawyer, but Schuman pressed for something new: the economist Alfred E. Kahn, who as a Cornell University professor and chairman of the New York State Public Services Commission was both a leading scholar of regulation and a leading practitioner of reform. When Carter's chief of staff insisted on a list of three potential nominees, Schuman responded: "Alfred Kahn, Alfred E. Kahn and Fred Kahn."[41]

Kahn was an effervescent eccentric. He walked around his New York office in socks, lectured members of his staff during daily swims, and held long hearings where he entertained himself, and sometimes the audience, by reeducating the expert witnesses.

He maintained a wry distance from the politicians he served. During his time in Washington, he called the President "naive" and the members of OPEC "schnooks." When the White House asked Kahn to please stop predicting an imminent recession, he gathered reporters and told them he would start referring to recessions as "bananas." This drew a protest from the United Fruit Company, a leading banana importer, so Kahn told the press that he had selected a new code word: "kumquat."

A sign in his office read "I Have Tenure at Cornell."[42]

Kahn was born on October 17, 1917, in Paterson, New Jersey — a factory city created by Alexander Hamilton in an early example of state-sponsored industrialization. Kahn's parents were Jewish immigrants from Russia; his father worked in one of the city's many silk mills. Kahn, a brilliant student, graduated from New York University at the age of eighteen and then earned a doctorate from Yale University in 1942. His subject was the "progressive ossification" of the British economy, which he attributed to "an almost unanimous abandonment of price competition."[43] During his graduate years, he also worked for a series of government agencies, laying the groundwork for his long career at the intersection of academia and public policy. He briefly served in the army and then landed at Cornell, where he remained for more than six decades, singing in student productions of light operas as often as he was invited onstage.

As a scholar of regulation, Kahn stood in the mainstream, rejecting the ideas being raised by the Chicago School. He subscribed to the conventional view that large companies were bad for the economy. In a 1940 paper, he warned that industrial giants like General Electric were taking advantage of patent laws to prevent the rise of potential competitors. The "great research laboratories are only incidentally technological centers," he wrote. "From the business standpoint, they are patent factories: They manufacture the raw material of monopoly."[44]

In a 1954 book, *Fair Competition*, he defended the idea that the government should protect small business at the expense of consumers. "One cannot simply equate the 'public interest' in a democracy with the 'consumer interest,'" he wrote. Adam Smith had famously asserted that consumption was the purpose of production. Kahn rejoined that this was "not true, even though Adam Smith said it." People, he wrote, also had interests as producers and as "citizens of an urbanized civilization."[45] It was not good for a factory town to lose its factories.

Kahn's most important book, *The Economics of Regulation* (1970), was a sweeping critique of the practice of regulation — and a defense of the value of effective regulation. The book read a bit like a job application. Regulatory agencies then were run by lawyers, and Kahn argued economists would do a better job. Describing the virtues of economists, and surely with one particular economist in mind, he wrote, "Who can have given more thought than he to the ultimate ethical and political implications of alternative public economic policies?"[46]

In 1974, Kahn got his wish: he was appointed New York's chief utilities regulator. Thomas McCraw argued in his brilliant *Prophets of Regulation* that Kahn's arrival marked the advent of a new era, an "economists' hour." McCraw calculated that in 1974 lawyers occupied more than half the seats on every federal regulatory commission.[47] Economists occupied virtually none. As economists filled more of the seats, the conduct of regulation began to change. Lawyers emphasized the importance of a fair process that produced fair outcomes. Economists like Kahn, by contrast, regarded economic efficiency as the primary goal of regulation.

Kahn's focus as a utilities regulator was on tying prices more closely to costs. He required the phone company to charge ten cents for directory assistance and he allowed electric utilities to vary prices depending on demand: they could charge more for power on hot summer days, and offer discounts to factories operating at night. Costs rose during periods of high demand because utilities needed to use their least efficient generators. In Kahn's view, charging a constant price for power without regard to generating costs encouraged the inefficient use of power, and it also meant that everyone ended up paying higher prices.

Critics of the new system argued that Kahn was allowing utilities to soak customers precisely when people needed electricity the most. The first adopter, the Long Island Lighting Company, was soon charging customers twelve times more for electricity during the hottest hours on the hottest days. New York, moreover, did not emulate some other states by offering reduced rates to lower-income households. Kahn opposed the use of regulation to redistribute wealth. "If prices are set in some fashion other than on the basis of cost," he said, "then it's the political process which will set the prices."[48] He did not feel it necessary to explain that in his judgment economics was superior to politics as a method of decision-making.

Kahn's new agency, the CAB, was, to a remarkable extent, a police force devoted to a single crime: the sale of discounted airline tickets.[49] In 1972, the CAB reported that a "four-day investigation" had uncovered such outrages as an eighty-one-year-old woman traveling on a youth fare. The most hardened scofflaws were charter airlines, which offered prices as low as one third of regulated fares. This was legal so long as charter operators did not sell tickets to individual passengers. They had to sell all the seats on a flight to a single group, which in turn could sell seats only to people who had been members of the group for at least six months — and advertising was prohibited. In the real world, travel agencies openly advertised charter flights. In 1971, the *New York Times* reported in a shocking exposé that a Manhattan travel agency was selling half-price tickets to England to anyone who paid ten dollars to obtain instant membership in the "Caledonian Friendship Society."[50]

To change the focus of regulation, Kahn first moved to change the regulators. Declaring it was "simply incredible" that the office charged with policy analysis was staffed entirely by lawyers, he created a new Office of Economic Analysis led by Darius Gaskins, an economist he hired from the Federal Trade Commission. Kahn's explanation was not calculated to flatter the legal profession: "I wanted to have objective economists watching carefully what we are doing and how it works out, prepared to identify problems, rather than simply to shut our eyes and rely on faith."[51]

Kahn also objected to the CAB's emphasis on due process, which he described as unfair because delays preserved the status quo at the expense of consumers.[52] He said lawyers were "timorous beasties," forever objecting to every change. He did make one exception, however. Concluding he needed a lawyer to fight lawyers, Kahn hired Michael Levine, who had been teaching at USC and puttering around on weekends in his own orange four-seater airplane.[53]

Kahn even objected to the way lawyers talked. He issued a memo in June 1977 demanding that the board's public statements should be written "as though you are talking to or communicating with real people." This was a matter of long-standing principle with Kahn, who told a reporter, "If you can't explain what you are doing to people in simple English, you are probably doing something wrong."[54] Kahn's memo went on for three pages, presumably to make sure he was being clear. "Every time you are tempted to use 'herein' or 'hereinabove' or 'hereinunder' or similarly, 'therein' and its corresponding variants, try 'here' or 'there' or 'above' or 'below' and see if it doesn't make just as much sense."[55] The memo caused a sensation. "Alfred Kahn, I love you," began one note published by the *Boston Globe*. "I don't care if you're fifty-nine and married and head of the Civil Aeronautics Board. Let's run away together."[56] The American Heritage Dictionary invited Kahn to join an advisory panel. Kahn, delighted, remained on the panel for the rest of his life.

The Hour

Deregulation began with air cargo. In the mid-1960s, a Yale undergraduate named Frederick W. Smith wrote a paper for an economics class proposing the creation of an express air delivery service. The business plan was literally illegal: at the time the government licensed three cargo airlines, which were allowed to charge for weight and distance, but not for speed. But Smith found a loophole. In 1973, he launched Federal Express, using a fleet of fourteen delivery planes so small they were not subject to federal regulation. Unfortunately for Smith, he soon found that the planes also were too small to sustain a profitable business. When he applied for a license to operate larger planes, the CAB predictably refused.

Smith pleaded with politicians to intervene, and the Carter administration saw an opportunity. In 1977, it pushed legislation through Congress opening the air cargo market to competition, and allowing companies to set their own prices. Smith bought seven Boeing 727s and began a rapid expansion. In 1985, United Parcel Service, a ground delivery company, launched its own air service, increasing competition. The real price of air shipping fell by an average of 2.52 percent each year during the first fifteen years of deregulation.[57] And price is an inadequate measure of the impact. Companies developed business models regulators had never imagined: "just in time" supply chains that delivered parts to factory floors at the moment of need; the rise of Amazon.com and online retail; the amazing fact that, in 2017, Chinese diners ate more than $100 million in lobsters flown live from Maine.[58]

Kahn did not wait for legislation to start deregulating passenger travel, declaring that he was determined "to remove the dead hand of the C.A.B."[59] Kahn's philosophy was simple: the laws of economics applied to aviation. He pointedly refused to embrace the mystique of air travel. In 1978, Eastern Air Lines introduced its newest and quietest jet in a ceremony at Washington National Airport. Kahn, in attendance, was asked what he thought. "I really don't know one plane from the other," he replied. "To me they are all marginal costs with wings."[60]

As an opening gambit, Kahn's board authorized discount fares. Continental Airlines responded by offering "chickenfeed fares" and reserving 30 percent of its seats for the chickens. Within a year, half of coach-class passengers were flying on discount tickets. When Senator Barry Goldwater, that old lion of less government, wrote Kahn to complain flights were too crowded, Kahn responded, "When you have further doubts about the efficiency of a free market system, please do not hesitate to convey them to me. I also warmly recommend some earlier speeches and writings of one Senator Barry Goldwater."[61]

Next the CAB granted blanket permission for airlines to establish new routes to and from the underused airport in Oakland, California. It did the same for Milwaukee; for Baltimore's airport, which had renamed itself Baltimore/Washington International in 1973 in a bid for business that failed to materialize; and for Midway Airport in Chicago, which at the time offered scheduled service to just a single destination: St. Louis.

United Airlines, the nation's largest air carrier, began to throw its weight behind deregulation, sensing opportunity in a competitive marketplace. This heightened fears among smaller carriers, but Kahn had set aside his earlier view that government should preserve small companies. In announcing the Oakland rules, the CAB said, "We cannot agree to define healthy competition as that state where the fortunes of the competitors fluctuate but no competitor ever goes to the wall."[62] Kahn had embraced consumer welfare as the goal of regulation. "My standard is, of course, what's good for the consumer," he said in a 1981 interview.[63]

William Thomas Beebe, Delta's chief executive, tried to go over Kahn's head, writing to Carter, a fellow Georgian, that deregulation would hurt consumers. "By cramming people into airplanes in large numbers and in great discomfort and by reducing frequencies so that people have to fly when you want them to fly rather than when they want to fly, you can reduce air fares," Beebe wrote. "All of us in the business have known this for a long time." But was that what Carter really wanted? It would be, Beebe said, "to the embarrassment of all and the tragedy of many."[64]

Carter took the risk. As Kahn improvised, the administration pressed Congress to legislate. The President lobbied aggressively and successfully, belying his reputation as a poor advocate for his own priorities.[65] When he signed the final bill on October 24, 1978, he declared, "For the first time in decades, we have deregulated a major industry."

Employees dispatched by the airlines were already camped on the sidewalk outside the CAB's Washington headquarters waiting for the next morning, when the board would begin to issue new route licenses on a first-come-first-served basis. Eastern Air Lines had arrived first, but its team lost its spot to United when an unfortunate employee needed to use the bathroom at a moment no one else was available to hold the company's place.[66]

Over the next five months, the board issued 3189 new route licenses; ticket prices fell and passenger volume climbed. "By every standard of economic measurement," Ted Kennedy enthused, "the results of airline deregulation have been phenomenal."[67]

The Civil Aeronautics Board closed on December 31, 1984. A Marine Corps bugler played "Evening Colors" while a staffer ceremonially removed the agency's seal from the wall of its boardroom. The last chairman, C. Dan McKinnon, banged a gavel he had received years before as a gift from Sam Rayburn, the Texas congressman who sponsored the legislation creating the board in 1938. "Competition is the rule and, because of it, the consumers are better served than ever," McKinnon declared. He added his hope that other regulatory agencies would close their doors.[68]

In the glow of victory, the Carter administration moved on to a thornier prize: trucking.

The industry employed three times as many people as airlines, and it was not struggling financially. In 1977, the eight largest trucking companies were twice as profitable as the average Fortune 500 company.[69] It helped that trucking firms, unlike airlines, got to set their own prices. The industry's milquetoast regulator, the Interstate Commerce Commission (ICC), allowed ten regional bureaus controlled by trucking firms to hold secret hearings and then issue binding prices. This system was also lucrative for the industry's employees, represented by the belligerent Teamsters union, which in 1976 negotiated a 30 percent wage hike — on top of inflation.

But Carter needed more victories. "Like it or not, we have failed to convince the public that the president is a strong economic chief," Treasury Secretary Michael Blumenthal wrote in March 1979 to White House Chief of Staff Hamilton Jordan.[70] And economists once again predicted tantalizing benefits. One study, by economists at the Department of Transportation, reported it was 10 to 25 percent cheaper to ship goods inside New Jersey, which did not regulate trucking prices, than to ship the same goods the same distance across the state line into Pennsylvania.[71] Carter's first transportation secretary, Brock Adams, opposed deregulation and threatened to fire his chief of regulatory policy for publishing that kind of research. Instead, Adams lost his job. When the new secretary, Neil Goldschmidt, arrived in the Oval Office carrying a yellow legal pad with a list of priorities, Carter took it and wrote "trucking" at the top.[72]

Carter's initial choice to head the ICC, A. Daniel O'Neal, also had doubts about deregulation. "There is something cavalier about the attitudes of those who appear willing for others to sustain serious losses so that we can test some economic theories," he had said in 1975.[73] Carter replaced him, too — with Darius Gaskins, the chief economist at Kahn's aviation board, who became the first economist to run the ICC.[74]

The Teamsters argued there was no need for changes, emphasizing the point by offering a bribe to the chairman of the Senate Commerce Committee, Howard W. Cannon of Nevada.* But Congress was in a free-

---

* Cannon and his neighbors in Nevada wanted to buy a parcel of land adjacent to their subdivision, to prevent construction of high-rise apartments. The union's pen-

market frame of mind. "There's no reason why we should be controlling capitalist acts by consenting adults," said Senator Bob Packwood, Republican of Oregon.[75] Trucking deregulation began in 1980; railroad deregulation started later that year.

Said one official, "The notion of deregulation is the new religion in this town."[76]

The deregulation of transportation largely delivered the benefits that economists predicted. The movement of goods became much cheaper: logistics as a share of the U.S. economy fell from 18 percent in 1979 to 7.4 percent in 2009.[77] The price of travel also declined. Average airline ticket prices on domestic flights fell by 45 percent during the quarter century following deregulation. Passenger volume soared, and the safety of flying improved.[78]

It was often a miserable experience, of course. American airlines treated customers so poorly that the Obama administration introduced a "Passenger Bill of Rights" in 2009 to discourage some of the worst abuses. But poor service was the argument for deregulation. The theory was that people would trade less service for lower prices. And they did. "There hasn't been a war in Europe for fifty years because they're all too busy flying on Ryanair," Michael O'Leary, the chief executive of that low-cost airline, boasted in 2011. "I should get the Nobel Peace Prize."[79]

Deregulation also succeeded in transferring money from workers to consumers, a goal Kahn and others acknowledged privately at the time. "I'd love the Teamsters to be worse off," Kahn said in an oral history recorded in 1981 but not made public until years later. "I'd love the automobile workers to be worse off. You may say that's inhumane; I'm putting it rather baldly but I want to eliminate a situation in which certain protected workers in industries insulated from competition can increase their wages much more rapidly than the average without regard to their

---

sion fund, which had acquired the land, offered to sell it to Cannon for $1.4 million, substantially below the market price. Five Teamsters were eventually convicted of attempted bribery; the government did not charge Cannon, but the scandal helped cost him his bid for reelection.

merit or to what a free market would do, and in so doing exploit other workers."[80]

Just so, the earnings of the average U.S. truck driver fell by 20 percent in real terms between 1980 and 2017. The average flight attendant in 2017 made 31 percent less. Executives, meanwhile, saw their compensation soar. The chief executive of American Airlines made $373,779 in 1980. The man who held the same job in 2017 made $11.33 million.

Kahn, who died in 2010, rejoiced in it all. "It's the greatest thing I ever did in my life, other than have children," he said.[81] Michael Levine, who died in 2017, also had no regrets, though he expressed a more nuanced verdict, saying the choice was between imperfect markets and imperfect regulation, and that he still preferred the flaws of the marketplace.[82]

Margaret Thatcher doubted the political wisdom of deregulation, so she made little mention of it during the 1979 campaign that made her Britain's first female prime minister. But her allies were eager to test the waters, especially Keith Joseph, known as the "Mad Monk" for the fervor of his faith in markets.[83]

Joseph was the son of a baronet who ran Bovis, one of the country's largest construction firms. First elected to Parliament as a Conservative in 1956, he began his political career as a conventional voice for business interests, but grew frustrated with the twice-chewed quality of the available ideas. In 1964, the well-dressed Joseph walked into the shabby offices of the Institute of Economic Affairs, a think tank created by a group of young economists who shared an enthusiasm for Friedrich Hayek's work and were trying to craft policy proposals based on his ideas. "We were out to have a little fun," said Ralph Harris, one of the group. "We were lads of thirty — put a firework down and see what happens."[84]

Joseph was not an immediate convert. The Conservative Party spent the early 1970s doubling down on liberal ideas, much like the Nixon and Ford administrations. The party platform declared the "fundamental problem" of public policy was a need for more government spending, and Joseph, named minister of social services, was on the front lines. But after the party lost power in 1974, amidst a sharp economic downturn, Joseph returned to the little think tank, declaring he wanted to launch a "crusade" for private enterprise.[85] Joseph was born again, publicly bemoaning his own earlier views and writing newspaper columns with titles like "Equality: An Argument Against." He said Britain needed more millionaires and more bankruptcies. "If we are to reduce poverty in this country and to raise our standard of living," he said, "we need more inequality than we have now."[86]

In the mid-1970s, Joseph created a new think tank, the Centre for Policy Studies, as a more pragmatic partner for the Institute of Economic Affairs. "My aim was to convert the Tory Party," he said.[87] In the service of that goal, he recruited a fellow Conservative politician, Margaret Thatcher, as vice chairman. Joseph soon sank his own chances to lead the party by publicly questioning whether poor mothers ought to give birth to so many children. Thatcher stepped into the leadership void, retaining Joseph as a key lieutenant and leaning on Harris and the institute for ideas.

In Britain, where the government owned the utility companies and large chunks of the industrial sector, the first step in deregulation was moving companies into the private sector. Joseph, named secretary of state for industry in Thatcher's new government, targeted British Telecom, the unpopular monopoly that often made people wait months for a new phone. In 1981, Parliament authorized a second phone company, Mercury Communications, and required British Telecom to let people buy handsets from other companies. British Telecom's executives, viewing this as the first step on a journey they did not want to take, predicted the changes would result in the electrocution of telephone linemen.[88] Instead, service began to improve.

In 1984, the Thatcher government sold a majority stake in the company, the largest offering to that time in the history of the London Stock Exchange. In the wake of the successful float, the government privatized the British Airport Authority, British Gas, British Rail, British Steel — everything but British Kitchen Sink. "Taken together," wrote one elated supporter, "the privatization programme in Britain probably marked the largest transfer of power and property since the dissolution of the monasteries under Henry VIII."[89] Between 1979 and 1997, the share of British economic output produced by state-owned companies fell from 12 percent to 2 percent.[90]

Thatcher's government made a point of selling shares in the privatized companies to their employees. Like many Conservatives, she saw labor unions as another form of monopoly, and she did not hesitate to use force to break their power — most prominently, in her government's brutal clashes with Britain's coal miners. But she also sought to realign the interests of workers, turning them at a stroke into petty capitalists as well as laborers. Similarly, the government sold much of Britain's public housing to its occupants. Nearly a third of British households lived in public housing in 1980; they were allowed to purchase their own homes at discounts of up to 50 percent off market price, based on years of occupancy.

The Labour Party's platform had long called for public ownership of the means of production, but it surrendered the fight. In 1995, the party's new leader, Tony Blair, won removal of the public ownership clause in the same Westminster hall where the party had adopted it in 1918.

In the early 1980s, American and Canadian airlines flying to Ireland were required to land in tiny Shannon, on the west coast, before flying on to Dublin. The inconvenient stopover was intended to protect Aer Lingus, the Irish flag carrier. Nor was that all of it: KLM, the Netherlands' flag carrier, was paid by the Irish government not to fly to Ireland.

Aer Lingus fares on a per-mile basis were four times higher than average fares in the United States. An Aer Lingus executive, dismissing the idea of deregulation, explained that Americans had an unhealthy obsession with low prices. "The important concept of public utility has been abandoned by these zealots and replaced by shortsighted consumerism," he said.[91]

The zealots were hard to keep away: American charter airlines saw Ireland as a ripe market. In 1984, the Irish government proposed to criminalize the sale of low-cost airline tickets. The penalty for competing with Aer Lingus was to be two years in prison and a fine of 100,000 Irish pounds.[92] The legislation finally exhausted the patience of Irish voters, who wanted to be shortsighted consumers. Chastened by the bill's defeat, the government granted permission to Tony Ryan, a former Aer Lingus executive, to start Ireland's second passenger airline.[93]

Ryan, who had spent years seeking approval from the Irish government, found it much easier to obtain permission from the British government to fly between Dublin and Luton, a little airport north of London. Thatcher's government was itching for the chance to extend deregulation to commercial aviation, but in Europe, unlike the United States, most flights crossed international borders. Britain needed other nations to climb on board.

A ticket on Ryanair's first route cost 95 Irish pounds, less than half the price of 208 Irish pounds on Aer Lingus. Travel between Dublin and London jumped 65 percent in the first year. Tourist visits to Ireland climbed for the first time in two decades. Irish construction workers commuted to London, where jobs were more plentiful; Catholic priests in London spread word of a cheap way home for weddings and funerals.[94]

The champions of open skies, including Kahn, predicted competition would thrive because every route was a discrete market in which airlines of various sizes could compete on even terms.[95] They did not anticipate the ways in which larger airlines would turn size into a competitive advantage, including the rise of hub-and-spoke route systems and frequent-flyer programs. The U.S. government allowed the industry to consolidate: during the Obama administration, the nation's eight largest airlines paired off and became the nation's four largest airlines, carrying more than 80 percent of domestic passengers.[96]

European regulators, by contrast, put limits on consolidation. They refused to let Ryanair buy Aer Lingus in 2007, and then refused again in 2013. As of 2018, the four largest European airlines — a list that includes Ryanair — controlled 45 percent of the market. Average airline ticket prices in the United States, in inflation-adjusted dollars, stopped falling around 2005.[97] For the first time since the dawn of aviation, it is generally cheaper to fly in Europe than in the United States.

The difference is symptomatic. Since the turn of the century, Europe has been more aggressive and successful than the United States in fostering and maintaining competition.

During the 1990s, both the British and American governments sought to require local telephone monopolies to share the use of their lines with rivals. In both countries, the initial experiment failed.

In 2005, the United States decided that phone companies no longer needed to share. The Bush administration said competition would come from the cable industry instead. The result was deregulation without competition. Three quarters of American households have, at best, a choice of two potential providers of high-speed internet service.[98]

In that same year, 2005, the United Kingdom tried again, adopting a new formula for leasing phone lines based on the work of the French economist Jean Tirole. The basic balancing act is to set rates high enough to reward investment by the company that owns the lines, but low enough to encourage competitors to lease the lines. Tirole's answer proved successful, and it has been adopted by a growing number of nations. When Tirole was honored with the Nobel Prize in 2014, a member of the prize committee told reporters, "Politicians would be stupid not to take his policy advice."[99] The United States has not, and so Americans pay more for internet access.[100]

It is easy to forget that markets are human creations, precisely because we have created so many markets. In the premodern world, markets were carefully circumscribed. A marketplace was a physical space: in British towns the boundaries often were marked by "market crosses." A market also was an event with a beginning and an end, often marked by the ringing of bells. Now we live in a marketplace that is always open, and that has no physical boundaries.

The ubiquity of markets, however, has only increased the importance of effective regulation. The experience of recent decades is a reminder that as surely as bad rules can damage markets, and society, so, too, can the absence of rules and enforcement.[101]

Chapter Seven

The Value of Life

We must not consider political economy as a subject for
statesmen. It is everyone's business.

—*Jean-Baptiste Say*, Catechism of Political Economy *(1815)*[1]

The U.S. military, responsible for more than half of federal spending
in every year from 1941 to 1969, was in the habit of deciding what it
needed and then looking at the price tag. The military said it was just trying to keep pace with the Soviet Union. "The Reds do not have their eyes
on the cash register, but on victory," said Ira C. Eaker, a general turned
defense contractor.[2] Politicians were not inclined to argue. Through much
of the 1950s, Congress allowed both the army and the air force to pour
hundreds of millions of dollars into separate efforts to develop anti-
aircraft missiles, despite general agreement that only one version was
needed. In 1958, Congress finally instructed the Pentagon to pick one,
but the army and the air force each refused to yield. Congress couldn't
muster the will to kill a weapons program. Instead, showing less wisdom
than Solomon, legislators cut some funding from both programs.[3]

During the 1960 presidential campaign, John F. Kennedy repeatedly
told voters the United States was losing its arms race with the Soviet
Union despite the government's open-checkbook policy. To overhaul
defense spending, Kennedy turned to Robert McNamara, a forty-four-
year-old whiz kid who had won a measure of fame by reviving the Ford
Motor Company. "You cannot make decisions simply by asking yourself

whether something might be nice to have," the new secretary of defense said. "You have to make a judgment on how much is enough."[4] And McNamara knew what kind of person he needed to make those judgments: he needed an economist.

He hired Charles Hitch, the head of the economics department at the Rand Corporation, a think tank created by the air force after World War II to keep some of the nation's best minds working on military problems. Though academics no longer could be compelled to take orders, they could be induced to work on interesting questions in beachfront offices in Santa Monica, California.

Hitch, one of the early recruits, was a conspicuously brilliant man. Born in Missouri in 1910, he became the first Rhodes Scholar offered a faculty position at Oxford University, then remained in Britain at the start of World War II, working on a team that picked targets for Allied bombers. After joining Rand in 1948, he pioneered the economic analysis of defense spending. A few months before the 1960 election, he published *The Economics of Defense in the Nuclear Age*, explaining how the United States could punch harder for the same price. It began, "Military problems are, in one important aspect, economic problems in the efficient allocation and use of resources."

McNamara, skiing in Aspen over the 1960 winter holidays, invited Hitch to meet at Denver's Brown Palace Hotel. The placid, pudgy, mildly unkempt Hitch and the forceful McNamara, his hair slicked tight against his scalp as if to minimize wind resistance, passed a long evening in conversation. A friend described it as "love at first sight."[5]

Hitch's approach to budgeting scarcely seems like something that was invented. He simply required the various branches of the military to write down their goals, the options for achieving those goals, and the costs and benefits of each option. But Hitch was not replacing some earlier system for making choices — he was introducing the discipline of making choices. He was imposing on the military an early version of what is now known as cost-benefit analysis. And Hitch and his lieutenants had little patience for the military's insistence that its decisions could not be judged by economists. Alain Enthoven, a thirty-year-old aide with a doctorate from MIT, ended an argument with an air force officer by declaring, "General, I have fought just as many nuclear wars as you have."[6]

The results were received with wonder. One can almost see the tears of gratitude rolling down the cheeks of Carl Vinson, the venerable chairman of the House Armed Services Committee, as he addressed McNamara. "I want to say this. I say it from the bottom of my heart," Vinson began. "I have been here dealing with these problems since 1919. I want to state that this is the most comprehensive, most factual statement that it has ever been my privilege to have an opportunity to receive from any of the departments of government. There is more information in here than any committee in Congress has ever received along the line that it is dealing with. It is so full of information all one has to do is just study it."[7]

The federal government in short order scrapped development of the B-70 bomber and accelerated development of the Polaris submarine, adopting Rand's judgment that it was a superior vehicle for the delivery of nuclear warheads. A host of missile systems with cartoonish names — Skybolt, Snark, Jupiter, Regulus, Hound Dog — were set aside in favor of one, the Minuteman.

The Soviets, curious about the Pentagon's new approach to budgeting, printed ten thousand copies of Hitch's book — although they did not pay royalties.[8] Charles Schultze, the economist who took over the White House budget office in 1965, also was impressed.* Weeks after his installation, he proposed that the rest of the government should adopt the new budgeting process. The memo landed on the desk of Joseph Califano, President Johnson's top domestic adviser. Califano was unhappy with the "unsystematic and chaotic and anarchic" state of budgeting in the rest of the executive branch, and he passed the memo on to Johnson with a strong

---

* The budget bureau, now known as the Office of Management and Budget, was created in 1921. Schultze's immediate predecessors were the first leaders of the bureau with any formal background in economics. David E. Bell, appointed in 1961, held a master's degree from Harvard. Kermit Gordon, appointed the following year, taught economics at Williams College. Schultze was the first director of the bureau to hold a doctorate in economics.

endorsement.[9] Two weeks later, the President issued the requested order, "so that through the tools of modern management, the full promise of a finer life can be brought to every American at the lowest possible cost."[10]

The United States had launched its first experiment with cost-benefit analysis in 1902, when Congress created a board of five engineers to review the costs and benefits of river and harbor projects undertaken by the Army Corps of Engineers, the nation's construction company.[11]

During the Great Depression, as government spending on public works projects rose to new heights, Congress tightened the rules, seeking to demonstrate that the money was being well spent. The new rules, passed into law in 1936, instructed the Corps of Engineers to build projects only "if the benefits to whomsoever they may accrue are in excess of the estimated costs."

These early efforts were largely unavailing. The government's ability to quantify benefits was quite limited, and its willingness to curtail public works spending was even more limited. In 1946, Congress authorized a plan to make the Arkansas River navigable all the way from the Mississippi River to Tulsa, Oklahoma — a river road of roughly the same length as a road from Boston to Washington, D.C. The railroads objected that the government, for the same price, could build two rail lines along the banks and run the trains at public expense. Better yet, one rail line already was there. But the governor of Oklahoma, Robert S. Kerr, urged Congress to take a broader view. "Let us not confine this hearing to the minor subject of comparative water-rail freight costs," he said. "Rather let us think about building a greater nation."[12]

That same year, the Corps prepared a particularly creative analysis to justify a proposed dam on Virginia's Rappahannock River. In calculating the acres of farmland that would be saved from seasonal flooding, it included the land on the bottom of the reservoir that would be created by the dam.[13]

Economists in the early twentieth century had cast doubt on the validity of cost-benefit analysis, arguing that it was impossible to compare the subjective preferences of individuals, and therefore it was impossible to aggregate costs and benefits. Consider, for example, a policy that cuts the price of corn. People are likely to spend less on corn, and more on other goods. Corn farmers will make less money while other producers will make more. But who is to say whether the pain experienced by the farmers outweighs the benefits for other producers?

In 1939, the Cambridge University economist Nicholas Kaldor built a bypass around this problem. In a short note in the journal of the Royal Economic Society, Kaldor asserted that any public policy that increased economic output could be structured so that it did not reduce anyone's welfare. Consider again the example of a reduction in the price of corn. The amount of money in the economy has not changed; the policy shifts the distribution of that money. It follows that the government can offset the shift — for example, by taxing other producers and giving the money to the corn farmers. But even if it does so, the price of corn still will be lower, providing a clear benefit. "In all such cases," Kaldor wrote, "it is *possible* to make everybody better off than before, or at any rate to make some people better off without making anybody worse off."[14]

This remains the logical foundation of the cost-benefit analysis of public policy.

It is important to recognize that Kaldor did not care whether everybody *was* left unharmed. It was sufficient, in his view, that everybody *could be* left unharmed. He thought government should cut the price of corn even if it did not attempt to ameliorate the farmers' pain. As the economic philosopher Amartya Sen has noted, the sole purpose of this standard, now known as Kaldor-Hicks, is to justify policies that hurt people; if everyone indeed benefits, the justification isn't relevant. Sometimes it is necessary or desirable for government to hurt people, but Kaldor-Hicks obscures both the fact of the harm and the identity of the victims. As with so much in economics, it ignores the question of distribution. It is a theory to gladden the hearts of winners; it is less clear that losers will be comforted by the possession of theoretical benefits.[15]

Jim Tozzi moved to New Orleans in 1963 after earning a doctorate in economics at the University of Florida. He taught by day and played jazz by night, but he soon concluded he wasn't cut out for either line of work. He decided to join the army — only to find himself shipped to Washington and put back to work as an economist. The army, its budget under attack by McNamara, was desperately seeking its own experts to fortify its defenses.

In 1966, Tozzi was promoted to lead a team of economists overseeing the Corps of Engineers' work on nondefense projects. The Corps regarded economic analysis as a nuisance. One Corps official wrote in the 1950s that he had picked the weakest member of his engineering staff to perform the economic analysis for a dam on the upper Columbia River in the Pacific Northwest because he wanted to keep the laggard "out of the hair of the project engineers."[16] Tozzi's job was to satisfy the Johnson administration's demands for greater rigor. As a lieutenant, he was at the bottom of the Pentagon's hierarchy, but as an economist, he wielded considerable power. He told me that he obtained permission to wear a business suit to the office, instead of a uniform, so those officers would take him more seriously.

A. Allan Schmid, a Michigan State economist who studied water projects, joined Tozzi's staff as a visiting professor in 1968. Before his first day of work at the Pentagon, Schmid's wife had to remind him to remove his "Stop ABM" button, protesting the development of antiballistic missiles.[17] Schmid spent much of the year fruitlessly trying to prevent the construction of a giant model of Chesapeake Bay, designed to study water flows but no longer necessary in the age of computers. But even as he struggled to impose cost-benefit analysis on construction projects, Schmid argued that Tozzi's office should expand its ambitions: he said it should also analyze the regulations that the Corps imposed on the private sector, like rules governing construction in floodplains. "A rule also directs the use of resources," Schmid wrote in a memo, which became a paper, which became the subject of a congressional hearing.[18] The idea, now conventional, was new to Tozzi and his team of economists. "The whole group was dumbfounded," he recalled. Yet the more Tozzi thought about it, the more he liked it. With permission from his superiors — but without clear legal authority — Tozzi began to review proposed regulations. "It's a good thing I'm not a lawyer," he said with a laugh, "because a lawyer never would have done that."[19]

This first expansion of cost-benefit analysis did not long survive the end of Johnson's presidency. After Nixon's election, Representative L. Mendel Rivers, Vinson's successor as chairman of the Armed Services Committee, told the Nixon administration he wanted power returned to the generals. Rivers, who loved a little drama almost as much as he hated economics, declared of cost-benefit analysis, "We have sworn by the eternal gods that it will not run this country any longer."[20] The new defense secretary, Melvin Laird, agreed to restrict economists to an advisory role. Tozzi was relocated from the Pentagon to an old building at a nearby Corps of Engineers facility.

But almost one thousand people, many of them economists, had been hired to meet Johnson's mandate or to defend agencies against it.[21] And most of them, including Tozzi, remained on the payroll. The war in Vietnam — which McNamara had conducted as a counting exercise, numbering enemy deaths as steps toward victory — diminished public trust in government but, somewhat ironically, increased demand for cost-benefit analysis. Numbers provided a reassuring sense of transparency and accountability. Within a few years, Tozzi was working in a more prominent office building.

The Scales

More than fifty thousand Americans died in car crashes each year during the mid-1960s, a spectacular volume of carnage that inspired its own sound track, most famously "Last Kiss," in which the singer heads "out on a date in my daddy's car." The government tried for years to reduce road deaths by emphasizing the personal responsibility of drivers, but the very word "accident" implies the limits of that approach.

In 1965, Ralph Nader's bestselling book, *Unsafe at Any Speed*, reshaped the public debate. Nader argued accident victims were hurt not by the initial crash but by the "second collision" with the interiors of their own vehicles. Accidents were inevitable, but injuries could be prevented — and car companies were hardly trying. The industry had an appalling record of indifference to the lives of its customers.[22]

Nader's attack on the car companies was an attack on the primacy of markets. He was rejecting the idea that unhappy consumers should simply buy other products. In the idealized world of economic models, consumer choice was a sufficient mechanism to force improvements in the safety of automobiles. In a nation with three big automakers, where driving had long passed from luxury to necessity for most people, Nader recognized the need to find another way of forcing companies to make safer products. He recognized the need for regulation.

In 1966, at the urging of the Johnson administration, Congress created the Department of Transportation and ordered the new agency to make driving less dangerous. Rules requiring seat belts, collapsible steering columns, and shatterproof windshields, among other changes, quickly began to save lives. Deaths in automobile accidents peaked in the late 1960s and early 1970s. Although the population of the United States has grown significantly, annual death tolls over the last half century have remained below those gory heights.

Building on the example of auto regulation, the federal government created an alphabet soup of agencies to watch over the American people — eleven health and safety agencies between 1964 and 1977, including the Environmental Protection Agency (EPA) and the Occupational Safety and Health Administration (OSHA). The government embraced responsibility for protecting the health and safety of consumers, and the quality of the environment, even as it began to back away from its role as an economic regulator. In 1970, the federal government employed 18,000 economic regulators and 9,700 health and safety regulators. A decade later, the federal government employed 24,100 economic regulators — and 66,400 health and safety regulators.[23]

Such regulation was not entirely new. The invention of steamboats in the early nineteenth century was followed by the invention of federal steamboat inspectors.[24] But the intensification was dramatic, reflecting a broad consensus that unfettered markets were producing unacceptable results. Coal dust blackened the shirts of Pittsburgh schoolchildren; in

Cleveland, the Cuyahoga River kept catching fire. The rise of mass media, particularly the evening news, which the major networks expanded from fifteen to thirty minutes beginning in 1963, made local problems into national problems. When an oil spill off Santa Barbara reached the California coast in 1969, the oil-coated birds died on television. An increasingly prosperous nation, which had once embraced smokestacks as symbols of prosperity, now saw those smokestacks as threats to its quality of life.

Public support for Nader swelled after General Motors conceded that it had hired private detectives to investigate Nader's personal life, in hopes of discrediting him. The company agreed to pay Nader $425,000, which he used to launch a small army of eager young lawyers known as Nader's Raiders, who pressed for more regulations to keep people from harm.

As the government expanded regulation, corporations sought to wield economics as a shield. Automakers pressed Congress to stipulate that safety rules could not be imposed unless regulators demonstrated that the benefits, measured in dollars and cents, exceeded the cost of compliance. Nader successfully prevented this use of economics to limit regulation, convincing Congress that companies should be required to do what was possible, not what was profitable.[25]

The victory set a pattern. The landmark laws of the late 1960s and the early 1970s mostly did not require agencies to calculate costs and benefits. Some specifically instructed agencies to ignore costs. "One may well ask, 'Too expensive for whom?'" Texas senator Ralph Yarborough, the last in a line of populist Democratic senators from that state, thundered during the debate over the creation of OSHA. "Is it too expensive for the employee who loses his hand or leg or eyesight? Is it too expensive for the widow trying to raise her children on a meager allowance under workmen's compensation and social security? And what about the man — a good hardworking man — tied to a wheelchair or hospital bed for the rest of his life? That is what we are dealing with when we talk about industrial safety. We are talking about people's lives, not the indifference of some cost accountants."[26]

* * *

In the early years of his presidency, Richard Nixon embraced the sweeping expansion of federal regulation, particularly to protect the environment. "The great question of the seventies," he said in his first State of the Union address, in January 1970, "is shall we surrender to our surroundings, or shall we make our peace with nature and begin to make reparations for the damage we have done to our air, to our land, and to our water?"[27]

The massive popularity of the first Earth Day celebrations in April 1970 appeared to answer that question decisively. Images of the Earth as seen from space — as an object, small and fragile — were widely displayed. There was also the experience of life on Earth: "In the summer of 1970, if you looked out at the horizon in Washington, D.C., you were looking at a very dark brown layer of pollution. It smelled. And there is no industry in Washington. It was all automobiles," recalled Christopher DeMuth, then a young aide in the Nixon White House.[28]

On the last day of 1970, Nixon signed the Clean Air Act, which required the government to establish air quality standards without regard to cost. DeMuth helped to draw up plans for a new environmental agency, the EPA.[29] Its first head, William Ruckelshaus, a lawyer plucked from civil rights work, introduced himself to the nation by demanding that Union Carbide sharply reduce emissions from a factory in Marietta, Ohio. The EPA, Ruckelshaus said, had "no obligation to promote agriculture or commerce; only the critical obligation to protect and enhance the environment."

But Nixon soon was having second thoughts. Economic growth began to falter, diverting the attention of voters. As the new rules began to bite, the squeals of the nation's executives were plainly audible in Washington. And some of the dirtiest industries, like automakers and steel mills, were the same industries under greatest pressure from foreign rivals.

The President signaled the rapid evolution of his views in August 1971 in an annual report on the environment that said the government needed to weigh the costs and benefits of regulation. "It is simplistic," the report said, "to seek ecological perfection at the cost of bankrupting the very taxpaying enterprises which must pay for the social advances the nation seeks."

In October 1971, George Shultz, the economist Nixon had installed as a kind of majordomo at the newly created Office of Management and Budget, issued a memo requiring agencies to submit cost-benefit analyses of major regulations to his office.[30] Jim Tozzi, one of the few people in the world with any practical experience in using cost-benefit analysis to assess regulations, was hired for the critical job of evaluating proposed environmental rules.

Congress, for example, had instructed the EPA to make the nation's waterways "fishable and swimmable by 1983," and the agency proposed to get there by requiring the elimination of some pollutants. "They didn't want any discharge," Tozzi told me, "and I said, 'Guys, are you out of your minds?' You didn't need a Ph.D. in economics to understand that we couldn't afford all of this shit."

Environmentalists said Tozzi was focused on what was rather than what could be. The Clean Air Act, for example, required sharp cuts in auto emissions that were impossible using available technologies. Lee Iacocca, then a Ford vice president, warned that enforcing the rules "could prevent continued production of automobiles."[31] Instead, General Motors created a filter called a catalytic converter to neutralize the pollution.*

The Value of Life

One of the first assignments the air force gave the Rand Corporation in the late 1940s was to figure out the best way to blow up the Soviet Union. Rand's experts carefully considered the problem and advised the air force to send wave after wave of cheap, slow bombers into the teeth of the Soviet defenses. They had put a price on the bombs and the airplanes, but not on the pilots.

The endorsement of kamikaze tactics did not amuse the air force,

---

* Believers in markets took for granted that companies would pursue any profitable opportunity for innovation, just as people do not leave ten-dollar bills on the sidewalk. In a brief note in *Scientific American* in 1991, the Harvard economist Michael Porter dismissed this view as "Panglossian" nonsense. He asserted that regulation could spur innovation, highlighting, for example, an EPA program that encouraged companies to install energy-efficient lighting. A review found that nearly 80 percent of those projects produced savings in two years or fewer. The evidence presented by Porter and others gradually overcame the theory.

which is run by pilots, and Rand found itself scrambling to salvage its credibility with its only major client. Some Rand economists argued for the necessity of a radical step: assigning a price to human life. "In many respects lives and dollars are incommensurable," one wrote, "but unfortunately the planners must compare them."[32]

The economists, however, couldn't figure out how to put a price on life. In those early years, Rand instead shifted its analyses to present costs in dollars and costs in lives side by side, allowing policy makers to set the exchange rate. But as the use of cost-benefit analysis expanded, economists gradually devised increasingly clever methods for estimating the prices of things not bought or sold. In time, economists claimed to know the dollar value of a lost hand, an hour spent in traffic, a clear view of the mountains — and the value of human life.

The expansion of cost-benefit analysis began at the National Park Service. The 1936 law requiring the Corps of Engineers to justify the cost of public works projects put pressure on advocates of new dams to quantify the benefits. The most valuable benefit — lives saved from flooding — remained beyond quantification. So advocates sought other ways of leaning on the scales. In 1946, the Interior Department, which oversaw some dam construction, ordered the National Park Service to put a price on fun, by estimating the recreational value of reservoirs created by new dams. This offended Park Service officials, who regarded parks as priceless, but the agency's director grudgingly instructed staff to certify the benefits of recreation equaled the cost of any improvements like boat ramps. Two years later, still under pressure, the Park Service agreed to value recreation at twice the cost of any improvements.

Seeking protection against further escalation, the Park Service also sent letters to ten distinguished economists requesting their views on the subject. Nine sided with the Park Service. "I don't think the overall utility or justification of the park system can be measured at all in statistical terms," one wrote, "and it would be dangerous to try to argue the issue in dollars and cents."[33] The tenth, Harold Hotelling, a professor at the University of North Carolina, proved there's always an economist on the other side of the argument. He said the government could estimate the value of a national park by calculating how much money people were willing to spend to visit the park. This, in turn, could be deduced by calculating the maximum amount anyone had spent to visit, and assuming everyone else would have been willing to spend just as much. For example, if the most expensive trip cost $100, and 10,000 people visited in a given year, the value of the park to the public was $1 million.[34]

The Park Service ignored Hotelling but, in 1956, a pair of California economists applied his idea to a cost-benefit analysis of a proposed dam project on California's Feather River. Their report tickled the interest of Marion Clawson, an economist at a young nonprofit called Resources for the Future. The nonprofit was created with funding from the Ford Foundation after a federal commission concluded the United States might run out of raw materials like minerals and oil. Clawson, one of the first hires, was interested in a different kind of scarcity: he thought the nation needed more parks, and he refined Hotelling's approach to demonstrate, as he put it, that "it is both theoretically possible and practically manageable to put monetary value on outdoor recreation."[35] Clawson proved an effective evangelist. In 1973, the federal government authorized the use of Hotelling's method.

It was opponents of federal regulation who first produced cost-benefit analyses that put a value on human life. In 1971, the Nixon administration quietly created a task force to evaluate automakers' complaints about regulation. One member, Howard P. Gates, a navy researcher who had worked for McNamara, pressed the panel to produce a cost-benefit analysis. That itself was still a new idea, but Gates went further, insisting a meaningful analysis required the panel to estimate the value of human life. "It was a shock to people," said Daniel K. Benjamin, then a junior economist on the Council of Economic Advisers who had been assigned to the task force, and who joined Gates in arguing for the analysis. "It was very clear in our discussions, from the pushback that we got, that we were doing something that was alien to the people who were making policy in the U.S. government."[36]

The idea of assigning a monetary value to human life is very old. The Code of Hammurabi is substantially a list of the sums that must be paid for killing people. Valuation also is inherent in the act of buying a slave.

And as wage labor became more common in the early modern era, the value of a person was equated with the market value of a person's output. "The Value, or Worth of a man," Thomas Hobbes wrote in his 1651 book, *Leviathan*, "is, as of all other things, his Price; that is to say, so much as would be given for the use of his Power."

Perhaps the most important precursor to the valuation of life in cost-benefit analysis was the rise of life insurance, which first became popular in Britain in the eighteenth century. Life insurance initially struck many people as morally objectionable, not least because early policies often were purchased on other people's lives, as a form of gambling. During the Jacobite Rebellion of 1745, agents did a lively business in contracts on Bonnie Prince Charlie. France banned life insurance in 1793; in the United States, life insurance was widely regarded as immoral until the mid-nineteenth century. But the industry gradually succeeded in elevating its product from immoral speculation to moral obligation, and it did so by explicitly equating the value of an insurance policy and the value of a life: a responsible adult was urged to purchase life insurance in an amount calculated to offset the economic consequences of untimely death. "In this age of commercialism, it is fitting and proper that everything, including human life, be reduced to a money equivalent," said a speaker at the first "World Insurance Congress," in San Francisco in 1915. Solomon S. Huebner, one of the first academics to study insurance, was particularly influential in popularizing the idea that life had a dollar value. "The most important new development in economic thought," he said in 1924, "will be the recognition of the economic value of human life."[37]

In assigning a value to accident victims nearly a half century later, Gates borrowed the insurance industry's logic. He calculated the difference between the age of the average victim and average life expectancy, and multiplied that by annual income per capita. The result was a figure of $140,000, or about $885,000 in 2019 dollars.[38] The National Highway Traffic Safety Administration added a few more items to the ledger later that same year, including the price of a funeral and the inconvenience to the victim's employer, which raised the value of life to $200,700. The agency described this as a minimum value. "We are not arguing that it is unwise to spend more than the amounts calculated," it said.[39] But numbers have a habit of shedding their footnotes.

Two years later, in 1974, the federal government rejected a regulation on the basis that the cost exceeded the value of the lives that would be saved. The story began with the death of the actress Jayne Mansfield in 1967 in a grisly accident outside New Orleans. A car carrying Mansfield slid under the tail of a truck that had been obscured by a cloud of pesticide. All three people in the front seat of the car were killed. Amid the public outrage provoked by the death of a celebrity, the Johnson administration proposed to require the installation of a metal bar under the tails of large trucks. Regulators estimated these "Mansfield bars" would save 180 lives per year. But after years of debate, the Ford administration shelved the idea in 1974. Estimating the value of life at $200,000, the administration concluded the bars would need to save four times as many lives to justify the cost.[40]

It should be obvious that life is worth more than life insurance: people who are fully insured usually prefer not to die, and their beneficiaries usually agree. But how much more? Thomas Schelling, an economist who encountered the issue while working as a visiting scholar at Rand in the 1950s, had never stopped chewing on it. Schelling was a theoretical economist with an abiding interest in human behavior, an oddity in a discipline then dominated by mathematicians. He was a pioneer in the field of game theory, which can be described crudely as the art of putting yourself in other people's shoes. An illuminating example, which he used in class: Tomorrow you have to meet a stranger in New York City. You have agreed to meet but you have not set a time or place. Where would you go, and at what time of day, to have the best chance of meeting?*

Schelling, born in 1921, was a decade younger than Friedman and Stigler, and by the time he received a doctorate from Harvard in 1951, the threat of depression had been overshadowed by the threat of nuclear war. Schelling's studies of Cold War dynamics led him to suggest to the

---

* The most common answer among Schelling's students in the 1960s: noon, Grand Central Station, under the great clock.

Kennedy administration that it should establish a hotline with the Kremlin to limit the chances of miscommunication. His expertise also brought the movie director Stanley Kubrick to Schelling's home outside Boston. The two men spent a long day in 1962 discussing the plot of Kubrick's black comedy *Dr. Strangelove*. And, in 1965, it led the Brookings Institution to invite Schelling to contribute a paper on the vexing problem of valuing human life.

The practical issue confronting policy makers, Schelling said, was how much to spend on problems that posed relatively small risks to large numbers of people, like the threat of disease, traffic accidents, or pollution. In a democratic society, he said, this was a decision that should be made by the polity. Did they want less risk? "It surely should be their privilege to have the program if they are collectively willing to bear the cost," Schelling wrote. "If they are not willing, perhaps it would be a mistake to ask anyone else to bear the cost for them."

Previous estimates of the value of life were based on the value to other people: the owner of a slave, the employer of a worker, the dependents of a wage earner. Schelling, by contrast, argued the value of life should be determined by "the people who may die."[41]

Schelling suggested asking people directly; several younger economists inspired by his paper sought instead to tease the answer out of wage data. Riskier jobs tend to pay higher wages: the people who clean the outside of windows on skyscrapers earn more than those who clean the inside of the same windows. Economists estimated the value that the workers placed on their own lives by comparing the difference in risk with the difference in pay.[42]

The new approach made its federal debut in the late 1970s. Warren Prunella, a professor of economics at Canisius College in Buffalo, followed a friend to Washington to work at one of the new crop of regulatory agencies, the Consumer Product Safety Commission. At first, Prunella's job was to justify decisions made by lawyers. As another member of that first generation later observed, "You almost had to take careful steps to make it clear you didn't take economics into account."[43] But Prunella gradually gained influence. The commission established a nationwide system for hospitals to report injuries caused by consumer products, and Prunella used the data to calculate which products were doing the most harm. He argued the commission should prioritize action on those products. "It took about five years of education on the rest of the staff and commissioners to convince them that doing cost-benefit analysis was the way to maximize the life-saving and the injury-saving," he said.[44]

In 1978, Prunella was asked to evaluate proposed standards for the flammability of furniture fabrics. Among the benefits, he included the value of the lives that could be saved, using a figure of $1 million per life. The rule was rejected. But in 1981, Congress required the agency to perform cost-benefit analyses on future rules, and it adopted the $1 million figure.

Regulating the Regulators

Workers who handled raw cotton often developed breathing problems that doctors in the 1970s attributed to the inhalation of cotton dust. The condition was called "brown lung," after the black lungs of coal miners. Under Nixon, federal regulators moved to require air filtration systems in textile plants, but the White House let the proposed rule languish. When Jimmy Carter was elected in 1976, textile unions assumed victory was at hand. Eula Bingham, the new head of the Occupational Safety and Health Administration, met with a group of textile workers suffering from brown lung. One of the workers asked her to join in a prayer; Bingham said that in the silence, she could hear the wheezing of workers struggling to draw breath.[45] Determined to help, Bingham dismissed concerns about the cost of the air filters. She said economics should not be a "paramount consideration" in setting safety and health standards.[46]

In May 1978, however, the Carter administration hit the brakes again. Carter had created a regulatory review system headed by Charles Schultze, the economist who had persuaded Johnson to embrace budgetary cost-benefit analysis, and who believed the job of an economist in government was to serve as a "partisan advocate for efficiency."[47] One of his colleagues, the economist William Nordhaus, had flagged the brown lung rule as a prime example of the government's indifference to efficiency. Nordhaus argued masks would protect workers at lower cost, and he urged Schultze to take a "dramatic and confrontational" stand.[48]

The fight between Bingham and the economists soon spilled into public view, as did a number of related efforts by the economists to delay or weaken proposed regulations. Senator Edmund Muskie, the author of the Clean Air Act, summoned Schultze before a Senate committee and lashed the economist for obstructing the will of Congress. "I take issue with the idea that we have to have lengthy economic analysis before we can have clean air and clean water," Muskie said. "Our standards of what is healthy are being compromised by economics."

Muskie said Congress already had weighed the merits of the nation's laws — as he put it, "Charlie Schultze isn't telling us anything we didn't know" — and it was undemocratic for economists to substitute their own tallies of costs and benefits.[49] In a 1979 speech, Muskie warned that the greatest threat to the environment was not pollution, but "anti-regulators who claim it is too costly and too burdensome to protect people from the hazards of pollution."[50]

House Democrats also staged a hearing to air their grievances with cost-benefit analysis, inviting Ralph Nader to provide the entertainment. He did not disappoint, decrying what he called the "ideological arithmetic" of elitists who lived in "air-conditioned buildings."[51]

Carter agonized, then decided in favor of Bingham, allowing the rule to move forward. But he thought that his economists also had a point. He pressed for legislation in 1979 to create a formal regulatory review process, telling Congress, "Society's resources are vast, but they are not infinite." The unspoken message was that cost-benefit analysis was a language for dealing with reality. The choices would be made; the question was only how.

Carter's party rejected his plan, but a backlash was building against regulation and, once again, Milton Friedman emerged as a leading spokesman. A key theme of Friedman's *Free to Choose*, the public television series that first aired in January 1980, was the vice of regulation. Friedman said competition was the best regulator: the quality of a restaurant was assured by the availability of other restaurants; the price of steel was limited by the existence of other steel mills. "Alternative sources of supply," Friedman wrote in the book that accompanied the series, "protect the consumer far more effectively than all the Ralph Naders of the world."[52]

And Friedman's view was about to become government policy.

"Good evening," Ronald Reagan told the cameras a few weeks after his inauguration in 1981. "I'm speaking to you tonight to give you a report on the state of our nation's economy. I regret to say that we're in the worst economic mess since the Great Depression." There would be tax cuts, but Reagan said he also was assigning Vice President George H. W. Bush to "carefully remove the tentacles of excessive government regulation which are strangling our economy."

Reagan and his aides did not share Nixon's ambivalence about the value of health and safety regulation. They were pretty sure it was bad. The chairman of Reagan's Council of Economic Advisers, Murray Weidenbaum, was the author of a much quoted estimate that regulations imposed an annual burden of $100 billion on corporations. Weidenbaum's work was funded by companies including General Electric, and his techniques included double counting.[53] But the new administration took the view that the burden of proof rested with proponents of regulation. "There is no reason," said the 1982 *Economic Report of the President*, "to think that commands from the government can do a better job of increasing an individual's economic welfare than the individual can by making choices himself." Indeed, a growing literature suggested that regulation often had unanticipated adverse consequences. An early classic in this genre was a 1975 paper by Sam Peltzman, George Stigler's protégé, arguing that seat belt laws killed pedestrians because drivers felt safer and therefore took larger risks.

In February 1981, the White House summoned representatives of regulatory agencies to a meeting in the old office building that sits on the west flank of the White House, an odd Second Empire confection in a city of neoclassical temples. Their host was James C. Miller III, who had been tapped by Reagan to lead a new office with a new mission: regulating the regulators.*

The lawyers were handed copies of an executive order requiring cost-benefit analysis of proposed rules, and allowing Miller's office to block rules it deemed inefficient. Miller watched as the lawyers began to make notes and to strike objectionable lines. Then, as they got to the last page, they saw Reagan's signature, and they realized they were not being asked for their opinions. These were marching orders. One of the regulators put down his pen, looked up at Miller, and said, "Jim, do you have a clean copy?"[54]

Miller, born in 1942 in Atlanta, Georgia, was a child of the free-market movement. As a graduate student in the late 1960s at the University of Virginia — then a hotbed of Chicago-style economics — Miller made a splash by editing a collection of essays advocating the end of military conscription. His dissertation was a critique of airline regulation, a subject that engaged his interest because his father was a Delta Air Lines pilot. It won Miller a job as an economist in the Nixon and Ford administrations. When that gig ended sooner than he had hoped, he retreated to the American Enterprise Institute, where he spent the rest of the 1970s honing plans to wield economics against regulation.

A stocky southerner with a booming voice, Miller was an obdurate advocate for free markets, insisting for example that consumers should be free to buy lower-quality products and describing the rise of consumer regulation as "national nannyism."[55] He was also given to homespun earnestness, peppering his public remarks with words like "heck" and "darn" and "hokey." Critics dubbed him Miller Lite.

---

* The position was Miller's first job under Reagan. The Office of Information and Regulatory Affairs was tucked inside the Office of Management and Budget. Later in the Reagan administration, Miller was named head of the Federal Trade Commission and then returned to the White House as the head of OMB.

It was a vogue among Reaganites, particularly the economists, to wear ties decorated with miniature cameos of Adam Smith, but few wore the ties as religiously as Miller. When he showed up at an event in New York in the summer of 1982 wearing something else around his neck, a federal newsletter reported it was the first time in eighteen months Miller had been seen in public without a Smith tie.[56]

Miller had watched as the Carter administration reliably found reasons to soften its economic objections to regulation; he was determined to set a different tone. "In the previous administration," he said, "there was good will, but a lack of backbone." In early 1981, a Treasury official testified that the Internal Revenue Service would not submit its regulations for Miller's review. Miller promptly got the official on the telephone. "I said in so many words, 'It is now ten thirty in the morning and by twelve thirty you will have a letter in each committee member's office confessing that you had the information totally incorrect,'" he said. And that is what Treasury did. "Here I was," Miller recalled decades later, still gleeful, "a thirty-seven-year-old economist, telling these agencies what to do."[57]

Miller hired Jim Tozzi, who had remained in the government through the Ford and Carter years, as the deputy in charge of reviewing proposed regulations. Tozzi relished the role, working seven days a week and reading rules on the bus as he commuted to his unassuming Virginia home. "You got a high, man," Tozzi said. "Every time you went to work. You could feel it. You were going to regulate the regulators."[58]

Miller left the White House in the fall of 1981 to lead the Federal Trade Commission, which had been a bastion of regulatory activism during the Carter years. "I went in with guns blazing," Miller told me, "and it was hand-to-hand combat for a while." In 1982, the FTC's Seattle office proposed a recall of Bayley "survival suits." These suits, mostly used by fishermen and by workers on deep-sea oil rigs, were supposed to keep people who fell into the water insulated and afloat, but a Coast Guard study found 90 percent had life-threatening defects. In an internal memo that found its way to the press, an official in the FTC's Seattle office said the agency's economics bureau had delayed the recall, advising, "If deaths actually occur, market forces — i.e. lawsuits by surviving heirs — may be adequate to remedy the problem."* Miller, hauled before an outraged congressional committee, defended the economics bureau, testifying that it had raised "a relevant question."[59]

Two-year-old Joy Griffith climbed onto her grandfather's reclining chair in October 1984 and fell between the seat and the leg rest, causing the chair to fold back up on her. Unable to breathe, she suffered permanent brain damage.[60] Griffith's injuries, and a number of similar incidents, prompted the Consumer Product Safety Commission to issue a "national consumer alert" in June 1985 warning about reclining chairs. But in December, the commission's staff concluded the agency should not require modifications to chairs already sold, or to new models. Warren Prunella calculated 40 million recliners were in use, each of which lasted about ten years. Design changes might prevent one death per year, so at $1 million per life — the figure the agency had adopted in the early 1980s — the estimated benefit of a successful recall was $10 million. At that price, changes were worthwhile only if each recliner could be fixed for less than 25 cents. Beyond the safety warnings, Prunella wrote, "it is our recommendation that nothing be done."[61]

Even the industry was taken aback: manufacturers voluntarily agreed to change the design of the chairs beginning in October 1986. Older chairs, however, were not recalled and, in 1987, an eighteen-month-old child climbed onto a recliner at a day-care center in Orange County, California, fell between the seat and leg rest, and suffered permanent brain damage.[62]

The government's growing reliance on cost-benefit analysis meant that economists like Prunella were exercising significant influence over life-and-death decisions. Cass Sunstein, a Harvard Law School professor who is a leading proponent of cost-benefit analysis — and who supervised regulation under President Obama — says the process enhanced democracy because it served "to translate social problems into terms that lay

---

* It is perhaps worth noting that the court system is not an example of "market forces." It is a form of government regulation.

bare the underlying variables and make them clear for all to see."[63] But cost-benefit analysis also displaced democracy, by elevating the judgments of economists above the judgments of politicians. And instead of clarifying those decisions, the government dressed the key choices in euphemisms and then wrapped the euphemisms in hundreds of pages of obscure language. The media in the 1980s, dimly aware that the government was doing something new, tried to wrap its mind around this math of life and death. A *New York Times* piece in 1985 asked a wide range of people to put a price on life, including a professor of anatomy who calculated that the raw materials in the average body, including five pounds of calcium, were worth about $8.37, and a police officer who testified the price of a contract killing began at about $10,000.[64] This was funny, but it did not dwell on the central facts: economists effectively were deciding whether armchairs should be allowed to crush children, and the decision rested on the dollar value the government assigned to human life.

Critics continued to focus on trying to make cost-benefit analysis disappear. "We don't like anything that prices out human life," a spokesman for the AFL-CIO said in 1981.[65] That same year, Al Gore, a third-term congressman from Tennessee, attacked cost-benefit analysis as "a cynical attempt to cripple important activities of the government." Shaking his head at the arrogance of economists, he asked, "What dollar figure can be assigned to the avoidance of birth deformities?"[66] The critics blocked passage of a law to require economic evaluation of all proposed regulations. They also found some success in the courts. In 1981, for example, the Supreme Court rejected the Reagan administration's efforts to terminate the brown lung rule. The court pointed out Congress had not required OSHA to balance benefits and costs.[67]

Judges similarly rebuffed efforts to set aside restrictions on pumping chemicals into public waterways, and to reverse a requirement for airbags in passenger vehicles. The regulations may have violated the laws of economics, but they did not violate the laws of the United States. Judges even ordered agencies to get back to work on new regulations. By the end of the 1980s, the pace of rule writing had rebounded.[68] But the new regulations increasingly were shaped by cost-benefit analyses.[69] "What's the alternative?" asked Christopher DeMuth, who had helped to create the EPA as a young Nixon aide, and who succeeded Miller as Reagan's regulator of regulators. "Flipping a coin? Consulting a Ouija board?"[70] There were undoubtedly theoretical imperfections and shortcomings but, in the words of Cass Sunstein, "a signal advantage of cost-benefit analysis is that we can actually engage in it."[71] By refusing to engage, opponents of cost-benefit analysis were allowing others to determine the rules used to make the rules.

Paralysis by Analysis

W. Kip Viscusi was determined to persuade liberals to embrace cost-benefit analysis.

Viscusi, born in New Jersey in 1949, developed an interest in cost-benefit analysis as a Harvard undergraduate in the late 1960s, during the early years of excitement. He wrote his senior thesis on "The Economic Evaluation of Water Resources Projects," and then landed a job working for Ralph Nader, co-authoring *Damming the West*, a 1973 critique of the government's penchant for building walls across western rivers. The book did not offer the standard liberal critique of cost-benefit analysis as inherently objectionable. Viscusi believed in the value of quantification; his argument was that the government needed to quantify a wider range of costs. He warned that environmentalists were making a strategic mistake by fighting the use of cost-benefit analysis rather than battling to shape the government's methodology. "Environmental impacts," he wrote, "will remain neglected impacts until they are quantified in dollar terms."[72]

Viscusi's doctoral dissertation in 1976 was one of the early papers that used wage data to estimate the value of human life. He leapt at the chance to join the Carter administration, but found it a frustrating experience. The first time he tried to persuade a federal regulator to put a value on human life, in 1980, the official responded, "We can't do that. That's immoral."[73] In Viscusi's view, the incomplete accounting of the benefits of regulation was the real sin.

During the 1980s, Viscusi continued to refine his assessment of the value of human life, and federal agencies began to take an interest. In 1982, DeMuth's office at the White House rejected an OSHA rule requiring warning labels on workplace chemicals. Both unions and industry groups supported the rule, but DeMuth compared it to what he regarded as the wasteful requirement for warning labels on cigarette packaging. Mary Ellen Weber, OSHA's head of regulatory analysis, sought an independent review from Viscusi. "I needed someone who the Democrats wouldn't think was a right-wing tool and the Republicans wouldn't think was a 'flaming, Commie, pinko liberal,'" she told the *Washington Post*. The agency's original analysis had valued human life based on lost wages, producing a figure of a few hundred thousand dollars. Viscusi put the value between $2 million and $3 million, or roughly ten times the agency's original figure — and just enough to show the benefits of the rule would exceed the costs. DeMuth continued to object, but the numbers were now on the side of regulation, and the rule went into effect.[74]

The debate over assigning a value to life was shifting from whether to how much. In 1985, OSHA pegged the price of life at $3.5 million to justify new safety requirements for construction equipment. The White House pressed OSHA to use a value of $1 million, a crucial difference because the estimated cost of the rule was about $1.1 million for each life saved. When the EPA proposed to ban asbestos — a mineral that breaks into little pieces that are easily inhaled and highly carcinogenic — the White House argued the agency should discount the value of each life that would be saved because it often took decades for cancer to develop.*

---

* Discounting is a formalization of the concept that sooner is better than later. A person with a dollar can either spend it — or invest it, and have more money tomorrow. The discount rate is the return on the investment a person requires to wait; a higher discount rate implies a stronger preference for immediate consumption. But even a very modest discount rate implies that people place a very low value on the future. For example, if saving a human life is worth $10 million today, a 3 percent discount rate implies that it's only worth spending $2.3 million in the present to save a life fifty years from now. American courts ultimately endorsed the argument that future asbestos deaths should be heavily discounted. As a result, asbestos

Viscusi could play that game, too. During the administration of President George H. W. Bush, the Federal Aviation Administration asked Viscusi to update his estimate of the value of life. He returned with a figure of $5 million, which he based partly on the argument that airline passengers tended to be relatively affluent. Automakers protested, fearing the rest of the Department of Transportation would adopt the figure. In 1992, the department settled on a compromise figure of $2.5 million. That still represented a significant increase. Among the consequences: in 1998, citing Viscusi's work, the department finally required "Mansfield bars" on the back of large trucks.

Many liberals hoped President Clinton would renounce cost-benefit analysis after taking office in 1993. But Clinton recognized that regulatory activity comprised a growing share of the work of government, and that the White House could exert greater influence by requiring agencies to submit rules for review.[75] Sally Katzen, the lawyer tapped as Clinton's regulatory czar, revived an old Carter administration line that regulation was good and cost-benefit analysis made it better. To draw a contrast with Reagan, she spent months building a consensus for changes to the regulatory review process. "We couldn't live with it. We couldn't scrap it. There's only one other alternative and that's to rewrite," she said. Before signing off, Clinton asked for any objections. "I sat there with my heart in my throat," Katzen said. But there were none. Even Vice President Gore had declared himself a convert to the value of cost-benefit analysis. So Clinton signed the executive order creating the new process and gave Katzen the pen.[76]

Republicans, after taking control of the House in 1994, once again sought to pass a law mandating cost-benefit analysis of environmental regulations, and other rules where it was not already required. The Harvard economist John Graham argued that making rules without regard to cost was "statistical murder," since the government might be able to save more lives by regulating more efficiently.[77] The new House Speaker, Newt Gingrich, said environmental regulations "misallocated resources on

_____

remains legal in the United States, although it is illegal in many other industrialized nations.

emotional and public relations grounds without regard to either scientific, engineering or economic rationality."[78]

Clinton, dryly observing that "the environment is still not able to protect itself," rallied Democrats against the changes. But the administration also announced that the EPA would begin voluntarily to put a price on the lives saved by its regulations. Environmental groups refused to participate. "Environmentalists without PhDs in economics from MIT aren't going to make headway in a room full of neoclassical economists," explained the head of one leading lobby.[79] Abstinence proved ineffective. Carol Browner, the head of the agency under Clinton, delivered a speech on the thirtieth anniversary of Earth Day, in 2000, emphasizing the EPA's mandate to reduce some kinds of pollution without regard to cost. "Let me repeat those last four words," she said. "Without regard to cost." Then the EPA published its guidelines, which Browner defended as necessary to demonstrate the value of regulation. The agency considered twenty-six studies — five by Viscusi — and decided to value life at $4.8 million, in 1990 dollars.

Under President George W. Bush, the EPA whittled away at the dollar value of human life. The first and most public assault came in 2003, when the agency proposed to apply a 37 percent discount to the lives of people over seventy. There was a certain logic: an intervention that added ten years to life surely was more valuable than an intervention that added five years, and it followed that saving the life of a twenty-year-old was, on average, more valuable than saving the life of a twenty-five-year-old. There also were reasonable counterarguments: For example, people approaching the end of life might place a greater value on their remaining years. These arguments were carefully considered.... No, actually the AARP protested loudly and furiously until a White House spokesman was sent forth to tell the American public, "The Bush administration's commitment to human life should not be questioned."[80]

The lesson learned was to cut the value of all lives. In 2004, the EPA quietly shaved 8 percent off the value of life in an analysis of air quality regulations. In 2008, the agency chipped off another 3 percent by not adjusting for inflation in an analysis of air pollution rules for boats and trains. In total, the value of life was reduced to $6.9 million (in 2008 dollars) — a cut of about $1 million from the 2000 guidelines, adjusting for inflation.[81]

Following the election of President Obama in 2008, the value of life rebounded. The Bush administration had rejected a plan to double the required roof strength of new passenger vehicles, which might have prevented 135 deaths per year in rollover accidents. Instead it required a smaller and less expensive increase in roof strength, estimated to prevent no more than 44 deaths each year. The Obama administration, citing the higher value it placed on life, required the stronger roofs. By 2016, the EPA was using a figure of $10.1 million — and it had committed to make regular inflation adjustments. The agency also launched a study of whether it should put a higher value on preventing cancer deaths, on the theory that cancer is a particularly unpleasant way to die, and therefore people may be willing to pay more to reduce the risk.

After the failure of a sweeping climate change bill in 2009, the administration also tried to strengthen environmental regulation by expanding the universe of quantifiable benefits. Many federal environmental regulations are justified primarily by a single kind of damage: the health effects of the emission of small particles. The administration set out to quantify a second kind of harm, from carbon emissions. In 2010, a government task force concluded one ton of carbon emissions caused about $21 in economic damage, including health effects, agricultural impacts, and flooding. In 2013, the administration increased this "social cost of carbon" to $33 per ton.

Both sides had accepted that battles over regulation would be fought in the language of economics. "The United States experienced a revolution," Sunstein wrote. "No gun was fired. No lives were lost. Nobody marched. Most people didn't notice. Nonetheless, it happened."[82]

Most industrial nations were suffering similar environmental degradation by the 1960s, but at first, the United States had been alone in responding forcefully. "We saw the Americans thrashing around from one pollution scare to the next, and we were mildly amused," the British journalist Stanley Johnson wrote in 1972 of the view from the United

Kingdom. "Over there they seemed set on working their way in a random manner through the whole periodic table."[83]

In recent decades, the dynamic has flipped. The United States was the first nation to regulate arsenic in drinking water, but when the World Health Organization in the 1990s recommended a new limit of 10 parts per billion, considerably stricter than the U.S. standard of 50 parts per billion, the European Union moved more quickly to the new standard. The Clinton administration proposed to follow, but the rule was not finalized before the 2000 election, and the Bush administration blocked its implementation. "Communities faced with the daunting task of finding the money to adhere to the stricter standards can breathe a sigh of relief," said Senator Pete Domenici, a Republican from Albuquerque, New Mexico, which then had the highest levels of arsenic in its water of any major American city.[84]

In 2002, Jeff Immelt, then the chief executive of General Electric, predicted "almost 99 percent" of the toughest regulations the company faced going forward would come from the E.U. rather than the United States. The company established a European headquarters in Brussels, the seat of the E.U., the better to cultivate its new overseers.[85]

One reason for the split is a difference over the role of economics. The European Union has taken a measured view of the value of cost-benefit analysis, particularly in environmental policy making. Its 1992 Maastricht Treaty enshrined a "precautionary principle" as the standard for regulation, meaning regulators do not require clear evidence of harm to impose restrictions. European regulators weigh costs and benefits, but they place a greater weight than their American counterparts on risks that can't be measured. "Those in public office have a duty not to wait until their worst fears are realized," Robert Coleman, the director general for health and consumer protection of the European Commission (the E.U.'s executive arm), said in 2002.[86]

In 2010, for example, the European Union banned baby bottles containing bisphenol A (BPA), a common ingredient in clear, hard plastics, citing "uncertainty" about its health effects. The U.S. Food and Drug Administration, by contrast, cited the same uncertainty as the reason it would not ban BPA. The FDA removed the chemical from a list of approved ingredients only after bottle makers voluntarily stopped using it. Europe similarly imposes tighter restrictions on antibiotics in animal feed, emissions from waste incinerators, and ingredients in cosmetics.[87]

Critics, including the U.S. government, warn that Europe is impeding the march of progress. "Excessive caution may be the biggest risk of all," the drug company Pfizer, barred from selling beef hormones, warned in a 2000 advertisement. Europe, it said, "could suppress the very forces of economic and technical innovation that make the current world possible."[88]

But as the ad itself suggests, cost-benefit analysis is inherently political. The precision of the results obscures the subjectivity of the underlying assumptions. It is a method for making choices with deliberation, and its widespread adoption has increased the rigor of policy making, not least by requiring policy makers to acknowledge inherent trade-offs. But societies can look at the same set of costs and benefits and reasonably make different choices. And societies can decide who makes those choices. Schelling's observation that cost-benefit analysis substitutes the judgment of the polity for the judgment of the expert is an opportunity, not a guarantee.

PART III

Chapter Eight

Money, Problems

The average [British] citizen wakes in the morning at the sound
of an American alarum clock, rises from his New England
sheets, and shaves with his New York soap and Yankee safety
razor. He pulls on a pair of Boston boots over his socks from
West Carolina, fastens his Connecticut braces, slips his
Waterbury watch into his pocket.... He sits on a Nebraska
Swivel chair before a Michigan roll-top desk, writes his letters on
a Syracuse typewriter, signing them with a New York fountain
pen, and drying with a blotting sheet from New England. The
letter copies are put away in files manufactured in Grand
Rapids.

—*F. A. Mackenzie, The American Invaders (1902)*[1]

In the final years of World War II, even as the United States and its
allies leveled the industrial heartlands of Europe and Japan, economic
policy makers laid plans for the revival of global trade. They wanted to tie
nations together, both to spur renewed economic growth and to render
war an unthinkable expense. Commerce would foster comity. "The main
prize of the victory of the United Nations is a limited and temporary
power to establish the kind of world we want to live in," the State Department wrote in a November 1945 white paper "presented for consideration
by the peoples of the world." The paper spoke of a new era in which
nations would "work together in every field of common interest, in particular the economic."[2]

The centerpiece of this plan was a deal negotiated in the summer of 1944, at the Bretton Woods resort in the White Mountains of New Hampshire, to fix the exchange rates of major currencies. The architects of the plan — led by the American economist Harry Dexter White — regarded fixed exchange rates as necessary to provide a stable environment for trade.* When foreign customers buy American goods, they must first exchange their own currency for dollars — or, if the buyer pays in a foreign currency, the company must make the exchange. Under the Bretton Woods Agreement, there was no need for airport signs listing the latest exchange rates. The dollar value of the British pound, for example, was fixed at $4.03.

The agreement also was intended to prevent nations from seeking an advantage at the expense of trading partners by unilaterally reducing the exchange value of their currencies to make their own exports cheaper and more attractive. White and his foreign counterparts, including John Maynard Keynes, who represented Britain at the Bretton Woods conference, thought that competitive currency devaluations in the early 1930s had driven a collapse in trade, which had plunged the world into the Depression and paved the road to war. In the words of an old saying, "When goods don't cross borders, soldiers will."[3]

And White had one more goal in mind: the agreement was designed to reinforce the economic dominance of the United States.[4] White shaped the terms to make the dollar the nearest thing to a universal currency. Before World War I, major trading nations had fixed exchange rates by promising to redeem their currencies for specified amounts of gold. Bretton Woods was an

---

* There are few theories that command such broad agreement among economists as the assertion that free trade benefits all participating nations. One of my favorite illustrations is a YouTube video featuring Andy George, a man who decided to make his own sandwich. George documented the process of growing his own lettuce and wheat, evaporating ocean water for salt, milking a cow, killing a chicken. The sandwich took six months to make and cost $1500. McDonald's, meanwhile, sells chicken sandwiches for less than $5. The point is that specialization saves time and money. One person writes for money and buys food, another makes food and buys books; the result is more food and books. The same logic holds for a community, for a nation, and for the global economy.

ersatz gold standard: other nations pledged to redeem their currencies for dollars, and the United States promised that it would redeem dollars for gold.[5]

The system largely succeeded in stabilizing exchange rates for three decades. The world experienced a recrudescence of prosperity the French fondly dubbed *Les Trente Glorieuses*. But the Bretton Woods system ultimately undermined the economic dominance of the United States.

The root of the problem was that the rest of the world needed dollars. In some ways this was a nice kind of problem: it meant the rest of the world was willing to trade goods for dollars, and then to sit on the dollars rather than using the money to buy goods from the United States.*

Moreover, the purchasing power of each dollar steadily increased. The West German and Japanese economies rebounded with American help. As they were barred from wasting money on conflict and colonies, their economic growth soon outpaced that of the United States, even as the dollar value of marks and yen held steady.[6] For American consumers, the result was a perpetual sale on German and Japanese goods, as each dollar, in effect, could be exchanged for a fixed percentage of the growing economic output of Germany or Japan. "The Japanese in particular have done more for the American consumer than Ralph Nader ever thought of doing," the Chicago-trained economist Martin Bronfenbrenner told a congressional committee in 1971.[7] The Japanese were pleased, too. Toyota's president referred to the U.S. market as "Toyota's salvation."[8]

For American manufacturers, however, the rise of the dollar was doubly painful. They faced an influx of foreign rivals on the home front even as they struggled in export markets. The American economy tilted toward consumption at the expense of production.

---

* Nations engage in trade for the purpose of obtaining imports. Most nations must sell exports to buy imports, but the United States was able to exchange dollars for imports — and many of those dollars simply remained in foreign hands because foreign nations needed to build reserves of dollars, just as they had built reserves of gold. American money is a claim on the U.S. government. If the owner sits on the claim, they are effectively lending the money to the government at no charge.

Bretton Woods barred unilateral currency devaluations, but it did allow nations to negotiate changes in exchange rates when it was necessary to adjust to changes in economic circumstances. This was seen as an important improvement on the rigidity of the gold standard. Keynes compared it to the difference between living under an absolute monarch and living in a constitutional monarchy.[9]

But the agreement did not define necessity. Per Jacobsson, the managing director of the International Monetary Fund, which was created to administer the deal, said necessity was like a pretty girl: "You can recognize one when you meet one." This was boorish and naive. A nation devalued its currency at the expense of its trading partners. Reducing the exchange value of the dollar would increase sales of American goods in Germany and Japan, and decrease sales of German and Japanese goods in the United States. It was not in the interest of other nations to accept devaluation of the dollar.[10]

Instead, the United States and its former enemies burrowed into a codependent relationship — Germans and Japanese producing; Americans consuming — entrenching economic patterns that persist up to the present.

Under pressure from labor unions, the Kennedy administration in 1962 created a program to compensate and retrain American workers who lost their jobs to foreign competition. But it was an empty gesture: not one dollar was distributed to workers over the next seven years.[11]

Foreign demand for dollars also caused the Bretton Woods system to collapse. The United States had promised to sell gold to foreign governments, on demand, at $35 per ounce, but the supply of dollars in foreign hands rose much faster than the supply of gold in the federal government's vaults. By 1963, foreign governments held enough dollars to claim every ounce of gold at Fort Knox, reducing the Bretton Woods Agreement to a convenient fiction that would last only as long as foreign nations refrained from calling those claims.[12]

The United States tried to postpone the day of reckoning by slowing the outflow of dollars. But in attempting to preserve the Bretton Woods system, the United States gradually pulled back from its stated purpose of increasing trade among nations. The government limited foreign lending by American banks and instructed the Pentagon to ship American coal to troops on foreign soil. In a news conference on New Year's Day in 1968, President Johnson asked Americans to refrain from vacationing in Europe for two years.[13]

The United States also sought to discourage foreign governments from redeeming the dollars that they already held. Beginning in 1963, the federal government sold bonds that were purchased with dollars but paid interest in other currencies—basically compensating foreign investors for agreeing to leave America's gold in Fort Knox. Alongside carrots, there were sticks. In 1966, Defense Secretary Robert McNamara suggested America might withdraw troops from West Germany if the Germans continued to withdraw gold from the United States. Karl Blessing, the president of West Germany's central bank, replied with a letter of assurance that West Germany would be delighted to hold on to its dollars.[14]

The federal government even flirted with prospecting for gold. In February 1968, a prominent California Republican, Representative Craig Hosmer, proposed the use of nuclear explosives to blast gold from the ground. Hosmer reckoned this improvement in mining technology could yield 100 million ounces of gold, more than three times the amount the United States had shipped to foreign nations the previous year. He borrowed the idea from Kennecott Copper, which was seeking permission to detonate an atomic bomb in an old Arizona copper mine.[15] The nuclear option remained on the drawing board. Instead, Washington launched Operation Goldfinger, a search for new sources of gold. Among other things, the federal government paid scientists to gather twenty-two samples of a plant called marsh horsetail to investigate a rumor that there was gold inside.[16]

All the while, the end of Bretton Woods drew nearer. The United States had made a promise it could not keep. By 1969, West Germany alone held enough dollars to drain Fort Knox.

*   *   *

Milton Friedman worked to end the Bretton Woods system almost from the hour of its creation, telling anyone who would listen that nations should let financial markets determine exchange rates.*

He was among the first to call attention to the fact that Bretton Woods was buttressed and preserved by limits on trade. He also warned, with considerable prescience, that the stability of the system was maintained only by deferring necessary economic adjustments. Countries with fixed rates could become trapped like continental plates trying to move in opposite directions — the longer the plates were locked together, the greater the eventual earthquake was likely to be.

His opening salvo came in 1948, on a radio panel with the deputy governor of the Bank of Canada, to whom Friedman offered the unsolicited advice that Canada should float its currency, effectively withdrawing from the Bretton Woods Agreement, which it had only just signed.[17]

Friedman offered the same advice to every other nation in a 1953 paper, "The Case for Flexible Exchange Rates." Terminating Bretton Woods in favor of floating rates, he wrote, was "absolutely essential for the fulfillment of our basic economic objective: The achievement and maintenance of a free and prosperous world community engaging in unrestricted multilateral trade."[18]

Under the Bretton Woods system, an American business was willing to accept 360 yen instead of $1 because the Japanese government guaran-

---

* Friedman's support for floating rates was distinct from many of his other positions in that it was not a counterrevolutionary effort to restore some version of the prewar economic system. He was advocating for something genuinely new. He opposed the gold standard as arbitrary, because it was based on the supply of gold, and wasteful, because gold needed to be removed from the ground and then stored in vaults. He also argued any system of fixed rates was inefficient, because it required the adjustment of prices and wages throughout the economy. He said it was easier to adjust a single price: the exchange rate. This he memorably compared to daylight saving time. Everyone could adjust his or her schedule, he said, "but obviously it is much simpler to change the clock." See Milton Friedman, "The Case for Flexible Exchange Rates," in *Essays in Positive Economics* (Chicago: University of Chicago Press, 1953), 157–203.

teed that 360 yen could be exchanged for \$1. Under a system of floating rates, governments do not guarantee exchange rates. The American business must decide on its own how many yen to accept for each dollar. It is likely to make this decision by checking the latest prices in currency markets where traders sell dollars for yen, and vice versa. Those prices, in turn, theoretically reflect the relative strength of the two economies because each dollar, or each yen, is a claim on that nation's economic output.

Friedman said relying on markets would correct the flaw at the heart of Bretton Woods, because exchange rates would adjust without political impediments. Better yet, he said these adjustments would be gradual and smooth, reflecting the slow pace of change in the relative strength of major economies. Reliance on the market, he said, would support trade and increase prosperity. In other words, markets would achieve the goals of Bretton Woods better than Bretton Woods.

Friedman and the policy-making establishment once again were wrestling over the best way to deal with uncertainty. The interdependence of national economies was increasing, as was the complexity and pace of commerce. Policy makers saw a need for stronger management; Friedman and his allies favored faith in markets.

In the spring of 1967, Friedman publicly debated Robert Roosa, a reasonable choice as the voice of the establishment.[19] Roosa had earned a doctorate at the University of Michigan and briefly taught economics at Harvard before serving in the Kennedy administration as under secretary of the Treasury for monetary affairs; later, he was a partner at the New York investment bank Brown Brothers Harriman. From that long experience, he had arrived at the conclusion that Friedman was a naïf. Proposals like Friedman's, he said, were "not either theoretically sound or operationally practicable." Currency markets would fail to converge on a single exchange rate, and the fluctuations would cripple trade. Governments could try to intervene unilaterally, but in the absence of an agreement, there would be "a continuous invitation to economic warfare" in the form of competitive devaluations, reprising the 1930s.

Friedman, in disbelief, asked if Roosa meant to deny that markets would set prices.

Roosa: I deny that an actual market would exist.
Friedman: You deny that a market will exist in exchange?
Roosa: I do, yes.
Friedman: In foreign exchanges?

Once more, Roosa said yes. "What it all comes down to is that the economic traffic among nations has become too vast and too complex," he maintained. "Individual foreign exchange traders and bankers would have an almost impossible task in groping for a going rate that could take all of these conflicting influences into account."[20]

By 1968, Paul Samuelson estimated 90 percent of academic economists accepted Friedman's argument in favor of adjustable rates (Samuelson numbered himself among the converts). The Bretton Woods system, in their view, was suppressing trade, as well as failing to allow for adjustments in exchange rates. Samuelson said, however, that he still saw no prospect of convincing politicians. "The chance that Professor Friedman even with his eloquence can make it happen is not one in ten billion," he said on a TV program called *The Dollar in Danger*. "I don't know whether we should waste the time of adults in discussing this."[21]

But markets did not leave the decision to politicians. Cross-border investment flows had grown even more quickly than international trade in goods and services; the quicksilver changes in those capital flows pushed the Bretton Woods system past its breaking point.

Britain surrendered first, announcing on November 18, 1967, that it would start selling pounds for just $2.40. The British economy was lagging its continental rivals, and the high price of the pound was making matters worse. Devaluation had become a necessary humiliation.

Prime Minister Harold Wilson reassured the public that "the pound here in Britain, in your pocket or purse," had not been devalued because it would still buy the same amount of British goods. This was a smoke screen — the effect of devaluation was to make foreign goods more expensive. Still, the leader of the Conservative Party, Edward Heath, may have gone a little far in declaring, "It will be remembered as the most dishonest statement ever made."[22]

The Johnson administration rushed out a press release "unequivocally" backing Bretton Woods. But Gardner Ackley, chairman of Johnson's Council of Economic Advisers, privately warned that America would need to devalue the dollar, too. It was only a matter of timing.

Economic Nationalism

During the 1968 election campaign, Richard Nixon asked Arthur F. Burns, his top economic adviser, to sound out European governments on the future of Bretton Woods. Burns reported the situation was "very precarious," but not beyond repair. He urged Nixon to seek a new set of fixed rates. "Let us not develop any romantic ideas about a fluctuating exchange rate," Burns instructed. Harking back to the 1930s, he warned, "There is too much history that tells us that a fluctuating exchange rate, besides causing a serious shrinkage of trade, is also apt to give rise to international political turmoil."[23] Nixon's chief diplomat for monetary policy, Paul Volcker, agreed with Burns. Asked about floating rates during his first official trip overseas, Volcker replied, "These ideas have had a lot of discussion in academic circles and that's where they can stay."[24]

Friedman tried to win Nixon's attention, delivering a memo in the fall of 1968 urging him to float the dollar as soon as he took office. Friedman argued any initial turbulence could be blamed on the outgoing administration, while the benefits would be credited to Nixon. "On the economic front, there appear to be only gains and no costs," Friedman wrote. On the other hand, he warned that if Nixon waited, there would be a crisis "in a year or two at most."[25]

Nixon was not interested. Like most people, he wanted the plumbing to work but he did not want to work on the plumbing. In a memo describing his foreign policy priorities, Nixon said he wanted to focus on the "big battles" — namely, relations with the Soviet Union and China. Also

Europe. And the Middle East. And Southeast Asia. Actually, when it came to foreign policy, the subject Nixon loved best, there was only one area he did not want to hear about. He was quite clear. "I do not want to be bothered by international monetary matters."[26] So, for two years, Nixon let Volcker conduct desultory talks with foreign governments.

Meanwhile, the Bretton Woods system continued to fall apart. France followed Britain, devaluing its currency in August 1969. The following spring, in May 1970, Canada became the first major nation to drop out of the system.[27] Friedman, trying to speed the collapse, told a German reporter that West Germany was "chained to the dollar like a prisoner."[28] It was more like an umbilical cord, pumping prosperity into the German economy at the expense of a little inflation, but the Germans did have an abiding terror of inflation. In May 1971, West Germany fired a warning shot, briefly allowing the deutschmark to float against the dollar.

The fragility of America's position was underscored by a confidential White House report in the spring of 1971 that warned the United States was likely to run its first annual trade deficit since 1896 — the value of imports would exceed the value of exports for the first time since America's emergence as an industrial power. The report noted that one in every five cars sold in Los Angeles was from Japan.

The decision to end Bretton Woods began with Volcker, who concluded in early July 1971 that the crisis had arrived: the United States was about to run out of gold. Volcker wanted to maintain a system of fixed rates, but he had despaired of persuading other countries to accept a 10 to 15 percent devaluation of the dollar, the minimum reduction he regarded as sustainable. He told his boss, Treasury Secretary John Connally, that the United States should announce it would no longer exchange dollars for gold, to drive other countries to the negotiating table.

Connally, the former governor of Texas, was a charismatic conservative Democrat whom Nixon had brought into his administration not as an expert on economics but as a potential successor.[29] Connally understood the need to address the crisis, but what really seized his attention was the prospect that devaluation would create jobs. The unemployment rate had been hovering around 6 percent for almost a year, and the White House was under pressure to act.

On July 15, Nixon unveiled his plans to become the first American president to visit Communist China. But when he briefed Congress a few days later, the questions were about the domestic economy. "Connally and I concluded that the time had come to act," Nixon wrote in his memoirs.[30] Two weeks later, Connally returned with a sketch of the kind of "big play" Nixon loved: tax cuts, wage and price controls, and the end of Bretton Woods. The United States would suspend conversion of dollars to gold and invite other nations to negotiate a new set of exchange rates. To encourage cooperation, America also would impose a 10 percent tariff on imports until a deal was reached. On August 12, Nixon met in his hideaway office, in the building next to the White House, with Connally and George Shultz, the former Chicago professor who ran the Office of Management and Budget and who had displaced Burns as Nixon's favorite economist. They agreed that it was time to close the gold window. Shultz later described the plan as "an alliance with the market itself."[31]

During the Great Depression, the federal government bought large chunks of hardscrabble farmland on the eastern shoulder of the Allegheny Mountains, about sixty miles north of Washington, D.C. The land was denuded and rocky but not without charm. In that very different time, the Roosevelt administration decided to build a rustic retreat for federal workers. Most of the campgrounds at Catoctin Mountain Park eventually were opened to the public, but one was reserved for the president. Dwight Eisenhower dubbed it Camp David.

On the afternoon of Friday, August 13, 1971, President Nixon slipped out of hot and sticky Washington for a weekend at the mountain retreat. Gathering his advisers shortly after three o'clock in the Aspen Lodge, the president's cottage, he solemnly encouraged them to sign the guest book. Some already knew why they had been gathered; the rest did not have long to wait. Nixon told them they were about to embark on "the most significant economic action since World War II."[32] They were going to dismantle something else that Roosevelt had built: they were going to blow up the international monetary system.

The weekend at Camp David was memorialized in dramatic detail by the Nixon speechwriter William Safire, and so it is often portrayed as the decisive moment. It is more accurately described as thirty-six hours of Arthur Burns beating his head against a wall, trying to persuade the President to abandon Connally's plan.[33] Burns, who had been installed as the head of the Federal Reserve, warned that financial markets would convulse and trade would unravel, just as it had in the 1930s. "*Pravda* will headline this as a sign of the collapse of capitalism," he said. In his diary he used stronger language, writing, "The gold window may have to be closed tomorrow because we now have a government that seems incapable, not only of constructive leadership, but of any action at all. What a tragedy for mankind!"[34]

Yet Burns was not a man to stand on principle. He met privately with the President to make a final plea for the old system, and then pledged to support its abandonment. "When Arthur barks, he also wags his tail," one rival later wrote.[35]

While Nixon worked on his speech, the President's men gathered for dinner. Volcker, convinced some did not grasp the enormity of the decision, told them that if he had a billion dollars to invest before the President spoke, he could make enough money to retire the federal debt, then roughly $23 billion. H. R. Haldeman, the President's chief of staff, leaned forward with a mock-serious look and said, "Exactly how?"[36]

The phone rang. It was the President, calling to ask Safire to deliver the message that Burns was a "rare jewel" and a good man. The flattery continued in the morning: Burns wrote in his diary that when the President promised all present a Camp David jacket with their name on the front, he, Arthur Burns, received the additional gift of a pair of Camp David glasses.[37]

That Sunday night, Nixon began his televised speech to the nation by boasting the Vietnam War was going so well that it was time to talk about the economy. There were three problems, he said: unemployment, inflation, and Bretton Woods. To create jobs, Nixon announced billions of dollars in tax cuts. To curb inflation, he announced the first peacetime controls on wages and prices in American history. And to rebalance trade, he announced the United States no longer would guarantee the exchange value of the dollar. The price of a British pound, and every other currency tied to the dollar, was suddenly an open question. "There is no longer any need for the United States to compete with one hand tied behind her back," Nixon said.

The President made a point of reassuring Americans the devaluation of the dollar would not affect the prices of domestic goods — the same half-truth Wilson had told the British people four years earlier. Nixon closed the speech with a flourish, quoting a Philadelphia diarist who wrote in the summer of 1775, "Many thinking people believe America has seen its best days." Now, as then, Nixon said, "our best days lie ahead."

It was a declaration of economic nationalism, and in the United States, the initial reaction bordered on euphoria. The Dow Jones stock index posted its largest one-day gain; opinion polls showed such a jump in Nixon's popularity that one pollster compared it to the nation rallying behind Roosevelt after the attack on Pearl Harbor.

Just as Burns had predicted, the Communists also were delighted. Leonid Brezhnev, the leader of the Soviet Union, hailed "the possibility of a profound crisis of the capitalist system."[38]

The rest of the world was less enthused. "A Declaration of War in Trade Policy" read the banner headline in one of Germany's leading newspapers, *Süddeutsche Zeitung*.[39] Oil-producing states, which had long insisted on payment in dollars, threatened to raise prices, the initial step toward the first "oil shock" two years later. Japanese prime minister Eisaku Satō, already rocked by Nixon's decision to go to China, got a call from Secretary of State William P. Rogers just ten minutes before Nixon spoke. "Not again!" Satō said.[40]

Over the next few years, exchange rates jitterbugged and nations wasted vast amounts of money trying to make those rates stop moving. The Archbishop of Canterbury urged the British to "pray earnestly" for the pound sterling.[41] *The New Yorker* ran cartoons about exchange rates. The French finance minister, Valéry Giscard d'Estaing, said the subject of money had been elevated from obscurity: "At stake is the expansion of international trade, that is to say, the growth of the world economy."[42] Giscard d'Estaing found himself elevated, too, from relative obscurity to head of state, as were other finance ministers of his generation: West Germany's Helmut Schmidt, Great Britain's James Callaghan, and Japan's Takeo Fukuda. Economics was moving to the foreground, and policy makers faced the challenge of defining a new relationship between governments and markets.

Shifts and Shocks

"Well, you know what we have done," Connally told a roomful of economists summoned to offer advice three days after Nixon's speech. "What do we do next?"[43]

Volcker still hoped to negotiate a new set of fixed rates, but Shultz had a different plan in mind. He wanted to do nothing. He thought it was time to let markets set rates.

Shultz, gangly, courtly, and considered, was denigrated by some administration rivals as a water carrier for Milton Friedman. Burns, a more celebrated economist who lost the battle for Nixon's ear, wrote of Shultz in his diary, "What a pity that this quiet, persuasive but woefully ignorant ideologist has such influence with the president."[44] This mismeasured the man. Shultz was not a particularly original thinker, but he had a rare combination of economic and political sophistication. Henry Kissinger wrote in his memoirs, "If I could choose one American to whom I would entrust the nation's fate in a crisis, it would be George Shultz."[45] And Shultz knew his own mind. "I think no one should aspire to manage the economy," he told one interviewer. "I think the basic idea about our economy is that it manages itself."[46]

Shultz was born in New York in 1920, then, like Friedman, left the city for New Jersey at a young age. There the similarities ended. George's father, who worked on Wall Street, moved his family to leafy Englewood.[47] Shultz went to prep school and Princeton and then postponed graduate school at MIT to join the marines, fighting in the Pacific and rising to the rank of captain before resuming his studies in 1946. In Cambridge, Shultz fell in with a diverse group of academics interested in labor markets, including the former director of research at the United Steelworkers of America. Shultz's thesis examined why shoemakers in the city of Brockton, south of Boston, were slow to cut wages during the Great Depression. Keynesians viewed inflexible wages as evidence of the need for government intervention; Shultz found that markets had worked in a surprising way. Wages were tied to the price of a shoe. Instead of cutting those rates, companies had reduced total compensation by shifting production to cheaper shoes.

Shultz moved directly from graduate studies onto the MIT faculty, and then to the University of Chicago in 1957. His office was across the hall from George Stigler, with whom he played golf as often as possible, and through whom he became friendly with Friedman. Both men, particularly Friedman, had a deep influence on Shultz's thinking.

Chicago gave Shultz his first crack at management, making him the head of the business school. He also was gaining a reputation as a mediator in labor disputes. The secret, he said, was to get people to stop talking about principles and to start talking about problems.[48]

When President-elect Nixon asked Shultz to serve as labor secretary in the fall of 1968, Shultz accepted the job on one condition. He was convinced the government's frequent intervention in labor disputes was preventing compromises by teaching both sides to expect federal mediation. He asked Nixon to support a strategy of nonintervention. A test arrived almost immediately. The Johnson administration had won an injunction against a dockworkers strike, but the court order expired days before Nixon's inauguration, and the workers once again threatened to walk off the job. Shultz said he told the President, "This is going to cause a lot of kerfuffle in New York City, and it seems like a national emergency, but it isn't."[49] If the administration waited a few weeks, he predicted, management and workers would get the message. Nixon was true to his word, Shultz held firm, and the strike was settled.

But Shultz was frustrated in his broader objective. Both unions and management continued to seek government aid. At a meeting with executives in New York City in the summer of 1970, Shultz was pressed on what the government would do to prevent rising wages. The government? The mild-mannered Shultz exploded, telling the executives, "You're just a bunch of crepehangers."[50]

Nixon, taking notice of Shultz's talents, asked the economist to mediate the desegregation of schools in several southern states. Then he promoted Shultz to run the Office of Management and Budget. Shortly after that change, Senator Robert Dole mentioned to Nixon that he was having trouble contacting John Ehrlichman, one of the President's top advisers. "Ehrlichman?" Nixon responded. "Don't worry about him. I'll put you in touch with somebody who really counts: George Shultz."[51]

In September 1971, Shultz arranged for Friedman to meet with Connally at the latter's Washington home. Friedman lauded Connally for abandoning Bretton Woods and argued against any return to fixed rates. After the meeting, Friedman wrote Connally, "You deserve enormous credit for the courageous and determined stand you have taken." Two months later, when he heard Connally was negotiating a new set of fixed rates with the Europeans and the Japanese, Friedman sent a second letter, declaring himself "extremely depressed" and warning the new deal "would snatch defeat from the jaws of victory."[52]

Connally's efforts provide a useful illustration of the basic problem with negotiating exchange rates: the process was political, whereas the test of the resulting decisions was economic. During the talks, held at the Smithsonian, Connally and his Japanese counterpart, Mikio Mizuta, ducked into a room lined with sample jars. Connally wanted Japan to increase the dollar value of the yen by 20 percent, but he said he needed at least 18 percent. Mizuta told him this was impossible: the final number had to stay below 17 percent. Anything higher would be a "very, very ominous number for Japan," Mizuta said, because that was the magnitude of the yen's appreciation in 1930, when Japan returned to the gold standard just before plunging into an historic recession. Mizuta added, "The finance minister who decided upon this return to the gold standard was assassinated."[53] This was the verbal equivalent of punching Connally in the gut. The Treasury secretary had been shot and almost killed when Kennedy was assassinated in Dallas eight years earlier. Connally accepted an appreciation of 16.88 percent.

When Nixon announced the Smithsonian Agreement in December 1971, he called it "the most significant monetary agreement in the history of the world." Volcker turned to another Nixon aide and whispered, "I hope it lasts three months."[54]

It lasted six.[55] Markets remained unwilling to accept arbitrary prices.

The decisive turn toward floating rates came after Shultz replaced Connally in June 1972, becoming the first economist to serve as Treasury secretary. Shultz did not hesitate to accept his own advice that the United States should embrace floating rates. He ended the government's interventions in the foreign exchange market in support of the Smithsonian deal. Then he played his hand with patience, waiting for the deal to fall apart.

In February 1973, he let Volcker spend four days persuading the Japanese and Europeans to accept another U.S. devaluation. That deal lasted about a month. "I now realize that I was on a Mission Impossible," Volcker told me. "Nobody, certainly not a group of assistant secretaries, were going to devise a new monetary system."

Nixon, for his part, left the issue almost entirely in Shultz's hands. He was done thinking about exchange rates. "The only objective I heard him state about a reformed monetary system, and I heard him say it more than once, was that he just didn't want 'any more crises,'" Volcker said.[56] When Haldeman told the President that Britain had devalued the pound, Nixon said he didn't care. Haldeman pressed on, telling the President Italy might be next. Nixon, recording himself for the benefit of posterity, responded, "Well, I don't give a shit about the lira."[57]

The Europeans also were tired of negotiating. "The most urgent aspect of international monetary reform," one negotiator joked, "is to return to a system of fixed weekends."[58] By March 1973, the yen, lira, and pound all were floating against the dollar. The Germans kept buying billions of dollars, trying to maintain a fixed exchange rate. Finally, Shultz stopped returning phone calls from his West German counterpart, Helmut Schmidt.[59] At a meeting in Paris on March 16, Shultz allowed the Europeans to broach the idea of floating rates, then accepted.[60]

Shultz left the formalities to his successor, William Simon, who concluded an agreement legitimating floating rates in 1976. The Europeans included a mechanism for reconsideration. The United States included a clause granting the United States veto power and furthermore clarifying that it reserved the right to float the dollar irrespective of any vote. Washington had given Bretton Woods to the world, and Washington took it away.

Those like Robert Roosa and Arthur Burns who had predicted floating rates would cause a collapse in trade were spectacularly wrong. The value of exports and imports was equal to a quarter of the world's annual economic output in 1971. By 2008, with markets entrenched as the arbiters of exchange rates, the value of trade was 60 percent of global GDP.[61]

But Shultz and Friedman were wrong, too. Floating rates did not deliver balanced trade. Or stability.

The Chicago Mercantile Exchange was the second trading floor in America's second city. The Board of Trade ran the futures market for the most lucrative commodities, allowing sellers of wheat and corn to reduce risk by selling crops before the actual harvest. The Merc was for the leftovers. It began as the eggs-and-butter market, then gradually added onions, pork bellies, and cattle. Leo Melamed, the ambitious chairman of the exchange, was desperate for new products. "You can't invent another meat," he moaned to friends. Then, in 1967, he read a story about Milton Friedman in the *Wall Street Journal*. It said Friedman, concluding Britain was likely to devalue the pound, had started calling Chicago banks to see if anyone would take the other side of a bet on devaluation. There were no takers, but Friedman thought there should have been.[62]

Melamed agreed. He hired the Merc's first economist and told the man to write Friedman seeking advice, one economist to another, on how to create such a market. Friedman, who made a point of answering almost any letter from almost anyone, wrote back a few weeks later offering encouragement but pointing out the moment was not ripe because changes in exchange rates were rare events under the Bretton Woods system.

After Nixon's speech, Melamed himself wrote to Friedman, persuading the professor to travel from his vacation home in Vermont for a breakfast at the Waldorf-Astoria in New York. There he offered Friedman five thousand dollars to write an endorsement of a new financial market for trading in currency futures. It was not a hard sell. Friedman favored markets of all kinds, and he thought a futures market was a necessary complement to a system of floating exchange rates. It would provide a vehicle for investors to signal their views of the direction of currency prices. And just as farmers benefited from protection against fluctuations in crop prices, businesses would benefit from protection against fluctuations in exchange rates.

When Melamed announced the creation of the International Money Market on December 20, 1971, the press release had Friedman's name all over it. Melamed called the five-thousand-dollar endorsement deal "the best investment the Merc ever made."[63]

Friedman had predicted that floating exchange rates would change slowly over time, because the relative strength of national economies also changed slowly over time. Moreover, he said that speculators would contribute to stability, because they would make money by driving prices back toward the levels justified by those fundamentals.

But instead of floating, exchange rates soared and sank.

Economists offered a variety of tortured theories for the volatility, avoiding the actual and obvious explanation: there was gambling going on.[64] By 1985, daily currency trading topped $150 billion; by 1995, $1.2

trillion; by 2007, $3.3 trillion.[65] An industry popped into existence: currency managers for industrial firms, bankers to take their instructions, speculators to take advantage.*

The losers did not take long to start washing up onshore. Franklin National Bank, a midsized New York lender, failed in 1974 after losing its investors' money in the new world of currency trading. Also in 1974, German authorities shuttered Herstatt Bank — actual motto: "Saving Should Not Be a Gamble" — after it lost almost half a billion marks gambling on the dollar's gyrations.[66] And the worst was yet to come: in May 2015, four of the world's largest banks pleaded guilty to manipulating the dollar-euro exchange rate to book profits at the expense of clients.[67]

All of this — the insurance, the gambling, the outright theft — was the price of the new system.[68]

It is one of history's telling details that Keynes, who did not trust markets, was a successful investor, while Friedman, who loved markets, went largely unrequited. Melamed tells of getting a call from Friedman, who wanted to short the Canadian dollar because he was convinced markets would punish the profligacy of Liberal Party prime minister Pierre Trudeau. Melamed tried to talk him out of it — the Canadian dollar was rising — but Friedman was determined. He didn't give up until the value of the Canadian dollar rose by another 13 percent.[69]

Chimerica

The end of the Bretton Woods system reduced the trade value of the dollar for a time, with far-reaching consequences. Japan adjusted to the *Nixon shokku* by shifting into high-technology manufacturing. Shipyards shut down; carmakers started building better cars. Toyota, once a byword

---

* Proponents of floating rates often argue the availability of insurance significantly reduces the risk of the system. But insurance is expensive. Susan Strange, commenting on the issue, refers to a famous quip: "Ah yes, like the Ritz Hotel, open to rich and poor alike!" See Strange, *Casino Capitalism* (Oxford: Basil Blackwell, 1986), 116.

for clunkers, gradually became the envy of the American auto industry. For the nations of Europe, the end of the international monetary system spurred the creation of a continental monetary system — and, in time, the creation of a pan-European currency.

But the United States did not pursue any sweeping changes in economic policy, and the dollar soon rebounded. The end of the dollar's special legal status did not curb foreign demand. Instead, the dollar's dominance increased. In the chaotic new world of floating exchange rates, many nations expanded their dollar reserves as a cushion against volatility. The economic historian Barry Eichengreen notes that movie villains continued to demand payment in dollars. So did a wide range of international businesses. It was a network effect, much like Facebook: everyone used the dollar because everyone used the dollar.

Some members of OPEC, the oil cartel, tried and failed to find a viable alternative. Both West Germany and Japan resisted the international use of their currencies, determined to preserve export-oriented economic systems. Japan maintained rigid capital controls, while West Germany took a less formal approach. When Iran proposed in 1979 to convert some of its dollar reserves into marks, the Bundesbank protested publicly. It insisted the United States alone could play that role "without having its economic policy damaged."[70]

The Carter administration tried to chide West Germany for its perpetually undervalued currency. When Treasury Secretary Michael Blumenthal mused in an interview that the dollar was too strong, the German newspaper *Frankfurter Allgemeine Zeitung* opined the United States was playing a "selfish, risky game that shows little responsibility toward the world economy."[71]

When Ronald Reagan was sworn into office in 1981, the exchange value of the dollar was roughly the same as in 1973. By the end of Reagan's first term, the exchange value of the dollar was up by 50 percent.[72]

The 1981 tax cuts required a huge increase in federal borrowing even as the Fed squeezed the money supply to drive down inflation. Interest rates spiked and foreign investors raced to acquire dollars, so they could participate in the lucrative business of lending money to the United States. During the Bretton Woods years, America and other major nations had imposed strict limits on international capital flows to maintain the stability of exchange rates. But the United States had ended those restrictions in 1974 and encouraged other nations to follow its example. The interaction of Reagan's tax cuts, the Fed's monetarism, floating rates, and financial deregulation sent the dollar up, up, and away.[73]

Imports flooded into the United States, creating a windfall for American consumers and a disaster for domestic manufacturers. Kodak made 80 percent of the film sold in the United States in 1979; its largest foreign rival, Japan's Fuji, had a 4 percent foothold. By 1985, Kodak's share of the U.S. market was down to 64 percent; Fuji's was up to 11 percent.[74] The rise of the dollar also reduced sales of American goods in other countries. Caterpillar, the Illinois company that dominated the global market for heavy construction vehicles in the decades after World War II, reported in 1983 that the dollar's rise had cut its foreign sales in half. It fired twenty thousand workers and moved some jobs overseas. One million domestic mining and factory jobs were lost during Reagan's first term.

The decline of American manufacturing employment is a long-term trend caused mostly by automation rather than foreign trade. In the 1880s, factories and farms employed roughly three quarters of American workers. By the 1980s, those sectors employed roughly one quarter of American workers even as the output of factories and farms continued to rise. Increased productivity allowed workers to move into other jobs.

But the appreciation of the dollar accelerated and distorted the evolution of the American economy. The United States lost factories and jobs that would have remained viable at lower exchange rates. Meanwhile, Walmart, which began the 1980s with 276 stores in and around Arkansas, ended the decade as the nation's largest retailer, operating more than four times as many stores, each staffed by low-paid workers and stuffed with cheap imported goods.[75]

The Reagan administration imposed some limits on imports of textiles, cars, and steel. For the first time since World War II, America's trade barriers, in aggregate, began to rise. But those walls were easily skirted. To take just one celebrated example, a tariff on motorcycles with engines larger than 700 cubic centimeters prompted the Japanese to develop, exclusively for the American market, motorcycles with 699cc engines.

Meanwhile, the administration refused to do one thing that might have limited the speed of the economic changes racking the country: it refused to drive down the exchange value of the dollar. This was a remarkably pure example of economic ideology dictating public policy. "There is no external measure of what any currency is worth, other than what the market is telling us it is worth," was the summary offered by Donald Regan, the new Treasury secretary.[76]

America's aversion to intervention was not shared by its major trading partners. The Bundesbank bought $25 billion in dollars between 1981 and 1985; purchases by other central banks approached another $25 billion. During that same period, the United States bought just $754 million in marks and yen.[77]

Lee Morgan, the chief executive of Caterpillar, met five times with Treasury officials and twice with President Reagan between 1982 and 1985 to press the administration to reverse the rise of the dollar. The visits were not productive. Treasury officials, including Beryl Sprinkel, the under secretary for monetary affairs, "just kept saying 'markets determine values of currency,'" recalled one attendee.[78]

Round, round-faced, with round eyeglasses, Sprinkel was a cheerful man with a rigid mind. A Fed official recalled briefing Sprinkel about a policy Sprinkel did not like: "Logic was on my side, so I thought, but unshakeable belief was on his," the official said. "We never got much beyond that impasse."[79] When Sprinkel was appointed chairman of Reagan's Council of Economic Advisers in 1985, he told the *New York Times* he would hire only economists who shared his views. Of the other kind, Sprinkel said, "They're not useful to me because I won't listen to them."[80] Pressed by Congress about the dollar's rise, Sprinkel responded modestly that markets were much smarter than bureaucrats. "For the U.S. to tell the foreign exchange markets what the rate of the dollar, the yen, the mark, or any currency should be strikes me as the height of arrogance," Sprinkel said.[81]

America's faith in markets was a mixed blessing for many foreign nations, too. The rise of the dollar caused a third oil shock for the rest of the world, which had to buy dollars to buy oil. Pierre Mauroy, the French prime minister, complained bitterly that the United States was taking advantage of its "exorbitant privilege" as the issuer of the nearest thing to an international currency, reviving a phrase coined by one of his predecessors in the 1960s — though that dubious privilege was now being conferred by the market rather than the Bretton Woods system.[82]

Foreign companies that had borrowed in dollars also were punished. The British airline entrepreneur Freddie Laker had launched a daily "Skytrain" service between London and New York, advertised with lighthearted taglines like "The End of Skyway Robbery," and "I'm Freddie — Fly Me!" The flights were cheap and popular; Queen Elizabeth II knighted Freddie in 1978. But Laker's customers mostly paid in pounds, while he paid most of his bills in dollars. Among other things, the company had borrowed $355 million to buy airplanes. As the dollar climbed against the pound, Laker Airways couldn't earn enough pounds to pay its dollar bills. Sir Freddie's company filed for bankruptcy in February 1982.

The worst damage, however, was in Latin America. The story began shortly after the end of Bretton Woods, in October 1973, when the members of OPEC imposed an embargo on oil exports to countries allied with Israel, including the United States and the United Kingdom. The price of oil rose rapidly, producing a windfall that the oil states, including Saudi Arabia, rather ironically deposited in American banks. The banks, in turn, pumped the petrodollars into the developing world — particularly Latin American countries like Chile, Brazil, and Mexico that welcomed foreign investment as part of programs of economic liberalization. Between 1979 and 1982, Latin America's foreign debts more than doubled, from $159 billion to $327 billion.[83]

Citicorp's chief executive, Walter Wriston, said lending to governments was an ideal business — immensely profitable and quite safe.

"Countries, unlike businesses, don't go bankrupt," Wriston said.[84] But as the dollar soared, Mexico announced in August 1982 that it could not make its interest payments. Other Latin American nations followed. Federal regulators saved Citicorp, and some rivals, by allowing banks to count the loans as likely to be repaid someday.[85]

It was an early instance of an all too familiar pattern: private profits and public bailouts. One lender told the *Wall Street Journal*, "We foreign bankers are for the free market when we're out to make a buck and believe in the state when we are about to lose a buck."[86]

During the 1984 presidential campaign, a new term came into use to describe a vast swath of the industrial heartland. People called it the Rust Belt.[87] That was also the year Youngstown, Ohio, lost its carousel. The grand merry-go-round, a signature attraction at the local amusement park for sixty years, was sold at auction when the park closed; in time, it found a new home on the New York waterfront, in a transparent jewel box by the French starchitect Jean Nouvel.

Reagan swept to reelection in 1984, but the political pressure to arrest the decline of American manufacturing continued to build. A new Treasury secretary, James Baker, persuaded Reagan to treat the value of the dollar as a matter of policy; Baker began to seek concessions from Japan.

In April 1985, Prime Minister Yasuhiro Nakasone asked every Japanese to spend the equivalent of $100 on foreign goods. He then went shopping with reporters in tow, spending $280 on a French shirt, an Italian jacket and tie, and a British dartboard for his grandson. He did not, however, buy anything Made in the U.S.A.[88]

A few months later, Japan made a more substantive gesture, signing a deal with other major developed nations at the Plaza Hotel in New York to drive down the exchange value of the dollar. In his 1986 State of the Union, Reagan came close to acknowledging his error. "We must never again permit wild currency swings to cripple our farmers and other exporters," he said.

For Japan, the Plaza Accord accelerated a process of deindustrialization — the Japanese term was *kudoka*, or "hollowing out." Japanese companies started moving more manufacturing overseas, including to the United States. Honda had opened its first American auto plant in Marysville, Ohio, in 1982, and other carmakers followed.

As with Nixon's devaluation, the dollar remained at a lower level for about a decade and U.S. manufacturing staged a modest recovery. Caterpillar emerged from the 1980s as a more efficient and profitable company. In 1988, its revenues exceeded the previous peak set back in 1981. Caterpillar employed fewer Americans, and many of those at lower wages, but it regained its role as one of the nation's largest exporters.

But the United States soon fell back into its comfortable pattern of borrowing and consuming, and this time, it found a foreign partner willing to finance its habit on an even larger scale: China.

At Bretton Woods in 1944, the Roosevelt administration had made the fateful decision to resist pressure, especially from the United Kingdom, to impose limits on trade surpluses. The dominance of American manufacturing then was at its peak. The foreign appetite for American goods was likely to exceed the American appetite for foreign goods for the foreseeable future, and the United States could meet the demand by lending money to foreign buyers.

John Maynard Keynes argued for limits on such lending. His argument was self-interested: he wanted Great Britain and its colonies to reclaim market share. But he also argued that in the long term, maintaining relatively balanced trade was in everyone's interest.

American policy makers saw some wisdom in Keynes's argument. The United States sought a measure of balance by throwing open its markets to foreign goods, while allowing its trading partners to maintain greater restrictions on American goods. The United States, after all, needed strong allies, not least to staunch the spread of communism. Political support for opening the American market to imports was almost inconceivably broad by modern standards, encompassing business groups, farmers, and some trade unions. Henry Ford II endorsed the elimination of U.S. tariffs on imported automobiles.[89] And the policy-making elite showed little patience with those who did worry about the threat posed by foreign competition. George Ball, President Kennedy's under secretary of state for economic affairs, delighted in recounting that he had gone to a meeting with American textile executives "dressed in a British-made suit, a British-made shirt, shoes made for me in Hong Kong, and a French necktie."[90] But the United States prevented any permanent limits on trade imbalances. If other nations wanted to borrow dollars to buy American goods, the United States was only too happy to accommodate the demand.

Half a century later, America had become the country that borrowed money to buy foreign goods — and that found itself unable to convince its trading partners, notably China and Germany, that everyone ultimately would benefit from constraints on trade imbalances.

China tied its currency to the dollar in the mid-1990s, in effect signing a unilateral Bretton Woods agreement. Initially the Chinese were trying to suppress inflation and avoid the exchange-rate volatility then plaguing other Asian nations. But as the growth of the Chinese economy outpaced the U.S. economy, the Chinese government's decision to maintain the exchange rate amounted to an increasingly massive subsidy for exports.

China was emulating the strategy successfully employed by West Germany and by several of its own neighbors, including Japan, South Korea, and Taiwan.

To maintain the exchange rate, China took much of the money earned from sales to Americans and returned it to the United States in the form of investments in Treasuries and other dollar-denominated bonds. The effect of this savings program was to defer the benefits of economic growth, forgoing immediate consumption in pursuit of greater long-term prosperity.

The impact on the United States was minor until 2000, when the Clinton administration and Congress normalized trade relations with China. U.S. investment in China sharply increased, as did imports from China.[91] Other Asian nations, seeking to maintain their shares of the lucrative American market, responded by suppressing their currencies against the dollar, too. Federal debt held by foreigners rose from $1 trillion in 2000 to $2.5 trillion in 2008.[92]

The United States once again embraced the willingness of other nations to finance American consumption. And once again, America sacrificed its factories. Currency manipulation by China and other nations — and U.S. borrowing — cost up to 5 million American jobs.[93]

The pressure also shaped and distorted the growth of the American economy. A 2011 study found almost all of the increase in net employment in the United States between 1990 and 2008, some 27.3 million jobs, was in sectors sheltered from foreign competition — notably, health care and retail. There is a straight line from Bretton Woods to Celina, Ohio, where a Walmart Supercenter sits a stone's throw from a larger building where a thousand American workers once built 2 million Huffy bicycles each year. Huffy moved the work to China in 1998 to meet Walmart's demand for lower prices. The bikes are cheaper; the good jobs are gone.[94]

"There is surely something odd about the world's greatest power being the world's greatest debtor," Larry Summers harrumphed in 2004. Warnings about the federal debt, and particularly about borrowing from China, became the backbeat of every discussion about American economic policy. Yet there was no sign the rest of the world planned an intervention. The only binding limit on American borrowing appeared to be the appetite of the American people.

Milton Friedman had insisted in 1967 that a trading partner like China would be good for the United States. "They are saying to us, 'Look, if you'll take some of our goods for cheap, we'll give them to you,'" he said. "Well, let's not be fools, let's take it." He also maintained that floating rates would prevent sustained manipulation of exchange rates. "Are you afraid that we're going to import a lot from abroad? We can't," Friedman said. Any trading partner would spend the money it earned, causing exchange rates to adjust. The fear of currency manipulation, he said, was a nightmare "dreamed up to scare children with."[95]

Friedman was wrong and there were consequences. The center of global manufacturing, which had moved from the English Midlands to the American Midwest, moved again, to southeast China. Trade helped to lift hundreds of millions of Chinese from abject poverty, and it increased the size of the American economy, too. The problem was in the distribution: as American policy makers exchanged the concentrated pain of job losses for the broad benefits of lower prices, most Americans came out ahead, but a significant minority were left behind.[96]

One study calculated roughly two thirds of the American workers who lost jobs as a result of increased trade with China ended up finding new jobs at equal or better pay. But one third of the workers did not and, on average, they lost 30 percent of their income.[97]

George Carney drove forklifts in a refrigerator factory in western Illinois until the factory closed in 2004. When I met him a decade later, in 2015, he was living on federal disability benefits, nursing a beer in a windowless bar on the banks of the Mississippi River. Carney said he was willing to accept that trade boosted the American economy. But trade is basically a form of eminent domain — the state took his job in the name of the greater good. And that, to Carney, did not seem fair. He told me, "I don't believe in laying someone off, in taking away someone's livelihood, just so other people can make more money."[98]

In his memoirs, published in 2018, Paul Volcker wrote, "We failed to recognize the costs of open markets and rapid innovation to sizable fractions of our own citizenry."[99] The truth is more bitter. Many economists did predict the costs, including Paul Samuelson, who co-authored a 1941 paper showing that trade between developed and developing nations could reduce working-class wages in the developed world. Some took the Kaldor-Hicks view that trade, like cost-benefit analysis, was justified because government could compensate the losers. Others went so far as to suggest that government should compensate the losers. But seventy-five years after the United States embarked on its effort to encourage foreign trade, the reality is that government has made little effort to do so. "The argument was always that the winners could compensate the losers," the economist Joseph Stiglitz, a vocal critic of this failure, told me. "But the winners never do."[100]

Euphony

The nations of Western Europe understandably embraced with particular fervor the idea that increased international trade would discourage military conflict. In 1951, France, Italy, West Germany, and three smaller nations created the European Coal and Steel Community as a first step toward economic integration. "The solidarity in production thus established will make it plain that any war between France and Germany becomes not merely unthinkable, but materially impossible," said Robert Schuman, the French foreign minister, who was born in the borderlands where France and Germany meet — a region that is both the heart of the European coal and steel industries, and the field on which the continent's wars often have been fought.[101]

In the mid-1950s, as those nations negotiated a broader deal, the British economist James Meade published a much discussed paper arguing that the Bretton Woods Agreement would impede European integration. His argument closely resembled the case made by Friedman: Bretton Woods didn't allow nations to make necessary adjustments in exchange rates. It imposed the same straitjacket as the gold standard: if the productivity of German workers rose more quickly than the productivity of French workers, France would be forced to reduce wages and prices throughout the economy rather than simply adjusting the exchange rate. Meade, like Friedman, argued that European nations should let the market set exchange rates.[102]

Robert Mundell was studying under Meade at the London School of Economics at the time, and he found Meade's argument perverse. "I thought it very strange that countries that were bent on integrating their economies should move to disintegrate their monetary systems," he said.[103] In a 1961 paper, he attacked Meade by following Meade's argument to what he saw as its logical conclusion. Meade had argued a flexible exchange rate was the best way to facilitate an economic relationship between two nations with different economic circumstances. Mundell said the same logic surely applied within nations. If Meade was right, the

United States would benefit from creating one currency for the manufacturing regions of the Northeast and Midwest, and a separate currency for the agricultural South, and then allowing the markets to determine the exchange rate. Moreover, Mundell said, some economically integrated regions of different countries, like the northwestern United States and western Canada, would benefit from sharing a currency. Mundell's point was to argue against floating rates, not to argue for multiple American currencies — or multinational currencies. "It hardly appears within the realm of political feasibility," he wrote, "that national currencies would ever be abandoned in favor of any other arrangement." Yet he added there was one part of the world where both politics and economics might support an experiment with a multinational currency: Western Europe.[104]

Neither Mundell nor Meade made much of an impression on policy makers at the time. Europe remained committed to the Bretton Woods system. But the debate continued to smolder, and the University of Chicago inevitably was the place that kept the embers alive. Mundell, who had become one of the world's most prominent experts on international economics, joined Friedman on the Chicago faculty in 1966. One student recalled the sharp contrast between the two professors. Friedman dressed like a slob but lectured with great care, discussing papers page by page. Mundell wore the latest European fashions and lectured like an improvisational musician, asking many questions and offering few answers. "The air was ripe with thesis topics," another of Mundell's students observed. Sometimes the two professors clashed directly. Friedman insisted international economics was simple: free trade, floating rates, and get out of the way. Mundell, ever more skeptical about floating rates, did not conceal his disdain. "Milton," he said during one such debate, "the trouble with you is you lack common sense."[105]

By the late 1960s, Bretton Woods was no longer providing stability for Europe. In August 1969, France devalued the franc for the first time in a decade; a few months later, Germany increased the value of the mark. Mundell, watching from afar and finding his own theory increasingly convincing, proposed the creation of a new currency: the "EUROPA."

As with Mundell's advocacy for tax cuts, this plan was largely dismissed by other economists. Mundell was regarded as a brilliant theorist, but many of his peers were convinced they understood the practical implications of Mundell's models better than Mundell himself. His 1961 paper, in their view, had made the case that economically integrated regions might benefit from a single currency, but who could argue that France and Germany were economically integrated?

Mundell responded that the creation of a single currency would advance integration. He thought American economists, in particular, were too dismissive of the political benefits. "If the Europe of the 1930s had a democratically run common currency in the 1930s," he said later, "there would have been no World War II."[106] Moreover, and here it mattered that Mundell was Canadian, he argued everyone would benefit from a strengthened Europe able to meet the United States as an equal rather than as a dependent, in the realm of money and everywhere else.

Mundell ended his 1969 speech proposing the EUROPA in a language very different from the dry math of modern economics, declaring, "It is time for Europeans to wake up."[107]

The Europeans instead fought to preserve the Bretton Woods system. Volcker, the American point man in those negotiations, said the vice governor of Belgium's central bank waved a finger in his face and warned, "If all this talk about flexible exchange rates brings down the system, the blood will be on your American head."[108] But after Nixon's speech in 1971, Europe began to chart its own course. The Smithsonian Agreement Nixon announced that December allowed currencies to deviate from the specified exchange rates by as much as 9 percent. A core group of European nations — including France, West Germany, and the United Kingdom — agreed to limit fluctuations among their own currencies to just 4.5 percent.

This first attempt ended in failure. The arrangement was dubbed "the snake in the tunnel," since it left room for wriggling, but amid the economic volatility of the mid-1970s the snakes soon began to leave the tunnel. Britain pulled out after less than two months. Italy didn't quite make it to the end of the first year. France withdrew and returned and then withdrew again.

Yet Europe kept trying. The political imperative for European unity was strong, and in 1979, a core group of nations led by France and West Germany announced a new deal, the European Monetary System. This lasted longer, mostly because the French were willing to suffer. When the socialist François Mitterrand won the presidency in 1981, he promised to "break with capitalism," and France embarked on a last dance with Keynesianism. As Anglophone nations cut public spending and raised interest rates, France sought to revive prosperity by spending money. As Anglophone nations pursued deregulation, Mitterrand nationalized major companies, raised the minimum wage by 10 percent, and shaved an hour off the workweek.

But in 1983, with inflation rising and France's participation in the European Monetary System under pressure, Mitterrand closeted himself with advisers for ten days in the Élysée Palace, where a "modernizing minority," in the words of one member, Finance Minister Jacques Delors, persuaded him to place his faith in markets. Mitterrand announced what came to be known as the "turn toward austerity." Companies were returned to private ownership, public spending was slashed, and wage growth slowed as the state focused on reducing inflation. The unemployment rate hit 10 percent; France remained in the European Monetary System. "The Socialists were converted to ideas that they had previously suspected: the importance of private enterprise, the profit motive, and so on," said the political scientist René Rémond. "To replace the idea of socialism with the idea of modernization is an enormous change."[109]

In 1982, the Italian economist Tommaso Padoa-Schioppa, the European Commission's director of economic affairs, published a paper reviving the case for the creation of a pan-European currency. He wrote in a spirit of frustration, troubled by a resurgence of nationalism. Like many educated and affluent Europeans of his generation, he had been raised as a citizen of Europe. He spoke four languages fluently — he preferred to work in

English because he said that language was most concise and precise — and had lived in West Germany and Belgium.[110]

Padoa-Schioppa wrote that the European Monetary System (EMS), like the Bretton Woods system, was inherently flawed, and for basically the same reasons. It was not flexible enough to survive changes in economic relations among the major participating nations, nor was it rigid enough to force changes in their domestic policies. And the pressure on the system was about to increase, because the members of the EMS were eliminating capital controls, allowing the free flow of investments. The movement of money among European nations was one of the primary economic benefits of integration, but it also made it difficult to maintain fixed exchange rates. In the long run, there were only two viable choices: let rates float, or adopt a single currency.[111]

France wanted West Germany to accept responsibility for the economic health of the rest of Europe as a prerequisite for a unified currency, just as the United States conducted a single fiscal policy for all fifty states, transferring money from prospering to suffering regions. West Germany wanted the rest of Europe to emulate its own frugality and efficiency. But by the early 1990s, both nations were ready to make a deal. The French wanted a currency that would command greater respect in financial markets. Mitterrand told Italian prime minister Giuliano Amato that he was tired of living "at the mercy of volatile capital which does not represent any real wealth, or creation of real goods. It is an intolerable immorality."[112] The West Germans wanted a currency agreement that preserved their ability to make a living off exports, and they needed Europe's political support for the project of German reunification.

The deal was signed in the Dutch city of Maastricht on February 7, 1992.[113] The host, Ruud Lubbers, the Dutch prime minister, was an economist by training who called his country "The Netherlands, Inc.," and, under the slogan "more market, less government," slashed regulation, privatized state-owned companies, and cut spending.[114] But for Lubbers and his guests, the love of markets did not extend to floating exchange rates. As a band played Mozart, Lubbers raised a glass of champagne and invoked the refrain of the croupier as the roulette wheel spins: *"Les jeux sont faits; rien ne va plus."*[115]

The phrase loosely translates as "The die is cast," but Europe had yet to convince skeptics. One of Mundell's colleagues bet him a bottle of wine the plan would not come to fruition. Mundell won the bet. The skeptics continued to underestimate the political imperative. "The European Commission did invite economists to present their views," said Paul De Grauwe, professor of European political economy at the London School of Economics. "It was a Darwinian process. I was invited, but when I expressed my doubts I wasn't invited anymore. In the end only the enthusiasts were left."[116] The participating nations — even Germany — fudged the fiscal requirements so the euro could debut on schedule.* On January 1, 1999, the eleven participating nations fixed exchange rates against the new euro standard.

Mundell won the Nobel Prize later that year. The prize citation said he had provided the model used by both proponents and critics of the euro, but the award was widely interpreted as laurels for the creation of a new kind of currency.[117] Mundell stood before the audience in Stockholm and sang Frank Sinatra's "My Way." Three years later, Europe sent 6 billion euros in notes and 40 billion euros in coins into circulation. The Belgian finance minister took reporters to an ATM, withdrew 150 euros, and declared, "I'm going to start by buying myself a Belgian beer."[118]

The euro is a German currency in the most important respects. The European Central Bank (ECB) is based in Frankfurt, and it operates under instructions to keep inflation low. Moreover, in the deal creating the euro, Germany accepted limited responsibility for the economic health of its new partners. The rest of Europe got to dance with Germany; Germany got to pick the music.[119]

---

* Italy, for example, announced a special onetime "Europe tax" to reduce its fiscal deficit to the required level for a single year. France relied on a onetime payment from France Telecom.

At first, this seemed like a good deal. Sharing a currency really did increase trade. One clever study found former French colonies in Africa that adopted the euro enjoyed a 76 percent increase in trade with members of the eurozone.[120] European nations found they could borrow money at very nearly the same interest rates as the Germans. This, too, seemed like a good deal at first: they borrowed vast sums and spent quite a bit of the money on German goods. Prosperity increased across the eurozone, particularly in the less affluent periphery; inequality declined.[121]

But there was a catch. Padoa-Schioppa, who became a member of the ECB's board, was among the first to describe the euro as "a currency without a state." There was still no mechanism for the prosperous parts of Europe to ease the pain of inevitable downturns. If the economy falters in Mississippi, the Federal Reserve does not cut interest rates to revive growth, because that would cause inflation in Texas. Instead, the federal government spends more money in Mississippi. But in Europe, the only recourse for Mississippis like Greece and Spain was to punish workers. One economist surveying the European scene observed, "When things are going well, a fixed exchange rate system sings like a bird. When things are going badly, it shits like an elephant."[122]

After the 2008 crisis, peripheral European nations began to feel the weight of that lesson. Like the United States, they had borrowed and consumed and lived beyond their means. Unlike the United States, they could not revive growth by borrowing more money, or by reducing the value of a national currency. The ECB provided some assistance in the form of lower interest rates, but its policies were calibrated for the whole of the euro zone, which meant the stimulus was grossly insufficient for Spain or Greece. Germany and other nations with stronger economies mostly resisted calls to provide help in the form of government spending or debt relief. Excepting Germany and a few smaller neighbors, unemployment across the eurozone remained high and inequality increased. Much of Europe experienced a lost decade.

Yet the euro not only endured, but remained popular in the nations that suffered most. In Finland, economic output per capita in 2017 was 5 percent smaller than a decade earlier, adjusting for inflation, but Finns remained wealthier than before the country tied itself to Germany two decades earlier. The nation's leaders continued to bet on the benefits of monetary union. "Devaluation is a little like doping in sports," Alexander Stubb, Finland's finance minister, said in 2015. "It gives you perhaps a short-term boost, but in the long run, it's not beneficial. Just like anyone else, we need structural reform, structural adjustment; we need to increase our competitiveness, and a little bit of luck."[123]

Chapter Nine

Made in Chile

Two years ago an economist friend remarked that he and I were
the only economists of his acquaintance who had not developed
an underdeveloped country. Since he has spent the last year
developing one, I feel very much alone.

— *Charles Hitch, "The Uses of Economics" (1960)*[1]

In 1942, the United States shipped a Princeton graduate named Albion
Patterson to Paraguay as part of an effort to teach the secrets of prosperity to the rest of the New World.[2] Patterson's job was to help farmers
in the South American nation grow more food, but he was stymied by a
lack of the most basic information about existing agricultural conditions.
He wrote home requesting the aid of an economist to gather data, but he
received no response. "Economics had not been discovered by Washington," Patterson dryly recalled years later.[3] Next he went to the local university, but economists there did not share his views about economic
development. Most Latin American economists wanted to pursue prosperity through industrialization, as the United States had done in the
previous century. The United States, by contrast, wanted South America
to focus on exporting food and raw materials — and to import goods
from American factories. The greed of American policy makers was
intertwined with the conviction that state-sponsored industrialization
led to communism. Patterson considered Paraguay's economists "pink."[4]

When Patterson was promoted and sent to Chile in 1953, he decided the
first step in reshaping the Chilean economy was to reshape the local econo-

mists. "What we need to do is to change the formation of the men, to influ-ence the education, which is very bad," he told the American ambassador.[5] Serendipitously, just a few months later, Theodore W. Schultz, the chairman of the economics department at the University of Chicago, walked into Pat-terson's office. Schultz was visiting Chile as the head of a federal commission sent to investigate the best ways to promote development in Latin America, and his appointment prefigured the conclusion: he was perhaps the world's leading proponent of the theory that education is the highway to prosperity. Education had allowed Schultz to escape from a hardscrabble farm in the Dakotas, and he was convinced the rest of the world could do it, too. "Fewer steel mills and other big plants should be built in the underdeveloped coun-tries, and more invested in the people of those countries, as we have invested in ourselves," he wrote.[6] Schultz, who later won a Nobel Prize for these ideas, made a powerful impression on the rest of the U.S. delegation. William Ben-ton, a former senator from Connecticut, wrote upon returning home that there were "few ways to contribute to the well-being of mankind that can match the needed development of Latin America's universities."[7]

Patterson, also enamored, went to the University of Chile and pro-posed a partnership with the economics department at the University of Chicago, funded by the U.S. government. Patterson said he picked Chi-cago not just because of Schultz, but because he regarded its economics faculty as "the best free-market group" in the United States. Luis Escobar Cerda, the head of the University of Chile's economics department, declined for the same reason. He later compared the Chicago proposal to "sending all the students to the University Patrice Lumumba in the Soviet Union."[8] Seeking a middle road between faith in markets and faith in state planning, Cerda recruited an economics professor from Columbia University in New York to improve the curriculum.

Patterson, undeterred, next knocked on the door of Santiago's Uni-versidad Católica, a less rigorous institution that catered to the children of the conservative elite. The bishop who ran the place told Patterson that he'd welcome funding for agricultural instruction.

"Let us forget agriculture," Patterson replied. "Let's work together in economics."[9]

*   *   *

Of all the Spanish colonies in the New World, Chile was the most remote: a long, thin strip of land sandwiched between the Andes Mountains and the Pacific Ocean, and capped at the north end by the Atacama Desert, the driest place on Earth. Residents and visitors spoke of Chile as an island; the local version of Spanish remains difficult for outsiders to understand.

The early settlers found a little gold, then turned to raising animals and wheat, dividing the available lands into a handful of great estates worked by tenant farmers. Charles Darwin, visiting in the 1830s, observed that the "feudal-like" system kept most Chileans in extreme poverty.

In the decades that followed, Chileans found a measure of prosperity by exporting the ground beneath their feet, first mining nitrates and then copper.[10] But as the United States industrialized and prospered, Chile stagnated. In 1913, income per capita in Chile was 50 percent of income per capita in the United States. By 1975, the figure was 27 percent.[11]

After World War II, as Chile's population boomed — and as voting rights were expanded — political leaders began to pursue economic growth with greater urgency, attempting to break up the great agricultural estates and to promote industrialization.[12] Raúl Prebisch, an Argentine economist hired by the United Nations to run a think tank devoted to South America's development, advanced the influential view that the continent needed to turn inward. He said sustainable prosperity was built on manufacturing, and he recommended sheltering domestic industry from foreign competition through measures like high tariffs.

This emphasis on production, and on government as the nursemaid of industry, was the recipe Britain had used to become the world's first industrial power. It was also the recipe Alexander Hamilton wrote down for the young United States in his famous "Report on Manufactures" in 1791. "By enhancing the charges on foreign articles," Hamilton wrote, policy makers can "enable the national manufacturers to undersell all their foreign competitors." Modern economics began as a protest movement against this idea, which was known as mercantilism. The British economist David

Ricardo insisted nations would prosper by opening their borders to trade. He famously advised Portugal to focus on making wine and to buy its cloth from England. But Ricardo's proof that trade was more efficient than protectionism only applied to a moment in time. A nation that followed Ricardo's advice might remain a nation of winemakers, while a nation that invested in development might achieve greater prosperity.

The United States followed Hamilton's advice and surpassed Britain as the world's leading economy. The German economist Friedrich List absorbed Hamilton's ideas while spending several years in Pennsylvania as a political exile in the late 1820s and early 1830s. He then taught his own nation the value of sheltering its young industries from foreign competition. Of Britain's advocacy for free trade in the nineteenth century, List wryly noted, "It is a very common clever device that when anyone has attained the summit of greatness, he kicks away the ladder by which he has climbed up, in order to deprive others of the means of climbing up after him. In this lies the secret of the cosmopolitan doctrine of Adam Smith...and of all his successors in the British government."[13]

List, in turn, had a major influence on the leaders of the Meiji restoration in Japan, who followed the recipe to build another of the world's industrial powers.[14] Several of Japan's neighbors, including South Korea and Taiwan, followed its example in the twentieth century.

But the United States, like Britain, did not want other nations to emulate its path to prosperity. The American Empire, the largest and most powerful the world has known, was primarily a system of economic rather than political controls. The goal was not to rule other nations, but to make money. And in pursuit of that goal, the United States during the twentieth century repeatedly demonstrated the kind of freedom it was most interested in promoting was free trade. It helped to overthrow democratically elected governments in nations including Guatemala, Iran, and Indonesia because they were insufficiently excited about America's kind of capitalism. When Thomas Jefferson cribbed one of his most famous lines from the English political philosopher John Locke, he changed one crucial word. Locke said humankind's inalienable rights included life, liberty, and property; Jefferson replaced property with "the pursuit of happiness."* American foreign policy during the American Century reverted to Locke's version.

Chile tried to develop an industrial base. During the 1950s and the 1960s, the government took a stake in the nation's major copper mines, and state-subsidized factories cranked out Chilean cars, radios, and refrigerators, among other goods. But Albion Patterson, the University of Chicago, and the U.S. government all helped to make sure Chile did not succeed. Today the average Chilean earns half as much as the average resident of Taiwan.

When the first Chilean students arrived at the University of Chicago in the fall of 1956, they were taken under wing by Arnold Harberger, an economics professor who was an expert on international development and a fluent Spanish speaker. During World War II, the army had decided that Harberger could best serve his country by learning Spanish, but after completing graduate school, he was assigned to work at a German prisoner-of-war camp in Illinois. His Spanish proved more valuable during the Cold War. He oversaw a rapid expansion of the university's program for Latin American students; during the 1960s, one third of Chicago's graduate students in economics came from Chile and other Latin countries.

Harberger and other Chicago professors dissected Latin America's economic policies in their classrooms, elaborating free-market alternatives and encouraging their students to write in the same vein. Harberger described himself as a "missionary" for the utility of economics. "I believe, more than most economists, in the great strength and pervasiveness of economic forces, and in the power of economic policy to do all sorts of things," he said. The great lesson he sought to impart was a "firm, unshaking conviction that market forces really work." In his judgment, this was a matter of fact rather than faith. Ideology led people into error; economics was anchored in truth. "It is our job to see that the voice of sound economics is heard by those who make decisions," he said. "This is what I have been fighting for, for almost all of my professional life."[15]

---

* Locke's phrase was "life, liberty, and estate."

The Chilean students saw relatively little of Milton Friedman. All graduate students in economics took his course in economic theory, and some of the Chilean students participated in his monetary workshop, but only one, Rolf Lüders, wrote a thesis supervised by Friedman, predictably entitled "A Monetary History of Chile."[16] Even in that instance, Friedman was a disengaged mentor — he did not read the final version of Lüders's work. "He told me, 'There are economists who read and economists who write, and I am an economist who writes,'" Lüders recalled.[17]

In Chicago, the Chileans called themselves the "Chicago Tigers" and talked about reforming not just Chile, but the rest of Latin America. Back in Chile, they found a country with very little interest in their ideas. They had been guaranteed teaching jobs at Católica, but their doctrinaire, youthful arrogance did not go over well with students just a few years younger. The new professors were nicknamed "Los Chicago Boys." Even worse, outside the university, they were ignored. "The Chilean community does not appreciate the full potential value it can derive from the discovery of new knowledge about its economy," said an understated 1959 evaluation of the program's impact.[18] James O. Bray, an economist who spent a few years at Católica, said Chileans concluded "that the Chicagoans either were dishonest tools of Yankee policy or else they were very stupid."[19]

But as Chilean politics shifted to the left, the Chicago Boys began to find an audience among conservatives seeking a counterweight. In 1967, a group of businessmen provided money for the economics department to open its own campus, a few miles from the rest of the university. In 1968, the nation's leading newspaper, *El Mercurio*, created an economics section written and edited by Chicago Boys. But they remained outsiders. In the 1970 presidential election, Chileans faced a choice of three candidates: the socialist Salvador Allende, who wanted to double down on economic management; Radomiro Tomic, a centrist; and the conservative Jorge Alessandri, who met with some of the Chicago Boys and then told an aide, "Get those crazy people out of here. I don't want to see them again."[20]

After Allende's narrow victory, some of the Chicago Boys left Chile. One recalled being searched at the Santiago airport by a Communist youth group and thinking, "Thank God I'm leaving this shitty country."[21]

Freedom from Freedom

In Chile, as in the United States, the ascendancy of free-market economics began with a loss of confidence in the government's management of the
economy. Allende significantly expanded public spending, creating a brief
economic boom followed by an explosion of inflation. The government
responded by imposing wide-ranging price controls, with predictable
results: bread was so cheap that pig farmers bought loaves for animal feed
while thousands of housewives marched on the presidential palace banging pots and pans to protest food shortages.

The country was divided between those seeking redress for exploita-
tion and those seeking to avoid expropriation. Truck drivers, panicked by
rumors the government planned to take ownership of their trucks,
launched a paralyzing strike. The CIA, operating under instructions
from President Nixon to "make the economy scream," did what it could to
deepen Chile's misery — for example, by giving money to the striking
truckers — but the message that the United States wanted a new government was probably more consequential than the sabotage itself.[22] On
September 11, 1973, the Chilean military seized power; Allende shot
himself with a gun he had been given by Fidel Castro.

One of the Chicago Boys, Sergio de Castro, recalled feeling "infinite
happiness" as he watched the Chilean military bomb the presidential palace.[23] Anticipating the likelihood of a coup, de Castro had organized a
small group to refine the economic ideas that Alessandri had rejected
during the 1970 campaign. They raced to print and deliver to Chile's new
leaders copies of the document — which they had dubbed *"El Ladrillo"*
(The Brick), because of its size.

But the military junta, led by the army general Augusto Pinochet,
had seized power to reverse Allende's economic revolution, not to start a
new one.[24] A few days after the coup, Pinochet asked an aide what was
this "brick" he kept hearing about? The aide said he had not bothered to
bring it to Pinochet's attention "because it is the most free-market and

Manchesterian capitalism plan that has ever been written."* The military was not inclined to let the market make decisions. When one adviser proposed to end controls on the price of bread, Pinochet took him to an army barracks and said, "Now, explain to them why the price of bread is going up."[25]

As the Chilean economy continued to unravel, however, reversing Allende's policies began to seem insufficient as a corrective. Pinochet told advisers that over the previous few decades the country had tried various degrees of economic management, and none had worked.[26] Milton Friedman had often said the best way to sell an idea is to make sure that it's ready. When the general went looking for something new, the Chicago Boys were there to provide it.

To make the case, they turned to Friedman himself. One of the Chicago Boys, who had become a wealthy businessman, paid for Friedman and Harberger to travel to Chile in March 1975 for a week of public speeches and private meetings, including a forty-five-minute session with Pinochet. As was his custom, Friedman offered the same advice in public and private: Chile should sharply reduce the creation of new money, which in turn required a sharp reduction in government spending. He memorialized this monetarist prescription, which he called "shock treatment," in a letter to Pinochet after their meeting. Gradual change was "not feasible," he wrote, because the economic pain might induce second thoughts.[27] As he told *Business Week*, "My only concern is that they push it long enough and hard enough."[28]

Chile's conservative elite had a long history of seeking advice from foreign economists, and the advice had always been the same: the government needed to go on a diet. In the 1850s, Chile hired a French economist to provide this advice. In the 1920s, it was Edwin Kemmerer, a Princeton professor dubbed "the money doctor of the Andes."[29] In the 1950s, it was

---

* "Manchesterian" is a synonym for "free-market," deriving from the English industrial city's role as an early hotbed of advocacy for an end to protectionist policies like the Corn Laws and, more broadly, for trade as the engine of prosperity.

Julius Klein, a Harvard professor whom *Reader's Digest* called "the private-enterprise doctor to undeveloped nations."[30] The novelty of Friedman's visit was not the advice but that Pinochet took it to heart.[31] In April 1975, the general convened his economic advisers at the presidential retreat at Cerro Castillo and decided to subject Chile to shock treatment.

Economists like to compare themselves to doctors, willing to treat any patient. But doctors seek the consent of their patients. The Chicago Boys had failed to obtain the political consent of the Chilean people. They persuaded one man; the rest of Chile had no choice. The military junta killed more than three thousand of its opponents and thousands more went into exile. Orlando Letelier, Chile's ambassador to the United States under Allende, wrote in a 1976 article in *The Nation* that the Pinochet regime's brutal overhaul of the economy was enabled by its brutal suppression of dissent. One month later, Chilean agents acting on Pinochet's orders murdered Letelier by blowing up his car in the middle of Washington, D.C.[32]

Some of the most prominent Chicago Boys, including de Castro and Lüders, have since agreed with Letelier that the policies implemented under Pinochet required an authoritarian regime. De Castro told a documentary filmmaker in 2012 that he had not known about the regime's atrocities at the time. And if he had? He paused and said, "I would have helped just the same."[33]

For almost seven years, de Castro exercised wide-ranging authority to reshape the Chilean economy.

He was born on January 25, 1930, to Chilean expatriates who lived in neighboring Bolivia, although de Castro's mother returned to Santiago to give birth. His father worked for an import firm that specialized in English goods, then found success in the mining industry. The Great Depression hit Chile almost as hard as the United States, and Bolivia suffered, too, but de Castro's childhood was largely unaffected.[34] At the age of thirteen, he was sent back to Santiago to study at the Grange, an elite private school that emphasized the importance of learning English. After graduation, he studied in Canada before returning once more to Santiago and enrolling at Católica. He was in his fourth year of studies when Schultz and Harberger arrived to negotiate the Chicago exchange program. De Castro served as an interpreter, then was selected as one of the first students to go to Chicago. Returning to Católica with a master's degree, he led a coup against the old faculty and was named chairman of the economics department. He did very little research; from the outset, his interest was in government.

His sympathetic biographer, Patricia Arancibia Clavel, described him as "intelligent, without political ambition and convinced that his ideas were good for Chile."[35] He also had the courage of those convictions. At an early meeting with Pinochet, de Castro argued for the privatization of textile factories. Pinochet wasn't interested, declaring, "Gentlemen, I am the one who holds the pot by the handle." De Castro retorted, "Well, Mr. President, you might be left just holding the handle."[36]

Once de Castro came to power, first as economics minister and then as finance minister, he began as he had promised, by slashing government spending. The public sector's share of economic activity fell from 40 percent in 1973 to 26 percent in 1979.

De Castro also opened Chile to imports, reducing the top tariff rate to 10 percent and eliminating a wide range of other restrictions. Japanese cars and motorbikes poured into the country, as many as two thousand a week, doubling the number of passenger vehicles in Chile between 1975 and 1981.[37] Shops in downtown Santiago displayed designer clothing behind new glass windows; shops in less affluent neighborhoods sold used clothing from the United States.

In embracing trade, however, Chile was abandoning its dreams of industrialization. More than 100,000 factory jobs, about a fifth of the total, disappeared during the first decade of military rule.[38] A journalist surveyed the twenty-two families on a single block in the Santiago shantytown of Violeta Parra in September 1977 — Chileans called such places *callampas*, a local term for mushrooms — and found only eight men had regular jobs. "There are families here that only eat cornmeal once a day," said Julio Rocha, among the luckier men because he had part-time work as a wicker weaver. "No one here has any money to buy those Japanese TV sets that they say are so cheap."[39] In the *callampa* of Las Rejas, a mother who could not afford milk for her children said she was afraid to complain. "You must understand that before, although things were bad, we could go anywhere we wanted, and we could unburden ourselves," she said. "Now we cannot."[40]

The Chicago Boys and Friedman had warned Pinochet the shock treatment would cause considerable pain, but they also said the pain would be fleeting. "You'd be surprised how fast people would be absorbed by a growing private-sector economy," Friedman told Chileans during one of his public lectures in Santiago.[41] Lüders said he and his colleagues also fully expected growth would reduce economic inequality. Instead, official unemployment stayed above 10 percent for the rest of the 1970s, and inequality soared.

As the economy finally rebounded from recession in the late 1970s, supporters of free-market policies began to applaud what they called an economic miracle. Friedrich Hayek, after visiting in 1977, said Chile was benefiting economically and politically. "I have not been able to find a single person even in much maligned Chile who did not agree that personal freedom was much greater under Pinochet than it had been under Allende," he said.[42] But his methodology may have been compromised by his inability to interview the many thousands already killed or exiled.

Four years later, in 1981, Hayek's free-market Mont Pelerin Society held a meeting in Chile, a decision widely seen as a seal of approval. But there was little cause for celebration. The growth of the late 1970s and early 1980s only served to offset the recession of the early Pinochet years. In 1973, when Pinochet seized power, income per capita in Chile was about 12 percent higher than the average for Latin America. By 1981, the difference once again was approaching 12 percent.[43]

Then de Castro and the Chicago Boys crashed the Chilean economy for the second time.

Economists in the midcentury had supported the freedom to trade across borders, but not the freedom to invest across borders. They regarded limits on the international movement of money as necessary to preserve economic stability, especially in smaller countries. The sheer scale of capital flows could cause distortions; the volatility of the flows could cause crises. "Nothing is more certain," Keynes wrote in the 1940s, "than that the movement of capital funds must be regulated."[44]

Ending those restrictions was a goal dear to Friedman and the financial industry. Friedman's objections went beyond his normal distaste for government. He noted the Nazis had used capital controls to consolidate political power; in his view, it was one of the most powerful tools available "to enable the state to control its citizens."[45] Just as anything less than free trade was a step toward communism, anything less than the free flow of money moved society toward totalitarianism.

As Keynesianism crumbled in the 1970s, capital controls crumbled, too — a victim of the change in the ideological weather and of practical difficulties in checking the resurgence of finance. In January 1974, Friedman's friend, Treasury Secretary George Shultz, announced the elimination of America's limits on capital flows. "I rejoice," he told investors, in the restoration of "the freedom to invest your funds where you think the prospects are most promising."[46]

The first time Friedman met Margaret Thatcher, over dinner in 1978, he urged her to make elimination of Britain's capital controls, in place since World War II, her first priority upon taking office. Thatcher suspended the controls in October 1979, a few months after she became prime minister. "Hooray for Margaret Thatcher!" Friedman said upon hearing the news.[47]

Chile was one of the first smaller countries to get rid of its capital controls — just as the Latin American debt boom was ramping up. The country also sharply reduced financial regulation, among other things allowing the nation's two largest conglomerates to acquire the two largest banks. This had the unsurprising effect of significantly increasing borrowing. By the early 1980s, Chile's interest payments to its foreign creditors were the most burdensome of any Latin American country, requiring 12.9 percent of its annual economic output.[48]

The trouble began, somewhat ironically, because the United States embraced Friedman's advice on another subject. The Federal Reserve's campaign against inflation drove up interest rates, and Chilean borrowers found it impossible to pay their dollar-denominated debts. As the economy crashed, de Castro insisted the market should sort winners and losers. But public opinion, and Pinochet, turned in favor of intervention; de Castro was removed from office.

"Everyone here just went a little further than they should have — and in this, the state has a lot of blame. Because nothing was ever done to stop it," complained one Chilean businessman.[49] As the government stepped in, nationalizing much of the banking industry, raising tariffs, and restoring regulation, Chileans joked about the "Chicago road to socialism."

But Pinochet didn't stay on the new road for long. For one thing, Chile had discarded its supply of other kinds of economists. The Pinochet regime had purged the economics faculties at the major universities, removing professors who did not preach the free-market line. At the University of Chile, six economics students had been shot on campus in the early days following the 1973 coup.[50] Herberto Aguirre, a student at the time, was imprisoned and tortured. He told me that he was lucky, because he also was released. But when he left prison, he knew better than to resume his studies in economics. He earned a degree in computer science instead.

As the economy improved, Pinochet installed a new cadre of free-market economists. The Chilean government had socialized the cost of the downturn; now it allowed the wealthy to profit from the recovery. This path was reinforced by the International Monetary Fund (IMF) and the World Bank, which provided financial assistance to the Chilean government.[51]

Those institutions, created as part of the Bretton Woods system to encourage the development of the international economy, emerged in the 1980s as zealots in the cause of market freedom, including the free flow of investment dollars across borders. That this freedom was a cause of Chile's crisis did not alter their view that it was also a remedy.[52]

Interestingly, the radicalization of the IMF was catalyzed by French socialists — not the conservative governments in the United States and

Britain.[53] The French finance minister Jacques Delors argued that capital controls mostly punished the middle class, since the wealthy simply evaded the rules. Ending the controls, he said, was a blow against inequality.

West Germany had long shared Friedman's aversion to capital controls, and for the same historical reasons.[54] With the French on board, the European Community mandated an end to all controls in 1988. The next year, again at the behest of the French, the Organization for Economic Cooperation and Development (OECD), which seeks to coordinate the economic policies of developed nations with democratic governments, adopted an informal but influential commitment to eliminate capital controls.

As the OECD began to add some emerging economies as members in the 1990s, it required those countries to eliminate their capital controls. But it didn't have to press the issue — developing nations were eager to adopt the trappings of success. Mexico was the first to meet the requirements and join the club, in 1994, and it immediately suffered a financial crisis. The Czech Republic joined in 1995, and it, too, quickly suffered a financial crisis.

Michel Camdessus, the French socialist and economist who ran the IMF, which also backed the elimination of controls, responded by arguing strenuously against the obvious conclusion. "It would be an egregious mistake to seek to prevent financial crises by reverting to a closed economic system with exchange controls and less open markets," Camdessus said. "To do this would be to try to turn the clock back and forego the benefits of globalization."[55]

Camdessus won his point, but a quarter century later, economists have yet to find evidence that the free flow of capital has increased growth, or reduced inequality.[56] What the world has learned, repeatedly, is that capital flows can and do cause financial crises.[57]

Milton Friedman was widely portrayed as the godfather of Chile's economic transformation. Some regarded this as a mark of distinction. "It seems when Milton Friedman talked, someone in Chile listened," Ronald Reagan said in a December 1976 radio commentary. "Wouldn't it be nice if just once someone in Washington would ask, 'What did he say?'"[58]

Others saw it as a scarlet letter. When Friedman was awarded the Nobel Prize the year after his visit to Chile, four laureates in other disciplines wrote letters of protest; the ceremony was disrupted by a heckler.[59] Questions about Chile trailed Friedman for the rest of his life.

The focus on Friedman obscured the fact that his role in Chile was typical of American foreign policy. Suharto's bloody takeover of Indonesia in the mid-1960s was a particularly instructive precedent. Indeed, the word "Jakarta" was spray-painted on walls around Santiago in 1972 as a pointed warning to Allende's supporters.[60] The Ford Foundation had funded a training program for Indonesian economists at the University of California, Berkeley. Suharto studied under one of those economists in college; when he came to power, he installed several of those economists, known as the Berkeley Mafia, to pursue the standard menu of opening up trade, privatization of state-owned industries, and a painful crackdown on inflation.[61] While Indonesia's technocrats didn't push free-market measures as far as their counterparts in Chile, the similarity between the lessons taught at liberal Berkeley and conservative Chicago is a reminder that differences among mainstream American economists were easily overstated.

By Harberger's count, more than twenty of his students have served as central bank governors or finance ministers across Latin America. The Reagan administration regarded the University of Chicago's program as such a success that in the late 1980s, George Shultz, then serving as secretary of state, launched a program to train a new generation of Latin American economists. Consulting with Harberger, the administration chose four universities, including Santiago's Católica, with economics faculties dominated by professors trained in the United States.[62]

But neither Reagan nor Thatcher — nor any democratically elected government — sought to carry out the full measure of Chilean-style economic reforms in their own countries. In 1982, Hayek wrote to Thatcher urging the example of Chile. Thatcher responded, "I am sure you will agree that in Britain, with our democratic institutions and the need for a high degree of consent, some of the measures adopted in Chile are quite unacceptable."[63]

Chileans, too, seized the earliest opportunity to end the rule of the Chicago Boys. In 1988, Pinochet held a plebiscite, expecting the nation to ratify another eight years of autocracy. The general ran on his economic record; his opponents ran against it, and won by a wide margin, clearing the way for the election of a new government in 1990.

"Growth with Equity"

For most of Latin America, the 1982 debt crisis was the beginning of a "lost generation." Not until 1998 did the income of the average Mexican recover.[64]

For Chile, by contrast, the crisis marked the beginning of an economic boom driven by the export of its natural resources. This was a cornerstone of the Chicago Boys' economic plan. In the words of Álvaro Bardón, a Chicago Boy who served as president of Chile's central bank in the late 1970s: "If comparative advantage determines that Chile should produce nothing but melons, then we will produce nothing but melons."[65]

The rewards of that strategy are highly visible. Santiago, the capital, commercial center, and by far Chile's largest city, is a modern metropolis with a gleaming skyline, a financial district locals call "Sanhattan," and streets full of immigrants who have come to Chile in search of a better life. Even the country's problems increasingly are the problems of prosperity: obesity instead of hunger; consumer debt instead of deprivation.

Copper remains the most important export, but Chile has developed new lines in fruit, wood, and salmon. The pink fish is native to the Northern Hemisphere; there were no salmon off Chile's coast fifty years ago. But in 1974, the American company Union Carbide identified the cold, sheltered waters off Chile's southern coast as a promising venue for the new business of raising salmon in captivity. The military government, eager to attract investment, soon struck deals with Japanese and Norwegian companies, too. By the end of the century, Chile was the world's second-largest salmon producer, trailing only Norway. Nightly flights carried fresh filets to Miami, and from there to supermarkets and restaurants across the United States.

Chile's economic growth has drastically reduced extreme poverty in the country, and salmon farming has played the dominant role along the southern coast, where the industry employs more than seventy thousand people.[66] But the profits are distributed unevenly. Transporting salmon from Chile to the Northern Hemisphere is expensive; for Chile to compete with northern fish farms, production has to be cheap. Salmon workers in Norway are paid more than three times as much as their counterparts in Chile.[67] Under Pinochet's regime, employers prevented the formation of labor unions. After the return of democracy, some workers formed unions, but Chilean law still imposes some of the most restrictive limits on collective bargaining anywhere in the developed world. In 2001, female workers at a salmon processing plant who earned an average of $130 a month went on strike seeking a raise of $15 a month. The company responded by firing 10 percent of the women, a literal decimation.[68]

Chile also has struggled to build on its successes in the relatively low-value business of producing food. The Danish shipping giant Maersk opened a $200 million factory in the Chilean port city of San Antonio in 2015, to build the refrigerated containers that it needs to ship Chilean fruit to foreign markets. The factory was celebrated as a breakthrough — evidence Chile's economy was creating better-paying jobs. Although the Chilean constitution, written under Pinochet, tightly circumscribes the government's ability to support private enterprise, Chile funded training programs for the factory's workforce. But less than three years later, in the spring of 2018, Maersk announced it was closing the factory and moving production to China. The company said it had struggled to find local suppliers in Chile for the parts that it needed to make the containers.[69]

Similarly, a growing share of the copper mined in Chile is refined in other countries. Codelco, the leading copper company, is so important to the Chilean economy that it has remained under state ownership. But Patricio Meller, a former director of Codelco, said Chile has failed to take the long view. "We have 30 percent of the world copper market," he said. "How come 30 percent of research and development is not done here?

How come 30 percent of the machines are not made here? That's where you should develop competitive advantage."[70]

Instead, Chile has sought to hold down costs at the expense of its future. In the province of Petorca, between Santiago and the ocean, thick groves of avocado trees are spread like green carpets over the sere hills. Chileans eat the fruit—hot dogs are often dressed with mashed avocado—but most of the crop is exported, and demand is so high that growers are draining the region's rivers, leaving residents without water. Instead of constraining an important industry, the government delivers water to the villages by truck, and the water is often dirty. "In order to send good avocados to Europeans, we end up drinking water with shit in it," one of the villagers said.[71]

Unequal growth, however, is not the primary reason that Santiago remains a city with an abundance of helicopter pads on the roofs of its downtown skyscrapers and shantytowns on its fringes. Chile's inequality is primarily the result of the indifference of its political leaders.

The standard measures of inequality assess the distribution of household income after taxes are paid and government benefits are received. This, after all, is the lived reality of inequality. And by this measure, the extent of inequality in Chile is an extreme outlier among developed nations.

But the initial distribution of income, before taxes and government transfers, is highly unequal throughout the developed world. It is actually less unequal in Chile than in France or Germany or the United States. What makes Chile different is that its government does less than almost any other developed nation to reduce inequality.[72]

Chile, blessed with natural resources, could use the money to build a more generous social safety net. The Chilean central bank has estimated that government spending as a share of the economy is significantly below average.[73] But a striking feature of Chilean politics is the breadth of consensus that government should not do more.

The return of democracy produced only a modest shift in economic policy. The government took some steps to soften the inequities of the

Pinochet era, like raising the minimum wage and imposing controls on foreign capital. But the emphasis was on continuity. Indeed, the new government doubled down on free trade, reducing tariffs, and spending on social welfare programs remained austere by the standards of the developed world.

The Chicago Boys and their admirers say Chile's prosperity induced the political left to embrace markets. Actually, in 1990, Chile still was less prosperous than Cuba.[74]

Alejandro Foxley, the finance minister in the first post-Pinochet administration, told me the new government emphasized continuity because it judged that Chileans did not want to live through another period of disruptive change. "They did not want another shock," he said. "They wanted to feel good about their lives."[75] The government also was constrained by laws written under Pinochet — and by Pinochet himself, who remained the head of the nation's military until 1998.

But Chile's aversion to redistribution outlasted Pinochet. In 2000, the nation elected a socialist president, Ricardo Lagos, for the first time since Allende. But Lagos, who held a doctorate in economics from Duke, didn't sound like socialists in other places. As transportation minister in the early 1990s, he had expanded the nation's highway system by recruiting private companies to build toll roads. As president, he declared that fostering economic growth was his priority, "then we are going to discuss how are we going to distribute the outcome of that growth, and not the other way around."[76] He added, "It seems to me that it's extremely dangerous to have a general who likes to have a coup, but probably it's more dangerous to have a finance minister that is a populist." Even Chile's leading socialist preferred Pinochet to Allende.[77]

The situation has not changed much in the last two decades. Chile has alternated between liberal and conservative governments, but economic policy has mostly held steady.

The consequences of this indifference to inequality stretch from birth to death.

Wealthy Chileans are born in private rooms in private clinics. The leading newspaper, *El Mercurio*, publishes the names of newborns at the fanciest Santiago clinics. On the other side of town, at the city's best public hospital, twelve mothers share a room on the maternity ward. Infant mortality declined from 63 per 1000 births in 1973 to 9.2 per 1000 births in 2000 — only a little higher than in the United States. But that is an average. In Lo Espejo, an inner-city neighborhood of dense housing projects, infant mortality was four times higher in 2000 than in Lo Barnechea, where the wealthy live in mansions on the lower slopes of the Andes.[78]

The government does even less for the elderly. The social security system was privatized in the early 1980s. The architect, José Piñera, was a member of the second generation of Chilean free-market economists. He studied under the Chicago Boys, then earned a doctorate at Harvard and joined Pinochet's government on a mission to replace Chile's system of government-backed pensions.[79] He rolled out the new system on May Day 1981 because, he said, the plan "gave freedom and dignity to our nation's workers."[80] The system has been emulated by more than thirty countries, mostly developing nations in South America, Asia, and Eastern Europe. In 2001, President George W. Bush hosted Ricardo Lagos at the White House and said that the United States could "take some lessons from Chile."* Indeed, it is hard to imagine a better lesson in the nature of free-market policies. The system requires Chilean workers to invest at least 10 percent of their salaries with private companies, which has helped to deepen financial markets and to fuel the expansion of the corporate sector. But this pension system does not provide adequate pensions. The average monthly benefit, which is based on the worker's individual contributions, is a little more than $300 — less than a month's pay at the legal minimum wage. The basic reason is economic inequality: most Chileans don't make enough money to provide for their own needs in old age. (Pinochet, anticipating the failure of his own system, insisted that members of the military would continue to receive a minimum pension

---

* Bush did. In 2005, he proposed the partial privatization of America's Social Security system.

guaranteed by the government.) A compounding issue is that the Chilean government is sponsoring a cartel, a small group of investment companies that charge exorbitant fees on the savings plans. The result is a system that transfers wealth from the poor to the rich — exactly the opposite of the way that social security works in most developed nations.

In 2016, almost 10 percent of Chile's population poured into the streets of Santiago and smaller cities to protest the pension system in the largest political demonstration since Pinochet's fall. "I've worked my entire life and I'd like to stop and rest, but I can't," said Luis Montero, a sixty-nine-year-old whose pension benefits only amounted to about $150 a month. "I have no idea what I will do when I get older."[81]

Chileans are proud their country has become, by many measures, the most prosperous in Latin America, and they tend to regard free markets as the magic sauce. The agony of Venezuela, which once held the title of "most prosperous Latin nation," is widely seen in Chile as an object lesson in the dangers of government meddling in economic policy. During Chile's national elections in 2017, the right-wing candidate, Sebastián Piñera — the younger brother of José Piñera and, like his brother, an economist with a doctorate from Harvard — warned that his opponent would turn the country into "Chilezuela." Piñera won handily.

Chile's politics also are shaped by declining participation. The sociologist Alberto Mayol says that lower-income Chileans feel powerless to improve their lot. "You can shoot a landlord, but you cannot shoot a bank," he said. Middle-income Chileans, meanwhile, are statistically even less likely to vote than the poor. Mayol says that's because the middle class has little interaction with the government. Their water and electricity are provided by private companies; they send their children to private schools; they are treated at private clinics; they drive on private roads. The rich and poor want favors from the government, but Chile's middle class doesn't care.

Yet there are visible signs of frustration among the younger generation. In 2011, students poured into the streets to protest the high price of education, some carrying signs that read "Less Friedman and More

Keynes." Seven years later, in the summer of 2018, students at several universities went on strike, piling up desks at campus gates in a protest sparked by the handling of sexual assault cases, but reflective of a broader sense of disenfranchisement. I picked my way through a barricade and sat with students on the front steps of the University of Chile's law school, long an incubator for the nation's political leaders.

"No one can say that the country today is not more prosperous. It's data," said Maria Astudillo, a twenty-four-year-old student at the school. "But the way that growth was generated means that a lot of people don't have access to education, to health, to food." The political left, she said, has "fallen asleep," acquiescing in free-market policies instead of fighting inequality. Her friend Isidora Parra, twenty-one, chimed in that she has little hope for the current generation of political leaders.

"They are fixed in their ways," Parra said. "We are waiting for them to die."

Made in Taiwan

American officials in the years after World War II saw Chile as a country with considerable economic potential. They saw Taiwan, an island on the other side of the world, as a charity case.* The United States had backed the losing side in China's civil war. The Communists took control of the mainland in 1949 and the leader of the Nationalist army, Chiang Kai-shek, retreated across the Taiwan Strait with more than one million soldiers and supporters in tow.

Chiang struck the classic dictator's bargain with the population of his rump state: he pledged to deliver prosperity while brutally suppressing dissent, spilling far more blood than did Pinochet.[82]

The United States was looking for the exits when Communist China backed North Korea's invasion of South Korea in June 1950, and America decided that Chiang might still be a useful ally after all. As in Chile,

---

* The journey from Chile to Taiwan is almost halfway around the world. Taipei's antipode is closer to Asunción, Paraguay.

the United States sent missionaries to instruct Taiwan in the proper management of its economy. From there, however, the stories unfolded quite differently. In 1950, Taiwan's economic output per capita was roughly one quarter of Chile's. By 1980, Taiwan had drawn even. By 2010, Taiwan's income per capita doubled Chile's.[83]

Taiwan, in brief, made the jump to prosperity that Chile has been unable to complete. The average Taiwanese eats twice as much meat as her grandparents ate in the 1950s and lives in a space seven times as large.[84] She can expect to live significantly longer than an American of the same age. And Taiwan remains one of the most economically egalitarian societies in the developed world.

One reason is that Taiwan resisted the advice of economists. Engineers oversaw Taiwan's economic policy during the second half of the twentieth century.[85] They regarded the economy as a machine, and they were not afraid to tinker. One of Taiwan's technocrats described the economy as "a huge engineering system that requires extremely careful and elaborate planning."[86] They solicited advice from economists — and listened to advice they did not solicit. Their appreciation for the power of markets grew with time. But in Taiwan, the engineers remained in control.*

The opening act of Taiwan's development may have been the most important, for it created an environment conducive to economic growth. Chiang's political party, the Kuomintang (KMT), broke up the island's great sugar and rice plantations and distributed the land among the former tenants. The party's founder, Sun Yat-sen, had preached the concept of "land to the tiller," meaning that the person who worked the land should own the land. But on the mainland, where the KMT was beholden to the

---

* There are of course other relevant differences between the two countries. Chile was blessed with abundant natural resources, attenuating the urgency of its efforts to develop factories. Chile was also a richer country in 1950, and closer to the United States, and therefore a more appetizing target as an American export market. Taiwan, for its part, was located in a gentrifying neighborhood, and the arrival of the Kuomintang delivered an infusion of both capital and talent.

feudal landowners, the party had not delivered. In Taiwan, the promise was easier to keep. The island had been a Japanese colony for the first half of the twentieth century, and the new arrivals were eager to break the power of the colonial elite.[87] The KMT capped farm rents at 37.5 percent of revenue, well below the prevailing average of 57 percent. This sparked a marriage boom among tenant farmers who suddenly found they had enough money to start families; the women were known as "37.5 percent brides."[88] Next, the government sold public lands. Finally, in 1953, it began to subdivide private lands, increasing the proportion of farmers working their own land from 36 percent in 1949 to 82 percent by the end of the process.[89] In a brilliant stroke, the former landowners were compensated with shares in state-owned industrial enterprises, shifting wealth from agriculture to industry.

The first generation of American officials sent to Taiwan after World War II supported land redistribution; they pushed a similar program in South Korea. But the Eisenhower administration ended those efforts, firing the American economist who led the work on the suspicion that he might be a Communist. That brought an abrupt end to what one Republican congressman, protesting the decision, accurately described as "about the only successful anti-communist step we have taken in Asia."[90]

Looking back on the twentieth century, the critical difference between nations that made the jump from poverty to prosperity and those that fell short may well have been the distribution of landownership: nations comprised of homesteaders fared better than nations comprised of plantations.[91] East Asia's most prosperous societies, Japan and South Korea and Taiwan, all ripped apart the holdings of large landowners and distributed the pieces among the masses. Those that left landholdings largely intact, like Thailand and Malaysia — and the nations of Latin America — did not achieve comparable growth.

The immediate virtue of land reform was job creation. More hands can always be employed on a farm. By the mid-1960s, an acre of Taiwanese farmland produced eight times more food than an acre of U.S. farmland.[92] In the longer term, the redistribution of land had two important consequences for Taiwan's development. First, it created a broad base of consumers — and petty capitalists. Second, it minimized the numbers and political power of both rent-seeking elites and poor families dependent on the state.

The development economist Gustav Ranis has observed that his colleagues struggled to influence policy in many developing nations because they had their priorities backward. Economists emphasized efficiency as the most important goal of public policy, while regarding political stability and distributional equity as benefits of the resulting growth. Ranis said the list should be reversed. People must agree that policies are equitable and conducive to stability before they are likely to care about increasing efficiency. Taiwan's redistribution of wealth created a broad base of support for the pursuit of growth.

The mastermind of Taiwan's industrialization was K. Y. Yin, who was born in the mainland province of Hunan in 1903. Yin's mother was well educated, which was uncommon at the time. He followed in her footsteps, graduating in 1925 from the prestigious Jiao Tong University with a degree in electrical engineering. His work as a young bureaucrat caught the attention of T. V. Soong, a senior government official who was the brother-in-law of both Sun Yat-sen and Chiang Kai-shek.

During World War II, Soong posted Yin to Washington to negotiate aid. After the war, Soong brought Yin into the KMT's top economic planning circles. Seeking an education, Yin traveled to Japan in 1950 and again in 1951 to study the history of the Meiji restoration, the period of Japan's initial industrial development in the late nineteenth and early twentieth centuries. The lesson for a "backward nation," Yin wrote later, was that "a government must take the lead, at least in the beginning. Relying entirely on a free economy is not enough."[93]

Yin decided to focus narrowly on three industries: electricity, fertilizers, and textiles. These he regarded, with reason, as the building blocks of a modern economy. His first steps set a pattern. The government provided $2.5 million in financing for a fertilizer plant, and $1 million in financing for a hydropower plant to power the fertilizer plant. Then it sharply increased the tariff on imported fertilizer. It required farmers to pay for domestic fertilizer with rice, at an exchange rate favoring the government. And it plowed the proceeds into industrial development.[94]

Yin was even less subtle in his construction of Taiwan's textile industry, providing companies with yarn from the United States and loans for equipment, then promising to buy the finished cloth.

Sheltering these nascent industries from foreign competition jump-started Taiwan's industrialization: output nearly doubled between 1951 and 1954.[95] But almost from the outset, mainstream economists tried to persuade Yin — and his bosses — to unhand the economy. In 1953, the United States sent a mission to the island, including two Chinese American economists with close ties to Chiang's government. Their basic advice was the same as the prescription that Milton Friedman liked to write for foreign governments: they said Taiwan should float its currency to facilitate trade and open its marketplace to foreign competition.[96]

Yin could not afford to ignore the visitors because the United States was funding Taiwan's industrialization. The country was spending far more on foreign tools and raw materials than it earned from exports of agricultural products like sugar, asparagus, and canned mushrooms. The United States provided an annual average of $100 million in non-military aid to Taiwan between 1950 and 1965, which covered 91 percent of the cost of Taiwan's extra imports.[97] So instead of ignoring the visiting economists, Yin listened, then politely declined to take their advice. The frustrated Taiwanese economist Mo-huan Hsing declared that Yin was "a stubborn bureaucrat full of the command economy ideology."[98]

In the mid-1950s, however, Yin's thinking began to shift. He briefly lost his job in 1955 after he was implicated in a corruption scandal. He was cleared and reinstated but, during his involuntary vacation, he studied economics. One day he turned up at Hsing's door, wanting to discuss an article the economist had written. The two men became friends.

Yin was aware that his development strategy was reaching its limits. Taiwan's output of clothing, for example, was outstripping domestic demand, while its complicated system of trade controls discouraged companies from seeking foreign markets. Some textile factories were beginning to shut their doors. And U.S. officials warned that the spigot of aid would not stay open forever. Taiwan needed dollars to purchase the machines and raw materials necessary for its development, and that meant it needed to sell more goods to other countries.

In 1957, Yin proposed that the government should encourage the export of textiles and a small number of other carefully selected manufactured goods. At the time, this was regarded as a surprising idea. There were few obvious success stories for Taiwan to emulate, and many of Chiang's advisers resisted, arguing that domestic development should remain the focus. "How can Taiwan ever hope to compete with the advanced nations?" asked one government minister.[99] Yin rejoined that Taiwan had one important advantage: it could, in effect, export cheap labor.

Yin won. In 1960, the government signed off on a four-year plan to invest more than $1 billion in the development of export industries, with roughly a third of the money provided by the United States.[100] The senior American development official in Taiwan said in an exuberant speech at a local university that the plan would make Taiwan a role model for the development of Asia. Even the island's optimists dismissed this as pablum. "No one had any inkling that a more prosperous growth epoch was in the making," said Yin's top aide, K. T. Li.[101]

Over the next thirty years, however, Taiwan ascended from poverty to prosperity by exporting manufactured goods.* The coastal plain was covered in a dense patchwork of midrise housing and metal-roofed factories, a landscape that looked a little like a successful version of Cleveland. When Yin died in 1963, his friends blamed exhaustion and proposed for his epitaph the words inscribed on an astonishing variety of consumer products: "Made in Taiwan."

Behind the exporters, a domestic economy blossomed.[102] One company, Chu Chen, began in the 1950s as a maker of roach spray, then added

---

* Agricultural products comprised 92 percent of Taiwan's exports in 1952. By 1972, that share was 16.7 percent. In recent decades, the share has remained well below 1 percent.

cleaning products. As the economy grew, it introduced a line of coffees, called Mr. Brown, which was sold in the island's ubiquitous corner markets. Then Mr. Brown opened its own stores. And as Taiwan achieved genuine prosperity, the old roach spray company started making a single-malt whiskey called Kavalan.[103]

Proponents of the free-market revolution hailed Taiwan's rise. Hayek's Mont Pelerin Society met in the capital city of Taipei in 1978, which attracted much less notice than its gathering in Chile a few years later, though both were ruled by authoritarian dictatorships. Friedman wrote in *Newsweek* that Taiwan and other East Asian nations had grown "by relying primarily on market forces."[104] The World Bank published an influential report in 1987 describing the economic rise of East Asia in similar terms.

It's a little hard to understand how intelligent people could have arrived at that conclusion. Perhaps part of the explanation is that Taiwan told its sponsors in the United States what they wanted to hear while doing what it wanted to do.[105] The government reduced the exchange value of its currency between 1958 and 1961 to make exports more attractive to foreign buyers, but it did not float the currency. Instead, Taiwan maintained its dollar at the same exchange rate with the American dollar for the next quarter century. As Taiwan's economy expanded, so did the effective discount for American buyers of Taiwanese goods. By the mid-1980s, almost half of Taiwan's exports went to the United States.

Taiwan also reduced trade barriers strategically. It was willing to export almost anything, but tariffs on imports remained largely unchanged from the 1950s through the 1970s.[106]

Key companies remained under state ownership, and the government had no compunctions about directing private firms.[107] To increase textile exports, for example, the government required firms to export at least 60 percent of output, or face fines. The government also reserved the best loan terms for successful exporters. These policies injected market discipline into Taiwan's managed economy: instead of relying on government bureaucrats to pick which firms the state would support, Taiwan used the international marketplace.

*   *   *

Yin left a warning to his successors. While government had a critical role to play in seeding new industries, he said that it needed to avoid the creation of "greenhouses." The government could plant the seeds and nurse the sprouts, but companies needed to be planted in the market.[108]

Sun Yun-suan, who became economics minister in 1969, was, like Yin, an electrical engineer by training. He had worked for the Tennessee Valley Authority in the United States in the 1940s and then oversaw reconstruction of Taiwan's electrical grid. He was familiar with Ricardo's theory of comparative advantage, and he was not impressed. It did not say anything about what a nation could become by developing new areas of expertise. On a visit to South Korea shortly after taking the job, Sun was impressed by a government-funded research institute largely staffed by Korean scientists trained in the United States. In 1973, he persuaded Taiwan's government to fund its own version: the Industrial Technology Research Institute, which now employs more than five thousand researchers with advanced degrees, almost all of them focused on developing commercially viable ideas, either in partnership with existing companies or as the seeds of new companies. Sun referred to the institute as his sixth child.[109]

The early 1970s were a difficult period for Taiwan. The island faced isolation as China gained international diplomatic recognition, including a visit from President Nixon. In 1971, China replaced Taiwan as a member of the United Nations. And that pain was compounded by the global oil shock. Sun, shunning the advice of free-market economists, decided to revive growth through a program of massive investment in public works, including the construction of a new international airport, a steel mill, and a shipyard.

Sun also decided to create a new industry. In February 1974, Sun and several of his colleagues had breakfast at a soy milk shop in Taipei with Wen Yuan Pan, a Chinese American engineer who worked for the American electronics company RCA. Pan told Sun that Taiwan should get into the business of making semiconductors. It was an audacious suggestion. Taiwan's factories specialized in cheap knockoffs, not cutting-edge technology. But an official history records that Sun asked only two questions —

How long will it take? How much will it cost? — then nodded and said, "Okay."[110]

Working through the new research institute, Taiwan negotiated a licensing deal with RCA and sent thirty-seven engineers to the United States for training. In 1977, the institute opened an experimental factory. Two years later, it created a joint venture to build a full-scale factory. The government also funded a new business park, backed by special tax breaks, as a home for factories that used Taiwanese semiconductors in their products. By 1983, privately owned Taiwanese companies were making toys, watches, calculators, and computers — and electronics had surpassed textiles as the island's primary export product. More than thirty-five years later, semiconductors remain at the heart of Taiwan's economy.[111]

Success brought new challenges. To maintain the exchange rate between the Taiwanese dollar and the American dollar even as its economy grew, Taiwan needed to sit on a big chunk of the money it earned from the United States. As the dollar's value soared in the early 1980s, Taiwan accumulated around $1 billion a month. The tiny island's foreign reserves outstripped Japan's and approached West Germany's. It became increasingly difficult to explain to the Taiwanese people why the government wasn't spending that money on public services. One opposition politician proposed everyone should be given $2200.[112] It also became harder to explain to the United States why American imports were kept out of the Taiwanese market.

Taiwan had reached the end of its economic adolescence and, under the weight of these domestic and foreign pressures, the government began to reduce its role in the economy. Taiwan allowed the value of its currency to rise by almost 40 percent against the dollar, and it loosened controls on capital flows. Tariffs were sharply reduced; imports rose. And the Kuomintang began a slow shift toward democratic government.

One remarkable feature of Taiwan's rise to prosperity was the relatively even distribution of the new wealth. The government did not achieve this result through redistribution. Both taxing and spending were modest by the standards of developed nations. Instead, by creating a society of smallholders, and then investing in education, Taiwan provided a large share of its population with both the financial and intellectual capital that made it possible to build prosperous lives. The economist Simon Kuznets famously argued that economic growth caused inequality to rise and then fall. In Taiwan, it fell and then stayed down.[113]

Many economists remained convinced Taiwan was not a model for other countries. They shared the judgment offered by Larry Summers in the early 1990s, during his time as the World Bank's chief economist: "For most developing countries, relying on imperfect markets rather than imperfect governments has a greater chance for promoting growth."[114] Friedman was not alone in insisting that Taiwan and South Korea would have grown even faster with less management.[115]

This judgment, however, is not shared by the Taiwanese government, which continues to manage development. The state research institute's current campus features a pair of buildings designed to look like open arms — arms reaching out to embrace industry, my tour guide told me. Inside is a gallery featuring the fruits of the institute's partnerships with Taiwanese and foreign companies: lithium batteries that don't explode, an umbrella that purifies drinking water, a new device to test the quality of the world's smallest semiconductors. "The smaller the country, maybe we have to be more top-down," said Stephen Su, who is in charge of the institute's relationship with industry. "We can't afford to be like the United States."[116]

Neither can the United States. Nations have always managed industrial development. The long history of state-aided innovation includes telephones, railroads, airplanes, vaccines, and computers. If you are reading this book on paper, you are looking at a rare exception. Gutenberg invented printing by himself. If you are reading this book on any kind of electronic device, you are not.

The economist Mariana Mazzucato has pointed out that governments have unmatched resources to fund high-risk research; businesses, by contrast, tend to invest once the path is clear. "If it is in the public interest for innovation to occur," she wrote, "there is a role for the public sector to require it to happen, rather than sitting back and hoping."[117]

Chapter Ten

Paper Fish

If, as seems possible, both capitalism and democracy are soon to
be swept away forever by a resurgence of mercantilism...then to
commercial banking will belong the uncertain glory of having
precipitated the transition to a new era.

— *Henry Simons,* A Positive Program for Laissez Faire *(1934)*[1]

A customer who deposited $5000 at New York's Dollar Savings Bank
in June 1970 could pick from a list of thank-you gifts including a
blender, a coffeemaker, and an iron. The East New York Savings Bank
offered steak knives. At First National City, "golden girls" in gold-striped
dresses registered new customers for a "golden giveaway" with a top prize
of $2500.[2]

The banks wooed customers with gifts because they were not allowed
to woo customers with interest payments. The federal government had
maintained wide-ranging controls on the financial industry since the
1930s. Policy makers blamed the industry for causing the Great Depression, and they were determined to prevent any fresh malfeasance. The
rules included an upper limit on the interest rates banks could pay on
deposits and the rates that banks could charge on loans.* Pretty much

---

* Interest rate caps, also known as usury laws, long predated the Depression. They
were a standard feature of premodern legal codes, and remained in place well into
the modern era. But in the United States, such laws had gradually been relaxed or
erased in the decades before the Depression.

every bank in New York in 1970 advertised that it paid the maximum rate, but to get customers in the door, they had to offer something more.

And increasingly, the promise of free stuff was not enough. As inflation eroded the value of interest payments on bank deposits, customers moved large amounts of money into alternatives like Treasury bonds.[3] Similar problems beset other parts of the financial system. Many state and local governments were subject to laws limiting the interest rates they could pay on bonds, and they, too, were struggling to attract investors. In October 1969, California governments were unable to sell $1.3 billion in bonds, mostly for school construction, at the maximum legal interest rate of 5 percent. The fast-growing commuter suburb of Dublin, east of Oakland, was forced to suspend plans for the construction of two new schools.[4]

For much of the next decade, ad hoc efforts to rewrite the rules failed to keep pace with rising inflation.[5] Banks continued to lose deposits as clever entrepreneurs created more rewarding places to store money. Vast sums were stashed in "Eurodollar" bank accounts on the other side of the Atlantic, beyond the reach of U.S. regulators. Even more money was deposited in "money market" mutual funds designed to look like bank accounts.[6] The Wall Street brokerage Merrill Lynch created ersatz checking accounts paying higher interest rates.[7]

For Citicorp, one of the largest banks in New York, the slow-motion crisis tipped into a new phase after Paul Volcker turned to monetarism in the fall of 1979. As interest rates soared, the bank's borrowing costs increasingly exceeded the rates it was allowed to charge on loans. Citicorp was particularly vulnerable because its chief executive, Walter Wriston, bet interest rates would soon fall. He believed in the monetarism preached by his friend and sometime tennis partner Milton Friedman. As reality resisted his expectations, the bank lost money.[8]

Some of the largest losses were in a relatively new line of business: credit card lending. But Citicorp's chief lobbyist, Hans H. Angermueller, realized that credit card lending also might be the easiest part of the business to return to profitability, by exploiting a loophole in federal law. Just one year earlier, in 1978, the Supreme Court had ruled that a credit card company could charge customers anywhere in the United States the highest rate of interest allowed by the laws of its home state.[9] What Citicorp's credit card division needed was a new home state.

Charles E. Long, Citicorp's vice chairman, compiled a list of five states that had lenient laws or might be willing to write new laws. One of the five names on the list was South Dakota, which was already moving to get rid of its interest rate caps. In November 1979, the state bankers' association had petitioned the legislature to lift the limit on loan rates, arguing the combination of high inflation and rate caps was leaving local banks with no way to make a profit. The bill sailed through the legislature and was signed into law on February 19, 1980.[10]

But that wasn't enough. Under federal law, banks needed an invitation to enter a new state. Citicorp executives flew to South Dakota and promised to bring 400 jobs. The company gave the text of the desired invitation to South Dakota's governor, Bill Janklow. The necessary legislation was introduced on the last day of the legislative session in 1980, passed by both houses on that same day, and signed into law by Janklow before the sun went down. He also declared that the need for jobs was an emergency, so the law took effect immediately.

Citicorp kept its promise even after New York pushed through a similar law. The company moved 400 jobs from Long Island to Sioux Falls. In time, it added another 2600.

Other companies quickly emulated Citi, effectively deregulating credit card lending. The results set the pattern for later rounds of deregulation. Lending rose sharply, and for some, the easy availability of credit, even at high interest rates, was empowering. For others, however, it was catastrophic. By the mid-1990s, as credit card use expanded, the share of the population filing for personal bankruptcy each year had almost quintupled.[11]

Meanwhile, consumer groups campaigned for deregulation of interest rates on deposits. The Gray Panthers, an organization that represented senior citizens, sued federal banking regulators, arguing limits on bank rates were a form of discrimination against those with modest means, since the wealthy were able to keep savings in more lucrative places. The Panthers sarcastically proposed that banks should be required to post signs in the windows of their branches: "Warning: Savings Deposits May Be Dangerous to Your Wealth!" The campaign was backed by Ralph Nader and the AARP, among other consumer groups.[12]

President Carter, broadening his commitment to economic deregulation, asked Congress in May 1979 to phase out rate caps on bank deposits. Congress delivered legislation the following year that ended the caps by 1986. The Reagan administration then decided that wasn't fast enough. The new Treasury secretary, Donald Regan, pushed for deregulation "as quickly as possible" and, in 1982, Congress agreed to accelerate the timing.[13]

The removal of the interest rate caps bolstered the banks, but it wreaked havoc in the parallel universe of savings-and-loans — specialized banks that focused on mortgage lending and that had been allowed to pay higher rates than banks on deposits. Stripped of their privileges, many savings-and-loans sought to survive by making risky investments.

The cleanup, in the late 1980s and early 1990s, cost taxpayers about $210 billion. That seemed like a lot, but the bills for deregulation were just starting to arrive.

There is little foundation for the nostalgic narrative that policy makers could have prevented the modern era of financial crises by maintaining the midcentury system of banking regulations. Those rules, including interest rate caps, were broken before they were dismantled. The failure, instead, was that policy makers made little effort to write new rules for the rapidly changing industry. Financial regulators were openly contemptuous of financial regulation. They insisted that market participants would police misconduct and maintain financial stability.

This conviction was deeply influenced by economists, who love markets of all kinds, but who developed a special reverence for financial markets. The purest expression of this faith is known as "efficient markets theory." It treats financial markets as the nearest thing to the kind of perfection found only in textbooks. The University of Chicago economist Eugene Fama provided a justification of this faith in 1965. Fama examined a newly created database of stock prices for the period between 1926 and 1960 and concluded that the prices fully reflected all available information.[14] In the language of economics, the prices were said to be "efficient."[15] This, in turn, implied that markets were stable and self-correcting, and that regulation served little purpose.

For the financial industry, the last quarter of the twentieth century was a period of innovation and explosive growth, and Fama's utopian view of financial markets was influential in persuading policy makers that governments did not need to write new rules for emerging areas of financial activity. One of the largest and most important of these new markets was the burgeoning trade in credit derivatives.

A derivative is a bet on the movement of other prices. The earliest known examples are almost as old as the earliest instances of writing: the contracts of Mesopotamian farmers to sell future harvests at specified prices. Modern derivatives originated in America's fertile crescent, with the establishment of a futures market in Chicago shortly before the Civil War. These grain contracts were marketed as a form of insurance, allowing farmers to reduce risk by locking in prices ahead of the harvest. But derivatives can also be used to amplify risk. An investor, for example, can promise to deliver grain they don't own, betting that they will be able to buy the promised grain at a lower price than the price at which they have agreed to sell it.

As financial deregulation opened new markets, and created new risks, financial engineers created new kinds of derivatives — as insurance against those risks and as new opportunities for gambling. The deregulation of exchange rates in the mid-1970s triggered the first big boom. The deregulation of interest rates in the 1980s triggered a second boom. Both paled in comparison to the wave that began in the early 1990s, when clever bankers popularized credit derivatives, which let investors bet on the possibility that borrowers would fail to repay debts.[16]

The market for credit derivatives proved to be huge. The value of just one variety, known as credit default swaps, increased from literally nothing in the early 1990s to an estimated $62 trillion by 2007 — more than the value of the world's economic output in that year.[17]

The government's Depression-era regulations carefully limited the activities of commercial banks, but industry lawyers concluded those laws had not anticipated the new derivatives, and did not bar banks from diving into the market. This prompted some regulators to suggest the need for new rules. E. Gerald Corrigan, the president of the Federal Reserve Bank of New York — one of the nation's most important financial regulators — made a show of innocence in a speech to a crowd of bankers in January 1992, telling the gathering that he was having a hard time understanding why so many investors suddenly needed credit insurance. The message was to rein in the gambling. "I hope this sounds like a warning," he said, "because it is."[18]

The industry's response, delivered in 1993, was a massive report detailing best practices for derivatives trading that should have been entitled "Look How Responsible We Are." The bottom line, spelled out clearly, was that there was no need for the government to intervene. Instead, the bankers helpfully advised customers to be careful when dealing with bankers.[19]

Mark Brickell, the head of a new trade group created to represent the derivatives industry, was an earnest libertarian who liked to quote Hayek's warning that regulation was the death of innovation. "Markets can correct excess far better than any government," Brickell said. "Market discipline is the best form of discipline that there is."[20]

The next year, 1994, Orange County, California, filed for bankruptcy after its treasurer lost more than a billion dollars investing in derivatives in pursuit of higher returns. It took twenty-three years for the county's taxpayers to repay the losses.[21] Also in 1994, Procter & Gamble lost more than $150 million on derivatives and sued Bankers Trust, a leader in the new market. One piece of evidence was a videotape of a Bankers Trust training session in which the instructor presented the example of a derivatives transaction involving a pair of blue-chip companies, and then helpfully explained the role of Bankers Trust was to "rip them off."[22]

This was not mere hyperbole. Paul Volcker recounts asking William Sharpe, a Nobel laureate in economics for his contributions to the rise of finance, just how much all these innovations were adding to economic growth. "Nothing," Sharpe replied. He explained that in his view, derivatives merely allowed some people to take money from other people. But, he added, "it's a lot of fun."[23]

The high-profile cases of Orange County and P&G briefly caused some members of Congress to doubt the industry's reassurances. A few proposed legislation. Brickell attacked the bills with savage contempt, telling anyone who would listen that Congress was clueless. The policy establishment agreed. "Risks in financial markets, including derivatives markets, are being regulated by private parties," Fed chairman Alan Greenspan calmly told Congress.[24] Corrigan, too, had found a new perspective. After moving from the New York Fed to a top job at Goldman Sachs, he said the industry should be allowed to address its own problems. Frank N. Newman, Treasury's expert on the issue, came out against regulation and then took a job at Bankers Trust. Both men were fortunate that espousing the prevailing ideology was the express lane to personal enrichment.[25]

The bills went nowhere, nor was interest revived in 1995, when a trader in Singapore gambled in derivatives and destroyed Britain's venerable Barings Bank. Brickell, asked for lessons learned, suggested the bank should have managed its risks more carefully.[26]

The Drs. Gramm

Phil Gramm, a professor of economics at Texas A&M University, met Wendy Lee in 1969 when she interviewed for a job on the economics faculty. Six weeks after she arrived in College Station, they were married.[27] They shared a love of markets and a distaste for government.

Gramm said his views were rooted in his life experience, telling an interviewer, "I don't just have faith in the free enterprise system, I have evidence."[28] It was a curious kind of evidence. Born into a military family in Georgia in 1942, he graduated from the state university, got a government scholarship to earn a doctorate, then took a job at Texas A&M, where he was granted tenure at the tender age of thirty. The government had been carrying Gramm on its books for three decades, and he was assured of the government's support for the rest of his life.

Instead, Gramm decided to take a different kind of government job. In 1978, he was elected to the House of Representatives. He arrived as a Democrat, but made his first splash in 1981 by partnering with the Republican minority on the House Budget Committee to pass a package of spending cuts. When the top House Democrat, Tip O'Neill, removed Gramm from the committee in 1983, Gramm resigned from Congress, registered as a Republican, and won the same seat in a special election five weeks later. He told voters, "I had to choose between Tip O'Neill and y'all, and I decided to stand with y'all." O'Neill's verdict: "Gramm, in my opinion, is more responsible for the mess this country is in than any other person than Mr. Reagan."[29]

In 1984, Gramm won a Senate seat. Mark McKinnon, an adviser to a rival campaign, told the *Washington Post* Gramm was easily underestimated because "he looks like a turtle and he sounds like a rooster." But McKinnon added, "He has an uncanny ability to sense the public mood before anyone else does."[30] Gramm was the purveyor of a new kind of populism, channeling the frustration of Americans who were becoming increasingly dependent on the federal government and increasingly angry about that dependence.

Back in Washington, he wasted little time reclaiming the spotlight, winning passage in 1985 of the first federal legislation to impose mandatory spending limits on the federal government, backed by automatic spending cuts. The legislation was thrown out by the courts, but it pointed the way for later efforts. How did a new senator manage to produce a landmark bill? "I waited for everybody else to come forward with a way of dealing with the problem," Gramm said afterward. "Nobody did. It got down to No. 97, and I did have an idea. And the most powerful words in a political debate are, 'I have an idea.'"[31]

Wendy Gramm moved with her husband to Washington and took a job on the front lines of Reagan's campaign against regulation, joining the administration as an aide to James C. Miller III at the Federal Trade Commission. Her life story made a better case for free enterprise. Her grandparents were Korean immigrants who worked in the Hawaiian sugarcane fields. Her father rose to become an executive at a sugarcane company. Wendy, who was born in 1945, graduated from Wellesley and then earned a doctorate in economics at Northwestern. She spent less than a decade in Texas, but she spoke with a noticeable Texas accent.

She moved up quickly, taking Miller's former job reviewing proposed regulations, where her tough line led Reagan to describe her as "my favorite economist."[32] In December 1987, Reagan nominated Wendy Gramm to lead the Commodity Futures Trading Commission (CFTC). Gramm created a curriculum for the agency's workers, featuring speeches by commodities traders and conservative economists, to inculcate her view that regulations stifle growth. "A little bit of regulation here, a little there and pretty soon the economy is strangled by red tape," she said.[33] She also worked to limit the commission's oversight of the burgeoning derivatives marketplace. One of her last acts before stepping down in January 1993 was to finalize an exemption for certain kinds of bets on energy prices, a change sought by a fast-growing Houston energy company called Enron. Five weeks later, she joined Enron's board of directors, where she continued to oppose the regulation of derivatives. That fall she wrote a piece for the *Wall Street Journal* pushing back against the proposals for new rules. She urged her former colleagues, and Congress, not "to over-regulate what we just do not understand."[34]

Shortly after Brooksley Born became the head of the CFTC in August 1996, taking the job once held by Wendy Gramm, Born was invited to lunch by Alan Greenspan, who explained his view that markets would police fraud. Born was bemused: as a lawyer, she often had represented the victims of financial frauds. Her clients had included victims of the legendary effort by the Hunt brothers, a pair of Texas oil heirs, to corner the market in silver in the late 1970s. She knew the Hunts had not been stopped by the market; they had been stopped by the CFTC.[35]

The market in credit derivatives soon caught Born's attention. She was struck by the industry's adamant opposition to the most basic forms of regulation, like record keeping and reporting requirements. "That puzzled me," she said. "What was it that was in this market that had to be hidden? Why did it have to be a completely dark market? So it made me very suspicious and troubled."[36] In early 1998, her staff began to prepare a tentative first step toward regulation, a request for public comment. Before the industry even had a chance to object, however, the Clinton administration tried to shut down Born's plan. According to the *Washington Post*, Larry Summers, then a deputy to Treasury Secretary Robert Rubin, called Born and told her, "I have thirteen bankers in my office and they say if you go forward with this you will cause the worst financial crisis since World War II."[37] That April, Born was summoned to a meeting with Rubin, Greenspan, and Arthur Levitt, the chairman of the Securities and Exchange Commission. The men took turns telling her to drop the issue.

The aversion to regulation had reached such a pitch in Washington that a proposal to talk about proposing rules had caused a firestorm.

Born released the proposal, which did not cause the predicted crisis. It did, however, prompt her opponents in other parts of the government to issue an extraordinary public statement expressing "grave concerns," questioning the CFTC's authority and urging Congress to intervene. At a hearing in July, Summers told Congress that Born had "cast the shadow of regulatory uncertainty over an otherwise thriving market." He had a sympathetic audience: Phil Gramm. "I see no evidence whatsoever to suggest that this is a troubled market," Gramm said.[38]

Less than two months later, a fresh batch of evidence landed with a thud. Long-Term Capital Management, a massive hedge fund led by some of the very professors whose theories underpinned the case for deregulation, collapsed in spectacular fashion. The lack of regulation, rather than its prospect, had once again caused a crisis. Born described it as a "wake-up call," but no one else stirred. Summers and Greenspan already knew markets were prone to breakdowns. Neither believed that markets were perfectly efficient. Summers was the author of an immortal five-word rebuttal: "There are idiots. Look around."[39] Greenspan, contrary to some caricatures, had a healthy fear of financial crises. But both men regarded market discipline as the better of two imperfect options. When Congress summoned the wise men again in late 1998, following the collapse of

Long-Term Capital, Greenspan testified, "I know of no set of supervisory actions we can take that will prevent people from making dumb mistakes."[40]

The Clinton administration asked Congress to suspend Born's rule-writing authority.[41] Phil Gramm decided to go further. He had become chairman of the Senate Banking Committee in 1995, a role in which he was more successful in reducing regulation than he had been in reducing government spending.* He wrote a provision, quietly inserted into a broader bill in December 2000, that prohibited the government from regulating large portions of the market in derivatives. Brickell, the industry lobbyist, rejoiced that the law "nailed the door shut."[42]

Support for deregulation was heightened by the fear of foreign competition. Senator Charles Schumer, Democrat of New York, told colleagues that "the future of America's dominance as the financial center of the world" was at stake in a 1999 vote to let large banks become financial supermarkets.[43] Similar words were spoken against derivatives regulation.

On the other side of the Atlantic, policy makers advanced similar arguments. The London Stock Exchange, the red-hot center of global finance during the glory years of the British Empire, had faded from prominence in the decades after World War II. Membership was restricted to British firms, which traded the shares of British companies.

The brokerage firms, however, still were making a lot of money, in part because they had agreed not to compete with one another on the

---

* Gramm sponsored the Gramm-Leach-Bliley Act, the 1999 law that completed the dismantling of the wall between commercial banking and financial markets, allowing companies like Citigroup to create financial supermarkets that sought profits in a broad range of financial activities, from predatory mortgage lending to financing corporate consolidation. "We are here to repeal Glass-Steagall because we have learned government is not the answer," Gramm said at the time, referring to the Depression-era law that the new bill erased. "We have learned that freedom and competition are." Both the celebrations and condemnations of the 1999 law have been overdone. Regulators already had demolished most of the wall.

basis of price. Customers could choose a broker, but the fees were the same. In the mid-1970s, American regulators had forced Wall Street firms to stop setting prices collectively, and competition had reduced prices. Inspired by that example, British regulators had launched an investigation of the London exchange.

Thatcher's government, which inherited the issue, preferred to let the exchange write its own rules. John Redwood, the head of the "Policy Unit," Thatcher's internal think tank, was a devoted champion of market-oriented policies. In a June 1984 speech, he compared London's brokers to "a chivalrous group of knights in a great big castle" who treated one another with great courtesy, and robbed everyone else.[44] Extending the metaphor, he said that the solution was not to conquer the castle, but to persuade the knights to lower the drawbridge.

By the mid-1980s, the leaders of the exchange were ready to modernize. They agreed to scrap fixed commissions and to open its floor to foreign firms.

Some of Thatcher's advisers warned the new emphasis on price competition would encourage unethical behavior. This was an acute reading of the human condition. Consider an example from the Israeli city of Haifa in the 1990s, where day-care centers typically closed at 4:00 p.m. Parents rarely came late to pick up children; they understood they would be imposing on the teachers. Still, it happened often enough, and it tended to be the same people. An economist named Uri Gneezy persuaded six day-care centers to announce that parents who came late would be fined. He then compared the results with four centers that continued to operate on the honor system. What happened? Late pickups roughly doubled at centers that punished late arrivals: parents facing a fine were more likely to come late. Parents felt they could purchase a few extra minutes to spend at work or the market or the gym. They didn't need to feel guilty, because they had paid. And the shift in behavior outlasted the policy: parents continued to come late even after the fines were eliminated. A social norm had been replaced by a transaction.[45]

In financial markets, one of the most consequential shifts was the demise of the idea that a banker had an obligation to act in a client's interest. Bankers, to be sure, had devoted plenty of energy to robbing clients in the era before deregulation. But it is hard to avoid the conclusion that they have done so with greater enthusiasm and success in recent decades. John Reed, the former head of Citicorp, has argued that the integration of Wall Street trading firms and commercial banks replaced a cultural emphasis on long-term relationships with a focus on short-term profit taking.[46] The rewards for misbehavior also have multiplied, while the authorities have shown astonishingly little interest in punishing white-collar criminality.

As Thatcher's aides debated the issue, however, most came down on the side of price competition. Nigel Lawson, the chancellor of the exchequer, insisted the United Kingdom needed to keep pace with its rivals. Redwood said investors would police the market. "People are, on the whole, pretty canny about their own money," he said.[47]

The makeover of the London Stock Exchange, on October 27, 1986, was dubbed the "Big Bang." American and continental banks rushed into the City of London, the historic financial district, and gobbled up venerable British brokerages like so many Pac-Man pellets.[48] Wits compared the City with Wimbledon, the tennis tournament dominated by foreign players.[49]

Broker fees quickly dropped by half, and the volume of trading on the London market roughly doubled.[50] The longer-term impact was to restore London's place as a center of finance. London began to outstrip New York as the preferred marketplace for trading in a wide range of dollar-denominated financial assets, in foreign exchange and in highly leveraged gambling on the American housing market — all thanks to the important fact that in London, there was even less regulation. It may seem astonishing that any other government could have outstripped the laissez-faire attitude of the U.S. government. Yet it was so. The British consolidated regulation in a single agency in 1997; its first chairman later explained that its philosophy was not to interfere in private transactions: "Consenting adults in private?" he said. "That's their problem, really."[51]

As the money poured in, London built a new financial district on the wharfs where men had once loaded ships. The flow of money had become more important to the British economy than the flow of manufactured goods. The share of corporate tax receipts from financial firms rose from about 12 percent before the Big Bang to a peak of 36 percent in 2000.[52]

But the gains went to the few — the knights in the castle, to borrow Redwood's allegory. And in exchange for all that money, the knights blew up the global economy.[53]

Bubble Trouble

For almost a decade, beginning in the late 1990s, consumer advocates brought accounts of abusive mortgage-lending practices to the Fed's marble headquarters in Washington, D.C. They told Fed officials about old ladies cheated out of homes they'd owned for decades and young families sold first homes they could not afford. They brought copies of fraudulent loan documents. None of it mattered. The nation's most important financial regulatory agency simply wasn't interested in one of the largest outbreaks of white-collar crime in U.S. history.*

Fed officials told the advocates they were interested in lending abuses only if the health of the broader economy was threatened. And, as economists, they did not regard anecdotes as evidence. They wanted data.

As the stories piled up, so did the advocates' frustration. By refusing to launch a systematic investigation, the Fed was ensuring it would not discover systemic problems.

"I stood up at a Fed meeting in 2005 and said, 'How many anecdotes makes it real?'" one of those outraged consumer advocates recalled.

---

* This point remains surprisingly controversial. Many politicians and bankers prefer to describe the crisis as the result of irresponsible but, for the most part, legal behavior. The anecdotal and statistical evidence of widespread fraud, however, is simply overwhelming. See, for example, Atif R. Mian and Amir Sufi, "Fraudulent Income Overstatement on Mortgage Applications During the Credit Expansion of 2002 to 2005," February 2015, National Bureau of Economic Research Working Paper 20947.

"'How many tens or thousands of anecdotes will it take to convince you?'"[54]

The answer was that the Fed's chairman, Alan Greenspan, already had decided to do nothing. When Greenspan was sworn in as the Fed's chairman in August 1987, he had accepted responsibility for policing the banks and protecting their customers.

But he did not mean it.

Greenspan became the nation's most important financial regulator despite a profound and unshakable conviction that financial regulation was worse than doing nothing, because it encouraged a false sense of safety. He criticized what he saw as a tendency among proponents of regulation to assume that identifying a problem was tantamount to solving it. He thought market participants should protect themselves.

"I was certainly not hired to implement regulatory policy that I thought was misguided," Greenspan told me in a 2018 interview. "Presidents would not have appointed me as head of the Federal Reserve for regulation."

He said that he chose to honor his oath of office by allowing the rest of the Fed's board of governors to set policy on regulatory issues. He said he followed a personal policy of casting his vote with the majority of the board.

But Greenspan was not passive on regulatory issues. As in the case of derivatives, he advocated passionately for the government to leave the marketplace and to stay out. It was as if the local police chief decided that neither he, nor anyone else, would do any policing.

Alan Greenspan was born on March 6, 1926, in New York City. He liked playing music, so he went to Juilliard for two years, then dropped out to join a jazz band. He found that he was good enough to hold a job, but not to be a star. He read business books during breaks, prepared tax returns for the other band members, and, in 1945, quit show business to enroll in business school at New York University.

The school was a practical place that mostly trained people for careers in business. The economics instruction was empirically oriented, an approach denigrated by ivory-tower types as "measurement without the-ory."[55] It suited Greenspan. He was skeptical of economists who wrote theories without worrying about measurement.

Greenspan moved uptown for graduate school at Columbia Univer-sity, then dropped out to take a job with the National Industrial Confer-ence Board, a New York research group financed by large corporations. "It was presumed if you studied economics seriously in those days that you would go on to be a teacher," said Greenspan's lifelong friend Robert Kavesh, who became one of those professors. "There was a hierarchy: the highest level was to teach; second, to work for government; third, sully your hands in the business world. Alan chose the last approach."[56] Greenspan soon began to make himself valuable to the conference board's clients. In one widely circulated report, Greenspan calculated the scale of federal spending on the Korean War. The actual numbers were classified, but Greenspan worked backward from the public record to figure out, for example, the likely impact of the buildup on demand for aluminum. Years later, a colleague at the Fed, Alice Rivlin, went looking for Greenspan and found him holed up in a small conference room with a bunch of low-level economists from various federal agencies, arguing about data. "Alan had his coat off and his sleeves rolled up and the thing that struck me is that they were all on a first-name basis," Rivlin recalled. "This was a working meeting of the number crunchers, and he was one of them."[57]

In 1953, a bond trader named William Townsend, impressed by Greenspan's reports for the conference board, proposed a partnership with the younger man. Townsend died five years later, but a grateful Greenspan kept his name on the marquee and built Townsend-Greenspan into a leading economics consultancy.

Consulting was Greenspan's elevator to the top of the New York financial world. He was Jewish and, in the 1950s, he judged that his oppor-tunities inside major corporations were limited. "I knew that if I started at the lower rungs of management, I'd stay there," he said. "I thought that I had to go around the system and I very consciously did that."[58]

In 1952, Greenspan married a Canadian artist named Joan Mitchell, who introduced him to the libertarian novelist Ayn Rand. The marriage ended after about a year, but the relationship with Rand endured and shifted the focus of Greenspan's life. She placed his understanding of economics in a political framework. "What she did — through long discussions and lots of arguments into the night — was to make me think why capitalism is not only efficient and practical, but also moral," he said.[59]

In the winter of 1964, Greenspan made his debut as a public intellectual, delivering a series of ten lectures on "The Economics of a Free Society" at Manhattan's Roosevelt Hotel. The lectures were edited by Rand, and Greenspan spoke carefully, hewing to the prepared text. His purpose, he said, was to "show why a laissez-faire economy is the only moral and practical form of economic organization."[60] The speeches sketched an even more limited role for the government than Milton Friedman had proposed in *Capitalism and Freedom*, which had been published two years earlier. Notably, Greenspan denounced the existence of the Federal Reserve as "one of the historic disasters in American history."[61] He also fiercely opposed the government's efforts to restrain the growth of large corporations. In a 1965 essay, Greenspan inveighed against the antitrust prosecution of the aluminum giant Alcoa, which was one of his most important consulting clients. "Alcoa is being condemned for being too successful, too efficient, and too good a competitor," Greenspan wrote.[62]

Greenspan's politics colored his consulting work. "There was an absolute rule at Townsend-Greenspan," Lowell Wiltbank, a longtime employee, told the journalist Michael Hirsh. "No communication that came out of the firm should ever be interpreted to advocate any expansion of government interference in the economy. If we advocated anything in terms of government policy, it was deregulation."[63]

In the late 1960s, Greenspan put the firm to work in the service of his politics. He volunteered as an adviser to Nixon's 1968 presidential campaign, making his mark by using the Townsend-Greenspan computer to analyze polling data. He resisted taking a job with the new administration, although he served on the commission that recommended the end of the draft, and on a commission that recommended the end of interest rate regulation. In the summer of 1974, however, as Nixon teetered on the brink of impeachment, Greenspan agreed to chair the President's Council of Economic Advisers. "I have very considerable self-interest in the survival of our free political and economic system — and I think that is what is at stake now," he said.[64]

A few hours after Greenspan's confirmation hearing, Nixon resigned. Greenspan became Gerald Ford's chief economist instead. He invited his mother and Ayn Rand to the swearing-in.

His first stint in Washington was a lesson in the limits of an economist's influence. He helped persuade Ford to oppose a bailout of New York City — a stand immortalized by the *New York Daily News* headline "Ford to City: Drop Dead" — but was eventually overruled.[65] He opposed a law requiring banks to disclose the interest rates they charged on mortgage loans, and he was overruled. Yet Greenspan found the work fulfilling, and he retained a deep respect for Ford. Late in life, he displayed just two photos of politicians in his office: Thatcher and Ford.

After Ford's loss to Jimmy Carter in 1976, Greenspan finally completed his doctorate in economics by submitting a collection of his published articles to New York University. He returned to his old life as a well-paid consultant while maintaining an active role in Republican politics. He lent his reputation to Ronald Reagan's presidential campaign by endorsing the candidate's plan to cut taxes and spending. Reprising his relationship with Nixon, however, Greenspan kept a measure of distance from the Reagan White House, visiting regularly to offer advice but remaining in the private sector. There was one public sector job, however, that he was more than willing to take. James Baker, then secretary of the Treasury, called Greenspan in 1987 and asked him to stop by his house. When Greenspan arrived, he found another Baker there — Howard Baker, the President's chief of staff. The two Bakers asked Greenspan whether he would like to replace Paul Volcker at the Fed.

Greenspan and Volcker had essentially the same view of monetary policy: both men wanted to eliminate inflation. But they had very different views of financial regulation.

The federal government during the Great Depression had slammed a wall between two kinds of banking. The point of the wall was to safeguard the commercial banking industry, which was devoted to the staid business of collecting deposits and making loans. On the other side of the divide was the wild world of Wall Street: brokerage houses that traded in securities, investment banks that arranged mergers, and, in time, newer creatures like hedge funds.

By the mid-1980s, the nation's largest commercial banks were desperate to join the fun on Wall Street. In early 1985, three of New York's largest banks — J.P. Morgan, Citicorp, and Bankers Trust — sought the Fed's permission to make a limited return to the brokerage business, for the first time since the Depression. The Reagan administration was all in favor, but Volcker dragged his feet, refusing to schedule a vote. Finally the administration forced his hand by appointing new members to the Fed's board who shared the desire to tear down that wall. The episode soured relations between Volcker and the White House.[66]

Greenspan was a member of J.P. Morgan's board, and he had publicly endorsed the company's application to enter the securities market, saying, "I have never seen a constructive regulation yet."[67] The week he was nominated to head the Fed, the White House called for Congress to further reduce restrictions, to help American banks compete with foreign rivals. Greenspan, awaiting Senate confirmation, made clear he did not share Volcker's misgivings.[68]

Greenspan's long tenure as Fed chairman was celebrated as an era of low unemployment and low inflation. The Washington journalist Bob Woodward hailed Greenspan as the "maestro" of an economic golden age. A young cable channel, CNBC, showed live footage of Greenspan's arrival at the Fed on the mornings of policy meetings, and its analysts interpreted the size of his briefcase. His face was plastered on T-shirts and magazines.

His signature triumph fittingly involved doing nothing: he resisted pressure to raise interest rates in the mid-1990s, judging correctly that the economy could grow without inflation because technology was increasing the productivity of American workers even as globalization suppressed consumer prices and workers' bargaining power.

His great failure also involved doing nothing: he repeatedly declined to curb the excesses of the financial industry. He had a consistent explanation: market participants, he said, would learn from failure. Yet Greenspan never did.

In 1984, an Arizona real estate developer named Charles Keating hired Greenspan to vouch for the financial strength of Lincoln Savings and Loan, a thrift Keating had just acquired to finance development projects. Greenspan duly concluded that Lincoln's management was "seasoned and expert in selecting and making direct investments." Actually Keating and his company were engaged in a wide-ranging financial fraud that was spectacular even by the high standards of the 1980s, a decade that saw considerable innovation in the field of financial fraud. The thrift failed in 1989, costing taxpayers about $2 billion. "Of course I'm embarrassed," Greenspan told a reporter after Lincoln's failure. Then he apologized in language that strikingly foreshadowed his famous remarks after the 2008 financial crisis, when he told Congress that he was "very distressed" by the failure of market discipline. "I don't want to say I am distressed, but the truth is I really am," he said in 1989. "I am thoroughly surprised by what has happened to Lincoln."[69]

In 1987, after the Latin American debt crisis, Greenspan predicted that "international lending will be significantly more prudent in the years ahead." He added, "I don't think any new policies have to be implemented."[70] After the first round of wipeouts in credit derivatives in 1994, Greenspan described the damage as educational. "As a consequence," he said, "firms' models and judgments should be sounder today than those that prevailed in early 1994."[71] After the collapse of Long-Term Capital Management in 1998, Greenspan again insisted the government should not tighten regulation of the banks that funded the hedge fund's bets, nor of the credit derivatives that allowed the hedge fund to burn so much money so very quickly. It was a view Greenspan carried right up to the 2008 crisis. "In today's world, I fail to see how adding more government regulation can help," he wrote in his 2007 memoirs. "We have no sensible choice other than to let markets work."[72]

By the mid-1990s, banks were dabbling enthusiastically in the business of high-rate mortgage lending to "subprime" customers — people who did not qualify for loans at the best, or "prime," rates. The banks created subsidiaries to make these loans: most borrowers got mortgages from Fleet Bank or Wells Fargo; subprime borrowers went to Fleet Finance or Wells Fargo Financial. Consumer advocates began to document other differences, too. The subprime-lending arms charged exorbitant fees and imposed punitive conditions, and their lending was concentrated in lower-income and minority communities. The banks described the new business as an earnest effort to serve customers who didn't qualify for traditional loans. The numbers told a different story. Many subprime borrowers could have qualified for prime loans. Minority borrowers ended up getting subprime loans much more often than white borrowers with similar financial profiles.

Consumer advocates pressed the Fed, which regulated the banks, to regulate the subsidiaries, too. In January 1998, the Fed formally refused. Its board of governors voted unanimously not to examine the practices of banks' subprime-lending subsidiaries nor to investigate consumer complaints against those subsidiaries. The Clinton administration criticized the decision, but the Fed did not budge. The banking industry, drawing the logical conclusion, enthusiastically expanded its lending through subprime subsidiaries. In March 1998, First Union bought the Money Store, a California lender that hired former baseball players Jim Palmer and Phil Rizzuto to encourage people to call 1-800-LOAN-YES. The following month, in April 1998, Citicorp announced a merger with Travelers, an insurance company with a subprime lending business that was renamed CitiFinancial. By 2004, at least 12 percent of all mortgage loans with high interest rates were being originated by companies that the Fed refused to regulate. In August 2007, the former Fed governor Edward Gramlich lamented that the mortgage marketplace was "like a city with a murder law, but no cops on the beat."[73]

The idea of a marketplace regulated by its participants is fundamentally flawed. A half century of experience with "self-policing" has amply demonstrated that even the most sophisticated customers are frequently victimized by financial industry professionals. Markets run on information, and the insiders usually have more information. The absence of regulation is a license to steal. The average adult obtains a few mortgage loans in a lifetime, from bankers who make more loans before lunchtime.

The paperwork is overwhelming; the language is impenetrable. And the most vulnerable borrowers often are least equipped to parse the details.

Beazer Homes sold both homes and mortgage loans to first-time buyers in the 2000s. "$1 down gets you in," said a banner on the wooden perimeter fence at Southern Chase, a Beazer subdivision outside Charlotte. The fence started falling apart long before the neighborhood was finished. Mark and Lea Tingley bought a home there in 2001. Lea made $11 an hour weighing trucks at a Martin Marietta rock quarry. Mark made a little less driving a forklift at a building supply store. They didn't think they could afford a home, but the developer, Beazer, promised to take care of the down payment, and to pay part of the mortgage for the first two years. *Let's just do this*, the sales agent told Lea. *You're pregnant. You need a home of your own.*[74]

Lea didn't ask any questions when the agent told her to leave her car payment off the loan application. She listed her income accurately on the application she signed, but on the final version, prepared by Beazer, her income was inflated by $187 a month — just enough to qualify for a loan. Most of all, the Tingleys said they didn't think about what would happen when Beazer stopped helping to pay the mortgage two years later. Millions of Americans similarly found themselves in homes they could not afford; many of them ended up losing those homes.[75]

Education is often prescribed as the remedy for predatory lending, but it is insufficient. Not only do lower-income borrowers tend to have less education, they also tend to live more stressful lives. The economist Sendhil Mullainathan has shown that poverty is literally debilitating. "Being poor," he writes, "reduces a person's cognitive capacity more than going one full night without sleep."[76] Ben S. Bernanke, the Fed chairman during the crisis years, wrote in his memoirs that he finally reached a conclusion at odds with his intellectual upbringing. "We found it was almost impossible to write sufficiently clear disclosures for some financial products," he wrote. "Like flammable pajamas, some products should just be kept out of the marketplace."[77]

But that was after the crisis. The government's approach to regulation in the years before the crisis is encapsulated in a single photograph taken in 2003. It shows a pair of banking regulators posing with a pair of bank lobbyists, and a stack of paper wrapped in red tape. One regulator holds a chain saw; the other holds garden shears. Everyone is smiling.

James Gilleran, one of the regulators in the photo, said the role of his agency, the Office of Thrift Supervision, was to let thrifts "operate with a wide breadth of freedom from regulatory intrusion." Thrifts, also known as savings-and-loans, still tended to focus on mortgage lending. As the housing market boomed, Gilleran eliminated one fourth of his agency's employees. He also suspended examinations of compliance with consumer protection laws, instructing thrifts to conduct "self-examinations." It was during this period that IndyMac, a California thrift, made a loan with a $1482 monthly payment to a Brooklyn man named Simeon Ferguson, who was eighty-five, suffering from dementia, and living on a monthly income of $1126.[78] There were lots of these stories before the crisis — lots of anecdotes dismissed as insignificant.

Greenspan said economic forecasting was "the most important qualification for being chairman of the Fed."[79] The job of a central banker, in his view, was to see the future and get ready for it. But he did not foresee the collapse of the housing market. He repeatedly said there was no bubble in real estate prices, that real estate didn't lend itself to speculation, and that a decline in housing prices, if it happened, "likely would not have substantial macroeconomic implications."[80]

He did not understand that the great Wall Street banks had become housing-finance companies — conduits carrying money from foreign investors into mortgage loans as the vast reservoirs of savings accumulated by America's trading partners were pumped back into the United States, inflating home prices and financial markets.[81] He allowed those same banks to operate as casinos for investors to place elaborate bets on the future of the housing market, using derivatives to greatly increase the scale of speculation — and the size of the crisis that followed.[82]

He had plenty of company. At a conference in August 2005, shortly before Greenspan retired, he was celebrated as a great public servant. When one speaker, a Chicago economist named Raghuram Rajan, dared to suggest that financial innovation was making the world a riskier place, Larry Summers called Rajan "slightly Luddite." Summers, echoing his attack on Born a few years earlier, added that even talking about such things was disruptive.[83]

Paper Fish

Remote, austere, sparsely populated, Iceland rose to prosperity in the twentieth century by trading codfish for everything else: bread and wine, wood and windows, cars and gasoline.

The advent of jet travel in the 1950s allowed Iceland to develop a second profitable export: foreigners came to see the original geyser, the glaciers, the hot springs, the sheer rock face that is the edge of the North American continental plate. The country created one of the first discount airlines, Loftleiðir, which advertised cheap flights to continental Europe with a stopover in Reykjavík; Bill Clinton was among the young passengers.[84] In the late 1960s, Iceland created a third export. The country built dams across meltwater rivers to generate huge amounts of electricity, and it encouraged construction of two aluminum smelters, which required huge amounts of electricity.[85]

Fish, tourism, and aluminum — that was the economy until the 1980s, when Iceland discovered Milton Friedman.

Over the next two decades, Iceland embraced financial deregulation as fully as any country ever has done. One economist described the boom that followed as "the most rapid expansion of a banking system in the history of mankind."[86] During the seven fat years from 2001 through 2007, the income of the average Icelander roughly doubled in real terms, reaching $61,930 in 2017 dollars. Then came the crash.

Both boom and bust were snow-globe miniatures of the broader financial crisis.

Iceland was not an obvious candidate for an experiment in extreme liberalization. It was a democracy with a Scandinavian-style welfare state, and the economy was dominated by a few family-owned conglomerates. But by the late 1960s, Iceland was running out of fish.

First the country tried to chase away foreign trawlers. In 1972, Iceland claimed exclusive fishing rights in a zone extending 50 miles from its shores, and in 1975 it moved the boundary to the 200-mile mark. When British fishermen refused to abide by the rules, Iceland deployed ships designed to cut their nets. The "Cod Wars" ended in complete victory for Iceland, but did not solve the problem of overfishing: Iceland was putting itself out of business.

In the mid-1980s, Iceland decided to try something new: H. Scott Gordon, an economist at Indiana University, had proposed that fishermen were poor because everyone was allowed to catch as much fish as they could. To prevent overfishing, the Icelandic government set a limit on the total catch and then divided shares among its fishermen. In 1991, the government introduced a further innovation, allowing fishermen to buy and sell their rights, which were dubbed "paper fish." The most efficient fishermen soon consolidated the industry, because they could afford to pay the most for fishing rights. Oil use by the fleet declined by 30 percent because the surviving boats were better at catching fish. The value of the catch increased by 44 percent because they also were better at selling fish. The skin was mixed into cosmetics. Enzymes were extracted from fish livers. Dried cod heads were shipped to Nigeria for soup stocks.[87]

The 1991 changes were introduced by a new prime minister, David Oddsson, who also wanted to expand market reforms to the rest of the Icelandic economy. Oddsson was a member of a rising generation of intellectuals and politicians who admired the American and British turns toward the market. He liked to recount that when Milton Friedman visited Iceland in 1984, and was asked for the solution to Iceland's problems, he had responded, "The solution is freedom."[88]

Oddsson took the advice. He cut the corporate income tax rate to 18 percent from 45 percent, and sold the state-owned banks, telephone company, and fish-processing plants. Iceland also joined the European Economic Area, a trade agreement allowing free movement of goods, services, people — and money. On March 27, 2001, amid much talk about economic maturity, the government announced it would let markets determine the trade value of Iceland's currency, the krona.

This was a bold step. The krona was the world's smallest independent currency, and three decades of experience suggested that small countries were easily overwhelmed by the free flow of money across borders. But economists insisted that previous victims, like Chile in the 1980s or Thailand in the 1990s, had failed to fully embrace deregulation. Oddsson accepted their argument that Iceland needed to go further, opening its financial markets and floating its currency.[89]

When I first visited Iceland, in the summer of 2008, I paid the local equivalent of twenty dollars for a bowl of soup at a restaurant in Reykjavík that didn't seem particularly fancy, and found myself wondering what the rest of the diners did for a living.

Ármann Thorvaldsson could have explained. Born into a working-class family, he scrambled to earn a business degree at Boston University in the early 1990s. Iceland had just opened a stock market, and Thorvaldsson landed a job with one of the first brokerages, Kaupthing. By the early 2000s, Thorvaldsson was in charge of the company's London office and he was fabulously wealthy. What he did in between, entertainingly narrated in a postcrash memoir, can basically be described as pumping borrowed money into Iceland.[90] Thorvaldsson's explanation for the binge was that Icelanders were raised to expect deprivation. He wrote that the Icelandic word for loan, *lan*, is also the word for luck. Icelanders also were raised to expect inflation. The Icelandic krona was separated from the Danish krona in 1920; since that time, the Icelandic currency had lost 99.5 percent of its relative value.[91] The result was that people borrowed what they could and spent it as quickly as possible.

The government borrowed money to build a hydroelectric power plant in the remote eastern highlands. (Iceland's population is tiny but it is roughly the size of Ohio.) The electricity was pledged to a new aluminum smelter on the eastern shore, to provide jobs for former fishermen in the town of Reyðarfjörður, but the economy was doing well enough that most of the construction workers were imported from Poland and housed in a new town outside the old town.

The people of Iceland borrowed, too. The number of new cars registered each year nearly tripled between 2001 and 2005.[92] More Range Rovers were sold in Iceland in 2007 than in the rest of Scandinavia combined — though Iceland accounts for only about 1 percent of the region's population.[93] Many car loans were denominated in yen, the currency of a very different island nation on the other side of the world, because Japan's interest rates were low. Icelanders also borrowed heavily against the value of their homes, taking advantage of a battle for market share between the nation's private banks and a government-owned mortgage lender, the Housing Financing Fund.

And Icelanders used the abundant supply of cheap money to trade with one another. Paper fish were particularly popular. In 2000, the going price was about 800 kronur per kilo of cod. By 2008 it reached 4400 kronur. At that price, the stock of paper fish was worth about fifty times the value of the annual catch.[94] More adventurous Icelanders, dubbed "Venture Vikings," invested in foreign assets, too, including American Airlines, a British soccer team, and a Russian brewery. One installed a ten-foot statue of a Viking in his London office. For whatever reason, it held a guitar.[95]

Íslandsbanki, one of Kaupthing's rivals, passed the twentieth century earning modest profits from the necessary business of financing fishing trawlers. In the new century, as it chased a greater destiny, the bank renamed itself Glitnir, after a part of heaven described in an old Viking saga: "There's a hall called Glitnir / With pillars of gold / It's also roofed with silver."[96]

Már Wolfgang Mixa worked as a stockbroker in the United States before returning to Iceland in the mid-2000s. In America he had spent three months in training and completed a written exam before he could touch clients' money. In Iceland, the training lasted one day and there was no exam. Mixa said he and his colleagues often were forced to use English words because the development of the financial industry was outpacing the development of the Icelandic language.[97]

In 1998, the Icelandic banking system was about the same size as the Icelandic economy. A decade later, the banking system was roughly nine times larger than the economy.[98]

Iceland and its financial institutions remained relatively obscure. Not until November 2005 did a foreign bank publish a credit analysis on Kaupthing, the star of Iceland's financial scene. The early reports tended to be glowing. The free-market system was proving again that money can move faster than knowledge.

Lars Christensen, an economist at Danske Bank in Denmark, was one of the few public skeptics, publishing a 2006 report warning investors to keep their distance. In response, the Iceland Chamber of Commerce commissioned a report by Frederic Mishkin, a Columbia University economics professor, that certified the health of the Icelandic financial system. Mishkin and Geir Haarde, an economist who had succeeded Oddsson as Iceland's prime minister, appeared together at an event in New York billed as "The Real Story about Iceland." Two years later, in February 2008, the Iceland Chamber of Commerce dismissed the very idea Iceland could be compared with the rest of Scandinavia "because we are superior to them in most respects."[99]

Still, the flow of money from large investors began to dwindle, so Iceland's banks went after the retail market. The European Economic Area allowed banks to serve residents of the entire zone, and Icelandic banks offered high interest rates to encourage Europeans to open savings accounts. "Hi, I'm John Cleese, a very famous actor…," began one ad in which the former Monty Python front man tried to pronounce Kaupthing.

After the collapse of Kaupthing, an unapologetic Cleese grumbled that Iceland seemed unable to control either its banks or its volcanoes.[100]

On Monday, October 6, 2008, less than a month after the failure of Lehman Brothers in the United States had initiated the deepest phase of the global financial crisis, Haarde went on television to report that Iceland's economy was being sucked into a maelstrom that could end in "national bankruptcy." Then he really sounded the alarm, ending his speech with the words "God save Iceland." God was not regularly invoked in Iceland, certainly not by public figures as an alternative to self-sufficiency.

People still quote that line. It encapsulated just how badly Iceland had gone wrong.

Krona could not be exchanged for foreign currencies, so the government was forced to borrow from other Scandinavian nations to pay for food. Much of the wealth that Icelanders had acquired disappeared. Thousands lost their homes, their cars, their hopes for retirement. In Iceland, thousands is a large share of the population.

Europeans, in turn, lost much of the money they had pumped into Iceland. Germany alone had shipped about $21.3 billion to Iceland — or about $70,000 for every man, woman, and child on the island. Much of the money came from state-owned banks, which were bailed out at the expense of German taxpayers.* "They wasted billions that we could have spent on schools, police and streets," fumed one German legislator, perhaps forgetting that the government had allowed it to happen.[101]

Iceland's story, like the rest of the crisis, is easy to reduce to the irresponsibility of bankers and borrowers. As one banker told a reporter in 2009, "When car crashes happen, people don't blame cars or stop driving them. They blame the drivers! Derivatives are the same — it's not the tools at fault but the people who used those tools."[102]

This is the same mistake that impeded efforts to reduce traffic fatalities during the first half of the twentieth century. What finally began to save lives was the recognition that accidents happen, and cars need to be designed to limit the damage.

Even between crises, a bloated financial sector is weighing on economic growth in developed nations, including the United States. Economists long argued that financial growth produced economic growth, but more recent work suggests finance, like most things, is best enjoyed in moderation. A remarkable share of the world's highly educated population is basically employed in the business of toll collecting. High levels of debt weigh on demand. And the focus on short-term gains comes at the expense of investments that might increase long-term prosperity. Finance tends to focus on consumer lending because it's easier to take advantage of

---

* These were still small numbers in the context of the global financial crisis. One of the largest state-owned German banks, BayernLB, managed to lose about $1 billion in Iceland — and about five times that much on American mortgages.

individual borrowers; it tends to focus on short-term transactions because it prizes immediate rewards. And finance tends to prefer low-risk deals, like construction loans, rather than sinking money into the long-term development of promising ideas.[103]

Iceland, at least, seems to have taken the lesson. The country jailed thirty-six bankers and shrank its financial industry down to size, imposing strict limits on foreign investment.

The collapse of the krona sparked a rebound in Iceland's export industries, most of all tourism, which benefited from the island's new-found notoriety. Tourism increased from 18 percent of exports in 2010 to 31 percent in 2015, topping fish and aluminum for the first time.[104]

Sandra Thorbjornsdottir, who worked in the financial industry during the boom years, moved in 2010 from Reykjavík to Reyðarfjörður, the tiny town on the opposite side of the island where Alcoa operates Iceland's third aluminum refinery. She bought an old restaurant and guest house, Taergesen, that had closed eight months earlier. In 2013, she added a second building with twenty more guest rooms. In 2016 she added a neighboring hotel, doubling her room count to eighty. But Iceland increasingly has found itself wrestling with a new version of an old problem: instead of too much money, there are now too many tourists. Globalization is a fire hose. Nations need water. But they also have to be careful how much they drink.

Conclusion

All right, so you didn't promise us a rose garden without
thorns — but the thorns without the rose garden?
> — *Walter Heller*, The Economy: Old Myths and
> New Realities *(1976)*[1]

At a celebration of Milton Friedman's ninetieth birthday in 2002, Ben
S. Bernanke, then a member of the Federal Reserve's board of governors, offered a salute: "I would like to say to Milton and Anna [Schwartz]:
Regarding the Great Depression. You're right, we did it. We're
very sorry. But thanks to you, we won't do it again."[2] Friedman did not
live long enough to see Bernanke keep that promise. He died in November 2006, and his ashes were scattered in San Francisco Bay.[3] The
following year, the economy plunged into the worst crisis since the Great
Depression.

Friedman had as large a hand in causing the crisis as any man, but it is
a mark of the complexity of his legacy that he also left effective instructions
for limiting the damage. Bernanke had replaced Greenspan as the
Fed's chairman shortly before the crisis began and, true to his word, he
pumped money into the financial system until the big banks stood up and
started walking again. When Bernanke entered the Fed's boardroom in
December 2009, officials gathered around the long table gave him a
standing ovation. The recession was over, unemployment had begun to
decline, and Bernanke was widely regarded as singularly responsible.

That week, it was Bernanke's turn on the cover of *Time* magazine.

The Economists' Hour did not survive the Great Recession. Perhaps
it ended at 3:00 p.m. on Monday, October 13, 2008, when the chief

executives of America's nine largest banks were escorted into a gilded room at the Treasury. The government had tried to support the banks by purchasing bonds in the open market, but the market had collapsed, so the government decided to save the financial system by taking ownership stakes in the largest financial firms.

Or perhaps it was one of a dozen other moments during the financial crisis; it doesn't really matter which. In the depths of the Great Recession, only the most foolhardy purists continued to insist that markets should be left to their own devices.* Milton Friedman said of John Maynard Keynes that if he had lived long enough, he would have been at the forefront of the free-market counterrevolution. Perhaps if Friedman had lived a few years longer, even he would have recognized that the counterrevolution had gone too far. "The idea that the markets were always right was mad," said French president Nicolas Sarkozy. "Laissez-faire is finished."

But a generation of economists and policy makers raised on faith in markets remained in the grip of those ideas, many of which also were entrenched by law and habit. It was madness to persist in those policies and to expect better results. But it was not obvious what should come next. The world's leaders must surely have sympathized with President Carter's plaintive letter to a trusted adviser back in 1979. "I understand from this what will not work. What will?" As in the 1930s and the 1970s, the 2010s were a decade of confusion.

Barack Obama took office in the depths of the recession. Advised by a collection of mildly penitent technocrats, he briefly embraced the Keynesian claim that government could help. Larry Summers, who was installed as head of the National Economic Council, had said in 2001 that government stimulus spending during an economic downturn was "passé" because its merits had been "disproven." In 2009 he changed his mind. When a reporter asked Summers to describe the government's plans, he responded with one word: "Keynes."[4] The Obama administration pushed

---

* The congregation of foolhardy purists was, to be sure, both substantial and distinguished.

a $787 billion stimulus plan through Congress, including money to build more railroads.[5] Federal spending on safety-net programs like unemployment benefits also grew rapidly.

Governments across the developed world shoveled money into the breach. The leaders of the world's major economies, the G-20, met in Pittsburgh in September 2009, and then issued a joint statement declaring, "We cannot rest until the global economy is restored to full health and hard-working families the world over can find decent jobs." They were pretty clear about what that meant, too, adding, "We will avoid any premature withdrawal of stimulus."

Some economists howled in protest. The Italian economists Alberto Alesina and Silvia Ardagna published a study in October 2009 that said governments could spur economic growth by reducing budget deficits — in other words, by spending less money rather than more.[6] A few months later, in January 2010, the American economists Carmen Reinhart and Kenneth Rogoff published a paper purporting to identify a kind of red line for government borrowing: they said that when debts exceeded 90 percent of a nation's annual economic output, growth declined.[7] The European Commission's head of economic and monetary affairs, Olli Rehn, started talking about a "90-percent rule." The chief economist of the International Monetary Fund called the 90 percent threshold "a good reference point." Reinhart and Rogoff had made an important mistake in their math, but it took a few years before someone caught it.[8]

Meanwhile, the Keynesian moment quickly faded. In the United States, Obama made a sharp turn toward austerity in January 2010, just one year after his inauguration, promising to freeze nonmilitary discretionary spending. "Families across the country are tightening their belts and making tough decisions," Obama said. "The federal government should do the same." A few weeks later, he created a commission to recommend steps toward a balanced budget. In the fall of 2010, Republicans won control of the House, ending any chance of more stimulus.

Europe retreated even more quickly. In April 2010, Alesina was invited to address a gathering of the European Union's economic and finance ministers in Madrid. He told the group that "large, credible and decisive" reductions in government borrowing would spur economic growth. The ministers cited Alesina's work in their official communiqué after the meeting.[9]

That June, the leaders of the major economies gathered again, this time in Toronto, and completely disavowed their earlier promises. The Europeans, in particular, were badly rattled by the opening acts of the Greek debt crisis. This time, the joint statement said developed nations had agreed to reduce their budget deficits by half over the following three years.

David Cameron, who took office as British prime minister in May 2010, moved to raise taxes and cut spending. One of Cameron's ministers, Eric Pickles, explained that public spending had caused the crisis. "People blame the bankers, but I think big government is just as much to blame as the big banks," he said.[10] During Cameron's six years in office, Britain eliminated roughly one million public sector jobs. Cameron said the goal was to reduce spending "not just now, but permanently." Meanwhile, the British financial sector staged a spectacular rebound, widening the gap between the ostentatious wealth of London and the economic stagnation of the hinterlands.

Germany's deficits had grown more quickly than America's, because of more generous safety-net programs. In the spring of 2010, Germany also turned toward austerity. The largest cuts were in the defense budget — including the end of military conscription. Wolfgang Schäuble, the German finance minister, cited Reinhart and Rogoff's work in explaining the plan. Four years later, in 2014, Schäuble took obvious pleasure in telling the Bundestag that the German government planned no increase in its total debt, balancing its federal budget for the first time since 1969.

Germany and its allies in northern Europe also set about imposing austerity on the struggling south. The European Central Bank (ECB) pressed Spain to amend its constitution, inserting a balanced budget requirement. In Italy and Greece, the elected heads of government resigned and were replaced by austerity-minded economists. In Greece, it was Lucas Papademos, a former ECB vice president. In Italy, it was Mario Monti, a former European minister and head of Bruegel, a market-oriented economic think tank.

* * *

Almost the only policy makers willing to persist in efforts to revive growth were the small coterie of former economics professors who ran the Federal Reserve. In November 2010, with the unemployment rate still at 9.8 percent, the Fed ended four decades of single-minded focus on inflation and launched a campaign to stimulate job growth. Chairman Bernanke said the Fed was fighting against "a waste of human and economic potential." People who are out of work suffer a decline in health and life expectancy; they lose skills, including the ability to read; and, perhaps most depressing, some studies have found extended unemployment impairs the prospects and the lifetime earnings of the children of unemployed workers. The Fed already had reduced its benchmark interest rate nearly to zero, pinning down short-term interest rates. To further reduce long-term rates, the Fed started buying vast quantities of Treasuries and mortgage bonds, forcing private money into riskier markets, which had the effect of reducing borrowing costs. Greenspan was not impressed, complaining in 2013, "The spectacle of American central bankers trying to press the inflation rate higher in the aftermath of the 2008 crisis is virtually without precedent."[11] He predicted, incorrectly, that the effort could end in double-digit inflation.[12]

Bernanke's successor, Janet L. Yellen, who took office in 2014, was an even more forceful advocate for reducing unemployment. In her first speech as chairwoman, Yellen told the stories of three Chicagoland residents looking for work. "They are a reminder," she said, "that there are real people behind the statistics, struggling to get by and eager for the opportunity to build better lives."

In 2011, Mario Draghi, an Italian economist who went to graduate school with Bernanke, became the new head of the ECB. The following year, he declared in London that the ECB would do "whatever it takes to preserve the euro. And believe me, it will be enough." The ECB then began to emulate the Fed's stimulus campaign. Also in 2012, Japanese voters swept the Liberal Democratic Party into power after a campaign in which its leader, Shinzō Abe, promised dramatic efforts to invigorate the economy, including monetary expansion, fiscal stimulus, and supply-side reforms. The "Abenomics" patchwork was very nearly the photo negative of Milton Friedman's views on government economic policy, embracing everything he had fought to discredit.

Even New Zealand's government instructed its central bank to focus on unemployment.

But the efforts of the central banks were not enough. Economic growth remained slow; millions of people remained out of the workforce for years, many not even trying to find jobs.

The Western democracies might have taken a lesson from China, which would have been a fitting turnabout, because China confronted the crisis with lessons taken from the West.

Following the death of Mao Zedong in 1976, some Chinese policy makers and intellectuals began to assert cautiously that the nation could achieve greater economic growth by heeding what they described as "objective economic laws."[13] This was bold talk in a country that had only recently stopped imprisoning people for the crime of "economism," but China's new leader, Deng Xiaoping, had been deeply impressed by a 1978 visit to Japan, and wanted to bring intellectuals back into policy making. Deng described this approach as "seeking truth from facts." Chinese leaders cast a broad net. They invited economists from socialist countries in Eastern Europe and from the United States. In 1980, the Ford Foundation paid for a group of prominent American academics to spend seven weeks teaching economics on an island on the grounds of the Summer Palace in Beijing. Paul Samuelson's textbook was translated into Chinese and, in 1980, the government invited Milton Friedman to visit.

Friedman's trip was not a success. When one reads the accounts of the visit, it is hard to say whether Friedman or his hosts were the more dismayed. At least the Chinese learned what they did not want. Instead they sought advice from Keynesians who favored a market economy carefully managed by the government — the kinds of Western economists who were no longer heeded in their own lands. Alexander Cairncross, a British economist who traveled to China in the early 1980s to meet with Premier Zhao Ziyang, the senior Chinese official most committed to market reforms, wrote in his diary after the meeting that it all "seemed quite natural until one stopped to think that the speaker was the Prime Minister of the largest country on earth, canvassing advice from an assorted group of foreign economists, not all of whom could hope for equal attention in their own country."[14] Margaret Thatcher's government had no interest in Cairncross's advice, but Zhao did.

In 1985, Zhao invited academics including Cairncross, the Hungarian János Kornai, and the American James Tobin for a Yangtze River cruise. The discussions were not always easy. The historian Julian Gewirtz reports that at one point, an interpreter burst into tears because she could not find Chinese words to explain what was being said. But the visitors, particularly Kornai and Tobin, made a lasting impression. Wu Jinglian, one of China's most prominent economists, later recalled the trip as the moment he concluded "a market with macroeconomic management should be the primary objective of China's economic reforms."[15] One of Kornai's books was translated into Chinese the following year and quickly sold more than 100,000 copies.

As China regained its role as a self-confident power, its leaders spent less time listening to Western economists, and the role of the early exchanges was diminished in the retelling. But when the 2008 crisis came, China's response was Keynesian in all but name. The government went on a spending spree about 2.5 times as large as the Obama stimulus, measured as a share of the two economies — and China persisted as the rest of the world turned to austerity.

The Obama administration did not repeat Roosevelt's effort to overhaul the financial industry. Instead, the government renovated and expanded the rusted infrastructure of regulation. One of the most notable changes was the creation of a new agency, the Consumer Financial Protection Bureau, to do what the Fed would not.

Bankers were not held responsible for their role in causing the crisis. In March 2009, Obama summoned the nation's top banking executives to the White House and warned them to mind their manners. "My administration," he told them, "is the only thing between you and the pitchforks." In the old westerns, the virtuous sheriff protects his prisoners from the mob so they can stand trial. This time there were few trials. As of 2018, about 355 bankers, mortgage lenders, real estate agents, and borrowers had been convicted of crimes related to the crisis. But they were almost all small fry. No executives of the largest financial firms went to jail. And the total was only about a third of the number of convictions after the much smaller savings-and-loan crisis in the 1980s.[16]

The government bailed out the banking industry, but it did not mount a comparable effort to help borrowers. Obama decided to rely on mortgage companies to modify unaffordable loans. He eschewed direct intervention, the approach advocated by his chief political rivals in the 2008 presidential race, Hillary Rodham Clinton and John McCain. Moreover, the administration did not require companies to invest the necessary resources to meet their legal obligations, and it responded slowly to warnings of misconduct. SunTrust piled up unopened applications from homeowners seeking help until the floor of the storage room buckled under the weight. A federal investigation concluded, "SunTrust, rather than assist homeowners in need, financially ruined many through an utter dereliction" of its legal responsibilities.[17] For these crimes, the federal government did not prosecute SunTrust, nor hold any individual SunTrust employees responsible.

One reason for the failure to hold bankers accountable was that the Justice Department was worried about economic efficiency. Eric Holder, the attorney general for much of the Obama administration, was the namesake of the "Holder Doctrine" — the view that prosecutors should consider "collateral consequences" before filing charges against corporations. Holder had articulated this view in a 1999 memo while serving as deputy attorney general in the Clinton administration. The government's prosecution of the accounting firm Arthur Andersen for its role in Enron's frauds in the early 2000s became Exhibit A: the accounting firm shut its doors, and thousands of workers were forced to scramble for jobs at other firms. After the 2008 crisis, Holder and his deputies reiterated their view that economic considerations trumped old-fashioned ideas about justice. "It does become difficult for us to prosecute them," Holder testified before Congress in 2013, "when we are hit with indications that if you do prosecute — if you do bring a criminal charge — it will have a negative impact on the national economy, perhaps even the world economy."[18]

Holder did not seem as mindful of the impact of allowing crimes to go unpunished.

Financial crises have a long history of corroding faith in liberal democracy. A study of financial crises in developed nations since 1870 found far-right political parties often are the beneficiaries, winning popular support by blaming immigrants and minorities for the loss of prosperity.[19]

This time was no different. Nationalist sentiment in the West had been on the rise at least since the 9/11 terrorist attacks; the Great Recession intensified the trend.[20]

In June 2016, Britain voted to leave the European Union. That November, Donald Trump was elected president of the United States. In 2018, Brazilians elected a new president, the nationalist Jair Bolsonaro, who campaigned in Trump's image.

Trump's contempt for economics — and for its basic building blocks, statistics and reasoning — is without parallel among modern American presidents. The numbers in the new administration's first budget didn't even add up. The administration pushed a tax cut through Congress without bothering to present a formal analysis. Regulations were set aside without any attempt to analyze the costs or benefits. The President revived antitrust enforcement, after a fashion, by threatening to block mergers of companies he did not like.

Most of all, Trump rejected the economists' view of trade. Peter Navarro, Trump's trade adviser, held a doctorate from Harvard, but he was not a conventional economist. He said trade was a war among nations; he had directed a documentary, *Death by China*, that opened with an animation of a knife labeled "Made in China" stabbing a bleeding map of the United States. Trump's chief political adviser, Stephen Bannon, took a similar view. "The globalists gutted the American working class and created a middle class in Asia," Bannon said. "The issue now is about Americans looking to not get fucked over."[21]

Trade was in decline even before Trump arrived in Washington. The dollar value of global trade fell each year from 2012 through 2016, before beginning a modest recovery.[22] But the new president set out to do his part. After his inauguration, Trump redecorated the Oval Office in shades of gold and then sat down to sign an order withdrawing the United States from a proposed trade agreement among Pacific Rim nations. He also pressed American companies to reconsider moves to other countries. Mainstream economists regard outsourcing as good for the American economy, so long as companies are responding to market forces. The new administration did not. "The free market has been sorting it out, and America's been losing," said Vice President Mike Pence.[23]

In the summer of 2017, roughly 240 years after the birth of modern economics, Trump was on Air Force One, working through the text of an upcoming speech. He grabbed a pen and wrote in the margin, "Trade is Bad."[24]

After the Flood

Galesburg, Illinois, a small factory town set in the vastness of midwestern farmland, prospered for most of the twentieth century. Ronald Reagan spent part of his childhood there; one of his first-grade report cards is displayed in a reliquary in an antiques mall on East Main Street. But around 1970, Galesburg began to fade. Michael Patrick, who landed at the local refrigerator plant straight out of high school in 1959, told me in 2015 that Galesburg had been losing factories and jobs for as long as anyone could remember. Companies went out of business, mechanized, moved to new cities. What began to change in the 1970s, he said, was that new companies stopped coming. When factories shut down, buildings stayed empty; when people lost jobs, they struggled to find new ones. In 2016, almost half of the 10,500 working-age men in Galesburg were not working.[25] It's worth underscoring that astonishing number because the most familiar measure of joblessness, the unemployment rate, grossly understates the scale of unemployment in the United States. The government counts people who are looking for work. In 2016, that described about 6 percent of the men in Galesburg — but an additional 41 percent of the city's working-age men were neither working nor actively seeking work. Some were retired; some were happy; but many had simply given up.

Those who did find jobs often had to compromise: driving an hour each way to factories in Peoria, or accepting odd hours, or working for less money. After the refrigerator factory shut down in 2004, Tracy Warner found two jobs: teacher's assistant by day and janitor by night. In her last year at the factory, she earned about $37,000; in 2015, she made $21,000.

America's shift from shoe making to bond trading was mostly the inexorable result of forces beyond the control of policy makers, and many of the consequences are very good. Technological progress vastly reduced the number of workers required to make a car or a computer, and manufacturing spread more evenly across the face of the globe. There is no alternate version of history in which American politicians embraced different policies and thousands of Americans are still making refrigerators in Galesburg, or steel in Pittsburgh, or cotton sheets in the mills of the Carolina Piedmont.[26]

But it didn't have to be so painful. The transformation of policy during the Economists' Hour hastened the evolution of the American economy, and funneled the benefits into the pockets of a plutocratic minority. The high price of the dollar and a single-minded commitment to low inflation accelerated the decline of manufacturing and made it harder to find new jobs. The growing pool of nonworking workers held down wages. One obvious counterweight, the power of unions, was eroded by the antipathy of elites and by the government's tolerance for corporate concentration, which shifted bargaining power to employers.

The federal government passed a minimum wage law in 1938, but it was not tied to inflation, so increases depend on the grace of Congress. Adjusting for inflation, the value of the minimum wage peaked in 1968. During the Economists' Hour, it lost 40 percent of its value.

Economists regarded wages as the unerring judgment of the marketplace. In the words of John Snow, an economist who served as Treasury secretary under President George W. Bush, "People will get paid on how valuable they are to the enterprise."[27]

Even liberals like Paul Samuelson and James Tobin regarded unions as cartels and insisted that minimum wage laws increased joblessness, a consensus that made it easier for politicians to attack unions and ignore wages.[28] Meanwhile, in the real world, wages were determined by a tug-of-war between employers and workers — and employers were winning.[29]

The most important effect of these shocks and shifts is quite simple: workers are getting less of the American pie. As shown in the chart below, the share of economic output American workers take home in wages has been falling since the early 1970s.

The greatest problem confronting the American economy, however, is not the decline of traditional manufacturing or the loss of factory jobs. Rather, it is the way the service economy has grown. As jobs have shifted into areas like health care and retail, employers have taken advantage of the permissive landscape. The part of the economy that is now expanding most quickly is the work of caring for aging baby boomers. Half of the ten occupations projected to add the most jobs in the United States by 2026 are different ways of saying "nurse."[30] These jobs tend to be physically

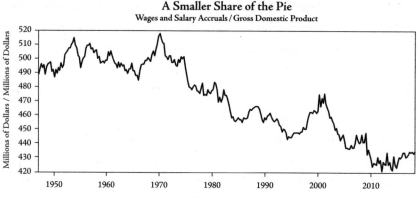

A Smaller Share of the Pie
Wages and Salary Accruals / Gross Domestic Product

Source: U.S. Bureau of Economic Analysis

demanding and emotionally draining; they also tend to be poorly paid, with meager benefits and little job security. The line of work projected to add the most jobs over the next decade, "personal care aides," offered an average annual salary of $23,100 in 2016.

If the iconic workplace of the midcentury was an automobile factory that lifted its workers into the middle class, the microcosm of the modern economy is a hospital staffed by a handful of highly paid physicians and a vast army of poorly paid support staff.

One consequence is the startling resurgence of inequality. Between World War II and the 1970s, economic growth in the United States lifted all boats at roughly the same rate. Since the early 1970s, growth has been erratic, and the benefits have gone mostly to the people who own the yachts. In 1971, the top 10 percent of households earned 31 percent of total income. By 2016, the top 10 percent took 48 percent.[31] Inequality has climbed to levels last seen in the days of Jay Gatsby.

Some degree of inequality is not just unavoidable, but desirable. Capitalism is a competition; money is the prize. George Stigler, who believed strongly in the moral value of markets, saw a benefit beyond this, too. He said the point of maximizing output "was with the maximizing, not with the output. The struggle of men for larger incomes was good because in the process they learned independence, self-reliance, self-discipline — because, in short, they became better men."[32]

But in the United States in the twenty-first century, the people who end up with the largest incomes tend to be the children of people with large incomes. Social mobility is ossifying; the lesson of the marketplace is that the same people usually win. And it's increasingly clear that inequality isn't even good for economic growth. A 2014 study by the Organization for Economic Cooperation and Development found that countries with more inequality had less growth.[33] One reason is that less affluent children often have less access to education, limiting their economic potential. In Chile, 33 percent of eighteen- to twenty-four-year-olds from the lowest income quintile were enrolled in college in 2017, compared with 53 percent of those from the top quintile.[34] In the

United States, differences in the quality of public education, and the rising cost of public universities, have produced similar, though less dramatic, effects.

Economic inequality also distorts public policy as politicians face greater pressure to accommodate rent-seeking elites and to provide help to the poor. And inequality attenuates a sense of shared purpose, which makes it more difficult to maintain political support for the necessary levels of public investment in education, research, and infrastructure.

The rise of inequality means the performance of the U.S. economy is not as strong as it may seem. Most Americans probably think the American economy outstripped the French economy during the Economists' Hour. They're right. But the picture is quite different if one excludes the top percentile of households in both countries. For the 99 percent, income growth in France was much faster than in the United States.[35]

A strong social safety net is necessary to sustain a market economy, just as a market economy is necessary to sustain a strong safety net. The economic historian Karl Polanyi observed that these imperatives — the reliance on markets and the commitment to provide a minimum standard of living — rose together in a "double movement" in the nineteenth century. Polanyi described the two forces as opposed: fairness eroding capitalism; capitalism eroding fairness.[36] A more optimistic view is that these forces can exist in productive tension, as during the mid-twentieth century, when the United States simultaneously expanded its safety net and its market economy. By contrast, in recent decades, America has pursued economic growth without sufficient regard to the strength of the safety net, and it is the imbalance that has proven destructive. The Georgetown economist Pietra Rivoli argues that opposition to trade is stronger in the United States, in comparison to other developed countries with higher levels of trade, because the social safety net is much weaker. The United States, for example, is the only developed nation that does not provide universal health care. If the people who lose jobs when a factory closes still have health insurance, if training is affordable, if they can find housing in the areas with new jobs and pay for child care, then transitions are manageable. If not, those people are likely to be angrier about globalization — and with ample justification.

Also, money is not enough. Unemployment is not just a lack of money; it is also a lack of purpose and of opportunity. Alfred Kahn was right to observe that "one cannot simply equate the 'public interest' in a democracy with the 'consumer interest.'" He was right to insist people also have interests as producers and as "citizens of an urbanized civilization."

Mohamed Bouazizi, the Tunisian fruit vendor whose self-immolation in 2010 set off the Arab Spring, lived in a nation with a rapidly growing economy. "Judging by economic data alone, the revolutions of the 2011 Arab Spring should have never happened," the World Bank noted in a 2015 assessment.[37] But Tunisians were not satisfied. They wanted freedom, health, happiness — and the Middle East is still burning. "Economic growth cannot sensibly be treated as an end in itself," Amartya Sen, an economist in an older tradition, has written. "Development has to be more concerned with enhancing the lives we lead and the freedoms we enjoy."[38]

In some cases, the answer is to make markets less efficient. Efficiency has no special claim as the primary purpose of a marketplace. Communities can decide what they want from markets. The market that matches medical students with training programs is structured to let married couples end up in the same place. That is not efficient, yet it was deemed important.

The government already shelters Americans from the marketplace in various ways — but the protections most often are afforded to affluent Americans, at the expense of everyone else. The antipathy toward unions has not extended to professional cartels like the associations of real estate agents that squeeze 6 percent commissions from home sellers. The government also lets medical doctors limit the number of training slots for new doctors, which is one reason doctors in the United States earn roughly twice as much as doctors in other wealthy nations. Zoning laws and other limits on construction raise housing prices in the areas where jobs are concentrated, which is good for current homeowners, and bad for everyone else.

How might the government extend protection to the less fortunate?

Policy makers should consider, for example, that the pain of losing one dollar generally exceeds the pleasure of gaining one dollar; that slowing the pace of change can reduce the pain; that markets "must be sometimes seasoned with mercy," in the words of the economist Frank Knight, a member of the University of Chicago faculty in the generation before the Age of Friedman and Stigler.[39]

Most important, in evaluating public policy, society would benefit from explicit consideration of the distribution of the potential costs and benefits. The rise of inequality has happened in large measure because policy makers haven't decided to stop it.

In a classic classroom game, a professor divides students into pairs. One student is given $10, and told to offer some to the other student. If the offer is accepted, the first student pays that amount and keeps the balance. If the offer is declined, the first student returns the $10 to the teacher. The second student benefits financially from accepting anything, even a single penny. But students routinely turn down anything less than about $3. They would rather watch the money burn than let the first student keep more. The British government obtained similar results in a 1970s survey. It offered the following choice: (A) Everyone gets £4 per week. (B) You get £5 per week, but some people get £6 per week. Eighty percent of respondents picked the first option, forgoing £1 per week because other people would get more.[40] "Homo economicus is usually assumed to care about wealth more than such issues as fairness and justice," says the behavioral economist Richard Thaler. "The research on ultimatum games belies such easy characterizations."[41]

Sometimes, the right answer is to do without a market. Congressional committees reserve at least a few seats at every hearing for the general public. The first people in line, however, generally have no interest in attending the hearing. They are paid to stand in line by companies that save seats, at a hefty price, for lobbyists or other members of the Washington elite. An economist might tell you that this is good for the person who waits in line, who has time and needs money, and it is good for the lobbyist, who would rather spend money than time. But it is not good for democracy. People do not have the same amounts of money, nor the same ability to earn money. Some people are born wealthy, some people become wealthy, and some people are born poor and stay that way. Reliance on the market grants priority to people who have money.

If that seems a petty example, consider another one: the United States is alone among developed nations in allowing income to determine who has access to health care. Or consider that in most metropolitan areas, a seat at a good public school is obtained by purchasing a home in an affluent suburb. Drivers in a growing number of cities pay to use less crowded highway lanes. Prisoners in some jurisdictions can pay for nicer cells. Citizens of other countries can purchase American citizenship by making a minimum investment in the United States.

Milton Friedman said markets strengthen society by limiting the number of issues on which people are required to reach agreement. "The widespread use of the market reduces the strain on the social fabric by rendering conformity unnecessary with respect to any activities it encompasses," he wrote in the 1960s. "The wider the range of activities covered by the market, the fewer are the issues on which explicitly political decisions are required."[42]

This misapprehends human nature. Relationships are like muscles rather than textiles. They are strengthened by use. The economist Albert O. Hirschman observed in his fascinating 1970 book, *Exit, Voice, and Loyalty*, that a person in a disappointing relationship — commercial, personal, or political — has three choices: she can leave, complain, or endure in silence. The easier it is to leave, he wrote, the less likely a disappointed person will complain. The easier it is to leave, the less likely that person will seek to improve the relationship. Wealthy parents, for example, do not seek to improve urban schools. They move to the suburbs. And America is a nation founded on the idea that it's better to move on. Our ancestors left the places they were born, and came here; they moved west, and west again. They left the cities for the suburbs, and the suburbs for the exurbs. They constructed a market society, and the defining feature of a market is the freedom to walk away.

Our problem is too many markets, and too much walking away. If you have taken anything from this book, I hope it is the knowledge markets are constructed by people, for purposes chosen by people — and they can be changed and rebuilt by people.

The market economy remains one of humankind's most awesome inventions, a powerful machine for the creation of wealth. But the measure of a society is the quality of life at the bottom of the pyramid, not the top. The willful indifference to the distribution of prosperity over the last half century is an important reason the very survival of liberal democracy is now being tested by nationalist demagogues, as it was in the 1930s.

I have no special insight into how long the rope can hold, or how much weight it can bear. The answers may well be "a long time" and "a lot," although the rising tide of popular discontent since 2008 should inspire some misgivings. I am confident, however, that our shared bonds will last longer if we can find ways to reduce the strain.

Acknowledgments

Some years ago, I read Thomas McCraw's *Prophets of Regulation*, which narrates the evolution of America's approach to economic regulation. The book stuck in my mind — particularly the idea that the current approach was relatively new. As I wrote about economic policy for a series of newspapers over the last fifteen years, I found myself frequently reminded of McCraw's view that regulation in the 1970s had entered a new era — what he called the Economists' Hour. I learned of similar revolutions in other areas of policy, and I began to learn more about what those revolutions had replaced.

The basic idea for this book kicked around in my mind for years. In the autumn of 2016, Chris Parris-Lamb persuaded me that it was time to write. Chris, who became my agent, helped me to shape the premise that the hour had ended, and that we now confront the question of what comes next. He also helped to shape everything else about this book, because he's awesome. My thanks also go to his colleagues at the Gernert Company.

Vanessa Mobley, my editor at Little, Brown, made a bet on a first-time author. I am deeply grateful for her enthusiasm for this project — and most of all for her skill as an editor, which made this book a lot better. Time and again, she helped me to see where I needed to go. I am also grateful to the many others at Little, Brown who helped to create and sell this book.

As a kid I dreamed of writing for the *New York Times*. In 2010, that dream came true and, almost a decade later, I still count myself incredibly fortunate to make my professional home among the world's best journalists. I am grateful to Elisabeth Bumiller and Dean Baquet for giving me the time to work on this book. I'm also grateful to my editors, who have encouraged my curiosity, including Tom Redburn, Damon Darlin, and Deborah Solomon, and to my colleagues on the economics beat. I learned from all of you.

Writing a book is a solitary enterprise, which I expected, and a communal enterprise, which I did not. The following is necessarily a partial list of the many people who contributed.

Tom Redburn agreed to an encore performance as my editor. His deep knowledge of the events described in this narrative, many of which he covered as a journalist, his grace and care as an editor, and his skepticism all left a mark.

Aaron Stagoff-Belfort performed valuable research on a wide range of subjects, particularly the history of antitrust enforcement, the rise of law and economics, and the contributions of George Stigler. I'm grateful for his enthusiasm, and his willingness to chase obscure anecdotes. Manuel Bautista González read the drafts of each chapter with particular attention to the description of economic concepts. He helped me to correct and clarify a number of issues, though of course he's not responsible for any remaining mistakes. He also translated primary sources from the original Spanish. Sam Dean was my eyes and hands at the Nixon Presidential Library.

The Library of Congress happens to be my neighborhood library, and I spent countless hours there. Ensconced in the grand reading room, working my way through a book and its sources, I sometimes felt like I was benefiting from the Victorian version of the internet. It remains wondrous to me how quickly the staff conjures texts.

My trips to Chile, Iceland, and Taiwan were some of the most rewarding parts of my research for this book, broadening my understanding of the real-world consequences of alternative economic policies. I am deeply grateful to Victor Herrero, who served as my guide in Chile. He contributed to this book as a journalist, as a translator, and as an inexhaustible source of information. In each of those roles, he was simply indispensable. I am also grateful to a number of other Chilean journalists for their help and hospitality, especially Isabel Reyes Bustos as well as Pascale Bonnefoy, Carola Fuentes, and Rafael Valdeavellano. In Taiwan and in Iceland, the language barriers were less binding, but I am grateful to Chris Horton for his hospitality and knowledge, and to Google Translate, which is amazing.

I'm grateful to all the people who read and commented on chunks of this book. Special thanks to Robert Litan, Yoni Appelbaum, Peter Conti-Brown, and Jared Bernstein, who gave a piece of advice good enough to put on a sticky note: "This is not a mystery novel."

Melvin Backman, Rachael Brown, and Hilary McClellen checked thousands of facts and quotes. I am amazed by some of the details they tracked down, and grateful for the many passages improved by their careful eyes. I am also grateful to Trent Duffy, who copyedited the final manuscript. It is both trite and true that none of them are responsible for my mistakes.

This book draws on my reporting as a Washington correspondent for the *Times*, and on my earlier work for the *Washington Post*, the *Boston Globe*, and the *Charlotte Observer*. One of the great joys of working at the *Times* is the opportunity to speak with policy makers and economists, including most of the living people named in this book. Quotes from interviews conducted for this book are cited in the endnotes.

My understanding of economic policy also is profoundly shaped by the hours I have spent as a reporter talking with people about the impact of economic policies on their lives. A few of those people appear in these pages. I am grateful to all of them for their willingness to speak with a stranger, often about painful experiences.

In addition to my own reporting and my historical research, this book stands on the shoulders of scores of earlier works that deeply informed my narrative and conclusions. I have cited the sources of specific quotes and facts. If you're interested in my recommendations for further reading, check out BinyaminAppelbaum.com.

My parents raised me in a house stuffed with books, including their own books. They encouraged my curiosity, taught me right from wrong, and gave me every opportunity to pursue my dreams. They are my heroes.

My children each wanted their own sentence in these acknowledgments, which surely is the least I can do for all the joy they bring me. Mila, I love you. Tomas, I love you.

I saved the best for last. My wife, Kytja Weir, made this book possible by shouldering an unequal share of our partnership, and she made it better in more ways than I can count. She has my love and my thanks, and my solemn commitment to wash all the dishes.

Washington, D.C.

April 2019

Notes

Introduction

1. Michel Houellebecq, *The Elementary Particles* (New York: Knopf, 2000), 4.
2. The anecdote is from William Neikirk's biography, *Volcker: Portrait of the Money Man* (New York: Congdon and Weed, 1987). Volcker told me in a 2018 interview he did not recall the conversation with his wife, but it was consistent with his feelings at the time. "I certainly thought I was in the bowels," he said. "I spent five years there and I don't know that I ever met the president [of the New York Fed]. You wrote a memorandum that you sent to your superior, who sent it to his superior."
3. There were no economists on the Fed's board when Volcker was hired in 1952. The only earlier example was Adolph C. Miller, a member of the Fed's board from 1914 to 1936, who held a master's degree in economics from Harvard and was a professor of finance for more than two decades. Men with a background in agriculture were regularly appointed to the board as representatives of an important sector of the economy. In 1952, that role was being filled by Rudolph M. Evans, an Iowa hog farmer. At that time, the presidents of two of the Fed's twelve regional reserve banks held master's degrees in economics: Malcolm H. Bryan, chosen as president of the Atlanta Fed in 1951, had worked as a Fed economist; Oliver S. Powell was chosen as president of the Minneapolis Fed in June 1952.
4. Martin made the comment on his final day as Fed chairman in January 1970, in a conversation with Richard T. McCormack, a young staffer in the Nixon administration. I am grateful to Richard Fisher, the former president of the Dallas Fed, who brought McCormack's account of his conversation with Martin to my attention. See Henry E. Mattox, *A Conversation with Ambassador Richard T. McCormack* (Xlibris, 2013), 56.
5. Keynes had developed his ideas with his native country in mind, but he met with similar rejection in the United Kingdom. "No finance minister, as far as I know, has ever deliberately unbalanced his budget," Neville Chamberlain, then serving as finance minister, told Parliament of Keynes's advice in 1933. For Roosevelt's quote, see Frances Perkins, *The Roosevelt I Knew* (New York: Viking, 1946), 215.
6. Michael A. Bernstein, *A Perilous Progress: Economists and Public Purpose in Twentieth-Century America* (Princeton, N.J.: Princeton University Press, 2001), 138.
7. Fritz Machlup, ed., *International Monetary Arrangements: The Problem of Choice* (Princeton, N.J.: Princeton University Press, 1964), 6.
8. The case, *U.S. v. Philadelphia National Bank*, is discussed in greater detail in chapter 5.
9. McCraw coined the phrase in his 1984 masterpiece, *Prophets of Regulation* (Cambridge: Belknap Press, 1984), to describe the rise of economics in regulatory policy.

10. From 1965 until 2009, economists held the majority of seats on the seven-member board. From 1973 until 2009, at least half of the regional reserve bank presidents were economists, too. And from 1978 until 2009, economists held a majority of the votes at all but two meetings of the Fed's monetary policy-making committee, the Federal Open Market Committee. The exceptions were a pair of meetings in 1995.

11. Three of Shultz's successors have also held doctorates in economics: W. Michael Blumenthal (1977–1979), Lawrence Summers (1999–2001), and John Snow (2003–2006).

12. Marion Fourcade, *Economists and Societies: Discipline and Profession in the United States, Britain, and France, 1890s to 1990s* (Princeton, N.J.: Princeton University Press, 2009), ebook loc. 1675.

13. Regulation of bread prices was a standard practice in medieval Europe. In France, it persisted well into the modern era. In the 1970s, the government set the price of a basic baguette — itself a twentieth-century innovation — but not of fancier breads. In 1978, the government announced the end of price controls. As in other industries, it turned out many consumers preferred lower-quality bread at lower prices.

14. Zhao Ziyang then was serving under Deng Xiaoping as China's premier, the titular head of the government. He was the chief architect of China's economic reforms until he lost power as a result of the Tiananmen Square protests in 1989. For the best account of that remarkable river cruise, and of China's broader engagement with Western economists and ideas, see Julian Gewirtz, *Unlikely Partners: Chinese Reformers, Western Economists, and the Making of Global China* (Cambridge: Harvard University Press, 2017).

15. Charles L. Schultze, "The Role and Responsibilities of the Economist in Government," *American Economic Review* 72, no. 2 (1982).

16. James Landale, "Thatcher's Mad Monk or True Prophet?," BBC Radio 4, April 7, 2014. Timothy Noah's *The Great Divergence: America's Growing Inequality Crisis and What We Can Do About It* (New York: Bloomsbury, 2012) surveys the causes of rising inequality in the United States. Angus Deaton's *The Great Escape: Health, Wealth, and the Origins of Inequality* (Princeton, N.J.: Princeton University Press, 2013) offers a broader view, including both the international context and the benefits of inequality.

17. The intermediate decennial averages are 2.160 percent in the 1970s, 2.156 percent in the 1980s, and 1.98 percent in the 1990s. Even excluding the crisis years of 2008 and 2009, the annual average for the first eight years of the 2000s is still just 1.7 percent. The numbers are from the official GDP estimates published by the U.S. Commerce Department's Bureau of Economic Analysis.

18. I turned thirty in 2008, but the decline in my generation's earning power is not a consequence of the recession. The average share of men earning more than their fathers for those born between 1973 and 1983 is 43 percent. In 2017, the Pew Research Center reported that just 37 percent of Americans expected their children would be better off economically. The figures are drawn from the work of the economist Raj Chetty and his collaborators, available at OpportunityInsights.org, and from Pew's Global Indicators.

19. "The Growing Gap in Life Expectancy by Income: Implications for Federal Programs and Policy Responses," 2015, National Academies of Science, Engineering and Medicine; available at https://doi.org/10.17226/19015.

20. Simon Schama, *The Embarrassment of Riches: An Interpretation of Dutch Culture in the Golden Age* (Berkeley: University of California Press, 1988), 222. The Harvard economist Dani Rodrik argues economic language is prevalent in political communication

because it synthesizes science and narrative. Economists reach conclusions that are purportedly scientific, and they are adept at communicating those conclusions in the form of stories "that lodge easily in the public consciousness," such as the simple story that taxation is enervating. The former Federal Reserve chairman Ben S. Bernanke, explaining his reasons for becoming an economist, wrote in his memoirs, "I found that I was good at explaining things." The need for effective explanation has increased in the era of mass communication. The political scientist Jeffrey K. Tulis has calculated that President Carter gave more public speeches during his four years in office than all of the American presidents gave during the entire nineteenth century.

21. Until 1840, postage was paid upon receipt, and the prices were quite high. William J. Bernstein writes in his history of trade, *A Splendid Exchange* (New York: Atlantic, 2008), that when Parliament approved the use of postage stamps, the era's leading advocate of free trade, Richard Cobden, "is said to have shouted for joy, 'There go the corn laws.'" For more on the role of *The Economist*, see Cheryl Schonhardt-Bailey, *From the Corn Laws to Free Trade: Interests, Ideas, and Institutions in Historical Perspective* (Cambridge: MIT Press, 2006).

22. Governments have been trying to count people for a very long time. The fourth book of the Bible is called Numbers because it records the details of a census. Many of the world's great empires, including ancient Egypt, China, and Rome, attempted enumerations with varying degrees of success. But population counts remained unusual, and more detailed surveys even less common. Britain did not attempt its first modern census until 1801. When Alexander Hamilton tried to gather information on the American economy for his 1791 "Report on Manufactures," he was frustrated repeatedly. The Hartford gunmaker Peter Colt wrote to Hamilton that he could estimate neither his annual production nor his annual revenues, and in this he was hardly unique. "It will be impossible to ascertain the requisite facts with precision," wrote Hamilton's friend Timothy Pickering, from whom he had requested information about Pennsylvania farmers. "For I doubt whether one American farmer in a thousand has determined by actual admeasurement, the sizes of his fields and their produce." See Eli Cook, *The Pricing of Progress: Economic Indicators and the Capitalization of American Life* (Cambridge: Harvard University Press, 2017).

23. De Bow was named professor of political economy at the new University of Louisiana in 1848 (the school is now called Tulane University). The historian Marion Fourcade reports that there were still just three professors of political economy in the United States in 1880. By 1910, the number had increased to fifty-one. As of 2017, there were almost thirteen thousand economics professors in the United States. Over the last half century, the share of the adult population employed as economics professors has more than doubled, although of course it remains quite small.

24. The Stanford historian George Fredrickson described Helper's book as quite possibly "the most important book, in terms of political impact, that has ever been published in the United States." It found a wide audience after the New York newspaper editor Horace Greeley bankrolled a second edition, in part to rebut an 1858 speech by the South Carolina politician James Henry Hammond, titled "Cotton Is King," in which he presented data purporting to show the superior productivity of the southern economy. By the time of the Civil War, more than 200,000 copies of Helper's book had been sold. De Bow's contribution was ironic; he was an ardent proponent of both slavery and secession. See Cook, *The Pricing of Progress.*

25. Diane Coyle, *GDP: A Brief but Affectionate History* (Princeton, N.J.: Princeton University Press, 2014), 13.

26. Arnold Harberger, "Sense and Economics: An Oral History with Arnold Harberger," conducted by Paul Burnett in 2015 and 2016, Oral History Center, Bancroft Library, University of California, Berkeley.

27. H. R. Haldeman Diaries, National Archives, August 16, 1971; available at nixonlibrary .gov/sites/default/files/virtuallibrary/documents/haldeman-diaries/37-hrhd -audiotape-ac12b-19710816-pa.pdf.

28. Hobart Rowen, "Juanita Kreps' Introspective Farewell," *Washington Post*, November 3, 1979.

29. J. H. Dales, *Pollution, Property and Prices* (Toronto: University of Toronto Press, 1968), 100.

30. A number of recent works have influenced my understanding of the relationship between the rise of the conservative movement in American politics and the rise of trust-the-market economics, including: Bernstein, *A Perilous Progress*; Kim Phillips-Fein, *Invisible Hands: The Businessmen's Crusade Against the New Deal* (New York: Norton, 2010); Lisa McGirr, *Suburban Warriors: The Origins of the New American Right* (Princeton, N.J.: Princeton University Press, 2001); Kevin Kruse, *One Nation Under God: How Corporate America Invented Christian America* (New York: Basic Books, 2015); and Rick Perlstein, *Before the Storm: Barry Goldwater and the Unmaking of the American Consensus* (New York: Hill and Wang, 2001).

31. McGirr, *Suburban Warriors*, 7.

32. The economist Brad DeLong calculates that a typical worker in 1500 CE was about 4.7 times more productive than the typical worker in 10,000 BCE. This is a glacial rate of change. As he points out, it meant progress generally was not visible in any single lifetime. Moreover, before the industrial revolution, increased productivity generally translated into larger populations, not a higher standard of living. See Brad DeLong, *Slouching Toward Utopia: The Economic History of the Twentieth Century* (New York: Basic Books, 2018).

33. The logic of the Alchian-Demsetz paper is a classic example of the pro-market genre. The authors stipulated that workers and employers reached agreements in an open market where each side was free to seek the best terms, and where everyone had full knowledge of the range of available opportunities. On that fantastic foundation, they built an elegant argument: workers needed a referee to determine the value of their labor and to prevent shirking, so they ceded property rights in their collective output to the referee — the corporation. The paper, in other words, assumed the absence of regulation to conclude that there is no need for regulation. In 2011, it was named one of the twenty most important papers ever published in the *American Economic Review*. See Armen A. Alchian and Harold Demsetz, "Production, Information Costs and Economic Organization," *American Economic Review* 65, no. 5 (December 1972).

34. "The groups in our society that have the most at stake in the preservation and strengthening of competitive capitalism are those minority groups which can most easily become the object of the distrust and enmity of the majority — the Negroes, the Jews, the foreign born, to mention only the most obvious." See Milton Friedman, *Capitalism and Freedom* (Chicago: University of Chicago Press, 1962), 21.

35. McGirr, *Suburban Warriors*, 253.

36. Ronald Reagan was the poet laureate of this new emphasis on individualism. Rodgers notes that Reagan "was fond of saying that his political opponents saw people only as members of groups; his party, to the contrary, saw the people of America as individuals." This was evident in his rhetoric. "In Reagan's very celebrations of the people, the plural noun tended to slip away, to skitter toward the singular." It was an emphasis shared by

many of the great rhetoricians of the free-market movement. "[George] Gilder's hero-
ically independent entrepreneurs, [Robert] Lucas's forward-looking utility maximizers,
[Jude] Wanniski's fish and coconut traders, the Coase theorem's rancher and farmer
maximizing the public good as they stood on the courthouse steps. To imagine the market now was to imagine a socially detached array of economic actors, free to choose." See
Daniel T. Rodgers, *The Age of Fracture* (Cambridge: Belknap Press, 2003).

37. J. R. Kearl et al., "A Confusion of Economists?," *American Economic Review* 69, no. 2
(1979).

38. Jonathan Schlefer, *The Assumptions Economists Make* (Cambridge: Harvard University
Press, 2012), 189.

39. George F. Will, "Passing of a Prophet," *Washington Post*, December 8, 1991.

Chapter 1. Markets in Everything

1. "The Intellectual Provocateur," *Time*, December 19, 1969.

2. Bernard Rostker's book *I Want You! The Evolution of the All-Volunteer Force* (Santa Monica, Calif.: Rand, 2006) was particularly valuable in the preparation of this chapter. The
book includes a digital archive of primary sources — a true public service. The records of
the retrospective conferences held roughly every decade since the end of the draft in
1973 are also a valuable resource. Anderson shared his recollections at the 2003 event.
See "The All-Volunteer Force: 30 Years of Service," September 16, 2003; available at
c-span.org/video/?178209-1/volunteer-force-30-years-service.

3. Martin Anderson, "The Making of the All-Volunteer Armed Force," in *Cold War
Patriot and Statesman: Richard M. Nixon*, ed. Leon Friedman and William Levan-
trosser (Westport, Conn.: Greenwood Press, 1993), 173.

4. Milton Friedman and Rose Friedman, *Two Lucky People* (Chicago: University of Chicago Press, 1998), 220. Friedman made the same point in a letter to a well-wisher in
1968: "The main function that people like myself serve is not to persuade anybody but
to throw ideas out in the open so that when circumstances arise that make them particularly relevant to current problems, they are available to be picked up": Friedman to
Zadon, November 19, 1968, Milton Friedman Papers, box 214, Hoover Institution
Archives, Stanford, Calif.

5. Friedman and Friedman, *Two Lucky People*, 381.

6. "We used to say that everyone loved to argue with Milton — when he wasn't there":
George Shultz, quoted in William Simon, *A Time for Reflection* (Washington, D.C.:
Regnery, 2004), 73.

7. "A Moynihan Report," *New York Times*, June 27, 1971. Moynihan added of Friedman,
"Not that I agree with everything he says, but simply that for a man who produces ideas
you really have to listen to, there is no equivalent at this time."

8. Solow's view of Friedman's work is summarized by his famous quip that everything
reminded Friedman of money. Well, Solow continued, everything reminded him
of sex, but he didn't put it in every paper. Robert M. Solow, "Review of *A Monetary History*," in *Modern Economic Classics — Evaluations Through Time*, ed. Bernard S. Katz
and Ronald E. Robbins (New York: Garland, 1988), 339–46.

9. Lawrence H. Summers, "The Great Liberator," *New York Times*, November 19, 2006.

10. Andrei Shleifer, "The Age of Milton Friedman," *Journal of Economic Literature* 47, no. 1
(2009): 123–35.

11. Friedman and Friedman, *Two Lucky People*, 29.

12. "Becoming an economist seemed more relevant to the burning issues of the day than
becoming an applied mathematician or an actuary": Milton Friedman, "Milton Friedman,"

in *Lives of the Laureates*, ed. William Breit and Barry T. Hirsch (Cambridge: MIT Press, 1986), 83.

13. Dress codes for college freshmen were common in the 1920s. Stanford freshmen, for example, were required to wear green caps with red buttons; at Columbia, black ties and socks; at Williams, blue ties. See "Princetonian Compares Freshman Rules of Discipline in United States Colleges," *Stanford Daily*, April 29, 1924.

14. Friedman and Friedman, *Two Lucky People*, 58.

15. Ibid., 81.

16. Ibid., 84.

17. Milton Friedman never conceded the point. He maintained that the advent of withholding had been necessary to win the war. More broadly, Friedman's libertarian views never took the form of isolationism or pacifism; he also supported the American invasion of Iraq in 2003, which his wife strongly opposed. He did express regret for co-authoring, during his time at Treasury, *Taxing to Prevent Inflation*, a book that took the Keynesian view of inflationary dynamics. "It's not something I'm very proud of," he said in a 2000 interview.

18. The issue is a trade-off between volume and power. The research group decided in favor of the small, high-volume guns. See Patricia Gates Lynch, "Interview with W. Allen Wallis," May 14, 1996, Association for Diplomatic Studies and Training Foreign Affairs Oral History Project, Library of Congress.

19. John B. Taylor, "Interview with Milton Friedman," in *Inside the Economist's Mind: Conversations with Eminent Economists*, ed. Paul A. Samuelson and William A. Barnett (Malden, Mass.: Blackwell, 2007), 133–34.

20. The most thorough and persuasive account of Friedman's intellectual development is an unpublished 2018 manuscript by Edward Nelson, a Federal Reserve economist, "Milton Friedman and Economic Debate in the United States, 1932–1972," 2018, books A and B; available at https://sites.google.com/site/edwardnelsonresearch/.

21. Friedman's doctorate was from Columbia, not Chicago. He spent his second year of graduate studies at Columbia on a fellowship, and returned there to complete the work. His adviser was Simon Kuznets, who won a Nobel Prize for his pioneering role in the development of statistical methods for measuring national economic activity. A version of the thesis was published as *Income from Independent Professional Practice* (New York: National Bureau of Economic Research, 1945). Friedman's views of the medical profession remained unchanged. He told an interviewer in 1969, "I often have fun by asking people, 'What do you suppose is the most powerful trade union in the United States?' And almost never does anybody give the right answer, which is the American Medical Association."

22. The liberal economist Paul Krugman, revisiting the pamphlet more than half a century later, wrote in admiration of Friedman that "his showman's flair combined with his ability to marshal evidence made him the best spokesman for the virtues of the free market since Adam Smith." See Paul Krugman, "Who Was Milton Friedman?," *New York Review of Books* 54, no. 2 (February 15, 2007).

23. The added note read, in part, "It means that, even from the standpoint of those who put equality above justice and liberty, rent controls are the height of folly." See Milton Friedman and George J. Stigler, *Roofs or Ceilings? The Current Housing Problem* (Irvington-on-Hudson, N.Y.: Foundation for Economic Education, 1946), 10. Both Friedman and Stigler thought free markets were the best redress for economic inequality, but they supported some forms of government intervention. "We should seek to make labor incomes more equal," Stigler said in a 1949 speech, "by enlarged educational systems, improvements of labor mobility, elimination of labor monopolies, pro-

vision of medical care for poor children, and the like": see George Stigler, *Five Lectures on Economic Problems* (London: Longmans, Green, 1949). Friedman was a longtime advocate for the creation of the earned-income tax credit.

24. Tony Judt, *Postwar: A History of Europe Since 1945* (New York: Penguin Press, 2006), 69.

25. Brian Doherty, "Best of Both Worlds: An Interview with Milton Friedman," *Reason*, June 1995.

26. Milton Friedman, "Neo-Liberalism and Its Prospects," *Farmand*, February 17, 1951.

27. Milton Friedman, *Capitalism and Freedom* (Chicago: University of Chicago Press, 1962), 36.

28. Friedman first wrote Goldwater in 1960, to complain about the senator's views on the regulation of international capital flows. In 1961, Goldwater reached out to Friedman after watching the professor debate Senator Joseph Clark, a Pennsylvania liberal who drove Goldwater to distraction. The two men first met in 1962, at the home of William J. Baroody Sr., the head of the American Enterprise Institute. For an account of Goldwater and his place in American history, see Rick Perlstein, *Before the Storm: Barry Goldwater and the Unmaking of the American Consensus* (New York: Hill and Wang, 2001).

29. Milton Friedman, "The Goldwater View of Economics," *New York Times Magazine*, October 11, 1964.

30. Milton Friedman, "Why Not a Voluntary Army?," *New Individualist Review* 4 (Spring 1967): 3–9.

31. Jefferson made this argument in a letter to James Monroe; he repeated it in other letters. Congress refused to authorize a draft during the War of 1812, and Jefferson believed Washington, D.C., had been taken and burned as a consequence. See *The Writings of Thomas Jefferson* (Washington, D.C.: Thomas Jefferson Memorial Association of the United States, 1905), 13:261.

32. John Lilburne, Richard Overton, Thomas Prince, and William Walwyn, "An Agreement of the Free People of England" (1649).

33. Robert Taft, "Compulsory Military Training in Peacetime Will Destroy Government by the People," in *The Papers of Robert A. Taft*, ed. Clarence E. Wunderlin Jr. (Kent, Ohio: Kent State University Press, 2003), 3:53.

34. Galbraith was a convinced opponent of conscription; like Friedman, he regarded it as a tax. He did not succeed in getting Stevenson to sound equally firm, but perhaps that is why Stevenson kept losing elections. Speaking on the courthouse steps in Youngstown, Ohio, the candidate told the crowd, "I noted in connection with this matter of meeting the increasingly urgent need for experienced and professional military personnel that this may well mean that we will need and want in the foreseeable future to turn to a method other than the draft for procuring such personnel." See "Text of Stevenson Talk at Youngstown," *New York Times*, October 19, 1956.

35. Thomas D. Morris, "Statement, Hearing Before the House Committee on Armed Services," Cong. Rec. H9942 (June 30, 1966).

36. Richard J. Whalen, "Here Come the Conservatives," *Fortune*, December 1963, 108–9.

37. Samuel Lubell, *The Future of American Politics* (New York: Harper and Brothers, 1952), 196.

38. Walter Y. Oi, "The Costs and Implications of an All Volunteer Force," in *The Draft: A Handbook of Facts and Alternatives*, ed. Sol Tax (Chicago: University of Chicago Press, 1967), 221–51. Men were required to register for the draft on their eighteenth birthday, but they were not eligible to be drafted until turning nineteen.

39. Tax, *The Draft*, 307–8.

40. "One of the major products of the Selective Service classification process is the channeling of manpower into many endeavors, occupations and activities that are in the national interest," read a brochure sent to local draft boards. "Many young men would not have pursued a higher education if there had not been a program of student deferment....Even though the salary of a teacher has historically been meager, many young men remain in that job, seeking the reward of a deferment." See Selective Service Administration, "Channeling," July 1, 1965, reprinted in *Columbia Daily Spectator*, October 24, 1967.

41. Austin Wehrwein, "Protesters End Chicago U. Sit-In," *New York Times*, May 14, 1966.

42. The organizers produced a detailed account of the proceedings: see Tax, *The Draft*.

43. I am deeply grateful to Marjorie Oi, Walter's wife, for sharing her recollections of her husband and a wealth of primary and secondary materials about his life and work.

44. Oi, "Costs and Implications of an All Volunteer Force," 221–51. The Pentagon had reasoned along the following lines: Imagine a nation with 100 young men. The nation asks each man to name his price to serve in the military. The first, a patriot, offers to serve for just $1 per year; the second says $2; the third says $3; and so on until the hundredth man says he'll serve only for $100. The nation must pay the same salary to each man. If it wants an armed force of 10 men, the tenth man wants $10 per year, so the total bill will be $100. To raise an army of 20 men, the government must pay the wage demanded by the 20th man, which is $20, so the total bill will rise to $400. Conscription was cheaper on paper. Let's say the nation wants an army of 10 men, and it decides to pay each soldier a token wage of $5 a year. It still gets 5 volunteers, and then it conscripts 5 men, at a total cost of $50. The savings on an army of 20 men are even larger.

45. Tax, *The Draft*, viii.

46. John J. Ford, "Looking Back on the Termination of the Draft," 2003; available at rand .org/content/dam/rand/pubs/monographs/MG265/images/webS0881.pdf.

47. Friedman was twenty-nine when the United States entered World War II, but he was exempted from the draft while he worked for the Treasury. In a 1996 interview, Friedman said that he stayed at Treasury to stay out of the war. "The only reason to stay on at Treasury was to avoid the draft," he said. His second wartime job, at Columbia, preserved his exemption. See "Rose and Milton Friedman: Our Early Years," *Hoover Digest*, 1996.

48. Martin Anderson, *The Federal Bulldozer: A Critical Analysis of Urban Renewal, 1949–1962* (Cambridge: MIT Press, 1964), 56.

49. Martin Anderson, *Impostors in the Temple* (New York: Simon and Schuster, 1992), 37.

50. Martin Anderson, "An Analysis of the Factors Involved in Moving to an All-Volunteer Force," April 1969 and July 10, 1969, Martin Anderson Collection, Richard Nixon Presidential Library, Yorba Linda, Calif.; available at nixonfoundation.org/2015/02/ towards-volunteer-force/. The presentations that Friedman and Oi made at the Chicago conference were reprinted in the *New Individualist Review*, a libertarian magazine published by students at the University of Chicago. See Milton Friedman, "Why Not a Voluntary Army?," 3–9.

51. Patrick J. Buchanan, "Memo to RN, October 23, 1967," in *The Greatest Comeback* (New York: Crown Forum, 2014), 376.

52. Robert B. Semple Jr., "Nixon Backs Eventual End of Draft," *New York Times*, November 18, 1967.

53. The Nixon White House tracked public opinion on the draft with understandable care. The first poll to find a majority of the public preferred an all-volunteer military

was a Harris poll in January 1970, which put the figure at 52 percent. See Memo from David J. Callard to Robert Odle, "Public Relations Regarding an All-Volunteer Force," March 11, 1970, reprinted in Rostker, *I Want You!*, G1133.pdf.

54. Richard Nixon, *RN: The Memoirs of Richard Nixon* (New York: Grosset and Dunlap, 1978), 522. This was a partial explanation. Nixon's great interest was foreign affairs. "I've always thought this country could run itself domestically without a president," Nixon told the journalist Theodore H. White. "You need a president for foreign policy." When it came to domestic policy, Nixon's North Star was the desire to win elections. Nixon acknowledged the political calculus in a 1985 letter, writing, "What really tipped the balance in my decision to support the voluntary army was the unrest over the draft because of the Vietnam war. But I would not have followed through after the election had I not become convinced that a voluntary army was economically feasible and militarily acceptable": see Richard Nixon to Robert K. Griffith, January 29, 1985, in Robert K. Griffith Jr., *The U.S. Army's Transition to the All-Volunteer Force* (Washington, D.C.: Center of Military History, 1997), 43.

55. The exact wording of the plank was "When military manpower needs can be appreciably reduced, we will place the Selective Service System on standby and substitute a voluntary force obtained through adequate pay and career incentives." See "Republican Party Platform of 1968," August 5, 1968; available at presidency.ucsb.edu/documents/republican-party-platform-1968.

56. "Humphrey Urges Bill of Rights for Draftees; Raps Nixon Plan," *Chicago Tribune*, August 18, 1968.

57. Richard Nixon, "The All Volunteer Armed Force," CBS Radio Network, October 17, 1968, reprinted in Nixon-Agnew Campaign Committee, *Major Speeches and Statements by Richard M. Nixon in the Presidential Campaign of 1968* (1968).

58. Rostker, *I Want You!*, 509.

59. This account is based on the written recollections of Wallis and Oi and my interview with Marjorie Oi. See Lynch, "Interview with W. Allen Wallis" (the transcription misspells Oi's name as "Hoig"). See also Walter Oi, "Historical Perspectives on the All-Volunteer Force: The Rochester Connection," in *Professionals on the Front Line: Two Decades of the All-Volunteer Force*, ed. J. Eric Friedland et al. (Washington, D.C.: Brassey's, 1996), 44. In an interview on March 10, 2017, I asked Marjorie Oi how she felt about the abrupt end of the trip. By then, she had a lifetime of experience with Oi in particular and economists in general. She laughed. "I don't know how closely you've been associated with academics who work at that level," she said. "It's not just a job; it's a whole lifestyle."

60. Richard Nixon, "Memorandum to Melvin Laird, February 2, 1969," Anderson Collection, box 1, folder 8, Nixon Library.

61. The quote is from Anderson's meeting notes. See Martin Anderson, "President's Office, 14 March 1969, 4:30 p.m.," Anderson Collection, box 1, folder 9, Nixon Library. Those notes are consistent with the President's public statement when he announced the creation of the commission: "I have directed the Commission to develop a comprehensive plan for eliminating conscription and moving toward an all-volunteer armed force." See "Statement by the President Announcing a Commission on an All-Volunteer Armed Force," March 7, 1969, in *The Report of the President's Commission on an All-Volunteer Armed Force* (Washington, D.C.: GPO, 1970), vii. Anderson related a different version of this meeting in a 1991 account. He said Nixon responded to Gates's doubts by declaring, "That's exactly why I want you as chairman. If you change your mind and think we should end the draft, then I'll know it is a good idea." See Anderson, *The Making of the All-Volunteer Armed Force*

(Palo Alto, Calif.: Hoover Institution, 1991), 5. Anderson's published writings, however, are chock-full of artistic liberties and verifiable inaccuracies.

62. "Memo from David J. Callard, August 28, 1969," Anderson Collection, box 38, folder 2, Nixon Library.

63. There is no transcript of the exchange because Westmoreland testified in a closed session. The earliest record I can find, quoted here, comes from a letter that Friedman wrote to President Reagan on June 2, 1981, which is available in Friedman's papers at the Hoover Institution. Friedman subsequently recorded a number of slightly different versions, including in his 1998 memoirs. The exchange was well rehearsed on both sides. General Hershey often invoked the specter of mercenaries, and his allies borrowed the line. Friedman, meanwhile, delivered a version of his rejoinder at the 1966 Chicago conference, and Senator Goldwater used similar language in a 1967 article.

64. Gates described the meeting in a letter to Friedman, who was unable to attend. He also thanked him for "the largest contribution both in terms of helping materially with the text and with resolving some of our most troublesome debates." See Thomas S. Gates to Milton Friedman, March 12, 1970, Friedman Papers, box 209, folder 7, Hoover.

65. Memo from Callard to Odle, "Public Relations Regarding an All-Volunteer Force," G1133.pdf.

66. *Report of the President's Commission on an All-Volunteer Armed Force*, 9–10.

67. "Draft Extended After War, Foreign Policy Debate," *CQ Almanac 1971*.

68. "Anti-War Senators Divided over Draft," United Press International, June 4, 1971.

69. David Rosenbaum, "Lottery Is Held to Set the Order of Draft in 1970," *New York Times*, December 2, 1969. The first lottery included men between the ages of nineteen and twenty-six who had not served in the military. Subsequent annual lotteries included just the new crop of nineteen-year-olds.

70. "We stay just about level rather than having this big peace dividend," White House Budget Director Caspar Weinberger told Nixon on January 26, 1973. Representative Gerald Ford, the House minority leader, chimed in, "Mr. President, the American people wanted the all-volunteer army, so they have to pay for it." See Douglas Brinkley and Luke A. Nichter, eds., *The Nixon Tapes, 1973* (Boston: Houghton Mifflin Harcourt, 2015), 26–28.

71. Melvin Laird, lecture at Department of Defense conference "The All-Volunteer Force: 30 Years of Service," Washington, D.C., September 16, 2003; available at c-span.org/video/?178209-1/volunteer-force-30-years-service.

72. On June 22, 1970, President Nixon signed a law lowering the national voting age to eighteen. When the Supreme Court ruled in December that states still could set a higher voting age, Congress responded with amazing rapidity. The Senate voted to amend the Constitution on March 10, 1971, and the House signed off, by a vote of 401–19, just two weeks later. Five states, including Connecticut, ratified the amendment on the day of the House vote. When the North Carolina and Oklahoma legislatures ratified the amendment on July 1, 1971, it became the law of the land.

73. "Last Draftee Glad He's Out," *New York Times*, May 31, 1982.

74. Griffith, *U.S. Army's Transition to the All-Volunteer Force*, 32.

75. Beth Bailey, *America's Army: Making the All-Volunteer Force* (Cambridge: Belknap Press, 2009), ebook loc. 1108–44.

76. Tax, *The Draft*, 459. The speaker was Timothy McGinley, a Labor Department official.

77. The size of the active-duty military has been cut in half, from the 2.6 million estimate used by the Gates Commission to roughly 1.3 million in 2017.

78. David Woods, "Last Draftee, Who Tried to Hide, Now Believes in Service," Newhouse News Service, June 22, 1993.
79. Martin Anderson, presentation at Department of Defense conference "The All-Volunteer Force: 30 Years of Service," Washington, D.C., September 16, 2003; available at c-span.org/video/?178209-1/volunteer-force-30-years-service.
80. Melvin Small and William D. Hoover, *Give Peace a Chance: Exploring the Vietnam Antiwar Movement* (Syracuse, N.Y.: Syracuse University Press, 1992), 117.
81. Scovill Wannamaker Currin Jr., "An Army of the Willing: Fayette'Nam, Soldier Dissent, and the Untold Story of the All-Volunteer Force" (Ph.D. diss., Duke University, 2015).
82. The proportions are similar for the more recent, but much smaller, deployment to fight ISIL in Syria. See "Department of Defense Contractors in Afghanistan and Iraq," May 13, 2011, Congressional Research Service.
83. *Report of the President's Commission on an All-Volunteer Armed Force*, 155. The United States has generally funded its wars with borrowed money, further limiting public concern about conflict. Many economists see little difference between borrowing money and raising taxes, because voters know the debt must be repaid, meaning that taxes eventually must be raised. Politicians have been ignoring this theory with considerable success through much of history. An intriguing proposal to make the cost of war more tangible, put forward by Representative David Obey (D-WI) in 2009, would require the government to impose an income tax surcharge to cover any spending on wars.

Chapter 2. Friedman v. Keynes

1. Karl Polanyi, *The Great Transformation: The Political and Economic Origins of Our Time* (1944; repr., Boston: Beacon Press, 2001), 35.
2. John Maynard Keynes, "An Open Letter," *New York Times*, December 31, 1933. When the letter was published, Keynes was fifty years old and already had been a prominent public intellectual and economic policy maker for several decades. Yet before 1933, he had left little mark on economic theory. His biographer Robert Skidelsky notes that his intellectual legacy rests primarily on the ideas he developed and espoused in the final years of his life.
3. The key to Keynesian economics is that saving is not the same as investing. This is true of money stuffed under a mattress; it is also true of money deposited at a bank. Increasing the amount of money in the banking system doesn't necessarily increase the willingness of banks to make loans, nor the demand for loans. When government takes money from the private sector, by taxing or borrowing, the money comes both from income and from savings. The portion that comes from savings is thus pulled back into use.
4. Samuelson defined the mainstream of American economics for thirty years in the successive editions of his standard textbook, *Economics*, which first appeared in 1948. He was also a dominant force in shaping the practice of economics, including the turn toward mathematics. "I can claim that in talking about modern economics, I am talking about me," Samuelson said in 1985. "My finger has been in every pie." But in this book, he makes only cameo appearances because he played relatively little role in public policy debates. When President Kennedy asked Samuelson to chair his Council of Economic Advisers, Samuelson refused. He explained later that he didn't want to impose upon his wife and children. When Kennedy asked James Tobin to serve, Tobin asked his wife why he couldn't emulate Samuelson and just say no. "Well," she replied, "Paul has to live with Paul Samuelson's conscience and you have to live with Jim Tobin's conscience." Tobin went to Washington — and later related his wife's remarks during

an oral history interview with the JFK Presidential Library. For Samuelson's quote, see his "Lord Keynes and the General Theory," *Economica* 14, no. 3 (1946).

5. Keynes wrote the letter to the *Times* at the urging of Felix Frankfurter. Frankfurter told Keynes the President would be receptive to the argument, and he sent Roosevelt an advance copy. See Nicholas Wapshott, *Keynes Hayek: The Clash That Defined Modern Economics* (New York: Norton, 2011), 157–60.

6. Frances Perkins, *The Roosevelt I Knew* (New York: Viking, 1946), 215. The account is often cited as evidence that Roosevelt didn't understand the argument Keynes was making. That was certainly the view taken by Keynes, who told Perkins he had "supposed the President was more literate, economically speaking." Keynes, who was fascinated by hands, later wrote that Roosevelt had "short round nails like a businessman's," which he did not intend as a compliment. In a 1965 article about Keynes, *Time* similarly reported that the President said after the meeting, "I didn't understand one word that man was saying." The historian Eric Rauchway, however, argues that Roosevelt understood Keynes, and was expressing a political judgment.

7. Roosevelt entered office with an orthodox commitment to balanced budgets, although from the outset he supported deficit spending on emergency relief programs. "We accepted the final responsibility of government, after all else had failed, to spend money when no one else had money left to spend," he said in a 1936 campaign speech. The following year, Roosevelt began to turn off the spigot, and the economy reversed its tenuous progress. This persuaded Roosevelt to embrace a more aggressive program of deficit spending in 1938. The beginning soon thereafter of America's transformation into the "arsenal of democracy" leaves open the question of how strongly Roosevelt would have embraced Keynesian ideas in the absence of war. While the government did not report unemployment data at the time, the Bureau of Labor Statistics estimated in 1948 that the jobless rate had been 17 percent in 1939, declining to 1 percent in 1944, the last full year of war. Some historians do emphasize the contribution of Roosevelt's New Deal spending programs. See, for example, Eric Rauchway, *The Money Makers: How Roosevelt and Keynes Ended the Depression, Defeated Fascism and Secured a Prosperous Peace* (New York: Basic Books, 2015).

8. Winston Churchill's wartime coalition government had previously issued a white paper in 1944 that said government was responsible for "high and stable levels of employment."

9. Edwin G. Nourse, the first head of the Council of Economic Advisers (CEA), was an agricultural economist, as were several of Roosevelt's economic advisers. That specialty was both more common at the time and known for a focus on practical questions. The Department of Agriculture was one of the first parts of the federal government to institutionalize the presence of economists, creating a Bureau of Agricultural Economics in 1921. The second chairman of the CEA, Leon Keyserling, was a lawyer who had done some graduate work in economics. Every subsequent chairman has held a doctorate in economics, with the exception of Alan Greenspan, the chairman from 1974 to 1977, who completed his doctorate in economics after leaving the job.

10. Wilder's biographer, Caroline Fraser, concludes that Wilder shared her daughter's political convictions. See Fraser, *Prairie Fires: The American Dreams of Laura Ingalls Wilder* (New York: Metropolitan Books/Henry Holt, 2017).

11. The textbook was written by a young Canadian economist named Lorie Tarshis, who had studied under Keynes at Cambridge. William F. Buckley launched a more famous assault on Tarshis in *God and Man at Yale* (1951), a polemic that was a shaping force in the resurgence of American conservativism. By the time it appeared, however, Tarshis

already had lost his audience. See Rose Wilder Lane, "Review of *The Elements of Economics*," *National Economic Council Review of Books*, August 1947, 1–8.

12. The Phillips paper was "The Relation Between Unemployment and the Rate of Change of Money Wages in the United Kingdom, 1861–1957," *Economica* 25, no. 100 (1958). The "menu" paper was Paul A. Samuelson and Robert M. Solow, "Analytical Aspects of Anti-Inflation Policy," *American Economic Review* 50, no. 2 (1960).

13. Daniel Stedman Jones, *Masters of the Universe: Hayek, Friedman and the Birth of Neoliberal Politics* (Princeton, N.J.: Princeton University Press, 2012), 191.

14. The quotes are from interviews conducted for a 1969 study of the Ways and Means Committee. The subjects are described as longtime committee members. See John F. Manley, *The Politics of Finance: The House Committee on Ways and Means* (Boston: Little, Brown, 1970), 92–93.

15. Julian E. Zelizer, *Taxing America: Wilbur D. Mills, Congress and the State, 1945–1975* (Cambridge, Eng.: Cambridge University Press, 1998), 84.

16. "The Federal Revenue System: Facts and Problems," Joint Economic Committee, 1956.

17. The Beatles' accountant in the 1960s has memorialized the band's largely successful efforts to avoid taxation, describing the members as "scruffy boys who didn't want to pay tax." The lyrics are from "Taxman," a song on the 1966 Beatles album *Revolver* written by George Harrison.

18. Republican campaign ads in 1960 noted Kennedy had failed to attend six consecutive sessions on fiscal policy. Paul Samuelson later said of Kennedy, "I testified many, many times before that committee.... He never was at a single meeting."

19. At an early meeting with economic advisers, one of the Harvard professors started talking fast and was urged by a colleague to slow down and treat the session like an introductory class. "Oh, Jack's had Ec A," the professor responded, referring to the fact that Kennedy had taken Harvard's introductory course in economics. Kennedy said, "It was in 1940, and I got a C." The professor slowed down. See "Council of Economic Advisers: Walter Heller, Kermit Gordon, James Tobin, Gardner Ackley, Paul Samuelson, Interview by Joseph Pechman on August 1, 1964," 43, John F. Kennedy Library Oral History Program, John F. Kennedy Presidential Library, Boston.

20. Charles Lam Markmann and Mark Sherwin, *John F. Kennedy: A Sense of Purpose* (New York: St. Martin's, 1961), 67. There are a number of slightly different versions of this quote in circulation, though the basic point is always the same. This is the earliest published version I can find.

21. "Council of Economic Advisers Interview by Joseph Pechman," 79–80.

22. Humphrey picked a bad example. Heller lived east of the river in a neighborhood called University Grove. The university owned the land and leased lots to faculty members, who were required to hire an architect. The result is a living museum of twentieth-century American architecture.

23. Heller narrated the meeting in several interviews, with a high degree of consistency. The quote here and the details of the encounter are from Robert Sobel, *The Worldly Economists* (New York: Free Press, 1980), 119.

24. Walter W. Heller, *New Dimensions of Political Economy* (New York: Norton, 1966), 15.

25. An example of Heller's felicity is his description of the federal deficit as "the black hole into which savings that ought to go into private investment and economic growth are relentlessly siphoned." See Kyle Crichton, "Walter Heller: Presidential Persuader," *New York Times*, June 21, 1987.

26. Walter W. Heller, "Activist Government: Key to Growth," *Challenge*, March–April 1986.

27. Some Keynesians saw enough value in government spending that they argued the government could increase economic growth by increasing taxation and spending that money. "The communists are telling the world that they alone know how to mobilize economic resources for rapid growth," the Keynesian economist James Tobin wrote in a 1960 essay published in the *New Republic*, based on a memo he wrote for Kennedy during the campaign. Tobin said economists knew a better recipe than Communists: more federal spending. And to raise the money, he said, the government should raise taxes. "Increased taxation," he wrote, "is the price of growth." Tobin was not in favor of burying money in old mines, however. He warned spending would work only if the government devoted the money to investment rather than consumption. See James Tobin, "Growth Through Taxation," *New Republic*, July 25, 1960.

28. Many traditional Keynesians, by contrast, hated Heller's plan. Leon Keyserling, Harry Truman's chief economic adviser, said Kennedy had embraced "trickle down" economics, invoking imagery that has a long history in American politics. William Safire, in his *Political Dictionary*, credits William Jennings Bryan, who blasted Republicans in his famous 1896 "Cross of Gold" speech for serving the rich and promising that "their prosperity will leak through on those below." Another common metaphor compared such tax policies to giving grain to horses as a means of feeding sparrows.

29. Mellon's argument prefigured the logic of supply-side economics. Of high tax rates, he said, "The taxpayers, through the many means available, avoid a taxable income and the government gets less out of a high tax than it would get out of a lower one": Andrew Mellon, *Taxation: The People's Business* (New York: Macmillan, 1924), 13. Modern analysts generally conclude the economic expansion, rather than the tax cuts, was the primary driver of revenue gains. See, e.g., Christina D. Romer and David H. Romer, "The Incentive Effects of Marginal Tax Rates: Evidence from the Interwar Era," February 2012, National Bureau of Economic Research.

30. Richard Reeves reports that DuPont's chairman, Crawford Greenewalt, told Kennedy in mid-August 1962 the company was operating at 80 percent of capacity, affirming Heller's argument that the problem was a lack of demand. See Richard Reeves, *President Kennedy: Profile of Power* (New York: Simon and Schuster, 1993), 333.

31. Kennedy had first broached the idea of a tax cut in a June 1962 speech, but he remained on the fence until the December speech. See Herbert Stein, *The Fiscal Revolution in America* (Washington, D.C.: AEI Press, 1996), 406–8.

32. Heller, *New Dimensions of Political Economy*, 35.

33. Dillon made the remarks in an oral history interview conducted by the John F. Kennedy Presidential Library on September 21, 1964, given on the condition the contents remained confidential until five years after Dillon's death.

34. Reeves, *President Kennedy*, 454.

35. Robert Caro narrates Johnson's negotiations in loving detail. See *The Passage of Power* (New York: Knopf, 2012), 466–83.

36. "The greatest psychological factor that we can create to control spending is the denial of additional revenues to the Treasury of the United States," Mills said in a 1963 speech urging support for the tax cut.

37. Rowland Evans and Robert Novak, *Lyndon Johnson: The Exercise of Power* (New York: New American Library, 1966), 372.

38. The Keynesian economist James Tobin defended the rising-tide-lifts-all-boats approach, even in retrospect: "The practitioners of the New Economics did not have to confront distributive issues squarely. It was apparent in advance that if their macro-economic policies took

effect and succeeded, recovery and growth during the 1960s would do much more to lift the incomes of the poor and disadvantaged than any conceivable redistribution and would be much less politically and socially divisive." See James Tobin, *The New Economics One Decade Older* (Princeton, N.J.: Princeton University Press, 1974), 53.

39. "We cannot relax our efforts to increase the technical efficiency of economic policy," Heller wrote in his 1966 book, *New Dimensions of Political Economy*. "But it is also clear that this promise will not be fulfilled unless we couple with improved techniques of economic management a determination to convert good economics and a great prosperity into a good life and a great society."

40. Lyndon B. Johnson, *The Vantage Point* (New York: Holt, Rinehart and Winston, 1971), 74.

41. "We Are All Keynesians Now," *Time*, December 31, 1965. Paul Volcker later told the British journalist Stephen Fay, "It is almost impossible to reconstruct the mood, but there was a feeling of exuberance in the economics profession, because it really thought it had the business of the cycle of boom-and-bust licked": see William Greider, *Secrets of the Temple* (New York: Simon and Schuster, 1987), 332. Johnson is sometimes misquoted as making the broader claim there would be no more recessions. He was not so bold. In a 1970 book, the liberal economist Arthur Okun phrased the argument better than his former boss: "Recessions are now generally considered to be fundamentally preventable, like airplane crashes and unlike hurricanes. But we have not banished air crashes from the land, and it is not clear that we have the wisdom or the ability to eliminate recessions." See Okun, *The Political Economy of Prosperity* (Washington, D.C.: Brookings Institution, 1970), 33–34.

42. In 2014, on the fiftieth anniversary of Johnson's declaration of war on poverty, Wisconsin Republican Paul Ryan, then chairman of the House Budget Committee, declared that the war had "failed." The available evidence suggests a different conclusion. See Christopher Wimer et al., "Trends in Poverty with an Anchored Supplemental Poverty Measure," December 2013, Columbia Population Research Center, Columbia University.

43. According to one congressional staffer, Heller "almost single-handedly made the profession [of economics] both respectable and useful in the eyes of government." See Michael A. Bernstein, *A Perilous Progress: Economists and Public Purpose in Twentieth-Century America* (Princeton, N.J.: Princeton University Press, 2001), 138.

44. Heller, *New Dimensions of Political Economy*, 3

45. Martin himself didn't claim authorship of the epigram. He first used it in an October 1955 speech before the New York chapter of the Investment Bankers Association of America: "The Federal Reserve, as one writer put it, after the recent increase in the discount rate, is in the position of the chaperone who has ordered the punch bowl removed just when the party was really warming up."

46. William McChesney Martin, "Does Monetary History Repeat Itself?" (commencement speech at Columbia University, June 1, 1965); available at https://fraser.stlouis fed.org/files/docs/historical/martin/martin65_0601.pdf.

47. The quote is from an account of the conversation that Martin related in January 1970. See Henry E. Mattox, *A Conversation with Ambassador Richard T. McCormack* (Xlibris, 2013), 56.

48. Joseph Califano, *The Triumph and Tragedy of Lyndon Johnson: The White House Years* (New York: Touchstone, 1991), 131–32.

49. Friedman described the incident as his only interaction with Keynes. The paper was a critique of work by Keynes's friend Arthur Pigou. Keynes declined to publish it in the

Economic Journal of the Royal Economic Society after showing the paper to Pigou, who did not appreciate the critique. It was then accepted for publication in Harvard's *Quarterly Journal of Economics*. See John B. Taylor, "Interview with Milton Friedman," in *Inside the Economist's Mind: Conversations with Eminent Economists*, ed. Paul A. Samuelson and William A. Barnett (Malden, Mass.: Blackwell, 2007), 122.

50. Leon Keyserling, "Testimony Before Subcommittee on General Credit Control and Debt Management of the Joint Committee on the Economic Report," March 12, 1952.

51. Milton Friedman and Anna Jacobson Schwartz, *A Monetary History of the United States* (Princeton, N.J.: Princeton University Press, 1963), 300.

52. A. A. Walters, "Milton Friedman," in *The New Palgrave: A Dictionary of Economics*, ed. John Eatwell et al. (London: Macmillan, 1987).

53. Recent scholarship, notably the work of Edward Nelson, makes clear that Friedman began to focus on the importance of the money supply — the core tenet of monetarism — by the mid-1940s. Earlier work generally dated the birth a decade later, in the mid-1950s. The earliest instance documented by Nelson is a 1946 radio broadcast in which Friedman said, "Limiting the money supply is a subject which has received far less attention than it deserves." See Edward Nelson, "Milton Friedman and Economic Debate in the United States, 1932–1972," 2018, book A; available at https://sites .google.com/site/edwardnelsonresearch/.

54. Milton Friedman, "Inflation and Wages," *Newsweek*, September 28, 1970.

55. Walter Stewart, the head of the Rockefeller Foundation, was an economist who had worked at the Fed in the 1920s. See Milton Friedman to Walter Stewart, January 12, 1949, Milton Friedman Papers, box 33, folder 35, Hoover Institution Archives, Stanford, Calif. The economic historian Beatrice Cherrier reports that Friedman made similar, and less qualified, remarks at a conference in 1947 or 1948. See Beatrice Cherrier, "The Lucky Consistency of Milton Friedman's Science and Politics," in *Building Chicago Economics: New Perspectives on the History of America's Most Powerful Economics Program*, ed. Robert Van Horn et al. (Cambridge, Eng.: Cambridge University Press, 2011), 353.

56. Friedman's conclusion was that the quantity of money was more important than the velocity, or the frequency with which money was spent. His critics often accused him of asserting that velocity was stable. His complex position instead is best summarized as the view that velocity is irrelevant. Robert L. Hetzel regards the 1952 testimony as the first statement of monetarist principles. See Robert L. Hetzel, "The Contributions of Milton Friedman to Economics," *Federal Reserve Bank of Richmond Economic Quarterly* 93, no. 1 (Winter 2007): 1–30.

57. Milton Friedman, "Discussion of the Inflationary Gap," in *Essays in Positive Economics* (Chicago: University of Chicago Press, 1953), 253.

58. Erin Jacobsson, *A Life for Sound Money: Per Jacobsson* (Oxford: Clarendon Press, 1979), 262. A few years earlier, Friedman had spoken at Harvard and received a note of thanks from his host, the liberal economist John Kenneth Galbraith: "So far as I can tell, also, the students seem to have suffered no permanent damage. I hope your colleagues perceive no disconcerting changes in you. On second thought, I hope they do." J. K. Galbraith to Milton Friedman, March 27, 1951, Friedman Papers, box 27, folder 13, Hoover.

59. The economic historian Daniel Stedman Jones describes Harrod's memo and the conflict in his *Masters of the Universe*. The full text of the memo makes fascinating reading: "The idea that you can reduce prices by limiting the quantity of money is pre-Keynesian. Keynes spent half his energy inveighing against precisely that idea. Hardly any econo-

mists under the age of 50 would subscribe to it. If it were supposed that the conservatives were associated with any such idea, that might drive many of the middle-of-the-way
economists into the ranks of Labour and, what is more, [Labour Party leader Hugh]
Gaitskell would probably succeed in galvanizing them all into lambasting and ridicul-
ing the policy. I do sincerely hope that no government speaker would use words
implying that the government subscribes to such an antiquated doctrine." Macmillan
was sympathetic to Keynes; his family's publishing firm, Macmillan, was the British
publisher of Keynes's works.

60. The document is commonly known as the Radcliffe Report. See *Report of the Committee on the Working of the Monetary System* (London: HMSO, 1959), 489.

61. Thomas Kuhn's classic book, *The Structure of Scientific Revolutions* (Chicago: University
of Chicago Press, 1962), concluded that adherents of a scientific paradigm rarely change
their minds. A new paradigm instead takes hold as the older generation is replaced.

62. Paul Douglas, a leading professor of economics at the University of Chicago, was
elected to the U.S. Senate in 1948 as a Democrat from Illinois, becoming one of the
first economists to serve in Congress. Douglas played the key role in forcing the Truman administration to grant the Fed its operational independence.

63. Robert Solow, "Friedman on America's Money," *Banker*, November 1964. This review
is reprinted in Bernard S. Katz and Ronald E. Robbins, eds., *Modern Economic Classics: Evaluations Through Time* (New York: Garland, 1988).

64. Milton Friedman and Walter Heller, *Monetary vs. Fiscal Policy: A Dialogue* (New York:
Norton, 1969), 16.

65. Milton Friedman described Rose Friedman as a "full partner" in the production of these
columns and his other popular writings. He may have understated her role. Edward Nelson quotes this account of the process: "They would turn on their reel-to-reel tape
recorder, and she would play an uninformed man-in-the-street and start asking him questions, and she kept pushing him to say it better, find a different way to explain it; and they
might tape for a couple of hours. And then she would transcribe the whole thing, edit it
down...and finally produce a column." See Edward Nelson, "Milton Friedman and Economic Debate in the United States, 1932–1972," 2018, book B, p. 123; available at
https://sites.google.com/site/edwardnelsonresesearch/. The *Newsweek* rotation also
included a third economist, a centrist slot occupied by the Yale professor Henry Wallich.

66. The official was Henry Wallich, who left Yale for a seat on the Fed's board in 1974. He
wrote in 1977, "The elected representatives of the people have discerned the attraction
of monetarist doctrine because it plays down the effects of fiscal policy." See James M.
Buchanan and Richard E. Wagner, *Democracy in Deficit: The Political Legacy of Lord
Keynes* (1977; repr., Indianapolis: Liberty Fund, 2000), 55.

67. Milton Friedman to Vermont Royster, December 3, 1963, Friedman Archives, box 32,
folder 15, Hoover. Three days later, Friedman sent Royster a note of apology, explaining, "My reaction was partly a consequence of high expectations. I have become accustomed to being either ignored or misinterpreted and misunderstood by the so-called
Liberal Establishment and have long since become inured to it. But for the *Wall Street
Journal* to do the same thing, that was and is a real disappointment."

68. Milton Friedman, "The Role of Monetary Policy," *American Economic Review* 58
(March 1968): 1–17.

69. Milton Friedman, *Dollars and Deficits: Living with America's Economic Problems* (Englewood Cliffs, N.J.: Prentice-Hall, 1968), 94.

70. James Tobin, "The Natural Rate as New Classical Macroeconomics," 1993, Cowles
Foundation Papers 1061.

71. A version of the speech was published the next year in the *American Economic Review* as Friedman, "The Role of Monetary Policy." The economic historian Robert Gordon argues intriguingly that Friedman was influenced by the close ties between the University of Chicago economics department and Latin America, where it was obvious that inflation and unemployment did not have a predictable relationship. See Robert J. Gordon, "The History of the Phillips Curve: Consensus and Bifurcation," *Economica* 78, no. 309 (2011): 10–50. Another economist, Edmund Phelps, separately arrived at conclusions similar to Friedman's at around the same time. Phelps's work was more technically sophisticated; Friedman was the better publicist. In any event, both men acknowledged they were reviving an older idea. The Scottish economist David Hume, for example, wrote in 1752, "It is easy to trace the money in its progress through the whole commonwealth; where we shall find, that it must first quicken the diligence of every individual, before it encrease the price of labour."

72. The story assumes that people initially don't know whether others have received a windfall. At first, therefore, they behave as if their own purchasing power has increased. Only with the passage of time does the realization dawn that Santa Claus came for everyone. Also, while the first windfall would come as a surprise, people presumably would be more likely to treat a second windfall as inflationary. This was an important piece of Friedman's theory. He argued experience would diminish the value of a continuing stimulus campaign, forcing the government to print even more money to achieve the same effect.

73. Friedman's view that the effects of monetary policy were felt after "long and variable lags" is a prime example of an idea that is now so conventional that Friedman is rarely given credit, nor is it widely remembered that his view was once controversial.

74. Friedman and Heller, *Monetary vs. Fiscal Policy: A Dialogue*, 30. Heller also pointed out that Friedman's approach would work only if the United States allowed the value of the dollar to float against foreign currencies. At the time, this seemed a serious objection because the value of the dollar was fixed against foreign currencies, but the United States floated the dollar beginning in 1973, a story told in chapter 8.

75. Robert Hall delivered these recollections at the American Economic Association's 2018 meeting in Philadelphia, at a panel on the fiftieth anniversary of Friedman's 1968 address.

76. Remarkably, from the modern perspective, Fed officials had ignored the distinction between nominal and real interest rates. The nominal rate is the stated interest rate of, say, 6 percent a year. If inflation is rising by 3 percent a year, however, then the real interest rate is just 3 percent. And if inflation rises to 4 percent the following year, then the nominal interest rate will rise to 7 percent without any increase in the real interest rate. Fed officials in the 1960s failed to understand that interest rates were rising because inflation was rising, and therefore the higher rates were not likely to restrain borrowing. This is another example of a battle Friedman won so completely that his victory is largely forgotten. He insisted during the 1950s and the 1960s that there was a significant difference between real and nominal rates. Conventional economists disagreed. The dispute was not resolved until the late 1960s because, in practice, there was little difference during the years inflation remained low. Today the distinction between real and nominal rates is universally understood to be significant.

77. Friedman's prediction reflected both the continued growth of the money supply and one of his most enduring contributions to economics, his "permanent income hypothesis." He argued that temporary changes in income had a limited impact on consumption because people tried to maintain a steady level of consumption based on their

income expectations over time. If people expected income to recover, they would initially dip into savings to maintain a stable level of consumption, adjusting only slowly. See Alan Blinder, *Hard Heads, Soft Hearts* (Reading, Mass.: Addison-Wesley, 1987), 74.

78. A. A. Walters to Milton Friedman, December 4, 1969, Friedman Papers, box 186, folder 3, Hoover.

79. Milton Friedman, "The Counter-Revolution in Monetary Theory," 1970, Institute of Economic Affairs, no. 33.

Chapter 3. One Nation, Under Employed

1. Alan Blinder, *Hard Heads, Soft Hearts* (Reading, Mass.: Addison-Wesley, 1987), 33.

2. This was a fine example of the warning that past results do not guarantee future performance. By the end of the decade, both Britain's Labour Party and Democrats in the United States would lose power in part because of high inflation. For Nixon's views, see Allan H. Meltzer, *A History of the Federal Reserve*, vol. 2, book 2, *1970–1986* (Chicago: University of Chicago Press, 2009), 791.

3. Nixon made the push on the advice of Herbert Stein, one of his economic advisers. See Allen J. Matusow, *Nixon's Economy: Booms, Busts, Dollars and Votes* (Lawrence: University Press of Kansas, 1998), 187–89.

4. *Public Papers of the Presidents of the United States, Richard Nixon, 1971* (Washington, D.C.: GPO, 1972), 608.

5. George Stigler, *Memoirs of an Unregulated Economist* (New York: Basic Books, 1988), 44.

6. Nixon made the comment to Georges Pompidou. He also said that Burns would quickly ossify into a typical bureaucrat, so it was important to harvest the ideas from his mind before it was too late. *Foreign Relations of the United States, 1969–1976*, vol. 3, *Foreign Economic Policy, 1969–1972; International Monetary Policy, 1969–1972* (Washington, D.C.: GPO, 2001), 91.

7. Rowland Evans and Robert D. Novak, *Nixon in the White House: The Frustration of Power* (New York: Random House, 1971), 13.

8. "Unfortunately, Arthur Burns turned out to be a good prophet," Nixon wrote in *Six Crises*, a 1962 memoir. "In October, usually a month of rising employment, the jobless rolls increased by 452,000. All the speeches, television broadcasts and precinct work in the world could not counteract that one hard fact."

9. Edward Nelson, "Milton Friedman and Economic Debate in the United States, 1932–1972," 2018, book B, p. 521; available at https://sites.google.com/site/edwardnelson research/.

10. Friedman was generally delighted by the choice of an economist to lead the Fed and specifically delighted by the choice of Burns. "The Chairmen since the beginning have all been admirable people, able people who were trying to do their best — I am not questioning their motives or their intent — but they have all had a background in an individual business or the individual bank," Friedman said. "Arthur Burns has a background in the economy as a whole." See Edward Nelson, "Milton Friedman and the Federal Reserve Chairs, 1951–1979," October 23, 2013, Federal Reserve Board, 26–27.

11. Arthur Burns, *The Business Cycle in a Changing World* (New York: National Bureau of Economic Research/Columbia University Press, 1969), 85.

12. Donald F. Kettl, *Leadership at the Fed* (New Haven: Yale University Press, 1988), 118. Anna Schwartz, who worked closely with both men, took the view that Friedman had

mismeasured Burns. Edward Nelson records Schwartz's impression: "Arthur had a place in Vermont, near Milton's, and Milton would talk to him about monetary theory and Arthur would smoke his pipe, nod, and Milton thought he was agreeing with him." For the view that Burns evolved in his thinking, see Nelson's own account in "Milton Friedman and Economic Debate in the United States, 1932–1972," 2018, book B, pp. 225–26; available at https://sites.google.com/site/edwardnelsonresearch.

13. "I want to make this perfectly clear. I don't think that our fiscal policy and our monetary policy are sufficient to control inflation," Burns told the Senate Committee on Banking, Housing and Urban Affairs in March 1971.

14. Burns repeatedly denied that he was influenced by White House pressure. The release of materials including his diary and Nixon's Oval Office tapes has rendered that defense untenable. Meltzer concludes, "Ample evidence cited above supports the claim that President Nixon urged Burns to follow a very expansive policy and that Burns agreed to do it." See Meltzer, *History of the Federal Reserve*, vol. 2, book 2, 798. The best remaining defense is offered by Matusow, in *Nixon's Economy*, who argues Nixon was motivated by a genuine belief that the economy required stimulus, and Burns was receptive for the same reason.

15. John Ehrlichman, *Witness to Power: The Nixon Years* (New York: Simon and Schuster, 1982), 254.

16. Stephen Axilrod, *Inside the Fed* (Cambridge: MIT Press, 2009), 61–62.

17. This was especially ironic because the two men first met at an Eisenhower administration cabinet meeting where Nixon, then vice president, spoke in favor of a minimum wage increase, arguing it would help Republicans woo the working class, and Burns, then head of the Council of Economic Advisers, replied with standard objections to government price controls. Burns continued to oppose price controls in public and in private right up to the moment when it became the alternative to doing his own job by raising interest rates. Nixon also had long professed an aversion to price controls, which he ascribed to his personal experience working on the rubber tire team at the federal agency that administered price controls during World War II. "There was a boilerplate paragraph on the horrors of wage and price controls" in almost every Nixon speech, recalled William Safire, who wrote many of those speeches. And years later, in his memoirs, Nixon wrote that the decision to impose controls in 1971 was "wrong." Yet he did so.

18. Milton Friedman and Rose Friedman, *Two Lucky People* (Chicago: University of Chicago Press, 1998), 387. Nixon continued to tend the relationship. When he heard Friedman would undergo open-heart surgery in 1972, the President called the Mayo Clinic to wish Friedman well. Nixon: "I said, 'What are they operating on?' And they said, 'We're operating on his heart.' And I said 'Fine! That's OK! Just don't operate on your brain.' Because we need you. We'll be expecting to see you back with a good heart and the same brain." Friedman: "Well I only hope they'll be taking as good care of me as you've been taking of the country." Fortunately for Friedman, the doctors did better.

19. "Baby Chicks Killed and Cooked for Feed," *New York Times*, June 25, 1973.

20. Iain Macleod, *Hansard Commons*, November 17, 1965, 1165.

21. Robert Samuelson, *The Great Inflation and Its Aftermath* (New York: Random House, 2008), ch. 3.

22. Stagflation can be explained in a Keynesian framework, but the explanation was not well understood at the time. The gist is that higher oil prices forced people to reduce consumption of oil, or of other goods, which increased unemployment. The United States responded with an economic stimulus, driving up inflation. Why was the stimu-

lus ineffective? The original problem was a decline in the supply of oil, so pumping money into the system drove up prices. It was a demand-side response to a supply-side problem. Nations that refrained from stimulating their economies, including Germany and Switzerland, experienced an economic downturn but did not experience higher inflation.

23. The move toward monetarism was influenced by the end of the Bretton Woods system of fixed exchange rates, which is described in chapter 8. The system of fixed rates created a target for the money supply; in its absence, countries needed a new target. The Bundesbank's choice was influenced by the Swiss American economist Karl Brunner, a monetarist who spoke German; in 1979, he launched the Konstanz Seminar, an annual conference that spread monetarist ideas in Germany. See Andreas Beyer et al., "Opting Out of the Great Inflation: German Monetary Policy After the Breakdown of Bretton Woods," September 2008, The Great Inflation Conference, National Bureau of Economic Research.

24. At the Nobel awards dinner, Friedman joked that it was awkward to accept a prize sponsored by Sweden's central bank for proposing that central banks should be eliminated.

25. James Cooper, *Margaret Thatcher and Ronald Reagan* (Houndmills, Eng.: Palgrave Macmillan, 2012), 38.

26. The targets were announced as part of the conditions for a $3.9 billion emergency loan from the International Monetary Fund, and the decision has sometimes been portrayed as one imposed on the United Kingdom. However, the Labour government had announced its intention to create monetary targets in April 1976, well before the bailout.

27. *The Economists Conference on Inflation* (Washington, D.C.: GPO, 1974), 123.

28. Ford did begin to show some sympathy for Friedman's view. "Unemployment is the biggest concern of the 8.2 percent of American workers temporarily out of work, but inflation is the universal enemy of 100 percent of our people in America today," he said in a February 1975 speech. Congress, too, appeared to be taking Friedman more seriously, passing in 1975 a resolution directing the Fed to set money supply targets, and to report regularly on its performance. Friedman, always open to expedient alliances, optimistically called it "the most important and the most constructive change" since the end of the gold standard in the 1930s. But in fact, the point was to pressure the Fed to print more money, in the service of driving down unemployment. And in practice, Burns subverted the new requirements by providing reports to Congress in a form that made it all but impossible to track the growth of the money supply over time.

29. The quotes are from a letter to George Shultz. The final line read, "I am taking the liberty of sending a copy of this letter to Arthur." See Milton Friedman to George Shultz, November 5, 1971, Milton Friedman Papers, box 33, folder 15, Hoover Institution Archives, Stanford, Calif.

30. "As a matter of general philosophy, my own belief is that the best way to control inflation is not to make money scarce, not to try to drive interest rates up, and not to try and keep people out of work and depend on welfare and unemployment compensation benefits to meet those hardships, but rather to put our people back to work, to hold interest rates down, and keep our economy growing, at a reasonably high rate." See "Interview with Jimmy Carter," *Business Week*, September 20, 1976.

31. "I pledge that if I am elected, we will never use unemployment and recession as a tool to fight inflation," Carter said. "We will never sacrifice someone's job, his livelihood, for the sake of an economic game plan. We will put into place a set of programs which will

take on unemployment and inflation at the same time, because we're not going to make any progress trying to fight them separately. This kind of balanced, coordinated approach will reduce overall unemployment to 4 percent and inflation to 4 percent or less by the end of my first term." See "Inflation and Unemployment," October 5, 1976, reprinted in *The Presidential Campaign 1976* (Washington, D.C.: GPO, 1978), 631.

32. Miller ran Textron, an industrial conglomerate. Other finalists included the heads of General Electric and DuPont. See Meltzer, *History of the Federal Reserve*, vol. 2, book 2, 923. Friedman, ever optimistic, told the *New York Times* that he applauded the choice of Miller. When Burns was appointed, Friedman had hailed the installation of an economist as a change for the better. When Miller was appointed, Friedman declared that it was better for the Fed to be led by a non-economist. See Ann Crittenden, "The President's Choice," *New York Times*, January 1, 1978.

33. Donald Janson, "Rioting Follows Protests by Truckers in Levittown, Pa.," *New York Times*, June 26, 1979.

34. The cumulative change in U.S. prices from 1973 to 1979 was 49 percent; in wages, 54 percent. See Meltzer, *History of the Federal Reserve*, vol. 2, book 2, 848.

35. A wide range of government rules had not been written to account for inflation, which caused some real problems. People moved into higher tax brackets as nominal incomes increased, reducing real after-tax incomes. Inflation also eroded wealth because laws limited the interest rates banks could pay on savings. And inflation eroded the value of government benefits like Social Security. But by 1981, changes in federal law had addressed all three of these problems by mandating regular adjustments to offset inflation.

36. William Greider, *Secrets of the Temple* (New York: Simon and Schuster, 1981), 44.

37. McLamb said he earned $9,000 in 1973 and $15,000 in 1978 — the equivalent of earning $10,236 in 1973. See Steven V. Roberts, "Poll Shows Majority of Americans Altering Life Because of Inflation," *New York Times*, June 5, 1978. It was not an isolated example. Average wages for steelworkers, for instance, rose from $4.72 per hour in 1972 to $11.91 per hour in 1982. In real terms, that was a 10 percent raise. See John Hoerr, *And the Wolf Finally Came* (Pittsburgh: University of Pittsburgh Press, 1988), 113–14.

38. James M. Buchanan and Richard E. Wagner, *Democracy in Deficit: The Political Legacy of Lord Keynes* (1977; repr., Indianapolis: Liberty Fund, 2000), 66–67.

39. W. Carl Biven, *Jimmy Carter's Economy: Policy in an Age of Limits* (Chapel Hill: University of North Carolina Press, 2002), 54.

40. Miller was widely regarded as an ineffective Fed chair, but Carter compounded the problem. He first decided to get rid of his Treasury secretary, Michael Blumenthal, which unnerved financial markets. Unable to persuade a leading banker or business executive to step into that job, he moved Miller to the Treasury, leaving the Fed's vice chair, a Florida politician named Frederick Schultz, as acting chair, which further unnerved markets.

41. "Transcript of Federal Open Market Committee Meeting," July 18, 1978; available at federalreserve.gov/monetarypolicy/files/FOMC19780718meeting.pdf.

42. Samuelson, *Great Inflation and Its Aftermath*, 119.

43. Carter first offered the job to Tom Clausen, the chief executive of Bank of America. It is unclear how well the President understood what he had done in then choosing Volcker. "What was known about him? That he was able and bright and it was also known that he was conservative," Stuart Eizenstat, Carter's top domestic policy aide, told the journalist William Greider in an interview for the latter's 1987 book, *Secrets of the Temple*.

"What wasn't known was that he was going to impose some very dramatic changes." In his own 2018 memoir, however, Eizenstat portrayed Carter's decision as conscious and deliberate, and quotes Carter as saying, "I decided to go ahead with it, because I thought it was better for the country." It seems reasonable to assume Carter understood the direction he was choosing, but not how hard Volcker would push to get there. Volcker recalled being told during the 1980 campaign that Carter had remarked, "God, they didn't have to be quite that monetarist." See Stuart E. Eizenstat, *President Carter: The White House Years* (New York: St. Martin's, 2018), 338. Still, Volcker recounts that he asked Carter whether monetary policy had cost him the 1980 election. "A wry smile spread over his face and he said, 'I think there were a few other factors as well.'" See Paul Volcker and Christine Harper, *Keeping at It: The Quest for Sound Money and Good Government* (New York: PublicAffairs, 2018), 111.

44. Joseph B. Treaster, *Paul Volcker: The Making of a Financial Legend* (New York: John Wiley, 2004), ebook loc. 1752.

45. Paul Volcker, "The Problems of Federal Reserve Policy Since World War II" (senior thesis, Princeton University, 1949), 77.

46. William R. Neikirk, *Volcker: Portrait of the Money Man* (New York: Congdon and Weed, 1987), 54.

47. William Silber, *Volcker: The Triumph of Persistence* (New York: Bloomsbury, 2012), 31.

48. Paul Volcker and Toyoo Gyohten, *Changing Fortunes: The World's Money and the Threat to American Leadership* (New York: Times Books, 1992), xiv.

49. John Connally, Volcker's dapper boss at the Treasury during the Nixon administration, once threatened to fire Volcker unless he got a haircut and bought a suit that fit. See Greider, *Secrets of the Temple*, 68.

50. Robert Kavesh's recollection is from an interview with the author on April 5, 2018. The other anecdotes are from Neikirk, *Volcker: Portrait of the Money Man.*

51. Money was important, but, Volcker said, "it seems to me the essence of policy making in these circumstances is that judgments must be made in the presence of uncertainty." See Paul Volcker, "The Contributions and Limitations of Monetary Analysis," September 16, 1976; available at newyorkfed.org/medialibrary/media/research/quarterly_review/75th/75article7.pdf.

52. Paul Volcker, "The Role of Monetary Targets in an Age of Inflation," *Journal of Monetary Economics* 4, no. 2 (1978): 329–39. Central bankers then placed little value on clarity. To the contrary, they had long regarded surprise as a useful tool. The Fed didn't announce changes in policy; traders were left to infer decisions from the movement of interest rates. Volcker was early to suggest there was value in managing expectations.

53. Burns delivered his speech, entitled "The Anguish of Central Banking," at a meeting of the International Monetary Fund. He wasn't wrong. A clever analysis by the Fed historian Donald F. Kettl counted ninety-one instances between 1961 and 1975 in which the White House Council of Economic Advisers reported to the president on the state of monetary policy. In forty-four instances, they judged the Fed was doing a good job; in forty-seven instances, they judged monetary policy was too tight. There was not a single instance in which they concluded that interest rates were too low. Congressional Democrats, too, had carped throughout the decade at any sign the Fed was restraining growth. If the Fed had tried to assert its independence, Congress could have taken that independence away. Not until 1980 did polls show that voters consistently regarded inflation as a larger problem than unemployment. See Kettl, *Leadership at the Fed*, 138. A few years after Volcker stepped down, in 1990, he spoke before the same conference. Volcker's speech was entitled "The Triumph of Central Banking?"

54. Silber, *Volcker: The Triumph of Persistence*, 168.

55. Volcker had stopped in West Germany on his way to Belgrade, where officials urged him to crack down on inflation. Some accounts describe this as influential; Volcker says it simply affirmed the importance of the course he already had chosen. See Volcker and Gyohten, *Changing Fortunes*, 168. See also Axilrod, *Inside the Fed*, 99.

56. Only ten presidents made the meeting. A replacement for Volcker had not yet been installed at the New York Fed, and Mark Willes of the Minneapolis Fed, a vocal proponent of the new policy, also was not present. See "Transcript of Federal Open Market Committee Conference Call," October 5, 1979; available at federalreserve.gov/monetary policy/files/FOMC19791005confcall.pdf.

57. Volcker's embrace of monetarism is often described as a stratagem to raise interest rates more quickly, both because the Fed did not need to approve the rapid increases, and because it could deny direct responsibility. The mechanical benefits were real, but I find the explanation unconvincing. Everyone understood that the Fed was raising interest rates, and I see no reason in the record to doubt Volcker's own account that (1) he saw some truth in monetarism; and (2) he wanted to send a message that the Fed was determined to bring inflation under control. One of Volcker's first acts as chairman was to reply to a congratulatory note from Friedman, who had written that it would not be difficult for Volcker to outdo his predecessors if he turned to monetarism. Volcker responded with a wink. "I will not be unhappy to have you preaching the doctrines of monetary rectitude as we move ahead," he wrote. He expected Friedman to circulate the response; Volcker was eager to convince people the Fed was changing course. See Silber, *Volcker: The Triumph of Persistence*, 149.

58. Treaster, *Paul Volcker*, ebook loc. 2669.

59. The joke had a kernel of truth: a rumor of Volcker's resignation had circulated on Wall Street the previous day, causing enough of a disruption in trading that the Fed had issued a formal denial.

60. Volcker and Gyohten, *Changing Fortunes*, 170.

61. The pain was exacerbated by financial deregulation, a story told in full color in chapter 10. In previous recessions, the Fed had removed the proverbial punch bowl by driving interest rates above the level banks were allowed to charge on loans. But Congress had recently removed those caps, allowing banks to raise rates in step with the Fed. That meant the Fed had to raise rates much higher to achieve the same decline in borrowing. Unable to prevent people from purchasing homes, the Fed drove them into bankruptcy.

62. Louis S. Jacobson, Robert John LaLonde, and Daniel Gerard Sullivan, "Earnings Losses of Displaced Workers," *American Economic Review* 83 (September 1993): 685–709.

63. "Transcript of Federal Open Market Committee Meeting," July 9, 1980, 76; available at federalreserve.gov/monetarypolicy/files/FOMC19800709meeting.pdf.

64. Greider, *Secrets of the Temple*, 461.

65. Volcker insisted at his Saturday night press conference in October 1979 that he did not expect to drive the economy into recession. "Well, you get varying opinions about that," Volcker said in answer to a reporter's question. "I don't think it will have important effects in that connection." He has since conceded this was misleading: he thought a recession was inevitable, and he thought the Fed's actions would accelerate the onset. "Deliberately designed? No," he wrote in his memoirs. "Designed with a clear understanding that sooner or later the accelerating inflation process would culminate in a recession? Certainly." See Volcker and Harper, *Keeping at It*, 138–39.

66. Other officials reported similar angst. The Fed's vice chairman, Fred Schultz, told William Greider, "Did I get sweaty palms? Did I lie awake at night? The answer is that I did both. I was speaking before these groups all the time, home builders and auto dealers and others. It's not so bad when some guy gets up and yells at you, 'You SOB, you're killing us.' What really got me was when this fellow stood up and said in a very quiet way, 'Governor, I've been an auto dealer for thirty years, worked hard to build up that business. Next week I am closing my doors.' Then he sat down. That really gets to you."

67. Treaster, *Paul Volcker*, ebook loc. 171.

68. "Interest Rates," *CBS Evening News*, December 20, 1981, Vanderbilt TV News Archive.

69. Beryl Sprinkel, "U.S. Approaches to Monetary Issues" (speech given in Paris, September 1981), in *The Political Economy of the United States*, ed. Christian Stoffaës (Amsterdam: North-Holland, 1982), 85.

70. Greider, *Secrets of the Temple*, 363.

71. In a 1975 piece, "Recession vs. Inflation," delivered in the midst of an economic downturn, Reagan wrote, "As one of our finest economists has said, reflation cannot sustain full employment in the long run except by faster and faster inflation." Those who seek to portray Reagan as ignorant of Friedman's views must grapple with this and other items in Reagan's long record. Friedman's own judgment was straightforward. "There's no question that Reagan understood the relation between the quantity of money and inflation." See John B. Taylor, "Interview with Milton Friedman," in *Inside the Economist's Mind: Conversations with Eminent Economists*, ed. Paul A. Samuelson and William A. Barnett (Malden, Mass.: Blackwell, 2007), 118.

72. A wide range of Reagan's advisers share the view that Friedman was preeminent among the President's economic advisers. Donald Regan said, "It was clear first of all that he was influenced by the economic theories of Milton Friedman." Edwin Meese said, "Of special importance among the academic advisers was Professor Milton Friedman." For Harlow's quote, see Michael Hirsh, *Capital Offense* (Hoboken, N.J.: John Wiley, 2010), 31.

73. Some authors take Reagan's interest in gold more seriously. See, for example, Sebastian Mallaby's detailed account of Reagan's views on monetary policy in *The Man Who Knew: The Life and Times of Alan Greenspan* (New York: Penguin Press, 2016). For the Wanniski/Reagan exchange of letters, see Greider, *Secrets of the Temple*, 418. The friend Wanniski wrote to in 1983 was Donald Rumsfeld; see Jude Wanniski to Donald Rumsfeld, February 1, 1982, Jude Wanniski Papers, box 18, folder 6, Hoover.

74. Rowland Evans and Robert Novak, *The Reagan Revolution* (New York: E. P. Dutton, 1981), 69.

75. The Stanford economist John Taylor, a leading scholar of monetary policy, has argued that Volcker and Reagan were influenced by the rise of rational expectations theory in the 1970s. Friedman argued that inflation expectations were based on past experience; the new school posited instead that people's behavior was shaped by expectations about the future path of policy. If people were convinced the government would keep inflation low, they would begin to behave that way—for example, by accepting smaller wage increases. This would allow the government to reduce inflation painlessly. Volcker was familiar with the theory, but he described its proponents as "screwballs." Martin Anderson, one of Reagan's most important advisers, presented the ideas to Reagan as evidence that curbing inflation might not be particularly painful. But there's no evidence Reagan bought it. Volcker and Reagan were ready for the pain.

76. The quote is from my interview with Volcker on April 5, 2018. Reagan's relationship with Volcker was never easy. At their first meeting, Reagan unsettled Volcker by asking why the nation needed a central bank. But he repeatedly declined to join in public criticism of the Fed's campaign during his first year in office. When he did voice concern in January 1982, it was to suggest that the Fed was deepening the recession by failing to properly control the money supply — in other words, by being insufficiently monetarist. Volcker is among those who credit Reagan.

77. Neikirk, *Volcker: Portrait of the Money Man*, 110.

78. Paul Volcker, "No Time for Backsliding" (remarks before the National Press Club, Washington, D.C., September 25, 1981); available at https://fraser.stlouisfed.org/title/451/item/8243.

79. "Income and Poverty in the United States: 2017," U.S. Census Bureau, September 2018; available at census.gov/content/dam/Census/library/publications/2018/demo/p60-263.pdf.

80. Greider, *Secrets of the Temple*, 403–12.

81. John M. Berry, "Volcker Defends Targets Under Heavy Senate Barrage," *Washington Post*, July 21, 1982. Even as Volcker noted the turn of the tide, he initially insisted the Fed would continue its campaign. At that same hearing, he said, "It would strike me as the cruelest blow of all to the millions who have felt the pain of recession directly to suggest, in effect, it was all in vain." Yet the Fed already had quietly started to reduce interest rates. The change is clear in the data, particularly in retrospect, but Volcker was at such pains to minimize its importance that the *New York Times* missed it completely. Its story about the hearing was headlined "Fed Will Stick to Tight 1982 Targets."

82. Velocity during those years increased at an average annual pace of 3.4 percent, with relatively modest annual deviations, thanks in part to the tight regulation of the financial system. Todd G. Buchholz, *New Ideas from Dead Economists* (New York: Plume, 2007), 247.

83. Margaret Thatcher, "Speech to the CNN World Economic Development Congress," September 19, 1992, in *The Collected Speeches of Margaret Thatcher*, ed. Robin Harris (New York: HarperCollins, 1997), 543. The economic historian Robert Skidelsky points out that monetarism took a different form in Britain. The government targeted a broader measure of the money supply that included credit creation, which is to say it took account of changes in velocity. In this respect, Thatcher's government ignored the lessons learned at Friedman's knee. The British form of monetarism, however, did not fare any better.

84. Margaret Thatcher, "Speech to Conservative Party Conference, October 10, 1980"; available at margaretthatcher.org/document/104431.

85. The Bundesbank, however, missed those targets more than half the time, suggesting that even in West Germany, the significance of monetarism was in the message it sent, not its practical application. See George M. von Furstenberg and Michael K. Ulan, *Learning from the World's Best Central Bankers* (Boston: Kluwer, 1998), 127.

86. Greider, *Secrets of the Temple*, 684.

87. See Milton Friedman, "Monetarism in Rhetoric and in Practice," Tokyo, June 22, 1983; available at imes.boj.or.jp/research/papers/english/me1-2-1.pdf. He elaborated on his conviction two years later, in testimony before the Joint Economic Committee of Congress in 1985: "It is widely believed that monetarism was tried in the United States from 1979 to 1984 and that it did not work in practice. This is very far from the truth. In October 1979 the Federal Reserve in desperation adopted monetarist rhetoric. It did not then and has not since adopted a monetarist policy." If the Fed had followed his

prescriptions, he said, "unemployment would never have risen as it did. Output would never have fallen as low."

88. *Hansard Commons,* vol. 191, May 16, 1991, col. 413.

89. Samuelson once famously declared, "Let those who will — write the nation's laws — if I can write its textbooks." There was much to this. But in this case, Friedman changed the nation's laws and so Samuelson had to change the textbook. By the 1990s, moreover, his textbook was being outsold by younger authors who said much less about Keynesian ideas. See Alan O. Ebenstein, *Milton Friedman* (New York: Palgrave Macmillan, 2007), 156–57.

90. George M. von Furstenberg and Michael K. Ulan, "A Sea Change for New Zealand," in *Learning from the World's Best Central Bankers,* 207–42.

91. Inflation in France was much higher than German inflation during the first half of the 1980s, and still a little higher during the second half of the decade. During the first half of the 1990s, inflation in France was significantly lower than inflation in Germany, but France continued to pay an inflation premium. By the second half of the decade, with monetary union looming and then realized, the gap was eliminated. See Don Brash, *Incredible Luck* (Auckland: Troika Books, 2014), ebook loc. 431.

92. Brash is sometimes described as a kiwi farmer. This contained a grain of truth. He bought a kiwi orchard in 1981 but, by his own account, it was a tax shelter.

93. The best available techniques for measuring price inflation tend to overstate inflation, generally by about 1 percentage point. One reason is the difficulty in measuring the changes in the quality of a given product. The most recent iPhone, for example, provides significantly more value than the original device. So the 0 to 2 percent target amounted to aiming for zero, with a margin for error.

94. Friedman, typically, scandalized the locals by calling for New Zealand to exit the business of making cars. He described the industry as a particularly egregious example of protectionist inefficiency. The last local car-making plant went out of business about a decade later. See "Interview with Donald Brash," *The Region,* Federal Reserve Bank of Minneapolis, June 1999.

95. Paul Goldsmith, *Brash* (Auckland: Penguin, 2005), 175.

96. Neal Wallace, *When the Farm Gates Opened* (Dunedin: Otago University Press, 2014), 21.

97. The Bank for International Settlements is a central bank for central banks, facilitating international movements of money and providing a forum for the establishment of international standards, such as the Basel standards for bank capital. It is also the only surviving example of the international institutions established after World War I. Adam LeBor narrates the history of the BIS in *Tower of Basel* (New York: PublicAffairs, 2013).

98. Greenspan was partial to the view that central bankers should sow a little confusion to inhibit financial speculation. "If I seem unduly clear to you, you must have misunderstood what I said," Greenspan told a gaggle of reporters early in his tenure at the Fed. That was not a frequent problem. "It's what central bankers do," said the economist Robert Solow. "They're like squid: they emit a cloud of ink and move away." See Linton Weeks and John M. Berry, "The Shy Wizard of Money," *Washington Post,* March 24, 1997. For Don Kohn's quote, see Mallaby, *The Man Who Knew,* 382.

99. Keith Bradsher, "Economics by Ripples," *New York Times,* May 30, 1994.

100. Greenspan explained that low inflation creates "an environment that forces productivity enhancements. It forces people who want to stay in business to take those actions — such as cutting down the size of the cafeteria, reducing overtime and taking away

managers' drivers — that they did not want to take before in the ordinary course of business in a modest inflationary environment because it was easier then just to raise prices to maintain margins." A quarter century later, there is still no evidence that reducing inflation from, say, 2 percent to 1 percent has significant economic benefits. Indeed, Greenspan told me in a 2018 interview that he has come to regard 2 percent inflation as optimal. Moreover, to the extent that low inflation comes at the price of higher unemployment, it may reduce innovation, because companies can rely on cheap labor rather than investing in machines. As I write, the United States is in an extended period of low inflation, and slow productivity growth. See "Transcript of Federal Open Market Committee, July 2–3, 1996," 67; available at federalreserve.gov /monetarypolicy/files/FOMC19960703meeting.pdf.

101. The economists Christina Romer and David Romer concluded the Fed behaved as if it was seeking to maintain an average unemployment rate of 7.3 percent, even though estimates of the lowest sustainable rate of unemployment averaged less than 6 percent during that seventeen-year period. The calculation of the delta's population is my own. See Christina D. Romer and David H. Romer, "The Evolution of Economic Understanding and Postwar Stabilization Policy," 2002, National Bureau of Economic Research.

102. The Council of Economic Advisers is staffed mostly by academic economists and serves as an internal think tank. The National Economic Council was created to coordinate the administration's domestic economic policies.

103. Bob Woodward, *The Agenda* (New York: Simon and Schuster, 1994), 73.

104. Blinder, *Hard Heads, Soft Hearts*, 33, 36, 51, 77.

105. Bob Woodward, *Maestro: Alan Greenspan and the American Economy* (New York: Simon and Schuster, 2000), 127.

106. Ironically, that did not keep Blinder from controversy. In a speech at the Fed's annual Jackson Hole conference, he suggested in careful language the Fed could stimulate job growth while maintaining control of inflation. The press, primed by his earlier work, portrayed it as an assault on Greenspan. The columnist Robert Samuelson, an absolutist in matters of inflation, opined that Blinder "lacks the moral or intellectual qualities needed to lead the Fed." See Robert Samuelson, "Economic Amnesia," *Newsweek*, September 11, 1994.

107. Clinton did reprise the Blinder gambit, nominating Alice Rivlin to serve as vice chairman. Rivlin told me that Clinton pitched her on the job by telling her that he was worried about Greenspan's inflation advocacy and wanted her to serve as the balance. Still, Clinton's most important decision was giving Greenspan a third term — and then a fourth term.

108. Some economists still deny that people are confused by inflation, or at least that such confusion has significant consequences. Meanwhile, in the real world, movie studios take advantage of inflation to advertise box office records — which are records only in nominal terms, since no movie has ever surpassed *Gone with the Wind* — because the studios think that people are confused by inflation. It seems likely that Hollywood has the better handle on human nature.

109. Binyamin Appelbaum, "Possible Fed Successor Has Admirers and Foes," *New York Times*, April 24, 2013.

110. In Yellen's view, the primary benefit of reducing inflation below 3 percent was to reduce distortions in taxation. Yellen said it made more sense to address those problems by changing the tax code. See "Transcript of Federal Open Market Committee, July 2–3, 1996"; available at federalreserve.gov/monetarypolicy/files/FOMC19960703meeting .pdf. Under Greenspan's successor, Ben S. Bernanke, the Fed adopted a 2 percent

inflation target in 2010. Interestingly, it did so to make clear that it was determined to push inflation back up to that level. Greenspan was appalled, writing, "The spectacle of American central bankers trying to press the inflation rate higher in the aftermath of the 2008 crisis is virtually without precedent." He predicted, incorrectly, that the effort could end in a return to double-digit inflation. See Alan Greenspan, *The Map and the Territory* (New York: Penguin Press, 2013), 269.

111. The worldwide decline in inflation was driven in large measure by globalization, rather than the specific policy choices of central banks. See Kenneth S. Rogoff, "Globalization and Global Disinflation," in *Monetary Policy and Uncertainty: Adapting to a Changing Economy* (Kansas City, Mo.: Federal Reserve Bank of Kansas City, 2003), 81.

112. Greg Ip, "Is Bernanke an Inflation Dove? Yes, but…," *Wall Street Journal*, October 31, 2005.

113. Lawrence H. Summers, "The Great Liberator," *New York Times*, November 19, 2006.

114. Robert E. Lucas, "Macroeconomic Priorities," *American Economic Review* 93, no. 1 (2003): 1–14. Lucas was a leading figure in a group of clever economists who by the mid-1970s had extended Friedman's work to argue that monetary policy could not exert consistent influence even over short-term economic conditions. Interference wasn't just inadvisable; it was impossible. This, in effect, revived John Stuart Mill's old description of money as nothing more than a veil. The problem with these mathematically elegant proofs is that they were arrant nonsense. It was perfectly evident that monetary policy had consequences; the work of economists was to explain and, better yet, to harness those consequences. As Robert Solow put the matter in his 1980 presidential address to the American Economic Association, "I remember reading once that it is still not understood how the giraffe manages to pump an adequate blood supply all the way up to its head; but it is hard to imagine that anyone would therefore conclude that giraffes do not have long necks." These more extreme formulations, however, exerted relatively little influence on policy makers. Laurence H. Meyer, who served as a Federal Reserve governor during the late 1990s, wrote in his memoirs that everything Fed officials needed to know had been said by Friedman, and that everything said since was irrelevant.

115. Robert Lucas Jr., "The Industrial Revolution: Past and Future," in *2003 Annual Report* (Minneapolis: Federal Reserve Bank of Minneapolis, 2004); available at minneapolisfed .org/publications/the-region/the-industrial-revolution-past-and-future.

116. The unemployment rate does not include people who are not actively seeking work. In 1979, at the height of stagflation, roughly 3.5 million American men in their prime working years, ages 25 to 54, were on the sidelines. By 2007, in the midst of the Great Moderation, roughly 8.5 million prime-age American men were on the sidelines. In percentage terms, the Bureau of Labor Statistics says the rate of non-employment among men ages 25 to 54 rose from 8.9 percent in January 1979 to 14 percent in January 2008. Until roughly the turn of the century, this trend was offset by increased female workforce participation. Since then, female participation also has declined. See Robert Skidelsky, *Money and Government: The Past and Future of Economics* (New Haven: Yale University Press, 2018), 202.

117. The concentration of wealth in the hands of the top 10 percent peaked at 84.4 percent in 1928, on the cusp of the Great Depression, then declined through much of the twentieth century, reaching a nadir at 63.6 percent in 1986. It has been climbing ever since. See Emmanuel Saez and Gabriel Zucman, "Wealth Inequality in the United States Since 1913: Evidence from Capitalized Income Tax Data," October 2014, National Bureau of Economic Research Working Paper 20625.

118. Richard W. Fisher, "Balancing Inflation and Growth," London, England, March 4, 2008; available at dallasfed.org/news/speeches/fisher/2008/fs080304.aspx.

Chapter 4. Representation Without Taxation

1. John Kenneth Galbraith, *Money: Whence It Came, Where It Went* (Boston: Houghton Mifflin, 1975), 86.

2. A record of the proceedings is preserved in Randall Weston Hinshaw, ed., *Inflation as a Global Problem* (Baltimore: Johns Hopkins University Press, 1972), 127.

3. Robert Mundell, "On the History of the Mundell-Fleming Model," *IMF Staff Papers* 47 (2001).

4. Robert A. Mundell, "The Appropriate Use of Monetary and Fiscal Policy for Internal and External Stability," *IMF Staff Papers* 9, no. 1 (March 1962). The paper argued for fiscal stimulus without differentiating between tax cuts and spending increases. He subsequently added a footnote specifying that tax cuts were the preferred instrument. Still, Mundell later told the historian Brian Domitrovic that he did not firmly embrace tax cuts as superior to spending increases until the early 1970s. "This is a difficult question to answer but the issue was not finally resolved until the early 1970s. In the early 1960s in my models I stressed the tax cuts and fiscal stimulus without distinction between supply-side effects and budgetary effects. The economics world at that time was almost universally Keynesian and that is why my policy mix ideas were so readily accepted. But I was aware of the supply-side effects of tax rates from my earliest writings, which were entirely in a classical international framework." See Brian Domitrovic, *Econoclasts: The Rebels Who Sparked the Supply-Side Movement and Restored American Prosperity* (Wilmington, Del.: ISI Books, 2009), 307.

5. Howard R. Vane and Chris Mulhearn, "Interview with Robert A. Mundell," *Journal of Economic Perspectives* 20, no. 4 (Fall 2006): 93.

6. Explaining a decision to raise corporate taxes in 1969, one of Nixon's economic advisers, Herbert Stein, wrote to a colleague, "There were more important things at this juncture in history to do with the federal budget, with the national output, than to make even more rapid a rate of growth that is already very rapid." See Allen J. Matusow, *Nixon's Economy: Booms, Busts, Dollars and Votes* (Lawrence: University Press of Kansas, 1998), 42.

7. Domitrovic, *Econoclasts*, 91. When Mundell was awarded the Nobel Prize in 1999, he said he would use the money to keep working on the castle — then entering its fourth decade of renovations. See also Sylvia Nasar, "Nobel Economics: Spending the Check," *New York Times*, December 5, 1999.

8. Robert A. Mundell, "The Dollar and the Policy Mix: 1971," *Essays in International Finance*, no. 85 (May 1971). The paper is a version of Mundell's remarks at the Bologna conference. As a technical matter, the earlier 1962 paper was about an economy with fixed interest rates. The 1971 paper extended the argument to an economy with floating exchange rates.

9. Hinshaw, *Inflation as a Global Problem*, 123.

10. Robert L. Bartley, *The Seven Fat Years: And How to Do It Again* (New York: Free Press, 1995), 59.

11. John N. Turner, "Budget Speech in the House of Commons," February 19, 1973; available at budget.gc.ca/pdfarch/1973-sd-eng.pdf.

12. Robert Lucas, another young member of the Chicago faculty, said in a 1998 oral history interview that he was offered the job before Laffer, but turned it down to focus on

his research, which ultimately won him a Nobel Prize. Laffer, for his part, launched a career in public policy that permanently reshaped the government's approach to taxation. "My guess would be that I, Art and the U.S. economy were all better off as a result," Lucas said. See Bennett T. McCallum, "An Interview with Robert E. Lucas Jr.," in *Inside the Economist's Mind: Conversations with Eminent Economists*, ed. Paul A. Samuelson and William A. Barnett (Malden, Mass.: Blackwell, 2007), 66.

13. The poem was attributed to one "Alfred Priori"; see "Money Machine," *New York Times*, May 16, 1971. Beyond gamesmanship, the mockery was motivated by the fact that Laffer's model was decidedly not a Keynesian model. Laffer used several methods to evaluate likely economic growth, including one that treated asset prices as an accurate barometer of the economic expectations of investors. This idea, a facet of "efficient markets theory," was just being developed at Chicago, and it remained far outside the mainstream. Laffer had the last laugh: his forecast hit the bull's-eye. But he says — quite rightly — that a bull's-eye in forecasting is a matter of luck. In his view, criticisms of the model were misguided without regard to the accuracy of the prediction for that particular year.

14. Domitrovic, *Econoclasts*, 106.

15. George Melloan, *Free People, Free Markets: How the Wall Street Journal's Opinion Pages Shaped America* (New York: Encounter, 2017), 183.

16. Jude Wanniski to Donald Rumsfeld, February 12, 1975, Jude Wanniski Papers, Hoover Institution Archives, Stanford, Calif.

17. The quote and anecdote are both from Alfred Malabre Jr., *Lost Prophets* (Cambridge: Harvard University Press, 1994), 180.

18. Jude Wanniski, "Theory and Policy: Mundell to Reagan," October 22, 1999; available at polyconomics.com/ssu/ssu-991022.htm.

19. Jude Wanniski, "It's Time to Cut Taxes," *Wall Street Journal,* December 11, 1974. As time passed, Wanniski devoted less space to quoting others and more space to his own outlandish claims about the benefits of tax cuts, insisting for example that "the drugs and alcoholism and divorce and personal abuses may begin to recede." Better yet, he said, tax cuts could win the Cold War — by commanding the respect of the Russians. See "The No. 1 Problem," *New York Times*, February 27, 1980.

20. This account of the celebrated meeting is based on Wanniski's written accounts, on interviews with Laffer and Grace-Marie Arnett Turner, who was also present, and on archival research. The napkin at the Smithsonian, which the museum presents as authentic, is dated September 13, 1974, and is dedicated to Donald Rumsfeld, Cheney's boss at the time. Wanniski, Laffer, and Turner agree that the meeting happened in November 1974, and that Rumsfeld was not present. Cheney wrote in his memoir that the meeting was in November and Rumsfeld was present. Rumsfeld wrote in his memoir that the meeting happened in 1975. It is my considered opinion that the Smithsonian, Rumsfeld, and Cheney are, to varying degrees, confused about the facts. See Binyamin Appelbaum, "This Is Not Arthur Laffer's Famous Napkin," *New York Times*, October 13, 2017.

21. Howard R. Vane and Chris Mulhearn, "Interview with Robert A. Mundell," *Journal of Economic Perspectives* 20, no. 4 (Fall 2006): 104. Laffer later advised a number of leading politicians, both Democrats and Republicans, on proposals to tax income at a single rate. He told me that there was a theoretical argument for going even further, and taxing lower-income people at a higher rate, because lower rates had the greatest economic effect on higher earners. But this, he said, was politically untenable.

22. Tyler Haggerty, "Forty Years Ago, a Mob of Students Stormed the Bank of America Building," *Daily Nexus*, February 25, 2010. Police beat a student who had just left a speech by the radical defense attorney William Kunstler. The beating, in public and in broad daylight, was the immediate precipitant of the riot that culminated in the burning of the Santa Barbara bank branch. Powell wrote in his memo (see the next endnote) that Bank of America branches had been attacked 39 times in the previous eighteen months, "22 times with explosive devices and 17 times with fire bombs or by arsonists."

23. Powell's memo, "Attack on American Free Enterprise System," was dated August 23, 1971. For the memo and the reaction, see Kim Phillips-Fein, *Invisible Hands: The Businessman's Crusade Against the New Deal* (New York: Norton, 2010), 156–65.

24. Lee Edwards, *The Power of Ideas: The Heritage Foundation at 25 Years* (Ottawa, Ill.: Jameson Books, 1997), 9.

25. Jacob S. Hacker and Paul Pierson, *Winner-Take-All Politics: How Washington Made the Rich Richer—and Turned Its Back on the Middle Class* (New York: Simon and Schuster, 2010), 116.

26. Morton Kondracke and Fred Barnes, *Jack Kemp: The Bleeding-Heart Conservative Who Changed America* (New York: Sentinel, 2015), 31.

27. Ibid., 38.

28. Wanniski first used the phrase as the headline of a *Wall Streeet Journal* editorial on April 9, 1976. In later usage, "fiscalists" was usually dropped.

29. Congressional Democrats legislated a number of changes to the budget process in response to the Nixon administration's refusal to spend some allocated funds, including the creation of budget committees, to oversee the process, and the Congressional Budget Office, to provide independent analysis.

30. Foxe, born Annabel Battistella, told the Associated Press, "When I met Mr. Mills I didn't even know who he was. And when they told me he was on the Ways and Means Committee, I didn't know what that was." Mills was reelected the following month. A few weeks after that, he appeared onstage at a Boston strip club where Foxe was the featured performer. That proved a little much; Mills agreed to surrender the chairmanship of the Ways and Means Committee and seek treatment for alcoholism. For Ullman's role, see "Alice Rivlin, Oral History," December 13, 2002, Miller Center of Public Affairs, University of Virginia, Charlottesville.

31. "Q&A with Alice Rivlin," *Bryn Mawr S&T*, October 21, 2009.

32. Martin Tolchin, "The Bearer of Bad News Has Fewer Friends," *New York Times*, July 4, 1982.

33. Judy Flander, "Top Government Economist Takes Over Congressional Budget Office," *Washington Star*, February 25, 1975. Of her husband, Rivlin said, "He never had any interest in running the household, not like some of the young husbands you hear about today." They were divorced two years later.

34. The first program that could perform large-scale simulations of the American economy was developed at Brookings in the late 1950s. By the late 1960s, a number of major institutions, including the University of Pennsylvania and Chase Manhattan Bank, had created their own economic models.

35. "It is far from clear that these effects are quantitatively important," Rivlin wrote. The infuriated congressman, John Rousselot of California, read the letter into the Congressional Record on July 11, 1978: 124 Cong. Rec. 20135 (1978).

36. "Backstage at the Budget Committee," *Washington Post*, April 11, 1980.

37. Paul Craig Roberts, *The Supply-Side Revolution* (Cambridge: Harvard University Press, 1984), 47.

38. The $250,000 contract went to Chase Econometric Associates, an arm of Chase Manhattan run by the economist Michael K. Evans. While working on the model, Evans freely opined in favor of lower tax rates on capital gains. A few months after Congress cut those rates, Evans parted ways with Chase, accepting a $1.8 million buyout of his shares in the company, thus making him a major beneficiary of the new law. See Lawrence Rout, "Forecaster's Fate," *Wall Street Journal*, March 4, 1981.

39. Milton Friedman, "The Limitations of Tax Limitation," *Heritage Foundation Policy Review*, Summer 1978, 11.

40. Edward Nelson, "Milton Friedman and Economic Debate in the United States, 1932–1972," 2018, book B, p. 222; available at https://sites.google.com/site/edwardnelson resesearch/.

41. Milton Friedman and Rose Friedman, *Two Lucky People* (Chicago: University of Chicago Press, 1999), 441.

42. Laffer no longer narrates his move to USC as a march into exile, but he did at the time. "It was horrible," he said in 1981. "I knew there was no way on God's earth that I could make it in the profession. So I went other routes — the press, the political process, consulting." See Paul Blustein, "Supply-Side Theories Became Federal Policy with Unusual Speed," *Wall Street Journal*, October 8, 1981.

43. Sue E. Jares, "Arthur Laffer Is a Man with All the Reasons for a Big Tax Cut," *People*, April 7, 1979.

44. Kit R. Roane, Joe Rubin, and Dan McKinney, "The Populist Politician and California's Property Tax Revolt," RetroReport.org, October 17, 2016.

45. Howard Jarvis and Robert Pack, *I'm Mad as Hell: The Exclusive Story of the Tax Revolt and Its Leader* (New York: Times Books, 1979), 107.

46. John Kenneth Galbraith, letter to the editor, *Newsweek*, December 18, 1978. The fire departments remained in business, but Proposition 13 constrained California's ability to fund public services. In 1978, the state ranked fourteenth in funding per student; in 2018, the state ranked forty-third. Proposition 13 also shifted the burden of taxation from the wealthy to the less wealthy as local governments replaced property tax revenues with sales and utility taxes. Levies on new development, another popular workaround, have contributed to the state's shortage of affordable housing. The measure was billed as protection for homeowners; in practice, it was a windfall for people who happened to own homes at that moment in time. Home ownership rates in California have declined. See Mac Taylor, "Common Claims About Proposition 13," California Legislative Analyst's Office, September 2016.

47. Kemp introduced legislation in April 1977 to cut personal income tax rates by 30 percent. He credited "the recommendations of Professor Robert Mundell on how to break free of the Phillips curve to reach low unemployment with low inflation." In June 1977, Roth, also a Republican, agreed to sponsor a Senate version on the condition that the cut was spread across three years. This had the effect of reducing the total tax cut to 27 percent, but not of eliminating the general practice of describing the measure as a 30 percent reduction.

48. Alan Greenspan, *The Age of Turbulence: Adventures in a New World* (New York: Penguin Press, 2007), 238.

49. Richard Cheney to Jude Wanniski, September 19, 1978, Wanniski Papers, box 25, Hoover.

50. Martin Feldstein and Shlomo Yitzhaki, "The Effects of the Capital Gains Tax on the Selling and Switching of Common Stock," *Journal of Public Economics* 9, no. 1 (February 1978).

51. The Steiger language passed as an amendment to a broader bill, the Revenue Act of 1978. The Carter administration accepted the language as an alternative to a version of the Kemp-Roth proposal, which was gaining momentum. Carter signed the bill one day before the 1978 midterm elections. Steiger died of a heart attack one month later, at the age of forty. See Domitrovic, *Econoclasts*, 161–73.

52. "Forecasting the Supply Side of the Economy," Joint Economic Committee, May 21, 1980.

53. The text of the radio ad is from an account of the campaign by the journalists Rowland Evans and Robert Novak, who took a greater interest in economic issues, and supply-side economics in particular, than the bulk of their peers. See their *The Reagan Revolution* (New York: E. P. Dutton, 1981), 61. Reagan's pollster Richard Wirthlin — who had a doctorate in economics — told the candidate that age was his greatest weakness with voters, and advocating for tax cuts was the only effective remedy. "Only when coupled with limiting taxes does the 70-year-old with 'Republican' economic beliefs achieve victory," Wirthlin wrote in a memo quoted by Monica Prasad, in "The Popular Origins of Neoliberalism in the Reagan Tax Cut of 1981," May 2016, New York University Tax Policy Colloquium.

54. The rise of payroll taxation is often overlooked. The rate rose from 9.6 percent in 1970 to 12.3 percent in 1980. The government also increased the amount of income subject to payroll taxation by 50 percent during the same period, after adjusting for inflation. Federal receipts as a share of GDP reached 19.1 percent in 1981, according to the White House Office of Management and Budget.

55. Jimmy Carter, *Keeping Faith* (New York: Bantam, 1983), 541.

56. Haynes Johnson, *Sleepwalking Through History* (New York: Norton, 1991), 19–20.

57. "Legality of Certain DOD Support for Activities Associated with the Inauguration of President Ronald Reagan," General Accounting Office, July 1, 1983.

58. The top tax rate reached 94 percent in a single year, 1945, and Reagan spent the first eleven months of that year in the army. The next year, when he returned to paid acting, the top rate was 91 percent. Also, Reagan wasn't paid per film. In 1945, he signed a contract with Warner Bros. that paid him $1 million over seven years. The quote is from a 1981 interview. Reagan made slightly different versions of the same point in other contexts: see Evans and Novak, *The Reagan Revolution*, 237.

59. The data is from the OECD. The 2017 figure for the United States was 27 percent. Reagan, wittingly or otherwise, was espousing a version of a theory that enjoyed a season in the sun in the 1940s after a British economist named Colin Clark published a paper asserting that nations crumbled if public spending exceeded about 25 percent of the economy. Clark was a pioneer in the development of national income accounting, but he got a little too excited about the uses of his measuring stick.

60. Ronald Reagan, "Reflections on the Failure of Proposition #1," *National Review*, December 7, 1973.

61. Dart broke into the drugstore business by marrying Charles Walgreen's daughter. After they were divorced, he left Walgreen's to run Rexall. His second wife, Jane Bryan, was an actress who had appeared in several movies with Reagan, and the two couples became close friends.

62. Ronald Reagan, "Taxation," November 28, 1978, reprinted in *Reagan, in His Own Hand*, ed. Kiron K. Skinner et al. (New York: Free Press, 2001).

63. David Stockman, *The Triumph of Politics* (1986; repr., New York: PublicAffairs, 2013), 53.

64. Evans and Novak, *The Reagan Revolution*, 97. Ture was named under secretary for taxation; Paul Craig Roberts was named assistant secretary for economic policy; Stephen J. Entin, another Chicago graduate, was installed as Roberts's deputy.

65. Referring to Reagan's economic advisers, Anderson wrote in his 1988 book, *Revolution: The Reagan Legacy* (Stanford, Calif.: Hoover Institution Press, 1990), "Neither they, nor Reagan, nor any of Reagan's senior aides ever made any such outlandish claim." Paul Craig Roberts, a founding father of supply-side economics, and the assistant secretary for economic policy in Reagan's Treasury Department, wrote in 2017, "The economic policy of the Reagan administration was most certainly not based on tax reductions paying for themselves in increased revenues." The Reagan quote comes from a speech he gave in Chicago, Illinois. It is perhaps the clearest imaginable refutation of the accounts offered by his aides.

66. Ronald Reagan, *The Reagan Diaries*, ed. Douglas Brinkley (New York: Harper, 2007), 34.

67. The early 1980s were a difficult time for macroeconomists with scientific pretensions. None of the major schools of thought correctly anticipated the broad effects of Reagan's policies, let alone the details. The failures of supply-side economics and monetarism are described in these pages, but Keynesians did not cover themselves in glory. James Tobin colorfully insisted in 1981 that Reagan's policies would produce a disaster. "If Amtrak hitched engines at both ends of a train of cars in New Haven station — we do still have a railroad there — one engine heading west to New York, the other east to Boston, and advertised that the train was going simultaneously to both destinations, most people would be skeptical," he wrote. "Reagan is hitching a Volcker engine at one end and a Stockman-Kemp locomotive to the other and telling us the economic train will carry us to full employment and disinflation at the same time." (The lines first appeared in an essay Tobin wrote for the Federal Reserve Bank of San Francisco's *Economic Review* in May 1981; see James Tobin, *Policies for Prosperity* [Cambridge: MIT Press, 1989], 113.) In the event, the short-term costs of monetarist and supply-side policies were more modest than the Keynesians had predicted, although the long-term damage was more consequential.

68. Alan Blinder, *Hard Heads, Soft Hearts* (Reading, Mass.: Addison-Wesley, 1987), 21. It is perfectly logical that tax rates influence human behavior. But the evidence suggests the magnitude is modest, and the effects are complex. Higher tax rates, for example, may induce some people to work harder, to maintain their incomes or to meet pre-existing obligations. For the same reasons, lower tax rates may cause some people to work less.

69. The average effective tax rate on corporate income fell from 51 percent in 1960 to 24 percent in 1985, but the 1985 calculation reflected a 35 percent rate from property taxes and personal income taxes, and a −9 percent rate from the corporate income tax. "In other words, the corporate tax system under 1981 law provides a net subsidy in the sense that its elimination would cause an increase in this total effective tax rate from 26 to 35 percent." See Don Fullerton, "Tax Policy," in *American Economic Policy in the 1980s*, ed. Martin Feldstein (Chicago: University of Chicago Press, 1994), 172.

70. Robert S. McIntyre and Robert Folen, "Corporate Income Taxes in the Reagan Years: A Study of Three Years of Legalized Tax Avoidance," 1984, Citizens for Tax Justice. Reagan extended his acting career by hosting a television program called *General Electric Theater* for almost a decade, beginning in the early 1950s. As part of the deal, he regularly visited GE factories, delivering speeches to the workers about the importance

of free-market principles. The experience was the crucible in which Reagan's political persona was formed.

71. National Research Council, "Understanding the U.S. Illicit Tobacco Market: Characteristics, Policy Context, and Lessons from International Experiences," 2015, National Academies Press; available at https://doi.org/10.17226/19016.

72. Friedman and Friedman, *Two Lucky People*, 171.

73. Phillips-Fein, *Invisible Hands*, 261.

74. The 1980s look a little worse without an adjustment for population. Average annual GDP growth was 3.2 percent in the 1970s and 3.1 percent in the 1980s. As the Congressional Research Service concluded in 2012, "Changes over the past 65 years in the top marginal tax rate and the top capital gains tax rate do not appear correlated with economic growth." Thomas L. Hungerford, "Taxes and the Economy: An Economic Analysis of the Top Tax Rates Since 1945," December 2012, Congressional Research Service.

75. Barton Gellman, *Angler: The Cheney Vice Presidency* (New York: Penguin Press, 2008), 259.

76. The Reagan administration's first budget estimated increased economic growth as a result of the tax cuts would offset about 20 percent of the initial revenue loss. That assessment was of course quite different from the President's own rhetoric.

77. Stockman, *The Triumph of Politics*, 31.

78. Ludwig Erhard, as minister of economics in West Germany from 1949 to 1963, and chancellor from 1963 to 1966, presided over West Germany's *Wirtschaftswunder*, or economic revival. He was one of the first Western policy makers to embrace the idea that economic growth should be the primary focus of public policy. His reforms included the end of postwar price controls and the creation of an independent central bank, the Bundesbank, that was instructed to focus on preventing inflation.

79. "Jim Miller, Oral History," November 4, 2001, Miller Center of Public Affairs, University of Virginia. The fiscal problems were exacerbated by a fundamental change in the 1981 legislation that attracted relatively little notice at the time. The United States introduced inflation-indexed tax brackets, just as Canada did in the 1970s, meaning that the income thresholds for higher rates of taxation rose with inflation. Before the change, inflation increased federal revenues in real terms by pushing people into higher tax brackets. That allowed the government to increase spending without raising tax rates, or to reduce tax rates without constraining spending. But the 1981 law was the last performance of that long-running show. During the 1980s, the federal government confronted a less pleasant reality: controlling deficits now required real spending cuts or real tax increases.

80. David Espo, "Senate Republicans Urge Economic Adviser to Quit," Associated Press, December 11, 1981. Reagan initially sided with the revolutionaries. "The recession has worsened, throwing our earlier figures off," the President wrote in his diary on December 22, 1981. "Now my team is pushing for a tax increase to help hold down the deficits. I think our tax cuts will produce more revenue by stimulating the economy. I intend to wait and see some results." It is the only economic issue on which he expressed strong feelings in the pages of that diary, which is mostly devoted to politics and foreign policy. He found support at the occasional meetings of an advisory group of conservative economists, including Friedman and Laffer. The economists praised the President, and the President told stories about Hollywood. "What they did for him more than anything else was to reassure him that the course he was following was right," said Martin Anderson, who organized the meetings.

81. Mundell's plan called for high interest rates, which he regarded as important in attracting foreign investors. Treasuries during the first half of the 1980s, for example, paid roughly 5 percent more than comparable Japanese securities. But time would show that foreigners were happy to invest in the United States even when interest rates were low.

82. Kenneth D. Garbade, *Treasury Debt Management Under the Rubric of Regular and Predictable Issuance, 1983–2012* (New York: Federal Reserve Bank of New York, 2015).

83. William Greider, *Secrets of the Temple* (New York: Simon and Schuster, 1981), 424.

84. Richard Ben Cramer, *What It Takes* (New York: Vintage, 1992), 66.

85. The top tax rate in the 1986 law is often reported as 28 percent, but the law included a 5 percent surcharge on some income taxed at the 28 percent rate. The legislation was celebrated as a triumph of efficiency and equality. Just as Wilbur Mills had proposed in the 1950s, the bill reduced tax rates while broadening the tax base, preserving both federal revenues and the distribution of taxation. The simplification of the tax code suited the temperament of the times: members of both parties said the government should seek to satisfy its need for money with a minimum of meddling in the marketplace. As the Treasury Department wrote in a 1984 report, "Any deviation from this principle represents implicit endorsement of government intervention in the economy — an insidious form of industrial policy based on the belief that those responsible for tax policy can judge better than the marketplace what consumers want, how goods and services should be produced, and how business should be organized and financed." But the ensuing celebrations overstated the purity of the new tax code. One effect of the bill was to shift tax preferences from the old economy of manufacturing to the new economy of technology and services. The effective tax rate on machinery, for example, bounced back up to 39 percent. And lots of less justifiable loopholes also survived. Special interests were learning to speak the language of economics. One economist, asked for his views by a client, responded that he had not been paid. The client, a lobbyist for real estate developers, paid and asked again. This time the economist replied, "What do you want us to find?" See Jeffrey H. Birnbaum and Alan S. Murray, *Showdown at Gucci Gulch: Lawmakers, Lobbyists, and the Unlikely Triumph of Tax Reform* (New York: Vintage, 1988), 111.

86. "The Distribution of Household Income, 2015," November 8, 2018, Congressional Budget Office.

87. The Gini coefficient, a standard measure of income inequality, rose by 5.17 percent between 1983 and 1988, the largest increase over any five-year period since World War II. See Wojciech Kopczuk, Emmanuel Saez, and Jae Song, "Earnings Inequality and Mobility in the United States: Evidence from Social Security Data Since 1937," *Quarterly Journal of Economics* 125, no. 1 (February 2010).

88. Keith Joseph, "Monetarism Is Not Enough," London, April 5, 1976; available at margaretthatcher.org/document/110796.

89. Alan Reynolds, "Marginal Tax Rates," *The Concise Encyclopedia of Economics*; available at econlib.org/library/Enc/MarginalTaxRates.html.

90. Robert Mundell, "Supply-Side Economics: From the Reagan Era to Today," March 24, 2011, Ronald Reagan Presidential Foundation, Simi Valley, Calif.; available at https://youtu.be/drvRxf-Kxf0.

91. "Historical Tables, Fiscal Year 2019 Budget," White House Office of Management and Budget.

92. Paul Blustein, "Supply-Side Theories Became Federal Policy with Unusual Speed," *Wall Street Journal*, October 8, 1981.

93. Ture resigned in protest against the 1982 law. By 1986, the corporate tax cuts had been almost completely reversed. See Dennis S. Ippolito, *Deficits, Debt and the New Politics of Tax Policy* (Cambridge, Eng.: Cambridge University Press, 2012), 122.

94. The lobbyist, Charls Walker, was described by one of his own colleagues as "the classic caricature of the cigar-smoking super-lobbyist with a limo." An economist by training, with a doctorate from the University of Pennsylvania, he cut his teeth on tax policy in the Nixon administration, and from the outset, he was unabashed in his sympathy for corporations. He told *Congressional Quarterly* that when he left for private practice, Nixon told him, "You're going to be doing what you have been, but now making money at it." During the 1980 campaign, Walker served as Reagan's top adviser on tax policy, pushing for corporate tax cuts. Then he returned to work as a lobbyist, pushing the same changes from the outside. See Charls Walker, "Comment on Tax Policy," in *American Economic Policy in the 1980s*, ed. Feldstein, 209.

95. In the 1982 law, 75 percent of the benefits came from tax hikes; in the 1984 law, 82 percent came from tax hikes. In 1987, the figure was just 39 percent. See Kathy Ruffing, "The Composition of Past Deficit Reduction Packages," 2011, Center on Budget and Policy Priorities.

96. Jack Kemp, "Shaping America's Economic Course," Colorado Springs, April 16, 1993.

97. David Maraniss, "Armey Arsenal: Plain Talk and Dramatic Tales," *Washington Post*, February 21, 1995.

98. Ibid.

99. Jason Horowitz, "Grover Norquist, the Anti-tax Enforcer Behind the Scenes of the Debt Debate," *Washington Post*, July 12, 2011.

100. The numbers are from "Historical Tables" of the FY2019 federal budget. Federal spending continued to rise, even after adjusting for inflation. But the decline of spending as a share of GDP still diverged sharply from the pattern in other developed nations. Excluding defense and health care, government spending as a share of economic activity has remained about 30 percent smaller in the United States than the average in other developed nations. (The United States spends more heavily on defense than every other developed nation except Israel. Strikingly, it also spends a larger share of national income on health care, even though the United States is alone among developed nations in allowing many of its citizens to live without reliable access to health care.)

101. The ellipsis is in the original version of the quote. See Rick Weiss, "NIH Cancer Chief Vents Frustration," *Washington Post*, December 24, 1994. The declines in federal spending on research, infrastructure, and social welfare are measured as shares of GDP.

102. Bush's initial argument for the tax cut was crafted by Lawrence B. Lindsey, an economist who tutored the Texas governor on economic issues in the late 1990s and then became the chief economic adviser for Bush's presidential campaign. Lindsey spent his career at the intersection of economics and politics. He studied under Martin Feldstein at Harvard, worked under Feldstein in the Reagan administration, and then returned to Washington as an adviser to President George H. W. Bush. He was a Fed governor from 1991 to 1997 and then joined the American Enterprise Institute. Karl Rove, George W. Bush's chief political adviser, admired a book Lindsey wrote that celebrated the Reagan tax cuts, and he invited Lindsey to visit Bush in Austin. After the 2000 election, Lindsey became the head of the National Economic Council, helping to push through Bush's 2001 tax cuts.

103. O'Neill told his side of the story to the journalist Ron Suskind. See Suskind's *The Price of Loyalty: George W. Bush, the White House and the Education of Paul O'Neill* (New York: Simon and Schuster, 2004).

104. There was an economic case against contingent tax cuts — the same as the argument against onetime rebates. Both rested on a paper that many economists regard as Milton Friedman's most important scholarly contribution, in which he argued that shifts in spending were tied to enduring changes in income, not short-term fluctuations. That suggested uncertainty about the duration of a tax cut would sap some of the stimulative benefit. "It's bad economics, especially if you're trying to influence economic growth," said Dick Armey, the House majority leader.

105. Greenspan, *The Age of Turbulence*, 221.

106. Gellman, *Angler*, 265.

107. Richard Cheney, *In My Time* (New York: Threshold, 2011), 308.

108. Gellman, *Angler*, 274.

109. The quotes are from Suskind, *The Price of Loyalty*, 284–91. Cheney acknowledged and sought to explain the remark in his memoirs. "Of course I thought deficits mattered. I just believed that it was important to see them in context, to note that while Ronald Reagan's dramatic increases in the defense budget and his historic tax cuts did push the deficit from 2.7 percent of the gross domestic product in fiscal year 1980 to 6 percent in fiscal year 1983, his spending on defense helped put the Soviet Union out of business, and his tax cuts helped spur one of the longest sustained waves of prosperity in our history. The result was a peace dividend, increased federal revenues, and, eventually, lower deficits." See Cheney, *In My Time*, 311.

110. "It is one of the supreme ironies of the information revolution of the late 20th Century that a public offered access to larger and larger sets of data is, at the same time, less and less capable of judging their veracity and using them effectively." See Michael A. Bernstein, *A Perilous Progress: Economists and Public Purpose in Twentieth-Century America* (Princeton, N.J.: Princeton University Press, 2001), 191.

111. "I am one of the few people who still are not as yet convinced that stimulus is a desirable policy at this particular point," Greenspan told Congress on February 11, 2003.

112. The analysis was later published: see Thomas Laubach, "New Evidence on the Interest Rate Effects of Budget Deficits and Debt," May 2003, Federal Reserve Board. In 2015, Laubach was named the Fed's top staff economist, director of the Division of Monetary Affairs.

113. Interview with Cesar Conda, September 28, 2017.

114. John Cassidy, "Tax Code," *The New Yorker*, September 6, 2004.

115. William G. Gale and Andrew A. Samwick, "Effects of Income Tax Changes on Economic Growth," 2016, Brookings Institution.

116. The data is taken from a remarkable and groundbreaking study published in 2018. The group described as highest income is the top 0.1 percent of the population, which comprised roughly twice as many people in 2011 as in 1961. The reduction of income tax rates is just one factor. The mix of taxation also has shifted: both personal and income taxation have declined, while regressive taxes, like the federal payroll tax and state and local sales taxes, have increased. See Thomas Piketty, Emmanuel Saez, and Gabriel Zucman, "Distributional National Accounts: Methods and Estimates for the United States," *Quarterly Journal of Economics* 133, no. 2 (May 2018). The study does not consider the effects of the tax increases passed under President Obama in 2013, nor of the tax cuts passed under President Trump in 2017. Other estimates, however, suggest the combined effect has been a further flattening in the distribution of taxation.

117. The data is from Gallup. The figure remained at 62 percent in April 2018, the most recent data at the time of writing. See https://news.gallup.com/poll/1714/Taxes.aspx.

118. For the most recent available data—from 2012—see Tax Foundation, "Facts and Figures 2018."

Chapter 5. In Corporations We Trust

1. Peck is quoted in Paul MacAvoy, *Unsettled Questions on Regulatory Reform* (Washington, D.C.: American Enterprise Institute, 1978), 13.

2. Michael Riordan and Lillian Hoddeson, *Crystal Fire: The Birth of the Information Age* (New York: Norton, 1997), 195–224.

3. The government had filed suit against AT&T three years earlier, demanding the sale of its manufacturing arm, Western Electric. The company's decision to license the transistor was a peace offering, intended to demonstrate AT&T was not using the profits from its telephone monopoly to pursue dominance in other industries. It proved insufficient. In 1956, AT&T agreed to license all of its existing patents free of charge and all of its future patents at a reasonable price.

4. "I.B.M. Trust Suit Ended by Decree; Machines Freed," *New York Times*, January 26, 1956. The business historian Alfred D. Chandler Jr. charts the role of antitrust policy in the computer revolution in his 2001 book, *Inventing the Electronic Century* (New York: Free Press, 2001).

5. F. M. Scherer, "The Political Economy of Patent Policy Reform in the United States," *Journal on Telecommunications and High Technology Law* 7, no. 2 (Spring 2009).

6. Eli Cook, *The Pricing of Progress: Economic Indicators and the Capitalization of American Life* (Cambridge: Harvard University Press, 2017), 232.

7. 21 Cong. Rec. 2457 (1890). Senator Sherman's brother, General William Tecumseh Sherman, had struck his own blow against market power in January 1865, when he ordered the redistribution of 400,000 acres of coastal plantations to freed slaves in 40-acre chunks. Sherman also authorized the army to lend mules to the farmers, a policy immortalized as "40 acres and a mule." The effort didn't last. President Andrew Johnson reversed the process, returning most of the land to its former owners in the fall of 1865.

8. Louis Brandeis, one of the great advocates for the preservation of small business, told Congress in 1911, "I think we are in a position, after the experience of the last twenty years, to state two things: In the first place, that a corporation may well be too large to be the most efficient instrument of production and of distribution, and, in the second place, whether it has exceeded the point of greatest economic efficiency or not, it may be too large to be tolerated among the people who desire to be free." See "Control of Corporations, Persons, and Firms Engaged in Interstate Commerce," Senate Committee on Interstate Commerce, November 29, 1911, 1174.

9. Standard Oil was famously portrayed as a predatory monopoly by the muckraking journalist Ida Tarbell, who was raised in the Pennsylvania oil fields and whose father, a small-time oilman, was driven from business by Rockefeller. The Supreme Court, in ordering the company's dissolution, accepted Tarbell's characterization; historians and economists continue to debate whether Rockefeller was a superior businessman or a cheat. One compelling piece of evidence that breaking up the company was justified, at least in economic terms, is that the aggregate market value of the constituent parts roughly quintupled after the breakup.

10. Mary Pilon's *The Monopolists* (New York: Bloomsbury, 2015) narrates the game's surprisingly tangled history.

11. "Amending Sections 7 and 11 of the Clayton Act: Hearings Before Subcommittee No. 2 of the Committee on the Judiciary," March 19, 1947, 7.

12. Lawrence J. White, "Economics, Economists and Antitrust: A Tale of Growing Influence," in *Better Living Through Economics*, ed. John J. Siegfried (Cambridge: Harvard University Press, 2010), ebook loc. 2945.

13. *Brown Shoe Co. v. United States*, 370 U.S. 344 (1962).

14. *United States v. Von's Grocery Co.*, 384 U.S. 270 (1966). Robert Bork made the same point more colorfully in his *The Antitrust Paradox: A Policy at War with Itself* (New York: Basic Books, 1978), writing that antitrust enforcement was "in the good old American tradition of the sheriff of a frontier town: he did not sift evidence, distinguish between suspects, and solve crimes, but merely walked the main street and every so often pistol-whipped a few people."

15. Mark J. Green et al., *The Closed Enterprise System: The Nader Study Group Report on Antitrust Enforcement* (New York: Grossman, 1972), 128–29.

16. Craig Freedman, "Insider's Story: Notes on the Claire Friedland and George Stigler Partnership," *History of Economics Review*, no. 55 (Winter 2012): 1–28.

17. George J. Stigler, *Memoirs of an Unregulated Economist* (New York: Basic Books, 1985), 6.

18. George J. Stigler, "The Economies of Scale," *Journal of Law and Economics* 1 (October 1958).

19. Stigler's dissertation "traced the evolution of theories of distribution between 1870 and 1895." It reflected his deep and enduring interest in the history of economic thought, a subject many economists, then and now, treat with profound indifference. See George J. Stigler, *Production and Distribution Theories: The Formative Period* (New York: Macmillan, 1941).

20. Interview with George Shultz, April 19, 2018.

21. I first encountered the letter on the Twitter feed of the economic historian Beatrice Cherrier, who was kind enough to send me a digital copy. The original source is Robert Solow to Paul Samuelson, n.d., Paul Samuelson Papers, box 70, folder "Solow, 46-2007," Rubinstein Library, Duke University, Durham, N.C.

22. Claire Friedland, "On Stigler and Stiglerisms," *Journal of Political Economy* 101, no. 5 (October 1993): 780–83.

23. Stigler's public comments on the influence of economists were maddeningly inconsistent. He was famously dismissive of the role economists played in ending the British Corn Laws in the nineteenth century, writing, "Economists exert a minor and scarcely detectable influence on the societies in which they live," and insisting the tides of history had determined the issue. On the other hand, his 1964 presidential address to the American Economic Association, entitled "The Economist and the State," included the following passage: "Our expanding theoretical and empirical studies will inevitably and irresistibly enter into the subject of public policy, and we shall develop a body of knowledge essential to intelligent policy formulation."

24. Craig Freedman, *In Search of the Two-Handed Economist: Ideology, Methodology and Marketing in Economics* (London: Palgrave Macmillan, 2016), 25.

25. Stigler, *Memoirs of an Unregulated Economist*, 211.

26. When word of the London lectures reached Chicago, Friedman sent his congratulations. "I am writing mainly to swell your head, though God Knows it must be big enough already." Milton Friedman and George Stigler, *Making Chicago Price Theory: Friedman–Stigler Correspondence, 1945–1957*, ed. J. Daniel Hammond and Claire H. Hammond (London: Routledge, 2006), 80.

27. George J. Stigler, "The Case Against Big Business," *Fortune*, May 1952. Stigler and his allies did not share the concern of antitrust proponents about the economic cost of corporate

concentration. One of Stigler's colleagues, Arnold Harberger, examined corporate profits in the 1920s and concluded that corporate concentration had allowed companies to extract from the average American a maximum of $2.25 per year in 1952 dollars, or about $21 in current (2018) dollars. See Arnold C. Harberger, "Monopoly and Resource Allocation," *American Economic Review* 2, no. 44 (1954): 77–87.

28. Friedman, who outlived most of his peers, offered an account of the friendship in "George Stigler: A Personal Reminiscence," *Journal of Political Economy* 101, no. 5.

29. Stigler was hired by W. Allen Wallis, who had been a friend of both Stigler and Friedman in graduate school, as well as their boss at Columbia during the war, and was then serving as dean of the Chicago business school.

30. Edward Nik-Khah, "George Stigler, the Graduate School of Business and the Pillars of the Chicago School," in *Building Chicago Economics: New Perspectives on the History of America's Most Powerful Economics Program*, ed. Robert Van Horn et al. (Cambridge, Eng.: Cambridge University Press, 2011), 121.

31. In this view, he had good company, including the Nobel Prize committee, which cited the paper prominently in making Stigler a laureate in 1982.

32. George J. Stigler, "The Economics of Information," *Journal of Political Economy* 69, no. 3 (1961).

33. George J. Stigler, "Monopoly," in *The Fortune Encyclopedia of Economics*, ed. David R. Henderson (New York: Warner, 1993). Stigler acknowledged that in markets with standardized products, policing could be less expensive, and therefore cartels would be more likely. The cost of policing also decreased with fewer sellers, or more buyers. It's obviously easier to police a smaller number of sellers. The point about buyers is more subtle. Stigler argued that a cheating company ran a given risk of exposure with each transaction. In a market with many small buyers, the price of exposure — probability times cost — might outweigh the profits from each small sale. Another interesting implication of Stigler's theory is that collusion is easier to enforce if sales are recorded publicly. This makes governments particularly vulnerable to collusion, since bids often are publicly disclosed. See George J. Stigler, "A Theory of Oligopoly," *Journal of Political Economy* 72, no. 1 (1964).

34. Director's acceptance to Yale was something of a fluke. In the early 1920s, Yale was under growing pressure from western alumni to admit more graduates of western public schools. Yale's dean of freshmen, Roswell P. Angier, visited Lincoln High School in Portland during Director's senior year as part of a new effort to encourage applications. Director seized the opportunity and secured a scholarship with the help of his history teacher, Norman C. Thorne, a Yale graduate. But Yale, along with other elite institutions, soon began an aggressive effort to limit Jewish enrollment. As a result, Director lost his scholarship after his first year at Yale. It is quite possible that 1921 is the only year in that era a Jewish student from a Portland public school could have secured admission. See Robert Van Horn, "The Coming of Age of a Reformer Skeptic (1914–1924)," *History of Political Economy* 42, no. 4 (2010): 601–30.

35. Director was not the first economist on the Chicago law school faculty. He took the place of Henry Simons, who played a formative role in the careers of Director, Friedman, and Stigler. See Rob Van Horn and Philip Mirowski, "The Rise of the Chicago School of Economics and the Birth of Neoliberalism," in *The Road from Mont Pèlerin*, ed. Philip Mirowski and Dieter Plehwe (Cambridge: Harvard University Press, 2009), 155.

36. Edmund W. Kitch, "The Fire of Truth: A Remembrance of Law and Economics at Chicago, 1932–1970," *Journal of Law and Economics* 26, no. 1. Coase's comments are particularly interesting because his 1961 paper on transaction costs is often identified as

the beginning of "law and economics" analysis. Another popular candidate is a similar 1961 paper by Guido Calabresi, a Yale Law School professor. By then, Director had been teaching the approach for more than a decade.

37. The evidence of Director's influence is preserved in the memoirs and oral histories of his students, and sometimes more explicitly in the papers that he inspired. McGee's second footnote began, "I am profoundly indebted to Aaron Director...." See John S. McGee, "Predatory Price Cutting: The Standard Oil (N.J.) Case," *Journal of Law and Economics* 1 (October 1958). For a recent critique of McGee's work, see Christopher R. Leslie, "Revisiting the Revisionist History of Standard Oil," *Southern California Law Review* 85, no. 3 (2012).

38. *Utah Pie v. Continental Baking Co.*, 380 U.S. 685 (1967). The decision did not save the smaller company. Utah Pie filed for bankruptcy in 1972.

39. Bork, *The Antitrust Paradox*, 387.

40. Stigler, *Memoirs of an Unregulated Economist*, 127.

41. William Domnarski, *Richard Posner* (New York: Oxford University Press, 2016), 55.

42. Ibid.

43. Arthur Leff, "Economic Analysis of Law: Some Realism About Nominalism," *Virginia Law Review* 60 (1974).

44. Richard Posner, *Economic Analysis of Law*, 2nd ed. (Boston: Little, Brown, 1977), 22. For an example of what Posner meant, consider a law in most states in the early twentieth century that allowed lawsuits for the "breach of promise to marry" — a category of cases that generally involved women who agreed to have sex with men who agreed to get married. When the man reneged, the woman sued. Such laws were passed in the name of justice, but the law and economics movement saw the motive in economic terms. A 1990 paper reported that as states repealed the laws, couples substituted a new incentive to encourage fidelity: sales of diamond rings increased significantly. Margaret F. Brinig, "Rings and Promises," *Journal of Law, Economics and Organization* 6, no. 1 (1990).

45. Steven M. Teles, *The Rise of the Conservative Legal Movement* (Princeton, N.J.: Princeton University Press, 2008), 99–100. A 1999 study found that Posner was cited twice as often as any other legal scholar in the second half of the twentieth century.

46. *U.S. v. Pabst Brewing Co.*, 384 U.S. 546 (1966).

47. David G. Moyer, *American Breweries of the Past* (AuthorHouse, 2009), 9–11.

48. *Antitrust and Trade Regulation Reports*, April 17, 1973.

49. Lester G. Telser, "Why Should Manufacturers Want Fair Trade?," *Journal of Law and Economics* 3 (October 1960): 86–105.

50. Richard A. Posner, *Antitrust Law: An Economic Perspective* (Chicago: University of Chicago Press, 1976), 164. Posner's condemnation of the decision (*U.S. v. Arnold, Schwinn & Co.*, 388 U.S. 365 [1967]) was particularly striking because he was criticizing his own work. He had argued the case for the United States as an attorney in the solicitor general's office, and he had won.

51. These details come from Powell's papers, made available to scholars after his death in 1998 and first described in a 2002 article. In the margin of one memo on the case, Powell scribbled "Posner, Baxter, Bork." See Andrew I. Gavil, "Sylvania and the Process of Change in the Supreme Court," *Antitrust* 17, no. 1 (2002).

52. The case is *Continental T.V. v. GTE Sylvania*, 433 U.S. 36 (1977). A 1974 case was a significant precursor. The industrial conglomerate General Dynamics had acquired an Illinois coal mining company. In allowing the deal over the government's objections, the court ruled the company's market share was less important than the fact there

wasn't much coal left in the company's mines. It was the first time the court held market share was not sufficient evidence, but it had not yet embraced efficiency as an alternative standard. See *U.S. v. General Dynamics Corp.*, 415 U.S. 486 (1974).

53. Henry G. Manne, "How Law and Economics Was Marketed in a Hostile World: A Very Personal History," in *The Origins of Law and Economics: Essays by the Founding Fathers*, ed. Francesco Parisi and Charles K. Rowley (Cheltenham, Eng.: Edward Elgar, 2005), 315.

54. Gregory C. Staple, "Free-Market Cram Course for Judges," *The Nation*, January 26, 1980.

55. Manne, "How Law and Economics Was Marketed in a Hostile World," 320.

56. The first alumni of the program to reach the Supreme Court were Clarence Thomas and Ruth Bader Ginsburg. See Elliott Ash, Daniell L. Chen, and Suresh Naidu, "Ideas Have Consequences: The Impact of Law and Economics on American Justice," November 2, 2017, National Bureau of Economic Research.

57. Judge Hauk was quoted in a *Washington Post* story that described the judicial seminars as funded by corporate donors. Manne said the report was inaccurate, insisting a different pot of dollars was used for the judicial programs. He later relocated his program, which also included seminars on law for economics professors, to Emory University in Georgia and then to George Mason University in Virginia, where he became the dean of the law school. See Fred Barbash, "Big Corporations Bankroll Seminars for U.S. Judges," *Washington Post*, January 20, 1980.

58. Ethan Bronner, "A Conservative Whose Supreme Court Bid Set the Senate Afire," *New York Times*, December 19, 2012.

59. Bork first made the argument in a 1966 paper, "Legislative Intent and the Policy of the Sherman Act," published in Director's journal. He wrote the book as a visiting scholar at the American Enterprise Institute, which provided financial support. In the opening pages, he paid tribute to Director. "Much of what is said here derives from the work of Aaron Director, who has long seemed to me, as he has to many others, the seminal thinker in antitrust economics and industrial organization." After reviewing the historical record, Bork concluded, "The legislative histories of the antitrust statutes, therefore, do not support any claim that Congress intended the courts to sacrifice consumer welfare to any other goal." See Bork, *The Antitrust Paradox*, 66.

60. Mason, who had introduced similar legislation, spoke at the end of the Senate's debate, summarizing the views of the proponents of the legislation. See 21 Cong. Rec. 4100 (1890). In the words of the Columbia University historian Richard John, "Few historians, if any, who have examined the 1890 antitrust act share Robert Bork's conviction that its original intent can be found in the determination of lawmakers to maximize consumer welfare. It's simply not true." See Richard John, "What Does History Tell Us? The Development of Antitrust in America" (presentation at Is There a Concentration Problem in America? [conference], Stigler Center for the Study of the Economy and the State, University of Chicago, March 27–29, 2017). See also the judgment of Herbert Hovenkamp, a University of Pennsylvania law professor and a leading authority on antitrust law: "Not a single statement in the legislative history comes close to stating the conclusions that Bork drew."

61. Stephen G. Breyer, "Judicial Precedent and the New Economics," in *Antitrust Forum 1983 — Antitrust Policy in Transition: The Convergence of Law and Economics* (New York: Conference Board, 1983), 9.

62. The court first articulated a similar view in a 1977 case, *Brunswick Corp. v. Pueblo Bowl-O-Mat*, in which the liberal justice Thurgood Marshall wrote that the limits on

mergers were "conceived of primarily as a remedy for '[t]he people of the United States as individuals,' especially consumers" (429 U.S. 477, fn. 10). The decision in the hearing aid case, *Reiter v. Sonotone Corp.*, 442 U.S. 330 (1979), affirmed the conclusion.

63. The Monopolization Reform Act specified that companies could not defend monopoly power as being the result of "superior product, business acumen, or historic accident." Hart died while it was under consideration, which probably did not help its cause.

64. Some of the shift likely reflects the increased aggressiveness of the Carter administration relative to its Republican predecessors. See Marc Allen Eisner, *Antitrust and the Triumph of Economics* (Chapel Hill: University of North Carolina Press, 1991), 179.

65. Some scholars regard a second set of revisions to the antitrust guidelines, in 1984, as more consequential. In combination, the changes made clear that economic efficiency was an acceptable justification for corporation concentration.

66. William Robbins, "A Meatpacker Cartel Up Ahead?," *New York Times*, May 29, 1988.

67. Average hourly wages fell from $9.06 in 1982 to $8.56 in 1992. Adjusting for inflation, the decline was 35 percent. One factor that helped companies reduce wages was a shift toward the employment of immigrants. See James M. MacDonald et al., "Consolidation in U.S. Meatpacking," February 2000, Department of Agriculture, Agricultural Economic Report no. 785, table 4-7.

68. Eisner, *Antitrust and the Triumph of Economics*, 214.

69. "Share of Federal Judges Appointed by Republican and Democratic Presidents Since Reagan," *Washington Post*, September 4, 2018.

70. Tamar Lewin, "The Noisy War over Discounting," *New York Times*, September 25, 1983. For an account of the crucial role economists played in the AT&T case, see Robert Litan, *Trillion-Dollar Economists: How Economists and Their Ideas Have Transformed Business* (Hoboken, N.J.: John Wiley, 2014). Some scholars argue the breakup of AT&T explains why internet use grew more quickly in the United States than in other developed nations like Japan.

Baxter had once taken a very different view of antitrust. In the 1960s, he authored model legislation increasing the government's power to break apart large corporations. In the mid-1970s, he made a public act of repentance, announcing in a speech at a lawyers' convention, "As one of the original drafters of the deconcentration act, it seems particularly appropriate that I recant.... The state of economic art has changed somewhat since 1968." See Eisner, *Antitrust and the Triumph of Economics*, 109.

71. For reassignment, see "Interview with William F. Baxter," *Antitrust Law Journal* 52, no. 1 (1983). For reeducation, see Eisner, *Antitrust and the Triumph of Economics*, 190. For private practice, see "Program of the 50th Anniversary Meeting of the Section of Antitrust Law," American Bar Association, 2003.

72. Michael Isikoff, "Chicago School Catches a Taxi," *Washington Post*, June 17, 1984.

73. The hourly rate for attorneys representing the indigent in Washington, D.C., was raised to $50 an hour in 1993, to $65 an hour in 2002, and to $90 an hour in 2009. As of 2018, that was 45 percent of the hourly pay in 1970, adjusted for inflation.

74. *United States v. American Airlines, Inc.*, no. CA3 83-032, filed February 23, 1983.

75. Kurt Eichenwald, *The Informant* (New York: Crown, 2001), 48–51.

76. Interview with Robert Litan, March 8, 2018.

77. William G. Christie and Paul H. Schultz, "Why Do NASDAQ Market Makers Avoid Odd-Eighth Quotes?," *Journal of Finance* 49, no. 5 (1994).

78. The Justice Department had previously received about one offer each year from a company willing to confess to participation in a cartel. Under the new policy, the offers came in at a rate of more than one per month. See Janet Novack, "Fix and Tell," *Forbes*, May 4, 1998.

79. "Our economy is more competitive today than it has been in a long, long time," Joel Klein, the head of the Justice Department's antitrust division, said in a January 29, 1998, speech in New York entitled "The Importance of Antitrust Enforcement in the New Economy"; see justice.gov/atr/speech/importance-antitrust-enforcement-new -economy.

80. Richard A. Posner, *Antitrust Law*, 2nd ed. (Chicago: University of Chicago Press, 2001), vii.

81. Linda Greenhouse, "Cigarette Antitrust Suit Is Rejected," *New York Times*, June 22, 1993.

82. *Brooke Group Ltd. v. Brown & Williamson Tobacco Corp.*, 509 U.S. 209 (1993).

83. James V. Grimaldi and Juliet Eilperin, "After Verdict, a Capital Welcome," *Washington Post*, April 6, 2000. The Bush administration settled with Microsoft in 2001. The company agreed to share with competitors the information necessary to write software for its operating system, and it was subjected to monitoring.

84. "Milton Friedman on Business Suicide," Cato Policy Report, March/April 1999, Cato Institute.

85. Is There a Concentration Problem in America? (conference), Stigler Center for the Study of the Economy and the State, University of Chicago, March 27–29, 2017.

86. The share of economic output paid to workers in wages has declined over the last half century. In a 2017 paper, "Declining Labor and Capital Shares," the economist Simcha Barkai found that the decline could be attributed to increased corporate concentration; see http://home.uchicago.edu/~barkai/doc/BarkaiDecliningLaborCapital.pdf.

87. James B. Stewart, "Steve Jobs Defied Convention, and Perhaps the Law," *New York Times*, May 2, 2014. Companies more commonly seek to restrict worker movement by imposing contractual provisions called noncompete agreements.

88. Milton Friedman to George Stigler, November 15, 1950, Milton Friedman Papers, box 33, folder 36, Hoover Institution Archives, Stanford, Calif.

89. Lina M. Khan, "Amazon's Antitrust Paradox," *Yale Law Journal* 26, no. 3 (January 2017).

90. Tim Wu, a Columbia Law School professor, argues the best way to improve antitrust law is not for courts to consider a broader range of consequences. Instead, he says courts should focus on a more basic question: Does a given example of corporate conduct promote or limit competition? The legal system should be focused on the process, not the outcome. As Supreme Court Justice Oliver Wendell Holmes Jr. wrote in 1905, "A constitution is not intended to embody a particular economic theory, whether of paternalism and the organic relation of the citizen to the state or of laissez faire." Khan's quote is from an interview on March 26, 2018.

Chapter 6. Freedom from Regulation

1. Marion Fourcade, *Economists and Societies: Discipline and Profession in the United States, Britain, and France, 1890s to 1990s* (Princeton, N.J.: Princeton University Press, 2009), ebook loc. 920.

2. Opponents of regulation brought their own celebrities to Washington, notably Amelia Earhart. See Lucile Sheppard Keyes, *Federal Control of Entry into Air Transportation* (Cambridge: Harvard University Press, 1951), 86–87.

3. There were eighty applications to start major airlines between 1950 and 1977. All were rejected. The government did license new regional airlines, which were allowed to fly smaller airplanes on shorter routes. By 1978, these accounted for about 9 percent of air travel. Unlicensed airlines, mostly intrastate airlines like Pacific Southwest, accounted

for another 2.4 percent of air travel. See "Air Carrier Traffic Statistics," 1978, Civil Aeronautics Board.

4. The Civil Aeronautics Authority was divided in 1940 into the Civil Aeronautics Board, to administer economic regulations, and the Civil Aeronautics Administration, to administer safety rules. The latter became the Federal Aviation Administration in 1966. See "Annual Report of the Civil Aeronautics Authority," 1940, 2.

5. The advent of economic regulation is sometimes narrated as a response to the Great Depression, especially by critics of government regulation. But the rise of regulation began significantly earlier, as a response to the excesses of capitalism in the late nineteenth century and early twentieth century. See William J. Novak, "A Revisionist History of Regulatory Capture," in *Preventing Regulatory Capture: Special Interest Influence and How to Limit It*, ed. Daniel Carpenter and David A. Moss (New York: Cambridge University Press, 2013).

6. See Philip M. Crane, "Regulatory Agencies," *Journal of Social and Political Affairs* 1 (January 1976): 21–42.

7. While this 1951 case holds the distinction of having the best name in the long history of American jurisprudence, a more important case was *Nebbia v. New York* (1934), which established the legality of economic regulation, including price regulation, so long as it was not capricious or discriminatory. Until that time, the courts had restricted regulation to industries of clear public importance, including the railroads.

8. Alfred Kahn, "Reflections of an Unwitting 'Political Entrepreneur,'" *Review of Network Economics* 7, no. 4 (2008).

9. The average flight was 52.8 percent full in the decade before deregulation; between 2007 and 2016, the average was 82.6 percent. Alfred Kahn, the "father of airline deregulation," regarded this as the best summary of the changes wrought by deregulation, both for better and for worse.

10. In 1960, the Air Transport Association of America reported that U.S. airlines carried 57.7 million passengers in a nation of 180 million people. In 2017, the most recent available data, the Federal Aviation Administration reported that airlines carried 799 million passengers in a nation of 320 million people.

11. George J. Stigler and Claire Friedland, "What Can Regulators Regulate? The Case of Electricity," *Journal of Law and Economics* 5, no. 2 (October 1962): 1–16.

12. George J. Stigler, "Public Regulation of the Securities Markets," *Journal of Business* 37, no. 2 (1964): 117–42.

13. Friedland said that after she learned of the error from Kevin J. Murphy, then a postdoctoral fellow at the University of Chicago, she took the news to Stigler. "George's answer was that there was no point in making a big fuss about this mistake because it was twenty years ago and nobody cared anymore." See Craig Freedman, *In Search of the Two-Handed Economist: Ideology, Methodology and Marketing in Economics* (London: Palgrave Macmillan, 2016), 108. The error was first reported in a 1986 piece that also critiqued the original study's methodological choices. See Amitai Etzioni, "Does Regulation Reduce Electricity Rates? A Research Note," *Policy Sciences* 19 (1986): 349–57.

14. Stigler gave Peltzman $12,000 in Walgreen funding. The quote is from a letter Stigler sent to Peltzman in 1972. See Edward Nik-Khah, "George Stigler, the Graduate School of Business and the Pillars of the Chicago School," in *Building Chicago Economics: New Perspectives on the History of America's Most Powerful Economics Program*, ed. Robert Van Horn et al. (Cambridge, Eng.: Cambridge University Press, 2011), 148.

15. Freedman, *In Search of the Two-Handed Economist*, 386.

16. James Allen Smith, *Brookings at 75* (Washington, D.C.: Brookings Institution, 2010), 89.

17. Martha Derthick and Paul J. Quirk, *The Politics of Deregulation* (Washington, D.C.: Brookings Institution, 1985), 34, 56.

18. Sam Peltzman, "Entry in Commercial Banking," *Journal of Law and Economics* 8 (October 1965): 11–50. The paper is a condensed version of Peltzman's dissertation. Peltzman later recounted Stigler told him he didn't like the results, but couldn't find any errors. See Freedman, *In Search of the Two-Handed Economist*, 380. The observation about taxi medallions was made by the economist Alfred Kahn.

19. George J. Stigler, "The Theory of Economic Regulation," *Bell Journal of Economics and Management Science* 2, no. 1 (Spring 1971): 3–21. Stigler's characterization of regulation is often described as an important insight, but Stigler himself acknowledged, in the paper, that it was already a "cliche."

20. It is important to note that the process was not evolutionary. New solutions not infrequently revived older solutions, as with the successive establishments of the first and second national banks of the United States and the creation of the Federal Reserve.

21. "A Conversation with Michael E. Levine," International Aviation Law Institute, April 17, 2006, DePaul University College of Law, Chicago.

22. Lucile Sheppard Keyes was one of the first economists to question the merits of sheltering companies from too much competition. Keyes, a student of Edward Chamberlin, the Harvard professor who saw monopolies everywhere, shared his view that competition tended to calcify over time. In her 1951 Harvard doctoral dissertation, she argued that regulation of the airline industry was expediting the process. By limiting competition, the government was driving up prices and restricting service. In her dissertation, and in subsequent papers through the 1950s, Keyes mocked the idea that limiting the number of airlines was necessary to preserve air travel, "any more than it is necessary to secure an adequate supply of soap, doorknobs, or automobiles." See Lucile Sheppard Keyes, "A Reconsideration of Federal Control of Entry into Air Transportation," *Journal of Air Law and Commerce* 22 (1955): 197.

23. California surpassed New York in 1964, although the *New York Times* noted in its rather crabby acknowledgment of the milestone that New York still had a larger civilian population: "California Takes Population Lead," *New York Times*, September 1, 1964.

24. Michael Levine, "Is Regulation Necessary? California Air Transportation and National Regulatory Policy," *Yale Law Journal*, July 1965. Ironically, shortly before Levine's article was published, Pacific Southwest persuaded California to restrict intrastate competition. See also "Conversation with Michael E. Levine."

25. Derthick and Quirk, *Politics of Deregulation*, 76.

26. Todd E. Fandell, "Aerial 'Happenings' Planned by United Air in Lounge War Sequel," *Wall Street Journal*, July 13, 1972.

27. George W. Douglas and James C. Miller, *The CAB's Domestic Passenger Fare Investigation* (Washington, D.C.: Brookings Institution, 1974), 220.

28. Merton J. Peck, "Deregulation of the Transportation Industry," in *Effective Social Science*, ed. Bernard Barber (New York: Russell Sage Foundation, 1987), 105–6.

29. Peter H. Schuck, *The Judiciary Committees* (New York: Grossman, 1975), 221.

30. Derthick and Quirk, *Politics of Deregulation*, 41. One of Breyer's colleagues at Harvard Law School, who had worked with Michael Levine and who knew Breyer was looking for ideas, put the two men in touch. The next time Levine passed through Boston, he

spent several hours talking with Breyer in the American Airlines lounge at Logan Airport. See "Conversation with Michael E. Levine."

31. Stephen Breyer, "Working on the Staff of Senator Ted Kennedy" (speech at New York University, February 1, 2011). Breyer later suggested that Kennedy was motivated by Jimmy Carter's interest in deregulation, viewing Carter as a potential opponent in the 1976 Democratic presidential primaries. "He said one thing once that was very interesting to me," Breyer recalled. "He said, 'Well, you know, this Governor Carter is going around talking about too much government, and he's getting a very good response.'" See "Stephen Breyer Oral History," June 17, 2008, Edward M. Kennedy Institute for the United States Senate, Boston.

32. Barbara Sturken Peterson and James Glab, *Rapid Descent: Deregulation and the Shakeout in the Airlines* (New York: Simon and Schuster, 1994), 34.

33. Laker, who operated a successful charter airline, wanted a license to offer scheduled service.

34. Stephen Breyer, *Regulation and Its Reform* (Cambridge: Harvard University Press, 1982), 330.

35. "Stephen Breyer Oral History."

36. Gerald R. Ford, *A Time to Heal* (New York: Harper and Row, 1979), 271.

37. Stuart Eizenstat, *President Carter: The White House Years* (New York: St. Martin's, 2018), 385–86. Every Democratic presidential nominee from Harry Truman in 1948 through Lyndon Johnson in 1964 attended the Labor Day rally. The next two nominees tipped their hat to the tradition. Hubert Humphrey in 1968 chose to march in a Labor Day parade in New York; George McGovern in 1972 made Labor Day appearances at union rallies in Ohio and California. Carter began Labor Day in 1976 with a press conference at the Georgia house where Franklin Delano Roosevelt died, then made an appearance at a NASCAR race in Darlington, South Carolina.

38. Alfred E. Kahn, *The Economics of Regulation* (New York: Wiley and Sons, 1971), 2:191.

39. "We had a meeting on airline deregulation, which will be the first test case. Later I hope to move on to deregulation of other industries. It's not going to be easy," President Carter wrote in his diary on June 20, 1977. See Jimmy Carter, *White House Diary* (New York: Farrar, Straus and Giroux, 2010), 65.

40. The report by the Government Accounting Office was released on February 23, 1977, although it was dated February 25. It was a rebuttal of a study released by an industry trade group that said deregulation would cause a sharp reduction in air service. See "Comments on the Study: Consequences of Deregulation of the Scheduled Air Transportation Industry," February 25, 1977, General Accounting Office.

41. When Hamilton Jordan, the President's chief of staff, called Mary Schuman to report that Carter had selected the second option, she responded, "That is the guy I would have picked myself." See Eizenstat, *President Carter*, 363.

42. Jonathan Rubin, "The Premature Post-Chicagoan: Alfred E. Kahn," *Antitrust* 25, no. 3 (2011).

43. Robert Sobel, *The Worldly Economists* (New York: Free Press, 1980), 236.

44. Alfred Kahn, "Fundamental Deficiencies of the American Patent Law," *American Economic Review*, September 1940, 485.

45. Joel B. Dirlam and Alfred Kahn, *Fair Competition: The Law and Economics of Antitrust Policy* (Ithaca, N.Y.: Cornell University Press, 1954), 18.

46. Kahn, *Economics of Regulation*, 1:15.

47. Thomas K. McCraw, *Prophets of Regulation* (Cambridge: Belknap Press, 1984), 244.

48. Douglas D. Anderson, *Regulatory Politics and Electric Utilities* (Boston: Auburn House, 1981), 127.

49. According to Breyer, 60 percent of the bureau's enforcement actions were fines for illegal discounts. See Derthick and Quirk, *Politics of Deregulation*, 44.

50. Robert Lindsey, "Airlines in Bitter Struggle on Atlantic Charter Rates," *New York Times*, January 31, 1971.

51. McCraw, *Prophets of Regulation*, 274.

52. "It seems to this layman that due process is defined in an inherently asymmetrical fashion," Kahn said in a speech on February 2, 1978. "It seems inherently to give protection to the parties who benefit from delay, and to be injurious to the parties — typically the public at large — who are adversely affected by delay.... In short, the requirements of legal due process, interposing the heavy hand of government between an idea and its application in the market, are directly antithetical to competition."

53. "A Conversation with Alfred E. Kahn," International Aviation Law Institute, October 27, 2006, DePaul University College of Law.

54. Ernest Holsendolph, "When Rules Work; When They Don't," *New York Times*, August 21, 1977.

55. Alfred Kahn, "Memo to Bureau and Office Heads, Division and Section Chiefs," June 16, 1977; available at lettersofnote.com/2011/04/on-bureaucratese-and-gobbledygook.html.

56. Susan Trausch, "The Demise of 'Whereas,'" *Boston Globe*, July 18, 1977.

57. David Hummels, "Transportation Costs and International Trade in the Second Era of Globalization," *Journal of Economic Perspectives* 21, no. 3 (2007): 131–54.

58. Penelope Overton, "Asians Help to Fill Sales Gap as Europe Eats Less Maine Lobster," *Portland* [Maine] *Press Herald*, February 16, 2018.

59. Richard E. Cohen, "The CAB's Kahn on Aggravations of Airline Deregulation," *National Journal*, January 14, 1978, 50. In November 1978, *Newsweek* ran a profile of Kahn, who was then leaving the aviation board, in which it quoted him as saying, when he arrived on the job the previous year, "I will consider it some measure of success in this job if there is no job when I leave it." But there is no earlier record of the comment, and Kahn insisted in later years that he arrived with an open mind. "Any implication that I came to the CAB, opportunistically and with a preconceived fixed commitment to flat-out economic deregulation, does an injustice to the complexities of the issue," he wrote in 2008; see his "Reflections of an Unwitting Political Entrepreneur." Indeed, Kahn's 1971 book on regulation included a brief discussion of the airline industry, in which he summarized Levine's paper on PSA but concluded he wasn't sure whether airlines were an example of a natural monopoly. Kahn thought the airline industry instead might resemble the automotive industry, where carmakers competed by adding features and raising prices. (In 1971, low-priced Japanese imports were just starting to flood the domestic market.) See Kahn, *Economics of Regulation*, 2:209–20. A number of Kahn's colleagues, notably Elizabeth Bailey, also have said or written that Kahn had to be talked into deregulation.

60. Carole Shifrin, "Airbus Debuts Here," *Washington Post*, April 13, 1978.

61. McCraw, *Prophets of Regulation*, 278.

62. Ernest Holsendolph, "C.A.B. Bids Airlines Pick Own Routes," *New York Times*, May 31, 1978.

63. "Alfred Kahn, Oral History," December 10–11, 1981, Miller Center of Public Affairs, University of Virginia, Charlottesville.

64. W. T. Beebe to Burt Lance, March 8, 1977; available at jimmycarterlibrary.gov /digital_library/sso/148878/11/SSO_148878_011_03.pdf.

65. The negotiations were facilitated by a budding romance between Kennedy's chief aide on the bill, David Boies, and Carter's point person, Mary Schuman. They were married in 1982.

66. "The Line Forms Here for Air Routes," *Business Week*, November 6, 1978, 66.

67. Derthick and Quirk, *Politics of Deregulation*, 129.

68. McKinnon had worked as a page for Rayburn decades earlier; Rayburn died in 1961. This account is based on newspaper reports and on footage of the final meeting included in *The Commanding Heights*, PBS, "Episode One: The Battle of Ideas." See Stuart Auerbach, "46-Year-Old CAB Goes out of Existence," *Washington Post*, January 1, 1985; and Irvin Molotsky, "C.A.B. Dies After 46 Years," *New York Times*, January 1, 1985.

69. Dorothy Robyn, *Braking the Special Interests* (Chicago: University of Chicago Press, 1987), 17.

70. Quoted in Michael J. Towle, *Out of Touch: The Presidency and Public Opinion* (College Station: Texas A&M Press, 2004), 51.

71. See W. Bruce Allen, Steven Lonergan, and David Plane, "Examination of the Unregulated Trucking Experience in New Jersey," July 1978, U.S. Department of Transportation. Another study found shipping rates for poultry fell by 33 percent during a brief period in the 1950s following a court decision that classified chicken as an "unprocessed agricultural good" that was not subject to federal regulation. When Congress restored the status quo ante, prices recovered, too.

72. "Oral History: Alfred E. Kahn, Ron Lewis and Dennis Rapp," December 10–11, 1981, Miller Center of Public Affairs, University of Virginia.

73. Derthick and Quirk, *Politics of Deregulation*, 71.

74. Gaskins was named chairman. Carter also appointed two new commissioners: Marcus Alexis, also an economist, and Thomas Trantum, an investment banker who provided reliable support for Gaskins on regulatory issues.

75. Packwood resigned from the Senate in 1995 after it emerged that he had failed to adhere to the "consenting adults" standard in his personal relations.

76. Derthick and Quirk, *Politics of Deregulation*, 29.

77. "2018 State of Logistics Report," Council of Supply Chain Management Professionals.

78. The average "all-in" ticket price, adjusted to 2017 dollars, fell from $632.92 in 1979 to $350.41 in 2005 — a decline of 45 percent, according to data aggregated by the trade group Airlines for America: see http://airlines.org/dataset/annual-round-trip-fares -and-fees-domestic/. Proponents of deregulation tend to cite the decline in airfares as the net benefit; in fact, fares in real terms were already in decline before deregulation. One reason was the gradual development of larger, faster, and more fuel-efficient airplanes. The 1970s were also a period of relatively high fuel prices, making subsequent decades look better by comparison. See also Paul Stephen Dempsey and Andrew R. Goetz, *Airline Deregulation and Laissez-Faire Mythology* (Westport, Conn.: Greenwood, 1992), who argue that deregulation did not significantly reduce fares.

79. Stuart Jeffries, "The Saturday Interview: Ryanair Boss Michael O'Leary," *The Guardian*, November 18, 2011.

80. Kahn, "Oral History."

81. Paul Solman, "Why Airline Profits Are Flying High," *PBS NewsHour*, PBS, April 20, 2017.

82. Michael Levine, "Why Weren't the Airlines Reregulated?," *Yale Journal on Regulation* 23, no. 2 (2006).

83. Thatcher's reticence has led some historians to conclude that privatization was not part of the Conservatives' original agenda. Key figures in the Tory government, including Nigel Lawson and Geoffrey Howe, insist that the goal was already in mind, and that it was not emphasized during the campaign because of Thatcher's concerns about its political appeal. See Nigel Lawson, *The View from No. 11* (London: Bantam, 1992).

84. "Interview with Lord Ralph Harris," *Commanding Heights,* July 17, 2000; available at pbs.org/wgbh/commandingheights/shared/minitext/int_ralphharris.html.

85. Ralph Harris, "Memorandum to: John Wood, Arthur Seldon," March 14, 1974, Archive of the Margaret Thatcher Foundation; available at margaretthatcher.org/document/114757.

86. James Landale, "Thatcher's Mad Monk or True Prophet?," BBC Radio 4, April 7, 2014.

87. Daniel Yergin and Joseph Stanislaw, *The Commanding Heights* (New York: Free Press, 1998), 130.

88. "Interview with Kenneth Baker," *Commanding Heights,* September 19, 2000; available at pbs.org/wgbh/commandingheights/shared/minitext/int_kennethbaker.html.

89. Madsen Pirie, *Privatization* (Aldershot, Eng.: Wildwood House, 1988), 4.

90. Richard Green and Jonathan Haskel, "Seeking a Premier-League Economy," in *Seeking a Premier Economy: The Economic Effects of British Economic Reforms, 1980–2000,* ed. David Card et al. (Chicago: University of Chicago Press, 2004), 48–49.

91. Sean D. Barrett, "Exporting Deregulation: Alfred Kahn and the Celtic Tiger," *Review of Network Economics* 7, no. 4 (2008).

92. The Civil Aeronautics Board, the U.S. regulator, had also proposed the criminalization of discounted airline tickets, in 1971. Congress declined to pursue the idea.

93. Ryan in 1971 hit on the idea of leasing Aer Lingus planes and crew to airlines in other countries during the winter months, when fewer people wanted to visit Ireland. Four years later, he went into the leasing business on his own. Deregulation in the United States provided a huge boost to the business as the new carriers needed airplanes. When Ryan signed a deal to provide seven planes to an upstart carrier called America West, he sent his son along with the airplanes. The son returned two years later to help his father launch Ryanair. See Richard Aldous, *Tony Ryan: Ireland's Aviator* (Dublin: Gill and Macmillan, 2013).

94. Siobhán Creaton, *Ryanair: How a Small Irish Airline Conquered Europe* (London: Aurum Press, 2014).

95. "I do not honestly believe that the big airlines are going to be able to wipe out the smaller airlines, if only because every study we have ever made seems to show that there are not economies of scale," Alfred Kahn said at a 1977 hearing.

96. The Obama administration was operating in a difficult legal environment, given the hostility of federal courts to antitrust litigation. In particular, courts have not allowed regulators to block mergers on the basis that consolidation will reduce the number of competitors that might enter new markets. Still, the administration made a political decision not to pursue the cases. See Justin Elliott, "The American Way," *ProPublica,* October 11, 2016.

97. In 2017 dollars, the average price of a domestic flight was $350.41 in 2005 and $362.61 in 2017, according to federal data compiled by Airlines.org.

98. "Internet Access Services," February 2018, Federal Communications Commission.

99. Karl Ritter and Nathalie Rothschild, "Nobel Prize for Economics Goes to France's Tirole," Associated Press, October 13, 2014.

100. "OECD Broadband Basket," June 2017, OECD Broadband Portal.
101. The economist Alvin Roth, perhaps the world's preeminent designer of markets — for kidneys and students, among other things — says that markets are like wheels: free movement requires an axle. Alvin Roth, *Who Gets What and Why* (New York: Houghton Mifflin, 2012), 13.

Chapter 7. *The Value of Life*

1. Jean-Baptiste Say, "Author's Note," *Catechism of Political Economy*, 3rd ed. (1815); available in the original French at https://fr.wikisource.org/wiki/Cat%C3%A9chisme _d%E2%80%99%C3%A9conomie_politique/1881/Avertissement.
2. Ira C. Eaker, "Weapons Selection Importance," *Los Angeles Times*, August 22, 1965.
3. Congress continued to fund both missile programs — the air force's Bomarc and the army's Nike-Hercules — over the following decade. Congress similarly funded the development of two midrange ballistic missiles in the 1950s: the army's Jupiter and the air force's Thor. See Ralph Sanders, *The Politics of Defense Analysis* (New York: Dunellen, 1973), 40.
4. Alain C. Enthoven and K. Wayne Smith, *How Much Is Enough? Shaping the Defense Program, 1961–1969* (New York: Harper and Row, 1971), 339.
5. Alain C. Enthoven, "Tribute to Charles J. Hitch," *OR/MS Today* 22, no. 6 (December 1995). Roswell L. Gilpatric, McNamara's deputy, said in a 1970 oral history that McNamara asked him to contact Hitch and that he interviewed Hitch in New York. This account is based instead on the Defense Department's official history of McNamara's tenure, which in turn draws on a 1968 book by Norman Moss. It says Hitch stopped in Denver on the way home from an economics conference. The records of the American Economic Association show Hitch was in St. Louis for its annual conference. See Norman Moss, *Men Who Play God* (New York: Harper and Row, 1968), 268.
6. Fred Kaplan, *The Wizards of Armageddon* (Stanford, Calif.: Stanford University Press, 1983), 254.
7. Enthoven and Smith, *How Much Is Enough?* 41.
8. Charles J. Hitch, *Decision-Making for Defense* (Berkeley: University of California Press, 1965), 46.
9. David Jardini, *Thinking Through the Cold War* (Seattle: Amazon, 2013), 167.
10. The quote is from Johnson's press conference on August 25, 1965. Enthoven said Hitch looked back on the decision with regret, describing it as "foolish." Hitch believed the success at the Pentagon had been built on the foundation of Rand's work on military spending, and that the rest of the government wasn't ready to use the same tools.
11. The legislation, sponsored by Representative Theodore Burton of Ohio, instructed the Army Corps of Engineers to consider "the amount and character of commerce existing or reasonably prospective which will be benefited by the improvement, and the relation of the ultimate cost of such work, both as to cost of construction and maintenance, to the public commercial interests involved, and the public necessity for the work": see U.S. Statutes at Large, 57th Congress, sess. 1 (1902), ch. 1079, p. 372. Burton, a lawyer by training, was ahead of his time as an economic policy maker. He also backed cost-sharing agreements with local governments that wanted waterway improvements, which he regarded as more likely to check dubious waterway projects than the new review process. Neither, in the event, had much of a restraining influence, but in 1914, Burton, who had become a senator, did succeed in blocking a $73 million package of particularly objectionable waterway projects by staging a twenty-one-hour filibuster.

Unsurprisingly, Americans were convinced that the idea of cost-benefit analysis was original to the United States. An early history of the technique describes it as "peculiarly, perhaps uniquely, American": see Richard J. Hammond, "Convention and Limitation in Benefit-Cost Analysis," in *Benefit-Cost Analysis and Water-Pollution Control* (Stanford, Calif.: Stanford University Press, 1960). However, the first instance may have come in 1901, when a Dutch engineer named Cornelis Lely published a table of costs and benefits with a proposal to build the largest seawall in the history of the Netherlands. Lely's table included the loss of fishing jobs and the value of new farmland. See Frits Bos and Peter Zwaneveld, "Cost-Benefit Analysis for Flood Risk Management and Water Governance in the Netherlands," 2017, Netherlands Bureau for Economic Policy Analysis. Some historians identify an earlier instance of modern cost-benefit analysis in the work of French engineers in the mid-nineteenth century, notably Jules Dupuit, who argued that toll revenues understated the economic value of bridges, and therefore the government should build more bridges and impose lower tolls on travelers. The historian Theodore M. Porter, however, argues that the French analyses are distinct because they were not intended for public consumption and debate.

12. Theodore M. Porter, *Trust in Numbers: The Pursuit of Objectivity in Science and Public Life* (Princeton, N.J.: Princeton University Press, 1995), 162–65.

13. Ibid.

14. Nicholas Kaldor, "Welfare Propositions of Economics and Interpersonal Comparisons of Utility," *Economic Journal* 49, no. 195 (1939).

15. Kenneth Arrow already had proved the new version of welfare economics was theoretically flawed. In his 1950 doctoral thesis, "Social Choice and Individual Values" — which was completed at Rand, where Arrow was working on Cold War game theory — Arrow showed that individual expressions of preference, in the form of rank ordering, could not be reliably translated into an accurate statement of collective preferences. This "impossibility theorem" remains a landmark contribution to economic theory, but it has had no discernible influence on public policy. Nor is it obvious that it should: as Arrow has said, "Most systems are not going to work badly all of the time. All I proved is that all can work badly at times."

16. Martin Reuss, "Coping with Uncertainty: Social Scientists, Engineers, and Federal Water Resources Planning," *Natural Resources Journal* 32, no. 1 (1992).

17. A. Allan Schmid, "My Work as an Institutional Economist," January 31, 2008; available at canr.msu.edu/afre/uploads/files/Schmid/My_work_as_an_Insitutional_Econo mist.pdf.

18. A. Allan Schmid, "Effective Public Policy and the Government Budget: A Uniform Treatment of Public Expenditures and Public Rules," in *The Analysis and Evaluation of Public Expenditures*, Joint Economic Committee, 1969.

19. Interview with Jim Tozzi, March 26, 2018.

20. J. Ronald Fox, *Defense Acquisition Reform: 1960–2009* (Washington, D.C.: Center of Military History/U.S. Army, 2012), 44–45.

21. The Corps of Engineers, for example, employed 51 economic analysts in 1963, about half of whom were credentialed economists; by August 1967, it employed 119 economists and was in the process of hiring another 30. The Corps also began to host visiting professors and to fund research at universities. See Gregory Graves, "Pursuing Excellence in Water Planning and Policy Analysis: A History of the Institute for Water Resources," 1995, Army Corps of Engineers.

22. Death rates at work, in the home, and on the road declined in every decade from the 1930s to the 1960s. But progress slowed in the 1960s, contributing to the pressure for

action. See W. Kip Viscusi, "The Misspecified Agenda," in *American Economic Policy in the 1980s*, ed. Martin Feldstein (Chicago: University of Chicago Press, 1994), 497.

23. *Regulation: Process and Politics* (Washington, D.C.: Congressional Quarterly, 1982).

24. The first commercial steamboat, Robert Fulton's *North River Steamboat*, launched in 1807, carrying passengers 150 miles between New York and Albany in just thirty-two hours. The drive now takes roughly three hours.

25. The Automobile Manufacturers Association had petitioned Congress to include language requiring that the cost of new regulations be "commensurate with the benefit to be achieved." After losing the legislative battle, the car companies sued, insisting that such analysis was necessary, and lost again. "We must decline to write into the Act," said the Sixth Circuit, "the very same suggestions which Congress declined to write into the Act." The court ruled, however, that the language of the act did permit the use of the technique. See *Chrysler Corp. v. NHTSA*, 472 F.2d 659 (1972).

26. 116 Cong. Rec. 37345.

27. Nixon's significant legacy of environmental protection was not rooted in the kind of love for the outdoors that motivated Teddy Roosevelt. His closest advisers on environmental issues generally agreed that he took little pleasure in nature. As with most issues of domestic policy, Nixon's calculus was political — which is not meant as a slur. He supported regulation because people wanted more regulation. He tried to strike a balance because there were competing interests. He sought to convince corporate executives that he was on their side, confiding to Henry Ford II, "We are fighting, frankly, a delaying action in many instances." But the bottom line is that he did more to protect the environment than any other American president.

28. "Interview with Christopher B. Demuth," January 14, 2008, Richard Nixon Oral History Program, Richard Nixon Presidential Library, Yorba Linda, Calif.

29. The administration's original plan was to create an Environmental Finance Agency that would fund the cleanup process. When Congress insisted that polluters should pay to clean up pollution, the administration next turned to the idea of pollution taxes. Nixon actually proposed such a tax in a 1970 speech, but the White House could not find a single member of Congress willing to introduce legislation. Congressional Democrats preferred the model of mandatory regulation, not least because it provided political cover. When businesses complained, Congress could point its finger at the relevant independent regulator.

30. George P. Shultz, "Agency Regulations, Standards, and Guidelines Pertaining to Environmental Quality, Consumer Protection and Occupational and Public Health and Safety," October 5, 1971, Office of Management and Budget. While Chicago School economists play a minor role in this chapter, particularly in comparison to the other stories told in this book, they were certainly proponents of cost-benefit analysis. A bastardized version of a quote from Lord Kelvin is carved into the social sciences building at the University of Chicago. "When you cannot measure, your knowledge is meager and unsatisfactory."

31. Richard L. Revesz and Michael A. Livermore, *Retaking Rationality: How Cost-Benefit Analysis Can Better Protect the Environment and Our Health* (Oxford: Oxford University Press, 2008), 135.

32. H. Spencer Banzhaf, "The Cold War Origins of the Value of Statistical Life," *Journal of Economic Perspectives* 28, no. 4 (2014).

33. H. Spencer Banzhaf, "Consumer Surplus with Apology: A Historical Perspective on Nonmarket Valuation and Recreation Demand," *Annual Review of Resource Economics* 2 (2010): 183–207.

34. This is a gross simplification of the economic concept of "consumer surplus." The visitor who spent the most might have been willing to spend even more; the others might not have been willing to spend as much. But it is not my gross oversimplification: it is the methodology Hotelling outlined in his original letter, in which he wrote, "If we assume that the benefits are the same no matter what the distance, we have, for those living near the park, a consumers' surplus consisting of the differences in transportation costs." See Harold Hotelling to Newton B. Drury, Director, National Park Service, June 18, 1947, in U.S. National Park Service, *The Economics of Public Recreation: An Economic Study of the Monetary Evaluation of Recreation in the National Parks* (Washington, D.C.: National Park Service, 1949).

35. W. Michael Hanemann, "Preface," in *Pricing the European Environment*, ed. Ståle Navrud (New York: Oxford University Press, 1992), 17.

36. Interview with Daniel Benjamin, March 22, 2018. Gates offered a similar account to the *Washington Post* in 1972: "When I came up with the idea of doing this, the other committee members were shocked. But they gradually became resigned to the idea." See William Greider, "The Economics of Death," *Washington Post*, April 9, 1972.

37. The quotes and details in this paragraph are drawn from Viviana Rotman Zelizer, *Morals and Markets: The Development of Life Insurance in the United States* (New York: Columbia University Press, 2017), 69–71.

38. "Cumulative Regulatory Effects on the Cost of Automotive Transportation," February 28, 1972, White House Office of Science and Technology. Lawrence A. Goldmuntz, the chairman of the Nixon task force on auto regulation, was explicit in justifying the methodology by referencing life insurance. "Do you have a life insurance policy?" he asked a reporter. "Does it represent the value you place on your own life? Of course not. On the other hand, it does represent a certain allocation of your resources, what you are willing to spend. That's what we're talking about — the allocation of resources." See Greider, "The Economics of Death."

39. "Social Costs of Motor Vehicle Accidents: Preliminary Report, April 1972," National Highway Traffic Safety Administration.

40. The government concluded the bars would cost $310 million, while the benefit would be only $36 million. See Joanne Linnerooth, "The Evaluation of Life-Saving: A Survey," 1975, International Atomic Energy Agency. The Nixon administration had rejected an earlier version of the regulation in 1971, finding that the costs exceeded the benefits, but not using a specific figure for the value of life. The official responsible for that decision, Robert Carter, later testified it was the first time the Transportation Department had used cost-benefit analysis as its primary basis for evaluating a regulation: see "Federal Regulation and Regulatory Reform," House Committee on Interstate and Foreign Commerce, 1976, fn. 73.

41. Thomas Schelling, "The Life You Save May Be Your Own," in *Problems in Public Expenditure Analysis*, ed. Samuel B. Chase Jr. (Washington, D.C.: Brookings Institution, 1966).

42. The early estimators included Robert Smith, an economist at Cornell; W. Kip Viscusi, a graduate student at Harvard; and Richard Thaler, a graduate student at the University of Rochester. Thaler's father, an actuary, provided him with data on occupational mortality rates, which Thaler combined with wage data to analyze what workers were paid to take larger risks. His conclusion, published in his 1974 doctoral thesis, was that workers valued their own lives at about $200,000. But Thaler was skeptical of his own results. He started surveying people to see whether their risk assessments were consis-

tent with the values implied by their job choices. The results showed a large gap. Thaler's adviser "told me to stop wasting my time and get back to work on my thesis," Thaler wrote in his memoir, *Misbehaving*. "But I was hooked." He continued to study the intersection of economics and psychology, work for which he won the Nobel Prize in 2017.

43. "William Ruckelshaus Oral History," April 12, 2007, Nixon Library; available at nixonlibrary.gov/sites/default/files/forresearchers/find/histories/ruckelshaus-2007-04-12.pdf.

44. Interview with Warren Prunella, March 29, 2018.

45. Jim Morris, "How Politics Gutted Workplace Safety," July 7, 2015, Center for Public Integrity.

46. "Eula Bingham Administration, 1977–1981," U.S. Department of Labor; available at dol.gov/general/aboutdol/history/osha13bingham.

47. Charles L. Schultze, "The Role and Responsibilities of the Economist in Government," *American Economic Review* 72, no. 2 (1982).

48. Paul Sabin, "'Everything Has a Price': Jimmy Carter and the Struggle for Balance in Federal Regulatory Policy," *Journal of Policy History* 28, no. 1 (2016).

49. Margot Hornblower, "Muskie Criticizes White House Meddling with EPA Rules," *Washington Post*, February 27, 1979.

50. Edmund S. Muskie, "Remarks at the University of Michigan" (speech, University of Michigan, Ann Arbor, February 14, 1979).

51. "Use of Cost-Benefit Analysis by Regulatory Agencies: Joint Hearings Before the Subcommittee on Oversight and Investigations and the Subcommittee on Consumer Protection and Finance," July 30, October 10 and 24, 1979.

52. Milton Friedman and Rose Friedman, *Free to Choose* (New York: Harcourt Brace Jovanovich, 1980), 225.

53. The Congressional Research Service judged Weidenbaum's work "suspect and of doubtful validity." See Julius W. Allen, "Estimating the Costs of Federal Regulation: Review of Problems and Accomplishments to Date," September 26, 1978, Congressional Research Service.

54. Interview with James C. Miller, March 21, 2018. Contemporary accounts include Peter Behr, "OMB Now a Regulator in Historic Power Shift," *Washington Post*, May 4, 1981.

55. Colman McCarthy, "Consumers According to Miller," *Washington Post*, November 8, 1981. Miller said, "Consumers are not as gullible as many people, as many regulators tend to think they are. They make intelligent choices. The thing that concerns me is that if we are so tight in our regulation that we can only produce the top-of-the-line kind of product…then people who would like to purchase a much lower-priced and perhaps not as high a quality product would be deprived of that opportunity. And I want to make sure that doesn't happen."

56. Miller, whose alternate neckwear featured the seal of New York, explained, "New York is special to everyone." See Clyde H. Farnsworth, "Neckties with an Economics Lesson," *New York Times*, July 7, 1982.

57. Miller interview. Miller was born on June 25, 1942, so he was actually thirty-eight at the time.

58. Dan Davidson, "Nixon's 'Nerd' Turns Regulations Watchdog," *Federal Times*, November 11, 2002.

59. Stuart Auerbach, "Seattle Fisherman Bobs Up at FTC Hearing," *Washington Post*, December 14, 1982.

60. Joy Griffith's case attracted particular attention because the comatose child was killed by her father at a Miami hospital in June 1985, one week after the CPSC issued the alert. Griffith told police that he could not bear his daughter's suffering. He was convicted of first-degree murder.

61. Bill McAllister, "Formula for Product Safety Raises Questions About Human Factor," *Washington Post*, May 26, 1987.

62. Bill Billiter, "Family Settles for $5 Million in Recliner Suit," *Los Angeles Times*, September 7, 1991.

63. Cass Sunstein, *The Cost-Benefit Revolution* (Cambridge: MIT Press, 2018), ebook loc. 932. In 1981, Sunstein, then working as a young lawyer at the Justice Department, was tasked with preparing the official opinion on the legality of Reagan's order requiring cost-benefit analysis. He approved.

64. William R. Greer, "Value of One Life? From $8.37 to $10 Million," *New York Times*, June 26, 1985.

65. Clyde H. Farnsworth, "Move to Cut Regulatory Costs Near," *New York Times*, February 14, 1981.

66. See "Role of OMB in Regulation," House Committee on Energy and Commerce, June 18, 1981.

67. The textile industry sued to block the rule. When the case came before the Supreme Court on the day after Reagan's inauguration, the government's lawyers, operating under old instructions, argued in favor of the rule. Two months later, a Florida building contractor named Thorne G. Auchter was installed as the new head of OSHA, and one of his first acts was to ask the court to refrain from ruling on the case. Auchter announced that his agency now subscribed to the necessity of cost-benefit analysis, and that it intended to issue a new and improved rule. Auchter also ordered the destruction of thousands of copies of "Cotton Dust: Worker Health Alert," a pamphlet about the dangers of brown lung (formally known as byssinosis), because the cover featured Louis Harrell, a North Carolina textile worker killed by byssinosis in 1978. "That photo makes a dramatic statement that clearly establishes a biased viewpoint in the cotton dust issue," Auchter explained. The Supreme Court refused to play along. In June 1981, it upheld the Carter brown lung rule. Pointing to the law that created OSHA, the court said Congress had decided that the health of workers was the primary consideration in the regulation of workplace toxins. There was, it said, no requirement for the agency to balance benefits and costs. Auchter, unwilling to concede defeat, next pursued the idea of revisions that would achieve the same benefits at a lower cost. But the industry no longer wanted relief. Most companies had spent the money required to comply with the new rules; they now wanted competitors to face the same expense. Still Auchter wasn't done. He authorized a North Carolina company that had not installed filters to experiment with alternative safeguards. The premise of the experiment has since been vindicated by scientific evidence that byssinosis is caused by bacteria, not the dust itself, and can be mitigated by washing raw cotton. But the politics were impossible. The company quickly foreswore the experiment and paid for filters.

68. W. Kip Viscusi, "Health and Safety Regulation," in *American Economic Policy in the 1980s*, ed. Feldstein, 460–61.

69. A federal court had ruled in *Sierra Club v. Costle* in April 1981 that the review process was legal, even if it was not required.

70. Robert Pear, "Fiscal Plans Bear the Telltale Signs of Cost-Benefit Analysis," *New York Times*, February 14, 1982. After leaving the Nixon administration, DeMuth enrolled

at the University of Chicago Law School, attracted by its emphasis on economics. After a few years in the private sector, he became director of a center at Harvard devoted to the study of regulation. He returned to Washington determined "to improve the efficiency of regulatory programs by hewing to economic thinking as much as possible" — and eager to demonstrate the value of that approach to a skeptical public. He argues that cost-benefit analysis sometimes led the Reagan administration to endorse more stringent regulation. A noteworthy example is the administration's decision to sharply reduce the permissible levels of lead in gasoline, which was the result of an EPA analysis that found the benefits would vastly outweigh the costs.

71. Sunstein, *Cost-Benefit Revolution*, ebook loc. 149.

72. Richard L. Berkman and W. Kip Viscusi, *Damming the West* (New York: Grossman, 1973), 242.

73. W. Kip Viscusi, *Pricing Lives: Guideposts for a Safer Society* (Princeton, N.J.: Princeton University Press, 2018), 1.

74. Pete Earley, "What's a Life Worth?," *Washington Post*, June 9, 1985.

75. Presidents are perpetually frustrated by the independence of the federal bureaucracy, a history encapsulated by the apocryphal but apposite reply President Kennedy is said to have made to a petitioner: "I agree with you, but I don't know if the government will." Elena Kagan described Clinton's embrace of cost-benefit analysis in a classic article, "Presidential Administration" (*Harvard Law Review*, 2000). Kagan, later a Supreme Court justice, described regulatory review as "the least significant and the most foundational" of the techniques Clinton used to assert control. That is probably true, as Clinton's other techniques included the simple expedient of telling agencies what to do.

76. Sally Katzen, "Perspectives on Modern Regulatory Governance: Oral History Project," 2012, Kenan Institute, Duke University, Durham, N.C.

77. Douglas Jehl, "Regulations Czar Prefers New Path," *New York Times*, March 25, 2001.

78. John H. Cushman Jr., "Congressional Republicans Take Aim at an Extensive List of Environmental Statutes," *New York Times*, February 22, 1995.

79. Revesz and Livermore, *Retaking Rationality*, 35.

80. Katharine Q. Seelye and John Tierney, "E.P.A Drops Age-Based Cost Studies," *New York Times*, May 8, 2003. The government has continued to wrestle with the implications of age, but more recent efforts have taken the form of emphasizing the value of children's lives rather than discounting the value of the elderly. Thus, for example, the Department of Transportation emphasized that a rule requiring rearview cameras in cars had greater value because it would save the lives of children. Similarly, the Consumer Product Safety Commission paid a consultant to study the value of children. The 2018 report concluded that children are roughly twice as valuable as adults, but the CPSC had not used that conclusion in a cost-benefit analysis as of mid-2018. See "Valuing Reductions in Fatal Risks to Children" (Industrial Economics report), 2018, Consumer Product Safety Commission.

81. W. Kip Viscusi, "The Devaluation of Life," *Regulation and Governance*, no. 3 (2009).

82. Sunstein, *Cost-Benefit Revolution*, ebook loc. 230. The courts also appear to be moving in the direction of requiring cost-benefit analysis of regulations in any case where Congress has not specifically directed an agency to ignore questions of cost. In *Michigan v. EPA* (2015), the Supreme Court held by a 5–4 majority that the EPA acted unreasonably in proposing to regulate some kinds of air pollution without considering the cost. The minority agreed that the EPA needed to consider cost, but said it had met that burden. In effect, all nine judges signed on to an interpretation of the Clean Air Act quite different from the prevailing view in the 1970s.

83. Stanley Johnson, *The Politics of Environment* (London: Tom Stacey, 1973), 172. Johnson, an advocate for stronger environmental regulation, thought his countrymen were being altogether too cautious. His son, Boris, became a prominent Conservative politician.

84. Political pressure ultimately forced the Bush administration to adopt the stricter standard. See Cindy Skrzycki, *The Regulators: Anonymous Power Brokers in American Politics* (Lanham, Md.: Rowman and Littlefield, 2003), 213.

85. Brandon Mitchener, "Rules, Regulations of Global Economy Are Increasingly Being Set in Brussels," *Wall Street Journal*, April 23, 2002.

86. Samuel Loewenberg, "Old Europe's New Ideas," *Sierra Magazine*, January–February 2004.

87. My treatment of this trend draws on David Vogel, *The Politics of Precaution: Regulating Health, Safety and Environmental Risks in Europe and the United States* (Princeton, N.J.: Princeton University Press, 2012).

88. Pfizer's full-page ad was published in *European Voice* the week of February 17, 2000. See Andrew Jordan, "The Precautionary Principle in the European Union," in *Reinterpreting the Precautionary Principle*, ed. Tim O'Riordan, James Cameron, and Andrew Jordan (London: Cameron May, 2001), 154.

Chapter 8. Money, Problems

1. F. A. Mackenzie, *The American Invaders: Their Plans, Tactics and Progress* (London: Grant Richards, 1902), 142–43.

2. The idea that trade would discourage military conflict was in broad circulation in the 1930s and 1940s. Thomas Watson Sr., the chief executive of IBM, put a plaque at the entrance to the company's Manhattan headquarters, opened in 1938, that said "World Peace Through World Trade." For the State Department's thoughts, see "Proposals for Expansion of World Trade and Employment," November 1945, U.S. State Department.

3. Economic historians continue to debate the role of trade policy in the collapse of the global economy. Recent scholarship has tended to treat the currency devaluations of the early 1930s as a consequence or accelerant of other economic problems, not a primary cause of the Depression. See, however, Douglas Irwin's *Peddling Protectionism: Smoot-Hawley and the Great Depression* (Princeton, N.J.: Princeton University Press, 2011).

4. White, a complicated figure, was both a dedicated and effective advocate for what he saw as the national interest of the United States — and a spy for the Soviet Union. John Maynard Keynes is often credited as the primary architect of the agreement, or at least as White's partner. In reality, Keynes, in one of his final acts in public life, obtained few of the concessions he sought to constrain the power of the United States. See Benn Steil, *The Battle of Bretton Woods* (Princeton, N.J.: Princeton University Press, 2013).

5. The rules allowed other nations to fix their currencies in dollars or gold. No one chose gold.

6. General Douglas MacArthur set an exchange rate of 360 yen to the dollar in April 1949, and there it stayed for almost a quarter century. For West Germany, the 1949 exchange rate was set at 4.2 deutschmarks to the dollar. This was revalued modestly in 1961 and again in 1969, when the dollar was pegged at 3.66 marks.

7. "The Balance of Payments Mess," Joint Economic Committee, June 1971, 246.

8. Judith Stein, *Pivotal Decade* (New Haven: Yale University Press, 2010), ebook loc. 246.

9. Under the gold standard, the theory was that nations would adjust while exchange rates remained the same: to increase exports, nations needed to drive down domestic wages

and prices. This painful option was still available under Bretton Woods, but it had become politically untenable. The expansion of suffrage and labor unions, among other trends, had shifted the balance of political power across the developed world. Proponents of fixed exchange rates argue that its rigor improved long-term economic growth. In this view, nations that chose to adjust exchange rates rather than adjusting domestic economic conditions were refusing to take their medicine. "Exchange rate stability was a public good; no country was willing to pay much to supply it," the economic historian Allan Meltzer wrote by way of an epitaph. See Allan H. Meltzer, *A History of the Federal Reserve*, vol. 2, book 2, *1970–1986* (Chicago: University of Chicago Press, 2009), 754.

10. The problem with unilateral devaluation is that trading partners could respond in kind. Indeed, that was exactly what happened in the early 1930s. John Kenneth Galbraith related in a 1964 essay that he asked a Swiss banker when the Swiss would respond to a U.S. devaluation, and the banker responded, "It might be late in the same afternoon": see "The Balance of Payments: A Political and Administrative View," *Review of Economics and Statistics* 46, no. 2 (May 1964): 115–22. The United States also wanted other nations to increase the value of their currencies in dollars rather than decreasing the value of the dollar in gold because America was reluctant to penalize its allies who were holding dollars — and even more reluctant to hand a windfall to two of the major gold-producing nations, the Soviet Union and South Africa.

11. The program, known as Trade Adjustment Assistance, finally began to make a small number of payments in the early 1970s, but it was still dismissed by the head of the AFL-CIO in 1973 as "burial insurance." When Congress broadened the president's authority to negotiate trade deals later that year, it also made the compensation program significantly more generous. By 1980, the program was helping 600,000 workers. The next year, the Reagan administration persuaded Congress to sharply reduce eligibility and benefits.

12. Total foreign dollar holdings exceeded the U.S. gold supply in 1960. Government holdings crossed the line three years later. See Barry Eichengreen, *Exorbitant Privilege: The Rise and Fall of the Dollar and the Future of the International Monetary System* (Oxford: Oxford University Press, 2011), 50.

13. Johnson was inclined to adopt a stronger proposal, limiting foreign travel by invoking the Trading with the Enemy Act of 1917. Cracking down on honeymooners does not seem like a great idea from a political perspective, but Treasury Secretary Henry Fowler had to write a memo explaining why the plan was illegal before Johnson grudgingly set it aside.

14. France, under the leadership of Charles de Gaulle, continued to convert dollars into gold as fast as it could, primarily to annoy the United States. See Meltzer, *History of the Federal Reserve*, vol. 2, book 2, 719.

15. "A-Blasts Studied as Way to Expand U.S. Gold Output," *New York Times*, February 26, 1968, 53.

16. James Ledbetter, *One Nation Under Gold* (New York: Liveright/Norton, 2017), 183.

17. Milton Friedman, Donald Gordon, and W. A. Mackintosh, "Canada and the Problems of World Trade," University of Chicago Round Table 526, April 18, 1948; available at https://miltonfriedman.hoover.org/friedman_images/Collections/2016c21/UCR_04_18_1948.pdf. Friedman, in his memoirs, claims that Donald Gordon, the deputy governor of the Bank of Canada, had never before heard a serious case made for floating rates. The transcript of the radio broadcast does not support that claim; it is Gordon who first mentions the idea. But Gordon Thiessen, a former governor of the Bank of Canada, said in a 2000 speech that Friedman deserved credit for stimulating

internal discussion, citing a number of memos on floating rates prepared in the after-math of the broadcast. Two years later, in 1950, Canada floated its exchange rate in violation of the Bretton Woods Agreement.

18. Milton Friedman, "The Case for Flexible Exchange Rates," in *Essays in Positive Econom-ics* (Chicago: University of Chicago Press, 1953), 157–203. The paper had its origins in 1950, when Friedman was hired as a consultant to the Marshall Plan and assigned to advise West Germany. At the time, the Germans were struggling to make enough money from exports to pay for needed imports. Friedman recommended a devaluation of the mark. A trade deficit, he said, indicated a nation's currency was too expensive. The Germans demurred. The 1953 paper generalized the advice.

19. That a member of the policy-making elite would engage Friedman was a coup for the American Enterprise Institute (AEI), which was struggling to emerge from the obscu-rity of life as a conservative think tank in 1960s America. The institute, founded in 1938 by the chief executive of the world's largest asbestos company, because he didn't like the New Deal, began to find a broader audience under the leadership of William J. Baroody Sr. Baroody spent the Great Depression on the government's payroll, working for the New Hampshire Unemployment Compensation Agency and the Veterans Administration, before joining AEI in 1954 and launching a second career as one of the most effective critics of his former employer. Baroody's signature strategy was pairing liberal and conservative experts to gain an audience for the conservative. The institute, for example, distributed popular analyses of pending legislation featuring both a respected liberal economist and a conservative view. Baroody persuaded donors that disseminating liberal views was the best chance to get liberal members of Congress to read something conservative, too.

20. Milton Friedman and Robert Roosa, *The Balance of Payments: Free Versus Fixed Exchange Rates* (Washington, D.C.: American Enterprise Institute for Public Policy Research, 1967), 185.

21. Robert Leeson, *Ideology and the International Economy* (Basingstoke, Eng.: Palgrave Macmillan, 2003), 114. Friedman biographer Edward Nelson makes clear that Samu-elson credited Friedman for the change: "I would like to pay personal tribute to Milton Friedman," Samuelson said in 1969. "He was a lone voice crying in the wilderness." Friedman's view, he said, "has now become the new orthodoxy in the academic profes-sion." See Nelson, "Milton Friedman and Economic Debate in the United States, 1932–1972," 2018, book B, p. 476; available at https://sites.google.com/site/edward nelsonresearch.

22. Anthony Lewis, "Commons Backs Wilson on Pound," *New York Times*, November 23, 1967, 17.

23. Meltzer, *History of the Federal Reserve*, vol. 2, book 2, 733.

24. Paul Volcker and Toyoo Gyohten, *Changing Fortunes: The World's Money and the Threat to American Leadership* (New York: Times Books, 1992), 144–45.

25. Milton Friedman, "A Proposal for Resolving the U.S. Balance of Payments Problem: Confidential Memorandum to President-Elect Richard Nixon," October 15, 1968, reprinted in *The Merits of Flexible Exchange Rates*, ed. Leo Melamed (Fairfax, Va.: George Mason University Press, 1988), 429–38.

26. On the domestic front, Nixon wrote that his interest in economic issues was limited to cases "where the decisions affect either recession or inflation." See Richard M. Nixon, "Memorandum for Mr. Haldeman, Mr. Ehrlichman, Dr. Kissinger," March 2, 1970; available at https://2001-2009.state.gov/r/pa/ho/frus/nixon/e5/55018.htm.

27. Canada previously had floated its currency between 1950 and 1962.

28. Leeson, *Ideology and the International Economy*, 132.

29. William Safire sketched the relationship in a chapter of his memoir entitled "The President Falls in Love." He quotes Nixon as saying of Connally, "Every Cabinet should have at least one potential president in it." See Safire, *Before the Fall: An Inside View of the Pre-Watergate White House* (New York: Doubleday, 1975), 498. Connally was openly skeptical of economics. He unblushingly told Congress that he didn't understand Ricardo's case for trade, but it was plainly wrong. Connally said, "That's the theory of comparative advantage. In the first place, the reason I do not understand it is that I am not an economist. But if I were an economist, I would not want to understand it because I do not believe it is going to work." Similarly, he initially dismissed devaluation as "monetary magic," insisting that the only cure for the value of the dollar was to strengthen the domestic economy. The rest, he said, would take care of itself.

30. Richard Nixon, *RN: The Memoirs of Richard Nixon* (New York: Grosset and Dunlap, 1978), 518.

31. George P. Shultz and Kenneth W. Dam, *Economic Policy Beyond the Headlines* (Stanford, Calif.: Stanford Alumni Association, 1977), 115.

32. Richard Reeves, *President Nixon: Alone in the White House* (New York: Touchstone/ Simon and Schuster, 2001), 356.

33. Meeting in the Oval Office on Thursday, August 12, Connally and Nixon agreed the discussions at Camp David would be held as if the outcome were an open question, to bring Burns gently into the fold. As the head of an independent agency, Burns had the potential to cause problems. See Douglas Brinkley, ed., *The Nixon Tapes, 1971–1972* (New York: Houghton Mifflin Harcourt, 2014), 233–72. George Shultz offered a similar account: "That wasn't a meeting to discuss something," he told me. "It was a meeting so Nixon could have a stage."

34. Robert H. Ferrell, ed., *Inside the Nixon Administration: The Secret Diary of Arthur Burns, 1969–1974* (Lawrence: University Press of Kansas, 2010), 49–53.

35. Wyatt C. Wells, *Economist in an Uncertain World* (New York: Columbia University Press, 1994), 206.

36. Safire, *Before the Fall*, 518. While Volcker did not elaborate on his plans, he presumably was referring to the possibility of placing bets on the movements of asset prices. There was no market in currency futures at that time, so Volcker would have needed to predict the impact of the President's speech on other financial markets.

37. Ferrell, *Inside the Nixon Administration*, 53.

38. Eichengreen, *Exorbitant Privilege*, 59.

39. The Germans had not missed anything in translation. Calling to congratulate Nixon, Nelson Rockefeller, the governor of New York, told the President that the first commercial after the speech was for Volkswagen, a coincidence the two men regarded as underscoring the importance of Nixon's decision. See H. R. Haldeman Diaries, National Archives, August 16, 1971; available at nixonlibrary.gov/sites/default/files/virtuallibrary/documents/haldeman-diaries/37-hrhd-audiotape-ac12b-19710816-pa.pdf.

40. "The Dollar: A Power Play Unfolds," *Time*, August 30, 1971, 17.

41. The *New York Times* reported that the archbishop's call to prayer was followed by "an immediate halt in the slide of the pound's value," although the article noted that "most observers attributed it to a wait-and-see attitude of traders pending the outcome of a British cabinet meeting." See "Notes on People," *New York Times*, July 2, 1975.

42. Robert Solomon, *The International Monetary System, 1945–1981* (New York: Harper and Row, 1982), 2.

43. John S. Odell, *U.S. International Monetary Policy* (Princeton, N.J.: Princeton University Press, 1982), 262.

44. Ferrell, *Inside the Nixon Administration*, 66.

45. Henry Kissinger, *Years of Upheaval* (New York: Simon and Schuster, 2011), 80–81.

46. "George Shultz: Looking Back on Five Years in Government," *Washington Post*, April 14, 1974.

47. Shultz likes to tell a story about starting a neighborhood newspaper when he was twelve. The price was five cents. He knocked on a neighbor's door and gave his sales pitch. The man went back inside and returned with a copy of the *Saturday Evening Post*, telling Shultz that was what a person could get for five cents. Shultz said it impressed upon him the logic of the market.

48. As a young professor at MIT, Shultz also helped Samuelson to write his famous economics textbook. Members of the faculty used drafts of the text in their classes, and then reported back to Samuelson on the parts that students had struggled to understand. See "Problems and Principles: George P. Shultz and the Uses of Economic Thinking," conducted by Paul Burnett in 2015, Oral History Center, Bancroft Library, University of California, Berkeley.

49. Interview with George Shultz, April 19, 2018.

50. A. H. Raskin, "Said Nixon to George Shultz: 'I Track Well with You,'" *New York Times*, August 23, 1970.

51. Rowland Evans and Robert Novak, *Nixon in the White House: The Frustration of Power* (New York: Random House, 1971), 369.

52. Soon after Connally started as Treasury secretary in February 1971, Friedman sought an introduction. He brought a copy of his 1968 memo to Nixon, telling Connally, "Here is a memo I wrote for you two years ago." For the two letters to Connally, dated September 30, 1971, and December 3, 1971, see Milton Friedman Papers, box 24, Hoover Institution Archives, Stanford, Calif.

53. The conversation was reported by Toyoo Gyohten, who was present as Mizuta's interpreter. Mizuta's account was misleading. The murdered finance minister, Junnosuke Inoue, was killed by an ultranationalist in 1932 as part of a terror campaign against political moderates. But by then, Inoue was no longer the finance minister, and the murder was not directly related to the gold standard. See Volcker and Gyohten, *Changing Fortunes*, 97.

54. Ibid., 90

55. Britain floated the pound on June 23, 1972, the first formal break.

56. Volcker and Gyohten, *Changing Fortunes*, 104.

57. "Transcript of a Recording of a Meeting Between the President and H. R. Haldeman in the Oval Office on June 23, 1972, from 10:04 to 11:39," White House Tapes, Richard Nixon Presidential Library, Yorba Linda, Calif.

58. Solomon, *The International Monetary System*, 336.

59. Harold James, *International Monetary Cooperation Since Bretton Woods* (New York: Oxford University Press, 1996), 242.

60. Shultz secured Nixon's permission at a meeting just before the conference where he told the President that the United States faced a choice between floating rates and ongoing massive intervention in currency markets. "You had to go whole hog one way or the other," Shultz said. See Odell, *U.S. International Monetary Policy*, 321. Shultz told me that he and Burns argued about the plan during most of the flight to Paris. When they arrived at the meeting, Shultz said he was relieved to find that Burns maintained a united front.

61. The global explosion in trade had many causes. The invention of the shipping container, surely one of the least heralded technological revolutions, played a leading role in reducing transportation costs. The invention of the internet, surely the most heralded of technological revolutions, played a leading role in reducing the cost of communication. The Soviet Union collapsed; China opened for business. As for floating rates, perhaps the most important contribution of the new system was that it allowed the United States to run almost unlimited trade deficits. The figures for 1971 and 2008 are from the Penn World Tables: see rug.nl/ggdc/productivity/pwt/. The World Bank estimates the change was from 27 percent to 61 percent over the same period.

62. This paragraph is drawn from Leo Melamed's memoir, *Escape to the Futures* (New York: Wiley, 1996).

63. Ibid., 177. Melamed has sometimes given $7500 as the sum paid to Friedman. Either way, the Merc got good value for its money.

64. In 1980, the economists Lars Peter Hansen and Robert Hodrick finally matched theory to reality, showing that speculation can be profitable because people are irrational. When Hansen won the Nobel Prize in economics in 2013, the paper was among his listed contributions. See Lars Peter Hansen and Robert J. Hodrick, "Forward Exchange Rates as Optimal Predictors of Future Spot Rates: An Econometric Analysis," *Journal of Political Economy* 88, no. 5 (October 1980).

65. For 1985, see Susan Strange, *Casino Capitalism* (Oxford: Basil Blackwell, 1986), 11. For the 1995 and 2007 figures, see "Triennial Central Bank Survey," March 2005 and July 2016 (respectively), Bank for International Settlements.

66. Marc Levinson, *An Extraordinary Time* (New York: Basic Books, 2016), 89.

67. The banks — Citigroup, JPMorgan Chase, Barclays, and the Royal Bank of Scotland — were engaged in a massive price-fixing conspiracy. The scheme was possible only because Robert Roosa turned out to be right: markets in foreign exchange do not coalesce around a single price. To address this problem, bankers create a daily benchmark rate by averaging the trades made in the thirty seconds on either side of 4:00 p.m., London time. Foreign exchange orders are often placed for execution at this benchmark rate, and investors often use that rate to calculate the value of their assets. But the rate is subject to manipulation. Traders for the major banks colluded in online chat rooms to "bang the close," the industry's term for flooding the market with orders during the benchmarking period to move the closing price. Wrote one Barclays trader, "If you aint cheating, you aint trying."

68. In a 1996 interview, Friedman acknowledged that volatility "was much greater than I would have anticipated," but maintained that it did not have "any serious negative effects." He did not live to learn that large banks were fixing the market at the expense of their own customers. See Brian Snowden and Howard R. Vane, *Conversations with Leading Economists: Interpreting Modern Macroeconomics* (Cheltenham, Eng.: Edward Elgar, 1999), 124–44.

69. Michael Hirsh, *Capital Offense* (Hoboken, N.J.: John Wiley, 2010), 46.

70. Eichengreen, the nearest thing to an official biographer of the dollar, downplays the importance of network effects. In his view, the dollar remains dominant because the United States still has the largest economy and the obvious alternatives, like the euro and the Chinese yuan, have significant shortcomings. He notes the dollar rose to dominance in about a decade, between 1914 and 1925, and he argues it could be replaced just as swiftly. See his history of the dollar, *Exorbitant Privilege*. The dollar, however, is deeply entrenched. For example, 72 percent of all the goods imported by Canada between 2002 and 2009 from countries other than the United States nonetheless were

paid for with U.S. dollars. See Linda S. Goldberg and Cedric Tille, "Micro, Macro, and Strategic Forces in International Trade Invoicing," November 2009, Federal Reserve Bank of New York. See also John M. Geddes, "Bundesbank Opposes Wider Role for Mark," *New York Times*, November 20, 1976.

71. It was not quite a case of pots and kettles, for while the Germans had not demonstrated any sense of responsibility for the health of the global economy, they also had not volunteered for the job. See Eichengreen, *Exorbitant Privilege*, 63.

72. The exchange value of the dollar is best calculated on a "trade-weighted" basis, meaning that the exchange rate of the dollar against each foreign currency is multiplied by the share of America's trade with countries using that currency. The calculation here is based on figures from the Federal Reserve's Trade-Weighted Index of Major Currencies.

73. Some conservative economists had steadily opposed the shift to floating rates, and found the failures of the new system unsurprising. James Buchanan, another Nobel laureate from the Chicago family, wrote in 1977 that floating rates "severed one of the constraints on internal monetary expansion. It does not seem to be entirely a coincidence that deficit spending and inflation have intensified since the shift to free exchange rates." He added that floating rates "make the economy considerably more vulnerable to unwise manipulation by domestic politicians." See James M. Buchanan and Richard E. Wagner, *Democracy in Deficit: The Political Legacy of Lord Keynes* (1977; repr., Indianapolis: Liberty Fund, 2000), 75.

74. Richard Friberg, *Exchange Rates and the Firm* (New York: St. Martin's, 1999), 41.

75. It remains the view of many economists that the decline of U.S. manufacturing was due to other factors and that the strong dollar, at most, influenced the timing. "The exchange rate is the expression of forces in the economy and saying that you wish it was different doesn't work," Maurice Obstfeld, the chief economist of the International Monetary Fund, said in 2017. The exchange rate, he said, is "overrated as a policy variable." Some studies of the decline of U.S. manufacturing in the 1980s, however, attribute more than half of the job losses in that decade to unbalanced trade. "The main problem facing manufacturers was not some deep-rooted structural issue, but an exchange rate that posed an enormous obstacle to its ability to compete in domestic and foreign markets," writes the economic historian Douglas Irwin. The evidence that exchange rates have damaged the U.S. manufacturing sector is even greater for the first decade of the present century.

76. John M. Berry and Jane Seaberry, "Regan, Feldstein in Opposition on Deficits' Impact," *Washington Post*, September 15, 1983. Lee Iacocca, the brash chief executive of Chrysler, lamented in 1985 that it was hard to muster political support for devaluation because the issue was difficult to explain. Money is ubiquitous and mysterious — both too common and too complicated to command attention. "People don't get excited about the high dollar," he said. "People don't really understand it, so nobody's going to get up in arms." See Yoichi Funabashi, *Managing the Dollar: From the Plaza to the Louvre* (Washington, D.C.: Institute for International Economics, 1989), 73. Iacocca's use of the word "high" was purposeful, because it also was painfully clear that politicians liked to talk about a "strong" dollar. "The strength of the dollar," Volcker later observed acidly, "came to be cited by some officials as a kind of Good Housekeeping Seal of Approval provided by the market, honoring sound Reagan economic policies."

77. The New York Fed — the operational arm of the central bank — issued a press release in December 1981 announcing that it had not intervened in currency markets during the previous six months, the first such stretch since the end of Bretton Woods. The Fed customarily defers to the Treasury on foreign exchange policy, carrying out the executive

branch's instructions, but Volcker wasn't inclined to move the dollar anyway. He was more worried than most U.S. officials about the loss of manufacturing jobs, but he believed fiscal deficits were the cause of the problem, and fiscal rectitude the solution. See Robert Solomon, *Money on the Move* (Princeton, N.J.: Princeton University Press, 1999), 15.

78. Funabashi, *Managing the Dollar*, 70.

79. Stephen Axilrod, *Inside the Fed: Monetary Policy and Its Management* (Cambridge: MIT Press, 2011), 103–4.

80. "Beryl W. Sprinkel Alive and Thriving in Economic Advice," *New York Times*, August 9, 1985.

81. "Why Reagan Bought Intervention in the Currency Markets," *Business Week*, June 28, 1982, 102–3. Sprinkel believed what he said. He persuaded the Reagan administration to eliminate his job as under secretary of the Treasury for monetary affairs in 1984. Five years later, the George H. W. Bush administration created a new position at Treasury, under secretary for international affairs, that was an effective successor, reflecting a swing back toward mindful management of floating exchange rates.

82. Solomon, *International Monetary System*, 365.

83. Paul Volcker and Christine Harper, *Keeping at It: The Quest for Sound Money and Good Government* (New York: PublicAffairs, 2018), 131.

84. "Latin IOU Struggle Is Triggering Jitters," *Miami Herald*, April 18, 1983.

85. "The LDC Debt Crisis," *History of the Eighties — Lessons for the Future*, vol. 1, *An Examination of the Banking Crises of the 1980s and Early 1990s* (Washington, D.C.: Federal Deposit Insurance Corporation, 1997).

86. Ha-Joon Chang, *Bad Samaritans: The Myth of Free Trade and the Secret History of Capitalism* (New York: Bloomsbury, 2008), 94.

87. Walter Mondale in a 1984 speech charged Reagan with "turning our great industrial Midwest and the industrial base of this country into a rust bowl," playing off the Dust Bowl of the Great Depression years. Journalists soon began referring to the "Rust Belt," preferring the contrast with the southern "Sun Belt."

88. Chieko Kuriki, "'Made in U.S.A.' Doesn't Sell," *Chicago Tribune*, April 22, 1985.

89. Douglas Irwin, *Clashing over Commerce: A History of U.S. Trade Policy* (Chicago: University of Chicago Press, 2017), ebook loc. 9908.

90. Ball is perhaps best remembered for his opposition to the Vietnam War, but he lost that fight. He made a much more significant contribution to American policy in the realm of trade, where he insisted on the classic liberal view that trade is good and more trade is better. Said Ball, "The concept that we must protect every American industry against the adjustments required by competition is alien to the spirit of our economy." See Stein, *Pivotal Decade*, ebook loc. 296.

91. Some accounts of the rise of trade with China downplay the role of U.S. policy, instead treating China's industrialization as an inexorable force. However, a 2016 paper by Justin R. Pierce and Peter K. Schott presents compelling evidence that one decision did matter. Until the turn of the century, the United States regularly reviewed China's eligibility for preferential tariff treatment. Pierce and Schott argued the decision to grant that status on a permanent basis in 2000 removed an important uncertainty, catalyzing increased capital and trade flows. See their "The Surprisingly Swift Decline of U.S. Manufacturing Employment," *American Economic Review* 106, no. 7 (2016).

92. In the early 2000s, the Fed held down interest rates to stimulate economic growth, and the dollar declined against most foreign currencies. But this process of equilibration did not affect the dollar-yuan exchange rate, nor the dollar's exchange rate with other Asian currencies effectively fixed against the dollar.

93. Other factors have of course contributed to the decline of manufacturing employment, including automation and globalization. But a 2012 study estimated that currency manipulation by twenty countries, China by far the largest, had cost the United States between 1 million and 5 million jobs. See C. Fred Bergsten and Joseph E. Gagnon, "Currency Manipulation, the U.S. Economy and the Global Economic Order," December 2012, Peterson Institute for International Economics.

94. Huffy is still based in Dayton, about two hours from Celina, where it employs about 120 managers and white-collar workers in areas like marketing and product development. For an account of Walmart's relationship with Huffy and other American manufacturers, see Anthony Bianco, *The Bully of Bentonville* (New York: Crown, 2009). See also Michael Spence and Sandile Hlatshwayo, "The Evolving Structure of the American Economy and the Employment Challenge," 2011, Council on Foreign Relations.

95. Friedman and Roosa, *Balance of Payments*, 92, 118.

96. A series of papers by a group of economists — including David Autor, Gordon Hanson, and David Dorn — that have reshaped the scholarly understanding of the impact of trade with China is available at ddorn.net/research.htm.

97. Lori G. Kletzer, "Job Loss from Imports: Measuring the Costs, 2001," Peterson Institute for International Economics.

98. Binyamin Appelbaum, "Perils of Globalization When Factories Close and Towns Struggle," *New York Times*, May 18, 2015.

99. Some of the other economists who appear in this book have similar regrets. Alice Rivlin, for example, told me, "We concentrated on the benefits of technological change and trade, but not on adjusting to those. We just didn't. Economists were much too focused on the average that we all benefit from technological change. A lot of people didn't — and we didn't do what we might have to help."

100. Appelbaum, "Perils of Globalization." Proponents of trade in the United States have caused their own problems by failing to ensure the gains of trade are shared broadly. But opposition to trade also draws strength from the triumph of sentiment over reason, because the pain of job losses is concentrated and the victims are visible, while the benefits of lower prices are diffuse. Douglas Irwin writes that in 1956, a New York congressman named John Ray voted against legislation to lower tariffs. Ray explained that his district included a birdcage factory that faced foreign competition and he had heard from almost every one of the factory's fifty workers. Ray's district also included a large chunk of the New York waterfront, where thousands of people worked in jobs tied to trade, but Ray said he had not heard from anyone who favored lower tariffs.

101. Schuman's father was born a Frenchman in Lorraine, then became a German citizen when the region was annexed in 1871, then moved to neighboring Luxembourg, where Schuman himself was born in 1886. Schuman moved to France, completing the circle.

    The other original members of the European Coal and Steel Community were Belgium, Luxembourg, and the Netherlands.

102. Devaluation is not free. It reduces the purchasing power of the nation's currency, and thus the value of workers' wages. But, like inflation, it avoids the need to reduce nominal wages. While Meade and Friedman agreed on the mechanism, they disagreed on the goal. Meade thought that floating rates would allow European countries to exercise greater control over domestic economic conditions; Friedman, of course, thought government should stay out of other aspects of economic policy, too. See James Meade, "The Case for Variable Exchange Rates," in *The Collected Papers of James Meade*, vol. 3, *International Economics*, ed. Susan Howson (London: Unwin Hyman, 1988).

103. Howard R. Vane and Chris Mulhearn, "Interview with Robert A. Mundell," *Journal of Economic Perspectives* 20, no. 4 (Fall 2006): 89–110.

104. Robert Mundell, "A Theory of Optimum Currency Areas," *American Economic Review* 51, no. 4 (September 1961).

105. See Rudiger Dornbusch, "The Chicago School in the 1960s," *Policy Options* 22, no. 5 (2001). See also Thomas J. Courchene, *Money, Markets and Mobility: Celebrating the Ideas of Robert A. Mundell* (Montreal: Institute for Research on Public Policy, 2002), 3.

106. Vane and Mulhearn, "Interview with Robert A. Mundell," 89–110.

107. Robert A. Mundell, "A Plan for a European Currency" (speech at the American Management Association Conference on the Future of the International Monetary System, New York, December 10–12, 1969), reprinted in *The Economics of Common Currencies: Proceedings of the Madrid Conference on Optimum Currency Areas*, ed. Harry G. Johnson and Alexander K. Swoboda (London: Allen and Unwin, 1973).

108. Volcker did not identify the official when he recounted the story in a 1992 book. In his memoirs, published in 2018, Volcker identified the speaker and reported a slightly different version of the quote; I have used the earlier version. See Volcker and Gyohten, *Changing Fortunes*, 68.

109. Michael Dobbs, "Socialist Metamorphosis," *Washington Post*, March 16, 1986.

110. Padoa-Schioppa's regard for public opinion is well illustrated by his complaint to German policy makers in the early 1980s that they were fanning the flames of public opposition rather than standing against it. See Ivo Maes, "Tommaso Padoa-Schioppa and the Origins of the Euro," March 2012, National Bank of Belgium Paper 222, 15.

111. Padoa-Schioppa, like Mundell, included the important caveat that regulation of international capital flows could allow countries to maintain fixed exchange rates and independent monetary policies. But the participants in the European project already were dismantling those controls, a process largely completed over the following decade. See Tommaso Padoa-Schioppa, "Capital Mobility: Why Is the Treaty Not Implemented?," in *The Road to Monetary Union in Europe* (Oxford: Clarendon Press, 1994).

112. The supply-side critique that regulation was impeding growth also had made its mark on the European debate. Proponents of a multinational currency regarded the constraints on fiscal policy as one of the benefits of the system, because it would force a focus on supply-side reforms like deregulation. See David Marsh, *The Euro: The Battle for the New Global Currency* (New Haven: Yale University Press, 2009), ebook loc. 4241.

113. Padoa-Schioppa served as one of the chief technocrats on the European commission that prepared the plan for the creation of a European currency. It was his suggestion the new system should begin on January 1, 1999. See Maes, "Padoa-Schioppa and the Origins of the Euro," 30.

114. Lubbers's phrases were "*de BV Nederland*" and "*meer markt, minder overheid.*"

115. Neil Irwin, *The Alchemists: Three Central Bankers and a World on Fire* (New York: Penguin Press, 2013), 77.

116. Eduardo Porter, "A Tempting Rationale for Leaving the Euro," *New York Times*, May 15, 2012.

117. Some European officials, notably Jean-Claude Trichet, the former head of the European Central Bank, describe Mundell as an important intellectual influence on the creation of the euro. Mundell himself has made the case that he deserves credit, too. See, for example, Vane and Mulhearn, "Interview with Robert A. Mundell," 89–110.

118. "The Euro's Arrival at a Glance," BBC, January 3, 2002.

119. Jacques de Larosière, governor of the Bank of France at the time of the Maastricht Treaty, pointed out that the new central bank was an improvement on the status quo. "Today, I am the governor of a central bank who has decided, along with his nation, to follow fully the German monetary policy without voting on it," he told a reporter. "At least, as part of a European central bank, I'll have a vote." See Hobart Rowen, "Of European Unity," *Washington Post*, October 25, 1990.

120. In a widely cited 2000 paper, Andrew Rose estimated sharing a currency could produce a threefold increase in trade among the participants. Studies of the eurozone generally find smaller but still significant effects. The Africa paper is particularly clever because the relationship between those countries and Europe had not changed except for the decision to use the euro. See Jeffrey Frankel, "The Estimated Effects of the Euro on Trade," 2008, National Bureau of Economic Research.

121. Germany's success as an exporter to other euro area nations was built on the country's remarkable discipline in restraining the growth of wages and consumption, in effect deferring the benefits of its economic success.

122. Arnold Harberger, "Sense and Economics: An Oral History with Arnold Harberger," conducted by Paul Burnett in 2015 and 2016, Oral History Center, Bancroft Library, University of California, Berkeley.

123. Neil Irwin, "Finland Shows Why Many Europeans Think Americans Are Wrong About the Euro," *New York Times*, July 20, 2015.

Chapter 9. Made in Chile

1. Charles J. Hitch, "The Uses of Economics," November 17, 1960, Rand Corporation.

2. The provision of technical assistance to Latin America, primarily in the areas of agriculture, geology, aviation, and child welfare, was initiated by President Franklin Roosevelt and expanded by Truman and Eisenhower. "We must embark on a bold new program for making the benefits of our scientific advances and industrial progress available for the improvement and growth of underdeveloped areas," Truman declared in his 1949 inaugural address. "More than half the people of the world are living in conditions approaching misery. Their food is inadequate. They are victims of disease. Their economic life is primitive and stagnant. Their poverty is a handicap and a threat both to them and to more prosperous areas. For the first time in history, humanity possesses the knowledge and skill to relieve the suffering of these people. The United States is pre-eminent among nations in the development of industrial and scientific techniques. The material resources which we can afford to use for assistance of other peoples are limited. But our imponderable resources in technical knowledge are constantly growing and are inexhaustible." It is hard to imagine a better name for one of the missionaries than Albion.

3. Juan Gabriel Valdés, *Pinochet's Economists: The Chicago School in Chile* (Cambridge, Eng.: Cambridge University Press, 1995), 110.

4. Ibid.

5. Ibid., 113.

6. Theodore W. Schultz, "Human Wealth and Economic Growth," *The Humanist*, no. 2 (1959): 71–81.

7. Valdés, *Pinochet's Economists*, 88.

8. Verónica Montecinos, "Economics: The Chilean Story," in *Economists in the Americas*, ed. Verónica Montecinos and John Markoff (Cheltenham, Eng.: Edward Elgar, 2009), 167–68.

9. Valdés, *Pinochet's Economists*, 116.

10. The world's largest deposits of sodium nitrate, also known as Chile saltpeter, are found in northern Chile. It was a key ingredient in both fertilizer and explosives until Germany began to produce synthetic saltpeter in commercial quantities during World War I. In the 1940s, copper overtook nitrates as Chile's major export.

11. José De Gregorio, "Economic Growth in Chile: Evidence, Sources and Prospects," November 2004, Banco Central de Chile.

12. Universal suffrage is a relatively recent phenomenon. Initially, republics including the United States limited voting to an elite minority of white, male, literate property owners. In Chile, the electorate expanded from roughly 15 percent of the population to roughly 30 percent of the population between 1958 and 1970. See Valdés, *Pinochet's Economists*, 243.

13. Friedrich List, *The National System of Political Economy*, trans. Sampson S. Lloyd (London: Longmans, Green, 1916), 295.

14. There is considerable disagreement among economists about the benefits of sheltering young industries. The conventional view is that the United States prospered despite its protectionist policies, a story told by the trade historian Douglas Irwin in *Clashing over Commerce: A History of U.S. Trade Policy* (Chicago: University of Chicago Press, 2017). Others see Hamilton's strategy as an important factor in America's rise, including the South Korean economist Ha-Joon Chang in *Bad Samaritans: The Myth of Free Trade and the Secret History of Capitalism* (New York: Bloomsbury, 2008).

15. Arnold Harberger, "Interview with Arnold Harberger," conducted by David Levy, *The Region*, Federal Reserve Bank of Minneapolis, March 1, 1999. Harberger's view of economics as an applied science was shared by Friedman. Asked what set Chicago's approach to economics apart in those years, Friedman answered, "The fundamental difference between Chicago at that time and let's say Harvard, was that at Chicago economics was a serious subject to be used in discussing real problems, and you could get some knowledge and some answers from it. For Harvard, economics was an intellectual discipline on a par with mathematics, which was fascinating to explore, but you mustn't draw any conclusions from it." See J. Daniel Hammond, "An Interview with Milton Friedman on Methodology," in *Research in the History of Economic Thought and Methodology*, ed. W. J. Samuels and J. Biddle (Greenwich, Conn.: JAI Press, 1992).

16. Leonidas Montes, "Friedman's Two Visits to Chile in Context," 2015, University of Richmond Summer Institute for the Study of the History of Economics.

17. Interview with Rolf Lüders, June 26, 2018.

18. Valdés, *Pinochet's Economists*, 140.

19. Ibid., 169

20. *Chicago Boys* (film), directed by Carola Fuentes and Rafael Valdeavellano, 2015.

21. Ibid.

22. The United States, for example, sought to cut off the Allende administration's access to credit, including by putting pressure on American banks. But the Chilean government was able to find new lenders in Western Europe.

23. *Chicago Boys*.

24. Admiral José Toribio Merino, head of the Chilean navy, encouraged the creation of The Brick, and was initially the member of the junta most sympathetic to the Chicago Boys. He said in a 1992 interview that he struggled to win the support of Pinochet and Air Force general Gustavo Leigh. "The original intention of Pinochet and Leigh, against my opinion, was to maintain a state-controlled economy," he said. The footage is shown in *Chicago Boys*.

25. Heraldo Muñoz, *The Dictator's Shadow* (New York: Basic Books, 2008), 67–68.

26. Lüders told me, in an interview on June 26, 2018, that he had heard this explanation from Pinochet: "I heard him say once, 'If you look at our history, we tried a mixed economy under Alessandri and it failed, then we tried the Christian Democrats, lots of reforms but the same thing happened, and then we tried socialism."

27. The letter is reprinted in Friedman's memoir: see Milton Friedman and Rose Friedman, *Two Lucky People* (Chicago: University of Chicago Press, 1998), 592.

28. "A Draconian Cure for Chile's Economic Ills?," *Business Week*, January 12, 1976.

29. Simon Collier and William F. Sater, *A History of Chile, 1808–2002* (Cambridge, Eng.: Cambridge University Press, 2012), ebook loc. 3176.

30. "Dr. Julius Klein, an Economist, 74," *New York Times*, June 16, 1961.

31. Lüders, who helped to arrange Friedman's trip, said he does not think that Friedman had an important influence on Pinochet, because in his view the general already had decided to adopt The Brick as the nation's economic policy. This judgment is shared by some Chilean historians who have studied the episode.

32. The Ford administration was aware that the military dictatorship in Chile, together with regimes in other South American nations, were collaborating on plans to assassinate political opponents. The State Department prepared a warning to those regimes, but on September 16, five days before Letelier's murder, Secretary of State Henry Kissinger decided that it should not be sent. See Peter Kornbluh, *The Pinochet File: A Declassified Dossier on Atrocity and Accountability* (New York: New Press, 2004).

33. *Chicago Boys.*

34. Histories of Chile often cite a League of Nations report that concluded the country was hit harder by the Great Depression than any other nation. The best available data suggests this is overstated. See Thilo Albers and Martin Uebele, "The Global Impact of the Great Depression," 2015, London School of Economics, Economic History Working Paper 218.

35. Interview with Patricia Arancibia Clavel, June 25, 2018. See also Patricia Arancibia Clavel and Francisco Balart Páez, *Sergio de Castro: El arquitecto del model económico chileno* (Santiago, Chile: Editorial Biblioteca Americana, 2007).

36. Muñoz, *Dictator's Shadow*, 72.

37. Exports rose from $1.8 billion in 1975 to $6 billion in 1980. Imports more than doubled, too. See Patricio Silva, "Technocrats and Politics in Chile: From the Chicago Boys to the CIEPLAN Monks," *Journal of Latin American Studies* 23, no. 2 (1991).

38. Albert O. Hirschman, "The Political Economy of Latin American Development," 1986, Center for U.S.-Mexican Studies, 12.

39. Juan De Onis, "Chile's Open-Door Economic Policy Admits a Flood of Luxury Goods, While Millions Live Hand to Mouth," *New York Times*, September 10, 1977.

40. Victor Perera, "Law and Order in Chile," *New York Times*, April 13, 1975.

41. Peter Dworkin, "Chile's Brave New World," *Fortune*, November 2, 1981.

42. Friedrich Hayek, letter to the editor, *The Times* (London), July 11, 1978.

43. Angus Maddison, *The World Economy: A Millennial Perspective* (Paris: Development Center of the OECD, 2001), 284–91.

44. The free flow of capital was the norm in the decades before the Great Depression. Keynes made the remark in a memo written on September 8, 1941, outlining his views on postwar financial regulation. See *The Collected Writings of John Maynard Keynes* (Cambridge, Eng.: Cambridge University Press, 1980), 25:26. Three years later, Keynes's views were written into the framework of the postwar monetary order and he told the House of Lords, "What used to be a heresy is now endorsed as orthodox."

45. Milton Friedman to Barry Goldwater, December 12, 1960, Milton Friedman Papers, box 27, folder 24, Hoover Institution Archives, Stanford, Calif.

46. Edwin L. Dale Jr., "U.S. Terminates Curb on Lending Dollars Abroad," *New York Times*, January 30, 1974.

47. John Campbell, *Margaret Thatcher*, vol. 1, *The Grocer's Daughter* (London: Jonathan Cape, 2000), 366.

48. Rudiger Dornbusch et al., "Our LDC Debts," in *The United States in the World Economy*, ed. Martin Feldstein (Chicago: University of Chicago Press, 1988), 166.

49. Jackson Diehl, "Fall of the 'Piranhas,'" *Washington Post*, April 17, 1983.

50. Andre Gunder Frank, a German Jew who immigrated to the United States after World War II, earned a doctorate in economics at the University of Chicago with Friedman as his adviser, and then became a left-leaning professor of economics at the University of Chile. He recounted the shootings in "An Open Letter About Chile to Arnold Harberger and Milton Friedman," August 6, 1974. Aguirre also recalled the incident.

51. Between 1983 and 1985, Chile received an annual average of $714 million in financial support from international institutions, equal to about 4 percent of GNP. See John Williamson, ed., *The Political Economy of Policy Reform* (Washington, D.C.: Institute for International Economics, 1994), 566.

52. Judith Teichman concludes that the IMF and the World Bank were particularly doctrinaire in the case of Chile. "The reluctance of some members of the World Bank's executive board to lend to Chile because of its problematic human rights situation strengthened the bank's and the IMF's ability to ensure orthodoxy. Officials at senior levels of the bank were willing to risk the opprobrium that involvement with Chile might bring only if the agreement with Chile was flawless on economic policy grounds." See Judith A. Teichman, *The Politics of Freeing Markets in Latin America* (Chapel Hill: University of North Carolina Press, 2001), 81.

53. Rawi Abdelal, *Capital Rules: The Construction of Global Finance* (Cambridge: Harvard University Press, 2007).

54. Ludwig Erhard, the architect of Germany's postwar recovery, was strongly opposed to capital controls. "Erhard had seen in Europe and especially Germany during the 1930s and 1940s what could happen when capital controls allowed governments to manipulate their currencies for political ends," Hans Tietmeyer, a former Bundesbank head, told Rawi Abdelal. See ibid., 49.

55. Michel Camdessus, "Drawing Lessons from the Mexican Crisis," Washington, D.C., May 22, 1995; available at imf.org/en/News/Articles/2015/09/28/04/53/spmds9508.

56. "Developed economies that borrowed more heavily from abroad did not grow more rapidly than those that did not depend as much on foreign finance," the economist Eswar Prasad wrote in a 2017 summary of the state of knowledge. See his *Gaining Currency: The Rise of the Renminbi* (New York: Oxford University Press, 2017), 45. As for inequality, the free movement of capital may well be exacerbating the problem by contributing to the growth of the financial industry, as well as by undermining taxation. There is striking evidence that the absence of capital controls is the reason that OECD nations — including Chile, which was admitted to the exclusive club in 2010 — are trapped in a race to offer the lowest rates of corporate taxation. See Michael P. Devereux et al., "Do Countries Compete over Corporate Tax Rates?," *Journal of Public Economics* 92, no. 5 (June 2008): 1210–35.

57. The first systematic study of the effects of free capital flows on financial stability, published in 1998, was co-authored by John Williamson, an economist best known for

coining the term "Washington consensus" in 1989 to describe the set of free-market policies that the United States regularly prescribed for developing nations with economic problems. Williamson pointedly omitted free capital flows from his original list; he and some other leading development economists never embraced the idea. Jagdish Bhagwati, one of the profession's most forceful and uncompromising advocates of free trade, is another longtime opponent of the free movement of capital. See John Williamson and Molly Mahar, *A Survey of Financial Liberalization*, Essays in International Finance (Princeton, N.J.: Princeton University Department of Economics, 1998).

58. Ronald Reagan, "Milton Friedman and Chile," December 22, 1976. See Kiron K. Skinner et al., *Reagan's Path to Victory: The Shaping of Ronald Reagan's Vision; Selected Writings* (New York: Simon and Schuster, 2004), 98.

59. Economists, even those who disagreed with Friedman's politics, generally regarded him as a deserving laureate for his academic work. Two letters opposing Friedman's selection, by laureates in other disciplines, appeared in the *New York Times* on October 24, 1976. The first was signed by George Wald and Linus Pauling; the second by David Baltimore and S. E. Luria. Friedman initially defended his trip to Chile as an example of his willingness to offer economic advice to anyone willing to listen, and indeed he made similar visits to right-wing dictatorships in Brazil and Spain and to left-wing dictatorships in China and Yugoslavia. "In spite of my profound disagreement with the authoritarian political system of Chile," Friedman wrote in a *Newsweek* column in 1976, shortly after his visit to Chile, "I do not consider it as evil for an economist to render technical economic advice to the Chilean Government, any more than I would regard it as evil for a physician to give technical medical advice to the Chilean Government to help end a medical plague." Later, Friedman also argued that where free-market policies took root, democracy tended to follow — and he and his supporters seized on Chile's turn toward democracy as a vindication of this philosophy. The idea that capitalism leads to democracy was quite popular in the 1990s and the 2000s, when it was frequently presented as a justification for Western engagement with China.

60. John Foran, *Taking Power: On the Origins of Third World Revolutions* (Cambridge, Eng.: Cambridge University Press, 2005), 180.

61. Karl Schoenberger, "Berkeley-Trained Group Plays Key Role," *Los Angeles Times*, June 1, 1992.

62. The program, called Advanced Training in Economics, was launched late in Reagan's second term and lasted about a decade. See Arnold Harberger, "Sense and Economics: An Oral History with Arnold Harberger," conducted by Paul Burnett in 2015 and 2016, Oral History Center, Bancroft Library, University of California, Berkeley.

63. Margaret Thatcher to Friedrich Hayek, February 17, 1982, Margaret Thatcher Foundation; available at margaretthatcher.org.

64. Maddison, *The World Economy*.

65. Bardón's observation in the original Spanish was *"Si las ventajas comparativas determinan que Chile solo tiene ventajas comparativas en la producción de melones, bueno, entonces tendremos que producir melones, y nada más."* See Stefan De Vylder, "Chile 1973–84: Auge, Consolidación y Crisis Del Modelo Neoliberal," *Ibero-Americana* 15, nos. 1–2 (1985): 5–49.

66. In 1987, 29 percent of the Chilean population had an income of less than $3.20 per day. By 2013, that share was 3 percent, according to the most recent World Bank data.

67. Alessandro Bonanno and Joseph Cavalcanti, "Globalization and the Time-Space Reorganization," 2011, Emerald Group, 185.

68. The company, Nutreco, fired 55 of the 560 workers at the plant "for reasons of loss of trust." See Sarah K. Cox, "Diminishing Returns: An Investigation into the Five Multinational Corporations That Control British Columbia's Salmon Farming Industry," 2004, Coastal Alliance for Aquaculture Reform, 51.

69. Chile invests significantly less in research and development than other countries with comparable economic resources, according to OECD data. Chileans also hold relatively few patents, an important measure of innovation.

70. Interview with Patricio Meller, June 26, 2018.

71. Alice Facchini and Sandra Laville, "Chilean Villagers Claim British Appetite for Avocados Is Draining Region Dry," *The Guardian*, May 17, 2018.

72. This passage is based on 2017 OECD data; however, measures of inequality are imprecise. The quality of data varies over time and among nations, and there is variability in methodology.

73. Chile's central bank has calculated that government spending, measured as a share of GDP, is about 5 percent lower than "the level that one would expect for a country with Chile's income per capita." The bank concluded this was evidence that the size of government was not impeding economic growth. The opposite conclusion appears at least equally viable. See De Gregorio, "Economic Growth in Chile."

74. Cuba's GDP per capita in 1990 was $2707, according to World Bank data; Chile's GDP per capita in 1990 was $2501.

75. Interview with Alejandro Foxley, June 21, 2018.

76. "Interview with Ricardo Lagos," *The Commanding Heights*, PBS, January 19, 2002.

77. Ibid.

78. Enrique Donoso, *"Desigualdad en mortalidad infantil entre las comunas de la provincia de Santiago,"* Revista Médica de Chile 132 (2004): 461–66.

79. Chen Yizi, a Chinese economist and government adviser who visited Chile in the early 1980s, was deeply impressed by Chile's technocratic government. He recorded approvingly that Pinochet had said, "Whoever can earn a doctorate from a famous European or American university can be a minister." The quote may be apocryphal — I've been unable to find an original source — but it certainly captures Pinochet's taste in bureaucrats. See Julian Gewirtz, *Unlikely Partners: Chinese Reformers, Western Economists, and the Making of Global China* (Cambridge: Harvard University Press, 2017), 199.

80. José Piñera, "How the Power of Ideas Can Transform a Country," 2001, JosePinera.org.

81. Pascale Bonnefoy, "With Pensions Like This, Chileans Wonder How They'll Ever Retire," *New York Times*, September 11, 2016.

82. The worst massacres were carried out by the Kuomintang before Chiang arrived on the island. Beginning on February 28, 1947, the government responded to protests by shooting thousands of Taiwanese, including targeted killings of political leaders. At one point, the government dropped leaflets, signed by Chiang and promising leniency, in the mountains where locals had fled. Many who returned were killed. Estimates of the death toll begin at ten thousand.

83. The comparison is of gross domestic product divided by population and adjusted for purchasing power. While calculations of purchasing power are imprecise, the concept is important: just as a dollar goes further in Buffalo than in New York City, so, too, the cost of living varies by country. Decennial data for 1950 through 1990 comes from Maddison, *The World Economy.* Decennial data for 1980 through 2010 comes from the International Monetary Fund. While there are differences in methodology the results are quite similar. The IMF's most recent numbers, for 2017, show the 2:1 ratio held steady.

84. The comparisons are between 1952, the earliest year for which data is available, and 2014, the most recent. See 2016 *Taiwan Statistical Data Book*, National Development Council, Republic of China.

85. Alan P. L. Liu examined the backgrounds of forty-four leading economic policy officials during the first three decades of Kuomintang rule, and found twenty-one had degrees in engineering while fifteen had degrees in the social sciences, including economics. Moreover, the economists tended to work for the engineers. "Of the fourteen ministers of economic affairs in the ROC from 1949 to 1985, ten had been trained in engineering." See Alan P. L. Liu, *Phoenix and the Lame Lion: Modernization in Taiwan and Mainland China, 1950–1980* (Stanford, Calif.: Hoover Institution, 1987).

86. The remark is attributed to K. T. Li, minister of economics in the 1960s. He was a physicist by training. See Fred Robins, "Taiwan's Economic Success," in *Emerging Economic Systems in Asia*, ed. Kyoko Sheridan (St. Leonards, N.S.W.: Allen and Unwin, 1998), 52.

87. Japan took control of Taiwan in 1895 under the Treaty of Shimonoseki after defeating China on the Korean peninsula. The Japanese made significant investments in infrastructure, but the progress was substantially erased during World War II. Agricultural productivity had roughly doubled during the first three decades of the twentieth century. By 1945, when China reclaimed control of the island, productivity was back to the level of 1910. See Tai-chun Kuo and Ramon H. Myers, *Taiwan's Economic Transformation: Leadership, Property Rights and Institutional Change, 1949–1965* (London: Routledge, 2012).

88. Kuo-Ting Li, *The Evolution of Policy Behind Taiwan's Development Success* (Singapore: World Scientific, 1995), 68.

89. Robert N. Gwynne, Thomas Klak, and Denis J. B. Shaw, *Alternative Capitalisms: Geographies of Emerging Regions* (Abingdon, Eng.: Routledge, 2014), 99.

90. The U.S. economist, Wolf Ladejinsky, had fled the Soviet Union in 1921 to escape from communism, and then devoted his life to fighting communism. See Joe Studwell, *How Asia Works* (London: Profile, 2013), 67.

91. For a more detailed version of this argument, see ibid. Among other evidence, Studwell cites a study of economic growth between 1960 and 1992 that identified only a few countries that sustained strong economic growth despite concentrated patterns of landownership: Brazil, which has since faltered, and Israel. The study is Klaus Deininger and Lyn Squire, "New Ways of Looking at Old Issues: Inequality and Growth," *Journal of Development Economics* 57, no. 2 (1998).

92. It was also true that an American farmer produced eight times more food than a Taiwanese farmer. Taiwan was taking advantage of abundant labor, while the United States was taking advantage of abundant land. See Li, *Evolution of Policy Behind Taiwan's Development Success*, 223.

93. The details are drawn primarily from Alan Liu's biographical sketch of Yin. See Liu, *Phoenix and the Lame Lion*.

94. This "rice tax," which the government monetized by selling the rice at the market price, was the government's largest source of revenue until 1963. Another interesting aspect of this early episode is that the United States in 1952 forced Taiwan to adopt the marginal pricing of electricity. The idea, proselytized by Alfred Kahn among others, was that utilities should charge more for electricity when generation costs rose during periods of high demand, like hot summer days, and less during periods of low demand, as at night, when generation costs declined. The idea was popular with economists but barely in use in the United States. See Kuo and Myers, *Taiwan's Economic Transformation*, 45–48.

95. Li, *Evolution of Policy Behind Taiwan's Development Success*, 269.

96. The economists, S. C. Tsiang and T. C. Liu, had met in Beijing as students in the 1940s and then settled in the United States, where they worked together at the IMF and then at Cornell University. They were lifelong friends and collaborators — Tsiang the more original thinker, Liu the better writer and speaker. For an account of the two men's relationship and work, see Jia-dong Shea, "The Liu-Tsiang Proposals for Economic Reform in Taiwan: A Retrospective," in *Taiwan's Development Experience: Lessons on Roles of Government and Market*, ed. Erik Thorbecke and Henry Wan Jr. (Boston: Kluwer, 1999). One interesting detail is that Liu came to the United States to study railroad engineering.

97. American military aid was even more substantial, guaranteeing the survival of Chiang's regime. One sign of the depth of America's influence is that the Kuomintang often held meetings in English for the benefit of the American advisers. See Neil H. Jacoby, *U.S. Aid to Taiwan* (New York: Praeger, 1966), 38.

98. Shirley W. Y. Kuo, "Government Policy in the Taiwanese Development Process: The Past 50 Years," in *Taiwan's Development Experience: Lessons on Roles of Government and Market*, ed. Thorbecke and Wan, 118. The government did adopt one critical piece of advice from the Cornell professors Tsiang and Liu. The conventional wisdom then held that developing nations should hold down interest rates to stimulate investment and to minimize inflation. Tsiang had long argued for the opposite approach, insisting higher interest rates would better accomplish both goals. Taiwan's first economics minister — a chemical engineer — adopted the suggestion, directing banks to offer high rates on savings accounts. Inflation ran about 500 percent per year from 1946 to 1948, then spiked as high as an annualized rate of 3000 percent in 1949. After the policy was introduced in March 1950, the share of the money supply held in savings accounts rose from 0.5 percent to 44 percent by 1952, and inflation slowed. Even as Friedman was developing his famous theory that governments needed to control inflation by focusing on the supply of money, Taiwan's engineers were controlling inflation by reducing velocity. See Kuo, "Government Policy in the Taiwanese Development Process," 48. Yin resumed the high-rate policy in 1960. Taiwanese saved 4.6 percent of total national income in 1952. By 1963, the figure was 11.6 percent—higher than the savings rate in the United States or the United Kingdom. By 1973, the savings rate was 29.6 percent. The money was plowed back into Taiwan's development, allowing the country to minimize its reliance on foreign borrowing. That independence, in turn, insulated Taiwan from the financial crises that rocked other developing nations as impetuous investors rushed in and out. See S. C. Tsiang, "Foreign Trade and Investment as Boosters for Take-Off: The Experience of Taiwan," in *Studies in United States–Asia Economic Relations*, ed. M. Dutta (Durham, N.C.: Acorn Press, 1984), 381.

99. Kuo, "Government Policy in the Taiwanese Development Process," 98.

100. The United States continued to push for market reforms. One condition of the aid was the establishment of a stock market. The Taiwan Stock Exchange opened on February 9, 1962. For the details of the four-year plan, see David W. Chang, "U.S. Aid and Economic Progress in Taiwan," *Asian Survey* 5, no. 3 (1965): 152–60.

101. Li, *Evolution of Policy Behind Taiwan's Development Success*, 243.

102. In the early phases of Taiwan's economic rise, the domestic market remained the predominant driver of growth. The contribution of exports to total growth was 22.5 percent in the late 1950s, 35 percent in the first half of the 1960s, 46 percent in the second half of the 1960s, and finally 68 percent in the first half of the 1970s. See Shea, "The Liu-Tsiang Proposals for Economic Reform in Taiwan."

103. I am grateful to Chris Horton for the example of Chu Chen.

104. While Friedman provided that judgment in passing, it was widely shared by contemporary scholars who had studied Taiwan more carefully. See Milton Friedman, "Election Perspective," *Newsweek*, November 10, 1980.

105. K. T. Li, for example, writes in his memoirs that Taiwan controlled inflation in the 1960s by keeping a firm handle on the growth of the money supply. In fact, the money supply expanded by 23 percent from 1952 to 1961, and by 20.9 percent from 1962 to 1972. During the first period, inflation averaged 12.3 percent per year; during the second period, inflation averaged 2.9 percent per year. See Erik Lundberg, "Monetary Policies," in *Economic Growth and Structural Change in Taiwan: The Postwar Experience of the Republic of China*, ed. Walter Galenson (Ithaca, N.Y.: Cornell University Press, 1979), 271. The obvious difference was instead Taiwan's embrace of high interest rates — a damper on velocity rather than quantity.

106. The share of imports subject to a tariff of at least 30 percent was 53.4 percent in 1955 and 60 percent in 1973. It did not begin to fall significantly until the early 1980s. Some scholars argue Taiwan eased other kinds of import restrictions during the 1970s, but the tariff rates alone are surely enough to qualify the claims about free trade.

107. In *Evolution of Policy Behind Taiwan's Development Success*, Li estimates the share of manufacturing output by state-owned companies at 57 percent in 1953, 38 percent in 1966, 20 percent in 1976, 15 percent in 1986, and 10 percent in 1991.

108. K. T. Li, Yin's deputy, put the point somewhat more felicitously. "What we as policymakers did in Taiwan was to help various parts of the economy first to start, and then to walk, and then we let go." See Robins, "Taiwan's Economic Success," 52.

109. Jean Yueh, "Sun Yun-suan: The Architect of Taiwan's Science and Technology Industry," *Taiwan Today*, July 31, 2009.

110. "The Industrial Heritage in Taiwan," 2009, Ministry of Economic Affairs, Republic of China, Taipei. The economist Dani Rodrik has estimated that developing nations advance toward the technological frontier in manufacturing at a rate of about 3 percent a year, almost irrespective of policy. This suggests Taiwan was closer to the cutting edge than was widely appreciated at the time.

111. There is no single replicable formula for economic development. Conditions vary and details matter. The Brazilian government sent scientists to RCA at the same time as Taiwan, but Brazil did not succeed in creating a semiconductor industry.

112. Nicholas D. Kristof, "Taiwan's Embarrassment of Riches," *New York Times*, December 21, 1986.

113. One measure of income inequality is the ratio of the top income quintile and the bottom income quintile. This ratio fell from 20.5 in 1952 to 4.4 by the early 1980s. It has since climbed to around 6, which remains lower than much of the developed world. In the United States, the ratio was 8.5 in 2016. In Chile, it was 10.

114. Michael Hirsh, *Capital Offense* (Hoboken, N.J.: John Wiley, 2010), 117. Summers was responding to an internal 1991 report criticizing the World Bank's approach to economic development. The report, commissioned on the insistence of Japan, documented the success of active management in East Asia.

A more recent caveat is of greater interest. The economist Dani Rodrik notes that automation is reducing the level of employment required even for basic manufacturing. Thus, nations that industrialized during the midcentury, like Taiwan, often saw manufacturing employment peak above 30 percent of the workforce. More recently, however, manufacturing employment peaked at just 16 percent in Brazil and at 20 percent in Mexico — and it may not reach even those levels in the next generation of industrial debutantes. "It is not implausible," Rodrik wrote in a 2017 book, *Straight Talk on Trade*, "that the East Asian tiger economies will be the last countries to ever experience industrialization in the manner to which economic history has accustomed us."

115. Friedman told an interviewer in 1978, "Taiwan has prospered not because of government planning, but in spite of it." Jagdish Bhagwati has made the same argument about South Korea's growth.

116. Interview with Stephen Su, July 24, 2018.

117. U.S. spending on research and development has held steady as a share of GDP, but the money comes increasingly from the private sector. The public share of R&D spending declined from 65 percent in 1963 to 29 percent in 2003. For the quote, see Mariana Mazzucato, *The Entrepreneurial State* (London: Demos, 2011), 13.

Chapter 10. Paper Fish

1. Henry C. Simons, *A Positive Program for Laissez Faire: Some Proposals for a Liberal Economic Policy* (Chicago: University of Chicago Press, 1934), 16.

2. These examples are taken from the Tuesday, June 23, 1970, edition of the *New York Times*, which included ads offering free gifts from more than a dozen different banks.

3. Regulators raised the top rate on bank deposits from 2.5 percent at the beginning of the 1960s to 7.5 percent at the end of the decade, but that was not enough. In every year after 1966, the real return on three-month Treasuries was higher than the top rate on bank deposits.

4. "Grassroots Hearings on Economic Problems," House Committee on Banking and Currency, December 1, 1969, 373–78.

5. In 1970, for example, regulators had made an emergency exception to the rate caps following the failure of the Penn Central Railroad. Concerned that other companies would struggle to access short-term credit markets, regulators allowed banks to offer higher interest rates on large deposits, basically creating an alternative intermediation process for companies to access funding. The measure remained on the books after the crisis passed.

6. A signature feature of these accounts is that shares were priced at exactly $1, fostering an illusion of stable value. The money market funds rose from almost nothing in 1978 to hold $200 billion — or 15 percent of all deposit dollars — by 1982.

7. Merrill Lynch introduced its "cash management account" in 1977, allowing investors in a money market mutual fund to write what were basically checks. The chief executive, Donald Regan, became Treasury secretary under Reagan — and in that role, a leading advocate of deregulation. For the rise of consumer finance, see Joe Nocera, *A Piece of the Action: How the Middle Class Joined the Money Class* (New York: Simon and Schuster, 1995).

8. The details about Citicorp and South Dakota are drawn primarily from two accounts: Robert A. Bennett, "Inside Citicorp," *New York Times*, May 29, 1983; and Stu Whitney, "What Really Happened to Land Citibank," *Argus* (S.D.) *Leader*, April 4, 2015.

9. In the early days of the credit card industry, banks mailed out cards to prospective customers — not applications, actual cards — and then sought to collect payment from anyone who took the bait. In 1969, an Iowa resident who had received a card from the First National Bank of Omaha sued the bank, arguing that it was illegal for the Nebraska company to charge higher rates than allowed by Iowa law. By the time the case reached the Supreme Court in 1978, it had been joined by a similar suit from Minnesota. The Omaha bank hired Robert Bork to make its case. His job was straight-

forward. The law was clear, and the court ruled unanimously that banks with national charters could legally make loans at the prevailing rates in their home state. Consumer advocates said Congress had not anticipated the advent of credit cards in writing the law. It was one thing to say a bank based in Omaha could offer loans to anyone who walked in the front door, and quite another to say that it could send loans to people who lived in other states. It would mean the effective end of usury laws. Justice William Brennan, writing for the court, said that this was a matter for Congress to address. It never has. See *Marquette Nat. Bank of Minneapolis v. First of Omaha Service Corp.*, 439 U.S. 299 (1978).

10. Bill Janklow, the governor at the time, recalled that in 1979 there were only seven housing permits issued in the state's largest city because banks refused to lend even at the highest legal rate. See interview with Bill Janklow in "The Secret History of the Credit Card," *Frontline*, PBS, November 23, 2004.

11. Diane Ellis, "The Effect of Consumer Interest Rate Deregulation on Credit Card Volumes, Charge-Offs and the Personal Bankruptcy Rate," March 1998, Federal Deposit Insurance Corporation no. 98-05.

12. Gretta R. Krippner, *Capitalizing on Crisis: The Political Origins of the Rise of Finance* (Cambridge: Harvard University Press, 2012), 80.

13. Edward Cowan, "How Regan Sees the Budget," *New York Times*, October 18, 1981.

14. The university constructed the database with funding from Merrill Lynch. It was the first database of its kind. Eugene Fama, in other words, was in the right place at the right time. Fama's original paper, "The Behavior of Stock Market Prices," was published in the *Journal of Business* in 1965. Five years later, he put forward his theory of efficient markets in a paper that synthesized several similar studies: see Eugene F. Fama, "Efficient Capital Markets: A Review of Theory and Empirical Work," *Journal of Finance* 25, no. 2 (1970).

15. The theory said nobody, no matter how smart, could predict the future movements of stock prices based on the information already in existence. The movement would be determined by what happened next. The economist Benoit Mandelbrot compared markets to a drunken man in an open field: he might stumble in any direction; he might double back on his own tracks. The only useful information about where he would end up was where he stood at the start. The theory actually comes in three progressively stronger formulations. The weakest version says past price movements cannot be used to forecast future price movements. The second extends that principle to all public information. The third includes nonpublic information. Particularly in its strongest form, the theory had a number of important implications. It suggested people should buy index funds rather than trying to beat the market. Somewhat counterintuitively, it also implied that markets were subject to a kind of natural order. The distribution of truly random events is surprisingly orderly: it looks like a bell curve. And this, in turn, suggested that risks could be quantified and managed. But markets are not always efficient. This has been demonstrated repeatedly in a wide variety of interesting ways. For example, the acquisition of information requires time and energy. That alone means markets can't be perfectly efficient, which Sanford Grossman and Joseph Stiglitz pointed out in 1975. Even Fama eventually conceded his theory was inaccurate, although it still had value as a rule of thumb. But Fama didn't go as far as some. Even after the 2009 crisis, he found it hard to accept that prices had been very wrong. True faith endures in the face of experience. "I don't even know what a bubble means," he told *The New Yorker*'s John Cassidy in 2010.

16. Credit derivatives can also be bets on intermediate events, like changes in a credit rating or in some other measure of the probability of eventual default. For the history of the market in credit derivatives, see Gillian Tett, *Fool's Gold* (New York: Free Press, 2009).

17. Gretchen Morgenson, "Credit Default Swap Market Under Scrutiny," *New York Times*, August 10, 2008.

18. Rob Wells, "New York Fed President Warns About Swaps Market," Associated Press, January 30, 1992.

19. Paul Volcker at the time was the chairman of the Group of Thirty, the trade group that issued the report on derivatives. He writes in his memoir that he insisted on toning down its conclusions. The final product, however, still took a hard line: "This study does not conclude that any fundamental changes in the current regulatory framework, such as separate regulation of this activity, are needed." See Global Derivatives Study Group, "Derivatives: Practices and Principles," July 1993, G-30, Washington, D.C. The episode deserves to be placed on the scales in weighing Volcker's reputation as an opponent of financial deregulation.

20. Tett, *Fool's Gold*, 30.

21. Teri Sforza, "We're Out! Orange County Pays Final Bankruptcy Bill," *Orange County Register*, June 30, 2017.

22. Frank Partnoy, *Infectious Greed: How Deceit and Risk Corrupted the Financial Markets* (London: Profile, 2010), 55.

23. Paul Volcker and Christine Harper, *Keeping at It: The Quest for Sound Money and Good Government* (New York: PublicAffairs, 2018), 238.

24. Alan Greenspan, "Testimony Before the Telecommunications and Finance Subcommittee of the House Energy and Commerce Committee: Impact of Derivatives on Financial Markets," May 25, 1994.

25. Testifying before Congress in 1994, Corrigan claimed not only that the industry had made significant progress, but that his famous warning two years earlier had played an important role. "My sentence, 'I hope this sounds like a warning because it is,' served a useful role in focusing attention, although we are not home free," he said. See Saul Hansell, "Panel Is Told Derivatives Are No Cause for Alarm," *New York Times*, May 11, 1994. Newman, then Treasury under secretary for domestic finance, wrote to the chairman of the House Committee on Financial Services, Representative Henry Gonzalez, on September 16, 1994, to suggest that the committee should "indefinitely postpone" any action on derivatives because "the administration has not identified a need for legislation regarding derivatives at this time." The following September, he joined Bankers Trust as senior vice chairman. See Lynn Stevens Hume, "House Banking Panel Shelves Derivatives Bill at Urging of Treasury, Committee Members," *The Bond Buyer*, September 20, 1994.

26. Brickell made the comments on *The Charlie Rose Show*, PBS, February 27, 1995.

27. Richard L. Berke, "Tough Texan: Phil Gramm," *New York Times*, February 19, 1995.

28. Steven V. Roberts, "Phil Gramm's Crusade Against the Deficit," *New York Times*, March 30, 1986.

29. Karen Tumulty, "Gramm's Politics of Controversy," *Los Angeles Times*, November 13, 1985.

30. George Lardner, "Phil Gramm: Risk-Taking Striver Sometimes Stumbles," *Washington Post*, February 7, 1996.

31. Tumulty, "Gramm's Politics of Controversy."

32. Robert D. Hershey Jr., "Wendy Lee Gramm: That Other Gramm of Power and Sway," *New York Times*, February 26, 1986.

33. Judith Havemann, "Wendy Gramm: Czarina of Federal Rules, Information and Statistics," *Washington Post*, April 7, 1986.

34. Wendy Lee Gramm, "In Defense of Derivatives," *Wall Street Journal*, September 8, 1993.

35. Manuel Roig-Franzia, "Credit Crisis Cassandra," *Washington Post*, May 26, 2009.

36. Interview with Brooksley Born in "The Warning," *Frontline*, PBS, October 20, 2009.

37. Roig-Franzia, "Credit Crisis Cassandra." There was a meaningful difference between the views of Greenspan and Rubin. In the words of one aide, "Greenspan was saying we shouldn't do it. Rubin was saying we couldn't do it." For a retrospective on the debate, see Noam Scheiber, *The Escape Artists: How Obama's Team Fumbled the Recovery* (New York: Simon and Schuster, 2012).

38. "Over-the-Counter Derivatives," Senate Committee on Agriculture, Nutrition and Forestry, July 30, 1998.

39. Justin Fox, *The Myth of the Rational Market* (New York: HarperCollins, 2009), 197. Summers can also claim credit for perhaps the second-best takedown of the efficient markets crowd: a 1984 presentation in which he described finance theory as akin to believing that the ketchup market operated under different rules than the rest of the world. He dubbed this "ketchup economics." See Lawrence H. Summers, "On Economics and Finance," *Journal of Finance* 40, no. 3 (July 1985).

40. "Hedge Fund Operations," House Committee on Banking and Financial Services, October 1, 1998.

41. Years later, President Clinton said he was wrong to trust in the market. "Sometimes people with a lot of money make stupid decisions," he told ABC News in April 2010. In other words, he should have listened to Professor Summers rather than Secretary Summers.

42. Tett, *Fool's Gold*, 75.

43. "Hedge Fund Operations."

44. John Redwood, "Tilting at Castles," June 11, 1984; available at nationalarchives.gov .uk/documents/prem-19-1199-part.pdf. The think tank was created by the Labour prime minister Harold Wilson in 1974. The first head was an economist from the London School of Economics. Thatcher's economic advisers were a more eclectic group, in part because there was no academic equivalent of the University of Chicago in the United Kingdom. Redwood held a doctorate in philosophy.

45. Uri Gneezy and Aldo Rustichini, "A Fine Is a Price," *Journal of Legal Studies* 29 (January 2000).

46. John Reed, "We Were Wrong About Universal Banking," *Financial Times*, November 11, 2015.

47. Jim Pickard and Barney Thompson, "Thatcher Policy Fight over 'Big Bang' Laid Bare," *Financial Times*, December 30, 2014. With regard to Redwood's views, suffice it to say that people are roughly as canny about money as Redwood was about people. Interestingly, price competition has turned out to require a larger regulatory apparatus than price controls, underscoring that more complex markets require more complex regulation. By one count, the ratio of regulators to bankers rose from 1 per 11,000 in 1979 to 1 per 300 in 2010. On the evidence, of course, the regulators still were badly outmanned. See Philip Booth, "Thatcher: The Myth of Deregulation," May 2015, Institute of Economic Affairs.

48. The British firms were helpless to resist. They were relatively small and they had no foothold in global markets. When a matchmaker tried to persuade the partners in one British firm to fly to New York to meet potential suitors, he was told that one of the

partners had no passport because he had never thought to go anywhere else. Danny Fortson, "The Day Big Bang Blasted the Old Boys into Oblivion," *The Independent* (London), October 29, 2006.

49. In the first year after the Big Bang, one quarter of the 300 members of the exchange came under foreign ownership.

50. Julia Tanndal and Daniel Waldenstrom, "Does Financial Deregulation Boost Top Incomes? Evidence from the Big Bang," *Economica* 85, no. 338 (2018).

51. Jesse Eisinger, "London Banks, Falling Down," *Portfolio*, August 1, 2008.

52. The rise of financial profits in the United States was even more spectacular, from about 15 percent of all corporate profits in the early 1980s to around 40 percent on the eve of the financial crisis. For the U.K. statistics, see Michael P. Devereux et al., "Why Has the UK Corporation Tax Raised So Much Revenue?," February 2004, Institute for Fiscal Studies.

53. Deregulation increased by about 20 percent the share of income delivered to the top 10 percent of the British population. Financial deregulation in Japan in the 1990s yielded a similar result. The sale of British firms to foreign investors provided an immediate windfall for London's bankers, and that was just a first taste. The eventual effect on income inequality was about the same as cutting the top income tax rate by 30 percent. See Tanndal and Waldenstrom, "Does Financial Deregulation Boost Top Incomes?," 232–65.

54. Binyamin Appelbaum, "As Subprime Lending Crisis Unfolded, Watchdog Fed Didn't Bother Barking," *Washington Post*, September 27, 2009.

55. The phrase is the title of a 1947 paper by Tjalling Koopmans, a Dutch American economist who was a leading figure in the marriage of math and economics. Koopmans and Friedman joined the Chicago faculty around the same time and became bitter rivals. Koopmans received the Nobel Prize in economics in 1975, one year before Friedman.

56. John Cassidy, "The Fountainhead," *The New Yorker*, April 24, 2000.

57. Interview with Alice Rivlin, September 27, 2018.

58. Interview with Alan Greenspan, March 14, 2008.

59. Soma Golden, "Why Greenspan Said 'Yes,'" *New York Times*, July 28, 1974.

60. The quote and other details about the speeches are from Sebastian Mallaby, *The Man Who Knew: The Life and Times of Alan Greenspan* (New York: Penguin Press, 2016), 90.

61. Mallaby, *The Man Who Knew*, 4.

62. Alan Greenspan, *Capitalism: The Unknown Ideal*, ed. Ayn Rand (New York: Signet, 1965), 55. He continued, "Whatever damage the antitrust laws may have done to our economy, whatever distortions of the structure of the nation's capital they may have created, these are less disastrous than the fact that the effective purpose, the hidden intent, and the actual practice of the antitrust laws in the United States have led to the condemnation of the productive and efficient members of our society because they are productive and efficient."

63. Michael Hirsh, *Capital Offense* (Hoboken, N.J.: John Wiley, 2010), 77.

64. Golden, "Why Greenspan Said 'Yes.'"

65. Kim Phillips-Fein makes the case in *Fear City* (New York: Macmillan, 2017) that New York's financial crisis was a defining moment in the rise of economic conservativism, helping to crystallize the view that government had overreached.

66. Volcker wrote in his memoirs that James Baker, then serving as Treasury secretary, "thought I would slow the momentum toward freeing the banks" from regulation. Baker also had frustrations with Volcker's handling of monetary policy. In the summer

of 1984, Reagan summoned Volcker to a meeting at which Baker instructed the Fed not to raise interest rates before the election. Volcker, stunned, left without responding. Two years later, Baker pressured Volcker to support a revaluation of exchange rates by pledging to hold down interest rates. Volcker once again refused to cooperate, and Baker may well have hoped that Greenspan would prove more pliant. That was certainly the hope of President George H. W. Bush when he handed Greenspan a second term in 1991. In the event, Greenspan lowered interest rates too late to revive the economy from a recession that probably cost Bush a second term as president. Said Bush, "I reappointed him, and he disappointed me."

67. Mallaby, *The Man Who Knew*, 724.

68. Nathaniel C. Nash, "Treasury Now Favors Creation of Huge Banks," *New York Times*, June 7, 1987.

69. Nathaniel C. Nash, "Greenspan's Lincoln Savings Regret," *New York Times*, November 20, 1989.

70. "Hearing on the Nomination of Alan Greenspan," Senate Banking Committee, July 21, 1987, 48.

71. Alan Greenspan, "Remarks Before the Economic Club of New York," June 20, 1995.

72. Greenspan offered a particularly remarkable expression of this worldview when he was asked by the Swiss newspaper *Tages-Anzeiger* in 2007 for his thoughts on the upcoming U.S. presidential election. Greenspan responded, "We are fortunate that, thanks to globalization, policy decisions in the United States have been largely replaced by global market forces. National security aside, it hardly makes any difference who will be the next president. The world is governed by market forces." See also Alan Greenspan, *The Age of Turbulence: Adventures in a New World* (New York: Penguin Press, 2007), 490.

73. Edward Gramlich, "Booms and Busts: The Case of Subprime Mortgages," Economic Policy Symposium, Federal Reserve Bank of Kansas City, August 31, 2007. Gramlich, stricken with leukemia, was too sick to deliver the speech at the Fed's annual symposium at Jackson Hole, Wyoming. Instead his remarks were read aloud. He died the following week. Gramlich has often been portrayed as the Fed's Cassandra, but he voted for the hands-off regulatory policy in 1998 as a member of the Fed's board of governors. In 2000, he told Greenspan at a private meeting that he thought the decision should be reconsidered. But Gramlich did not press the issue. In 2007, after the *Wall Street Journal* reported on the meeting, Gramlich sent Greenspan a note that read in part, "What happened was a small incident, and as I think you know, if I had felt that strongly at the time, I would have made a bigger stink."

74. Binyamin Appelbaum, Lisa Hammersly Munn, and Ted Mellnik, "Sold a Nightmare," *Charlotte Observer*, March 18, 2007.

75. The early waves of foreclosures were concentrated among subprime borrowers, but a 2015 study calculated that twice as many prime borrowers ultimately lost homes. Subprime borrowers never constituted more than about a fifth of the market, and fraud was common across all types of lending. See Fernando Ferreira and Joseph Gyourko, "A New Look at the U.S. Foreclosure Crisis: Panel Data Evidence of Prime and Subprime Borrowers from 1997 to 2012," June 2015, National Bureau of Economic Research Working Paper 21261.

76. Sendhil Mullainathan and Eldar Shafir, *Scarcity: Why Having Too Little Means So Much* (New York: Times Books, 2013), 13.

77. Ben S. Bernanke, *The Courage to Act* (New York: Norton, 2015), ebook loc. 1547.

78. Mike Hudson, "IndyMac: What Went Wrong?," June 30, 2008, Center for Responsible Lending.

79. Greenspan interview.
80. Alan Greenspan, "Testimony Before the Joint Economic Committee, June 9, 2005," Joint Economic Committee.
81. By some estimates, the inflow of global savings reduced interest rates in the United States by as much as a full percentage point. For more on the interplay of trade imbalances and the financial crisis, see Maurice Obstfeld and Kenneth Rogoff, "Global Imbalances and the Financial Crisis: Products of Common Causes," November 2009; available at https://eml.berkeley.edu/~obstfeld/santabarbara.pdf.
82. Much of the money came from Asia. In his book *Crashed*, Adam Tooze documents that Europe played a substantial role, too. Some economists argue the Fed could have limited the credit bubble by raising interest rates more sharply and quickly. While I do not discount this argument completely, the Fed tried to raise rates and it didn't make a dent in borrowing costs. The failure of regulation, in my view, was much more consequential than the precise level of interest rates. For the opposite viewpoint, see Mallaby's Greenspan biography, *The Man Who Knew*.
83. "General Discussion: Has Financial Development Made the World Riskier?," Economic Policy Symposium, Federal Reserve Bank of Kansas City, August 27, 2005; available at kansascityfed.org/publicat/sympos/2005/pdf/GD5_2005.pdf. The contretemps received no coverage at the time. The earliest account, published in the *Wall Street Journal* in 2009, quoted Summers as calling Rajan "lead-eyed." Fortunately for posterity, the meeting was recorded and a transcript was produced.
84. The airline merged with a state-owned airline in 1973, and was rebranded as Icelandair.
85. The British took possession of Iceland in 1940 after Denmark was conquered by Germany, then turned the defense of the island over to the United States, which built a large air base that remained in continuous use until the early twenty-first century. American investment in infrastructure, and jobs at the base, amounted to a fourth leg of the economy.
86. Michael Lewis, "Wall Street on the Tundra," *Vanity Fair*, April 2009.
87. The data is from Statistics Iceland. The reference years for the comparison are 1993 and 2013. See Kristján Skarphéðinsson, "Fishing Rights in Iceland," Food and Agriculture Organization of the United Nations, Global Forum on User Rights, Siam Reap, Cambodia, March 2015. See also Hannes Gissurarson, "Overfishing: The Icelandic Solution," June 2000, Institute of Economic Affairs.
88. David Oddsson, "Iceland's Economic Performance" (speech at the American Enterprise Institute, Washington, D.C., June 14, 2004); available at aei.org/publication/icelands-economic-performance/.
89. Iceland's central bank was instructed to focus on moderating inflation. The bank needed a model for determining how much money to circulate, so it borrowed Canada's. A model is a machine: you tinker with the settings, pop in some data, and it predicts the future. The Canadians calibrated their machine using historical data from Canada and the United States. The Icelanders added the United Kingdom and the euro area. Iceland's economy was quite different from the four chosen benchmarks. The result was a model that was reliably wrong. See Philipp Bagus and David Howden, "Deep Freeze: Iceland's Economic Collapse," 2011, Mises Institute.
90. Ármann Thorvaldsson, *Frozen Assets: How I Lived Iceland's Boom and Bust* (Hoboken, N.J.: John Wiley, 2009). Kaupthing helpfully engineered some of Iceland's early currency swaps, such as a deal between an Icelandic fishing company that sold its catch in foreign countries and wanted kronur, and Shell, which sold its oil in Iceland and wanted to get rid

of its kronur. Less helpfully, Kaupthing introduced "greenmail," the practice of buying a minority stake in a public company and then threatening to sell it to hostile interests.

91. "Iceland: Selected Issues," International Monetary Fund Country Report, April 2012, International Monetary Fund.

92. Statistics Iceland: see statice.is/statistics/business-sectors/transport/vehicles/.

93. Gylfi Magnússon, "What's the Lesson of Iceland's Collapse?," *Yale Insights*, May 22, 2009.

94. Níels Einarsson, "When Fishing Rights Go Up Against Human Rights," in *Gambling Debt: Iceland's Rise and Fall in the Global Economy*, ed. E. Paul Durrenberger and Gisli Palsson (Boulder: University Press of Colorado, 2015), 157.

95. Jón Ásgeir Jóhannesson, the owner of the statue, said he got the guitar at the Hard Rock Cafe, which does not quite constitute an explanation. See Kerry Capell, "The Icelander Who Wants Saks," *Bloomberg*, January 31, 2008.

96. Snorri Sturluson, *The Prose Edda* (Berkeley: University of California Press, 2012), 55.

97. Már Wolfgang Mixa, "A Day in the Life of an Icelandic Banker," in *Gambling Debt*, ed. Durrenberger and Palsson, 34.

98. Sigríður Benediktsdóttir et al., "The Rise, Fall, and Resurrection of Iceland: A Post-mortem Analysis of the 2008 Financial Crisis," Brookings Papers on Economic Activity, Fall 2017, Brookings Institution.

99. Thorvaldur Gylfason, "Iceland: How Could This Happen?," February 20, 2014, CESifo Working Paper Series 4605.

100. Durrenberger and Palsson, *Gambling Debt*, xxxvii. Iceland guaranteed domestic deposits only. When the banks failed, the money disappeared. The British and Dutch governments stepped in to cover losses, and eventually — after a protracted fight — were partially reimbursed by Iceland.

101. Jack Ewing, "Landesbank Losses May Bring Change to German Banking," *New York Times*, January 11, 2010.

102. Tett, *Fool's Gold*, 212.

103. For an overview of the problematic role of finance in the modern economy, see Rana Foroohar, *Makers and Takers: How Wall Street Destroyed Main Street* (New York: Crown Business, 2017). See also Stephen G. Cecchetti and Enisse Kharroubi, "Why Does Financial Sector Growth Crowd Out Real Economic Growth?," February 2015, BIS Working Paper 490.

104. Economists count foreign tourism as an export product: a country is selling goods and services to foreign buyers, even if those services are consumed domestically. Similarly, educating foreign students is a major source of export earnings for the United States and other developed nations. Recent economic research finds currency devaluations have a relatively weak impact on export volumes, because so much of international trade is priced in dollars. As a result, devaluation increases the profitability of exporters more than the volume of exports. The notable exception is tourism, which is more often priced in the local currency. See Camila Casas et al., "Dominant Currency Paradigm," December 2016, National Bureau of Economic Research Working Paper 22943.

Conclusion

1. Walter W. Heller, *The Economy: Old Myths and New Realities* (New York: Norton, 1976), 197.

2. Ben S. Bernanke, "Remarks at a Conference to Honor Milton Friedman," November 8, 2002.

3. In a 2005 interview, Friedman told a biographer that he wanted a headstone inscribed "Inflation is everywhere and always a monetary phenomenon." See Lanny Ebenstein, *Milton Friedman* (New York: St. Martin's, 2007), 233.

4. Summers's 2001 comments, in full, were: "The idea that a huge spending program is the way to stimulate the economy, or the idea that the way to get better at high tech is for the government to take over the technology industries, these kinds of ideas basically have become passé because they've been disproven." See *The Commanding Heights*, PBS, April 24, 2001. For the 2009 comments, see Stuart Eizenstat, *President Carter: The White House Years* (New York: St. Martin's, 2018), 285.

5. The embrace of Keynes was less than wholehearted. The stimulus was smaller than suggested by some of Obama's advisers. Also, the administration chose not to spend billions of dollars earmarked to help homeowners avoid foreclosure. For an account of the administration's decision-making, see Noam Scheiber, *The Escape Artists: How Obama's Team Fumbled the Recovery* (New York: Simon and Schuster, 2012).

6. Alberto F. Alesina and Silvia Ardagna, "Large Changes in Fiscal Policy: Taxes Versus Spending," October 2009, National Bureau of Economic Research Working Paper 15438. Alesina and Ardagna were graduates of the School of Economics at Bocconi University in Milan, founded by the conservative economist and politician Luigi Einaudi, who served as Italy's president from 1948 to 1955. The school became associated with the economic theory that deficit reduction could spur economic growth.

7. Carmen M. Reinhart and Kenneth S. Rogoff, "Growth in a Time of Debt," January 2010, National Bureau of Economic Research Working Paper 15639.

8. The error was discovered by Thomas Herndon, a graduate student at the University of Massachusetts, Amherst, who was doing his homework: The assignment was to pick a published economics paper and try to replicate the results. Herndon and two of his professors published a paper in the spring of 2013 pointing out the mistake in the Reinhart and Rogoff study. A furious dispute ensued, largely about the significance of the mistake. At a minimum, it's clear the 90 percent threshold has no special significance. See Thomas Herndon, Michael Ash, and Robert Pollin, "Does High Public Debt Consistently Stifle Economic Growth? A Critique of Reinhart and Rogoff," University of Massachusetts, Amherst, April 15, 2013; available at peri.umass.edu/fileadmin/pdf/working_papers/working_papers_301-350/WP322.pdf.

9. Peter Coy, "Keynes vs. Alesina," *Business Week*, June 30, 2010.

10. Peter Hetherington, "Outspoken Mayor Hits Out at Local Government Cuts," *The Guardian*, January 19, 2011. George Osborne, who soon became Cameron's finance minister, said in a 2010 speech that he accepted the crisis had been caused by the private sector. Austerity, he said, was necessary to prevent the next crisis. In support of this view, he quoted Harvard's Rogoff: "So while private sector debt was the cause of this crisis, public sector debt is likely to be the cause of the next one. As Rogoff himself puts it, 'there's no question that the most significant vulnerability as we emerge from recession is the soaring government debt. It's very likely that will trigger the next crisis as governments have been stretched so wide.'"

11. Alan Greenspan, *The Map and the Territory* (New York: Penguin Press, 2013), 269.

12. In a 2018 interview, Greenspan told me that he had since concluded that maintaining 2 percent inflation, the Fed's stated purpose, was economically beneficial.

13. The historical portions of this section are drawn primarily from Julian Gewirtz, *Unlikely Partners: Chinese Reformers, Western Economists, and the Making of Global China* (Cambridge: Harvard University Press, 2017), and from Friedman's accounts of his trips to China.

14. Gewirtz, *Unlikely Partners*, 138.
15. Ibid., 148.
16. The count of convictions comes from Sigtarp, a small federal agency created to investigate misconduct during and after the crisis. Some cases unrelated to Sigtarp investigations also have resulted in criminal convictions. See Sigtarp, "Quarterly Report to Congress," October 30, 2018.
17. "SunTrust Mortgage Agrees to $320 Million Settlement," July 3, 2014, Department of Justice.
18. "Oversight of the U.S. Department of Justice," Senate Judiciary Committee, March 3, 2013.
19. Manuel Funke et al.,"Going to Extremes: Politics After Financial Crises, 1870–2014," *European Economic Review* 88 (September 2016): 227–60.
20. Emil Verner and Gyozo Gyonyosi, "Financial Crisis, Creditor-Debtor Conflict and Political Extremism," November 2018; available at SSRN: https://ssrn.com/abstract=3289741. A study looking specifically at the rise of Hungary's far-right Jobbik Party since the 2008 crisis found support increased most sharply among Hungarians who borrowed in foreign currencies, and then faced much higher loan payments as the Hungarian currency crashed.
21. Michael Wolff, "Ringside with Steve Bannon at Trump Tower as the President-Elect's Strategist Plots 'An Entirely New Political Movement,'" *Hollywood Reporter*, November 18, 2016.
22. The data is from the Netherlands Bureau for Economic Policy Analysis, which keeps some of the best data on global trade flows. The Dutch have long taken trade very seriously.
23. Nelson D. Schwartz, "Trump Sealed Carrier Deal with Mix of Threat and Incentive," *New York Times*, December 1, 2016.
24. Bob Woodward, *Fear: Trump in the White House* (New York: Simon and Schuster, 2018), 208.
25. The employment rate among men in Galesburg between the ages of sixteen and sixty-five was 53 percent in 2016, according to the U.S. Census Bureau. Excluding those between the ages of sixteen and nineteen who were neither working nor looking for work, the rate was 56 percent. For more on Galesburg, see Chad Broughton, *Boom, Bust, Exodus: The Rust Belt, the Maquilas, and a Tale of Two Cities* (New York: Oxford University Press, 2015).
26. William A. Strauss, an economist at the Federal Reserve Bank of Chicago, has calculated that on average, what took 1000 workers to produce in 1950 took just 183 workers in 2010. Moreover, manufacturing in the United States has shifted toward products that require more technology and less manpower. A growing share of America's remaining factory workers hold college degrees. The result is that the value of America's manufacturing output continued to rise during the first decade of the 2000s even as employment declined. The Great Recession, however, reduced output, too. As of 2017, U.S. manufacturing output remained a little below the pre-recession peak.
27. Derrick Z. Jackson, "Income Gap Mentality," *Boston Globe*, April 19, 2006.
28. The 1989 edition of Paul Samuelson's economics textbook said that both unions and minimum wage laws caused unemployment. This was not a controversial view. A 1987 *New York Times* editorial called for the end of minimum wage laws, citing "a virtual consensus among economists that the minimum wage is an idea whose time has passed." One of the first attempts to study the actual effects of minimum wage laws, published in 1994 by the Princeton economists David Card and Alan B. Krueger,

found that a 1992 increase in New Jersey's minimum wage had not produced a measurable increase in unemployment. This was heresy, and the response was suitably overheated. The Nobel laureate James Buchanan wrote in the *Wall Street Journal* that allowing evidence to contradict theory was a disgrace. For good measure, he described his ideological opponents as "a bevy of camp-following whores." See Jonathan Schlefer, *The Assumptions Economists Make* (Cambridge: Harvard University Press, 2012), 4.

29. The idea that wages are set by social custom was propounded by early economists, notably David Ricardo, and remains, in my view, the most compelling theory of wage determination. For the argument that labor policies are a major driver of wage stagnation, see Frank S. Levy and Peter Temin, "Inequality and Institutions in 20th Century America," 2007, MIT Department of Economics Working Paper 07-17.

30. The projections, by the Bureau of Labor Statistics, are for the period between 2016 and 2026. The five occupations are: personal care aides, registered nurses, home health aides, medical assistants, and nursing assistants.

31. Moritz Kuhn, Moritz Schularick, and Ulrike I. Steins, "Income and Wealth Inequality in America, 1949–2016," June 2018, Opportunity and Inclusive Growth Institute, Federal Reserve Bank of Minneapolis, Working Paper 9.

32. George Stigler, *Five Lectures on Economic Problems* (London: Longmans, Green, 1949).

33. Economists had long assumed the existence of a trade-off between inequality and growth. The standard theory was that growth increased inequality. The OECD study suggests the relationship is not so straightforward. See Federico Cingano, "Trends in Income Inequality and Its Impact on Economic Growth," 2014, OECD Social, Employment and Migration Working Paper 163. The International Monetary Fund has reached the same conclusion: see "Fostering Inclusive Growth" (IMF staff presentation for the G-20 Leaders' Summit, July 7–8, 2017); available at imf.org/external/np/g20/pdf/2017/062617.pdf.

34. National Socio-Economic Characterization Survey (CASEN), 2017; available at http://observatorio.ministeriodesarrollosocial.gob.cl/casen-multidimensional/casen/docs/Resultados_educacion_casen_2017.pdf.

35. Real income growth for the average family in the United States was 32.2 percent between 1975 and 2006, compared with 27.1 percent in France over the same period. Excluding the top percentile, however, income growth was 17.9 percent in America and 26.4 percent in France. See Anthony B. Atkinson, Thomas Piketty, and Emmanuel Saez, "Top Incomes in the Long Run of History," *Journal of Economic Literature* 49, no. 1 (2011).

36. Karl Polanyi, *The Great Transformation: The Political and Economic Origins of Our Time* (1944; repr., Boston: Beacon Press, 2001).

37. E. Ianchovichina, L. Mottaghi, and S. Devarajan, *Inequality, Crisis, and Conflict in the Arab World: Middle East and North Africa (MENA) Economic Monitor* (Washington, D.C.: World Bank Group, 2015).

38. Amartya Sen, *Development as Freedom* (New York: Knopf, 1999), 14.

39. Frank H. Knight, *Selected Essays by Frank H. Knight*, vol. 2, *Laissez Faire: Pro and Con*, ed. Ross B. Emmett (Chicago: University of Chicago Press, 1999), 14.

40. Samuel Brittan, "The Economic Contradictions of Democracy," *British Journal of Political Science* 5, no. 2 (1975): 129–59.

41. Richard H. Thaler, "Anomalies: The Ultimatum Game," *Journal of Economic Perspectives* 2, no. 4 (1988): 195–206.

42. Milton Friedman, *Capitalism and Freedom* (Chicago: University of Chicago Press, 1962), 24.

Index

About the Author

Binyamin Appelbaum writes about economics and business for the editorial page of the *New York Times*. From 2010 to 2019, he was a Washington correspondent for the *Times*, covering economic policy in the aftermath of the 2008 crisis. He previously worked for the *Washington Post*, the *Boston Globe*, and the *Charlotte Observer*, where his reporting on subprime lending won a George Polk Award and was a finalist for the Pulitzer Prize. He lives with his wife and children in Washington, D.C.